Praise for *Overthrow*

"Do you think George W. Bush and the neoconservatives inducted 'regime change' into American foreign policy's hall of fame? Think again. Long before Iraq, U.S. presidents, spies, corporate types and their acolytes abroad had honed the art of deposing foreign governments. . . . Kinzer fills in the blanks."

—*The Washington Post Book World*

"Again and again, Mr. Kinzer shows the complex interaction between economic interests, media fervour, political idealism and racism that so often combined to inspire an eagerness to invade."

—*The Economist*

"*Overthrow* makes it abundantly clear that far from being some innovation devised in the aftermath of 9/11, 'regime change' has long been a mainstay of American statecraft. When targeting some offending potentate for retirement, Kinzer notes, Washington has seldom if ever acted for altruistic reasons."

—*The Nation*

"[A] fascinating and readable book . . . Provides a sobering opportunity to consider why—when many Americans think we're a wonderful democracy with a history of standing up for the little guy—so many countries hate and fear us. . . . [A] valuable analysis and history."

—*The Plain Dealer* (Cleveland)

"*Overthrow* is a primer for political progressives. . . . The trouble is, nobody in power seems to be listening."

—*The New York Observer*

"[A] wonderful chronicle of America's interventions in foreign countries . . . Kinzer's book is particularly enlightening about the consequences of such unilateral actions."

—*The New York Review of Books*

OVERTHROW

OVERTHROW

AMERICA'S CENTURY OF REGIME CHANGE FROM HAWAII TO IRAQ

STEPHEN KINZER

TIMES BOOKS   Henry Holt and Company   New York

Times Books
Henry Holt and Company, LLC
Publishers since 1866
175 Fifth Avenue
New York, New York 10010
www.henryholt.com

Henry Holt® is a registered trademark of
Henry Holt and Company, LLC.

Library of Congress Cataloging-in-Publication Data
Kinzer, Stephen.
Overthrow: America's century of regime change from Hawaii
to Iraq / Stephen Kinzer. —1st ed.
p.   cm.
Includes bibliographical references and index.
ISBN-13: 978-0-8050-8240-1
ISBN-10: 0-8050-8240-9
1. United States—Foreign relations—20th century. 2. Hawaii—History—
Overthrow of the Monarchy, 1893. 3. Iraq War, 2003–
4. Intervention (International law)—History—20th century.
5. Legitimacy of governments—History—20th century. I. Title.
E744.K49   2006
327.73009—dc22   2005054856

Henry Holt books are available for special promotions and premiums.
For details contact: Director, Special Markets.

Originally published in hardcover in 2006 by Times Books
First Paperback Edition 2007

Designed by Kelly S. Too

Printed in the United States of America
9   10   8

Time present and time past
Are both perhaps present in time future,
And time future contained in time past.

CONTENTS

OVERTHROW

Introduction

Why does a strong nation strike against a weaker one? Usually because it seeks to impose its ideology, increase its power, or gain control of valuable resources. Shifting combinations of these three factors motivated the United States as it extended its global reach over the past century and more. This book examines the most direct form of American intervention, the overthrow of foreign governments.

The invasion of Iraq in 2003 was not an isolated episode. It was the culmination of a 110-year period during which Americans overthrew fourteen governments that displeased them for various ideological, political, and economic reasons. Like each of these operations, the "regime change" in Iraq seemed for a time—a very short time—to have worked. It is now clear, however, that this operation has had terrible unintended consequences. So have most of the other coups, revolutions, and invasions that the United States has mounted to depose governments it feared or mistrusted.

The United States uses a variety of means to persuade other countries to do its bidding. In many cases it relies on time-honored tactics of diplomacy, offering rewards to governments that support American interests and threatening retaliation against those that refuse. Sometimes it defends friendly regimes against popular anger or uprisings. In more than a few places, it has quietly supported coups or revolutions organized by others. Twice, in the context of world wars, it helped to wipe away old ruling orders and impose new ones.

This book is not about any of those ways Americans have shaped the modern world. It focuses only on the most extreme set of cases: those in which the United States arranged to depose foreign leaders. No nation in modern history has done this so often, in so many places so far from its own shores.

The stories of these "regime change" operations are dazzlingly exciting. They tell of patriots and scoundrels, high motives and low cynicism, extreme courage and cruel betrayal. This book brings them together for the first time, but it seeks to do more than simply tell what happened. By considering these operations as a continuum rather than as a series of unrelated incidents, it seeks to find what they have in common. It poses and tries to answer two fundamental questions. First, why did the United States carry out these operations? Second, what have been their long-term consequences?

Drawing up a list of countries whose governments the United States has overthrown is not as simple as it sounds. This book treats only cases in which Americans played the decisive role in deposing a regime. Chile, for example, makes the list because, although many factors led to the 1973 coup there, the American role was decisive. Indonesia, Brazil, and the Congo do not, because American agents played only subsidiary roles in the overthrow of their governments during the 1960s. Nor do Mexico, Haiti, or the Dominican Republic, countries the United States invaded but whose leaders it did not depose.

America's long "regime change" century dawned in 1893 with the overthrow of the Hawaiian monarchy. This was a tentative, awkward piece of work, a cultural tragedy staged as comic opera. It was not a military operation, but without the landing of American troops, it probably would not have succeeded. The president of the United States approved of it, but soon after it happened, a new president took office and denounced it. Americans were already divided over whether it is a good idea to depose foreign regimes.

The overthrow of Hawaii's queen reignited a political debate that had first flared during the Mexican War half a century before. That debate, which in essence is about what role the United States should play in the world, rages to this day. It burst back onto the front pages after the invasion of Iraq.

No grand vision of American power lay behind the Hawaiian revolution of 1893. Just the opposite was true of the Spanish-American War, which broke out five years later. This was actually two wars, one in which the United States came to the aid of patriots fighting against Spanish colonialism, and then a second in which it repressed those patriots to assure that their newly liberated nations would be American protectorates rather than truly independent. A radically new idea of America, much more globally ambitious than any earlier one, emerged from these conflicts. They marked the beginning of an era in which the United States has assumed the right to intervene anywhere in the world, not simply by influencing or coercing foreign governments but also by overthrowing them.

In Hawaii and the countries that rose against Spain in 1898, American presidents tested and developed their new interventionist policy. There, however, they were reacting to circumstances created by others. The first time a president acted on his own to depose a foreign leader was in 1909, when William Howard Taft ordered the overthrow of Nicaraguan president José Santos Zelaya. Taft claimed he was acting to protect American security and promote democratic principles. His true aim was to defend the right of American companies to operate as they wished in Nicaragua. In a larger sense, he was asserting the right of the United States to impose its preferred form of stability on foreign countries.

This set a pattern. Throughout the twentieth century and into the beginning of the twenty-first, the United States repeatedly used its military power, and that of its clandestine services, to overthrow governments that refused to protect American interests. Each time, it cloaked its intervention in the rhetoric of national security and liberation. In most cases, however, it acted mainly for economic reasons—specifically, to establish, promote, and defend the right of Americans to do business around the world without interference.

Huge forces reshaped the world during the twentieth century. One of the most profound was the emergence of multinational corporations, businesses based in one country that made much of their profit overseas. These corporations and the people who ran them accumulated great wealth and political influence. Civic movements, trade unions, and political parties arose to counterbalance them, but in the United States, these were never able even to approach the power that corporations wielded. Corporations identified themselves in the public mind with the ideals of free enterprise, hard work, and individual achievement. They also maneuvered their friends and supporters into important positions in Washington.

By a quirk of history, the United States rose to great power at the same time multinational corporations were emerging as a decisive force in world affairs. These corporations came to expect government to act on their behalf abroad, even to the extreme of overthrowing uncooperative foreign leaders. Successive presidents have agreed that this is a good way to promote American interests.

Defending corporate power is hardly the only reason the United States overthrows foreign governments. Strong tribes and nations have been attacking weak ones since the beginning of history. They do so for the most elemental reason, which is to get more of whatever is good to have. In the modern world, corporations are the institutions that countries use to capture wealth. They have become the vanguard of American power, and defying them has become tantamount to defying the United States. When Americans depose a foreign leader who dares such defiance, they not only assert their rights in one country but also send a clear message to others.

The influence that economic power exercises over American foreign policy has grown tremendously since the days when ambitious planters in Hawaii realized that by bringing their islands into the United States, they would be able to send their sugar to markets on the mainland without paying import duties. As the twentieth century progressed, titans of industry and their advocates went a step beyond influencing policy makers; they *became* the policy makers. The figure who most perfectly embodied this merging of political and economic interests was John Foster Dulles, who spent decades working for some of the world's most powerful corporations and then became secretary of state. It was Dulles who ordered the 1953 coup in Iran, which was intended in part to make the Middle East safe for American oil companies. A year later he ordered another coup, in Guatemala, where a nationalist government had challenged the power of United Fruit, a company his old law firm represented.

Having marshaled so much public and political support, American corporations found it relatively easy to call upon the military or the Central Intelligence Agency to defend their privileges in countries where they ran into trouble. They might not have been able to do so if they and the presidents who cooperated with them had candidly presented their cases to the American people. Americans have always been idealists. They want their country to act for pure motives, and might have refused to support foreign interventions that were forthrightly described as defenses of corporate power. Presidents have used two strategies to assure that these interventions would be carried out with a minimum of protest. Sometimes they obscured the real reasons they overthrew foreign governments, insisting that they were acting only to protect American security and liberate suffering natives. At other time they simply denied that the United States was involved in these operations at all.

The history of American overthrows of foreign governments can be divided into three parts. First came the imperial phase, when Americans deposed regimes more or less openly. None of the men who overthrew the Hawaiian monarchy tried to hide their involvement. The Spanish-American War was fought in full view of the world, and President Taft announced exactly what he was doing when he moved to overthrow the governments of Nicaragua and Honduras. The men who directed these "regime change" operations may not have forthrightly explained why they were acting, but they took responsibility for their acts.

After World War II, with the world political situation infinitely more complex than it had been at the dawn of the century, American presidents found a new way to overthrow foreign governments. They could no longer simply demand that unfriendly foreign leaders accept the reality of American power and step down, nor could they send troops to land on foreign shores without worrying about the consequences. This was because for the first time, there was a force in the world that limited their freedom of action: the Soviet Union. During the Cold War, any direct American intervention risked provoking a reaction from the Soviets, possibly a cataclysmic one. To adjust to this new reality, the United States began using a more subtle technique, the clandestine coup d'état, to depose foreign governments. In Iran, Guatemala, South Vietnam, and Chile, diplomats and intelligence agents replaced generals as the instruments of American intervention.

By the end of the twentieth century, it had become more difficult for Americans to stage coups because foreign leaders had learned how to resist them. Coups had also become unnecessary. The decline and collapse of the Soviet Union and the disappearance of the Red Army meant that there was no longer any military constraint on the United States. That left it free to return to its habit of landing troops on foreign shores.

Both of the small countries Americans invaded in the 1980s, Grenada and Panama, are in what the United States has traditionally considered its sphere of influence, and both were already in turmoil when American troops landed. The two invasions that came later, in Afghanistan and Iraq, were far larger in scale and historical importance. Many Americans supported the operation in Afghanistan because they saw it as an appropriate reaction to the presence of terrorists there. A smaller but still substantial number supported the operation in Iraq after being told that Iraq also posed an imminent threat to world peace. American invasions left both of these countries in violent turmoil.

Most "regime change" operations have achieved their short-term goals. Before the CIA deposed the government of Guatemala in 1954, for example, United Fruit was not free to operate as it wished in that country; afterward it was. From the vantage point of history, however, it is clear that most of these operations actually weakened American security. They cast whole regions of the world into upheaval, creating whirlpools of instability from which undreamed-of threats arose years later.

History does not repeat itself, but it delights in patterns and symmetries. When the stories of American "regime change" operations are taken together, they reveal much about why the United States overthrows foreign governments and what consequences it brings on itself by doing so. They also teach lessons for the future.

PART ONE

The Imperial Era

1

A Hell of a Time Up at the Palace

Darkness had already enveloped Honolulu when a pair of well-dressed conspirators knocked on one of the most imposing doors in town. The man they came to visit held the key to their revolution. He was not a warrior or a warlord, not a financier, not a politician, not an arms dealer. John L. Stevens was the American minister to Hawaii, and that night he joined an audacious plot to overthrow Hawaii's queen and bring her country into the United States.

Stevens and the men who visited him on the evening of January 14, 1893, fully understood the seriousness of their mission, but they could not have known what a long shadow they would cast over history. They were the first Americans who ever met to plan and carry out the overthrow of a foreign government. That night they did much more than seal a country's fate. They also opened a tumultuous century of American-sponsored coups, revolutions, and invasions.

Hawaii was in the midst of an epic confrontation between tradition and modernity. Its tribal, land-based culture was collapsing under pressure from the relentlessly expanding sugar industry. A few dozen American and European families effectively controlled both the economy and the government, ruling through a succession of native monarchs who were little more than figureheads.

This system worked wonderfully for the elite, but it turned natives into underlings in their own land. Among those who wished to redress the balance was Queen Liliuokalani, and on that January day she convened her cabinet to make a shocking announcement. She would proclaim a new constitution under which only Hawaiian citizens had the right to vote. High property qualifications for voting would be eliminated, and the power of the nonnative elite would be sharply curtailed.

The queen's four cabinet ministers were aghast. They warned her that Americans in Hawaii would never accept such a constitution. She replied by insisting that she had the right to promulgate what she wished. As their debate turned angry, two ministers excused themselves and slipped out of the palace. One of them, John Colburn, the interior minister, rushed downtown to alert his lifelong friend Lorrin Thurston, a firebrand lawyer and antiroyalist plotter.

"Lorrin," he began, "we've been having a hell of a time up at the palace."

Thurston and other haole, as Hawaiians called their white neighbors, had been waiting for an excuse to strike against the monarchy. Now they had one. Stevens was on their side, and behind him lay the power of the United States. This was their moment.

The stage was now set for something new in history. Never before had an American diplomat helped organize the overthrow of a government to which he was officially accredited. The story of what led Stevens to do this, and the larger story of how the United States came to dominate Hawaii, are full of themes that would resurface time and again as Americans fell into the habit of deposing foreign leaders.

FOR NEARLY ALL OF THE FIVE MILLION YEARS SINCE IT VIOLENTLY EMERGED from the depths of the Pacific Ocean, Hawaii was defined by its isolation. Its first settlers, probably Polynesians from islands to the south, are thought to have arrived roughly around the time of Christ. Over the centuries, Hawaiians had little contact with anyone else because almost no one could cross the vast expanse of ocean that surrounded their islands. Thousands of unique plant and animal species evolved, more than almost anywhere else on earth.

Hawaii's human inhabitants developed a remarkably distinctive society that bound them together in elaborate webs of obligation, ritual, and reverence for nature. If not precisely a tropical Eden, this was a place where, over many generations, people maintained a well-balanced culture that sustained them both physically and spiritually. One historian has described it as "very successful" and "less brutish than were most of its contemporary societies throughout the world, even those of patronizing Europe, just as it was less brutal than are most of those that adorn our civilized world today."

That changed with astonishing suddenness, beginning on January 18, 1778. At daybreak that morning, off the coast of Kauai, a spectacle unfolded that stunned Hawaiians no less than the landing of a spaceship would stun them today. What seemed to be two floating islands appeared on the horizon. People became frenzied, some with excitement and others with terror. Many dropped their work and raced down Waimea Valley toward the shore.

"Chiefs and commoners saw the wonderful sight and marveled at it," according to one account. "One asked another, 'What are those branching things?' and the other answered, 'They are trees moving about on the sea.'"

These apparitions were actually British ships commanded by one of the century's most celebrated explorers, Captain James Cook. Awed natives at first took Cook for a god, but quite soon—perhaps inevitably, given the cultural differences between them—the two groups fell into violent conflict. Many islanders were happy when the foreigners sailed away, and pelted them with rocks when they returned a year later in desperate need of supplies. Hungry sailors began taking what they needed, and after they killed a Hawaiian chief, warriors took bloody revenge. They swarmed onto Cook and slashed his body to bits. Later they roasted his remains in an underground oven. It was one of the last times native Hawaiians were able to impose their will on whites.

Before long, Cook had his revenge. He and his men had left behind plagues more ferocious than even they could have imagined. Their few weeks of contact with natives, ranging from handshakes to sexual intercourse, produced the near-extinction of the Hawaiian race.

Cook's men, as he himself had predicted in his journal, set off an epidemic of venereal disease on the islands. That was just the beginning. Over the decades that followed, fevers, dysentery, influenza, lung and kidney ailments, rickets, diarrhea, meningitis, typhus, and leprosy killed hundreds of thousands of Hawaiians.

Once Hawaii was charted, it became a regular port of call for sailors of all sorts. They were not, however, the only ones who cast their eyes on this archipelago. So did a group of devout Presbyterians and Congregationalists from New England. From several sources—ship captains, a popular book about a Hawaiian orphan who made his way to Connecticut and embraced Christianity, and a series of articles published in a Maine newspaper called the *Kennebec Journal*—they heard that this remote land was full of heathens waiting to be converted. Between 1820 and 1850, nearly two hundred of them felt so moved by these accounts that they volunteered to spend the rest of their lives doing God's work in the Sandwich Islands, as Cook had named them.

Much of what these missionaries found appalled them. Hawaiian society, with its casual, communal nature and animist spirituality, could hardly have been more different from the stern, cold way of life to which these New Englanders were accustomed. Principles that the missionaries took to be cornerstones of civilization, such as ambition, thrift, individuality, and private property, were all but unknown to Hawaiians. They believed in the divinity of hills, trees, animals, wind, thunder, and even dewdrops. Some practiced incest, polygamy, infanticide, and *hanai,* a custom under which mothers would give their newborn infants to friends, relatives, or chiefs as a way of broadening their web of family relationships. Most were comfortable with nakedness and sexuality. To the dour missionaries, they seemed the most accursed sinners on earth. One found them "exceedingly ignorant; stupid to all that is lovely, grand and awful in the works of God; low, naked, filthy, vile and sensual; covered with every abomination, stained with blood and black with crime."

Armed with a degree of certitude that can come only from deep faith, missionaries worked tirelessly to impose their values on the people around them—or, as they would have put it, to save savages from damnation. "The streets, formerly so full of animation, are now deserted," reported a traveler who visited Honolulu in 1825. "Games of all kinds, even the most innocent, are prohibited. Singing is a punishable offense, and the consummate profligacy of attempting to dance would certainly find no mercy."

As the years passed, some missionaries lost their passion for enforcing this harsh moral code. So did many of their sons and grandsons, who were sent back to the United States for education and returned imbued with the restless spirit of their explosively growing mother country, where opportunity seemed to lie at the end of every wagon trail. Back in Hawaii, they looked around them and saw land that seemed to be crying out for cultivation. Several of them guessed that sugar, which the natives had been growing for centuries but never refined, would thrive there.

No one better symbolized the evolution of the haole community in

Hawaii than Amos Starr Cooke. Born in Danbury, Connecticut, Cooke arrived as a missionary in 1837 and served for several years as the notoriously strict director of a school for high-born Hawaiian children. The temptation of wealth eventually led him away from the religious path, and in 1851 he decided to try his hand at planting sugar. With another former missionary who had an eye for the main chance, Samuel Castle, he founded Castle & Cooke, which would become one of the world's largest sugar producers.

To begin large-scale farming, men like these needed land. Buying it was complicated, since native Hawaiians had little notion of private property or cash exchange. They had great difficulty understanding how a transaction—or anything else, for that matter—could deprive them of land.

In the late 1840s, Amos Starr Cooke helped persuade King Kamehameha III, a former student of his, to proclaim a land reform that pulled away one of the pillars of Hawaiian society. Under its provisions, large tracts of communal land were cut into small individual parcels, and most of the rest became the king's "royal domain." By establishing the principle of land ownership, this reform gave ambitious planters, including many missionaries and sons of missionaries, the legal right to buy as much land as they wished. Dozens quickly did so. Before long, the missionary and planter elites had blended into a single class.

One obstacle still lay between these planters and great wealth. The market for their sugar was in the United States, but to protect American growers, the United States levied prohibitive tariffs on imported sugar. In the 1850s, Hawaiian planters tried to resolve this problem by the simple expedient of making Hawaii part of the United States. Officials in Washington, however, had not yet developed a taste for overseas colonies, and brushed them aside. Later the planters tried to persuade American leaders to sign a free-trade agreement, or "reciprocity treaty," that would allow them to sell their sugar without tariffs in the United States, but that offer also fell on deaf ears.

Over the years that followed, a new generation of businessmen, politicians, and military planners in the United States became more interested in overseas trade. Hawaiian planters came up with an idea designed to appeal to their ambition: in exchange for a reciprocity treaty, they would grant the United States exclusive rights to maintain commercial and military bases in Hawaii. They arranged for the compliant monarch,

King Kalakaua, to endorse this plan and travel to Washington to present it. President Ulysses S. Grant found it too tempting to pass up. During the summer of 1876, the treaty was duly drawn up, signed, and ratified. This was its historic provision:

> It is agreed, on the part of His Hawaiian Majesty, that so long as this treaty shall remain in force, he will not lease or otherwise dispose of or create any lien upon any port, harbor, or other territory in his dominions, or grant any special privileges or rights of use therein, to any other power, state, or government, nor make any treaty by which any other nation shall obtain the same privileges, relative to the admission of articles free of duty, hereby secured to the United States.

This treaty preserved the facade of Hawaiian independence, but in effect turned Hawaii into an American protectorate. The preeminent historian of the period, William Adam Russ, wrote that it "made Hawaii virtually a sphere of influence of the United States, but the sugar planters in the islands were pleased. . . . The political consequences of this reciprocity agreement cannot be overestimated. When Hawaii was finally annexed in 1898, practically everyone agreed that the first real step had been reciprocity, that is to say, economic annexation."

News of this deal infuriated many native Hawaiians. When their protests turned violent, the alarmed king felt it prudent to ask for American protection. This the United States provided, in the form of 150 marines, who became his personal and political bodyguards.

The sugar industry quickly began to boom. In the first five years after the treaty was signed, the number of plantations in Hawaii more than tripled. Sugar exports to the United States, which totaled 21 million pounds in 1876, soared to 114 million pounds in 1883 and 225 million pounds in 1890. Money rained down on the white planters who controlled Hawaii's economy.

Growing sugar is labor-intensive, but neither whites nor native Hawaiians were willing to work in the fields. After considering several alternatives, planters began importing Japanese and Chinese laborers, whom they called "coolies." They came by the thousands after the reciprocity treaty was signed. That strengthened the planters' opposition to democracy, since universal suffrage would most likely have produced a government dominated by nonwhites.

. . .

THE RECIPROCITY TREATY WAS FOR A TERM OF EIGHT YEARS, AND WHEN IT expired, sugar growers from Louisiana tried to block its renewal. This greatly alarmed Hawaiian planters, whose fortunes depended on it. They arranged for King Kalakaua, who had fallen almost completely under their influence, to make a further concession. The renewed treaty included a clause giving the United States control over Pearl Harbor, on the island of Oahu, the finest natural port in the northern Pacific.

A few years later, King Kalakaua approved a constitution that secured the planters' power. It vested most authority in cabinet ministers, prohibited the monarch from dismissing any minister without the legislature's approval, and set wealth and property qualifications for election to the legislature. Called the "bayonet constitution" because it was imposed with the implied threat of armed force, it also gave all Americans and Europeans, even noncitizens, the right to vote but denied that right to Asian laborers. Its author was Lorrin Thurston, and after Kalakaua reluctantly accepted it, planters told him he also had to accept Thurston as his interior minister.

Kalakaua's inability to resist these impositions showed how fully the Hawaiian monarchy had come under white control. Whites reached this position not overnight, but through a steady series of steps. William Adam Russ wrote that they "slowly and imperceptibly wormed their way, year by year, into the King's favor until they were the power behind the throne. Controlling the business and wealth of the islands, they became the dominant minority amongst a people who only a few years before had welcomed them as visitors."

This system brought more than a decade of great prosperity to Hawaii's sugar planters, but two blows suddenly upset it. The first came in 1890, when Congress enacted the McKinley Tariff, which allowed sugar from all countries to enter the United States duty-free and compensated domestic producers with a "bounty" of two cents per pound. This wiped away the protected regime under which Hawaiian planters had thrived, and plunged them into what one of their leaders called "the depths of despair." Within two years, the value of their sugar exports plummeted from $13 million to $8 million.

As if that were not enough, the planters' puppet monarch, Kalakaua, died in 1891, leaving his independent-minded sister, Liliuokalani, to succeed him. The new queen had attended a missionary school and embraced Christianity but never lost touch with her native heritage. When her brother turned Pearl Harbor over to the Americans in 1887, she wrote in her diary that it was "a day of infamy in Hawaiian history." Later that year, while she was in London at the jubilee celebrating Queen Victoria's fiftieth year on the throne, she received news of the "bayonet constitution" and wrote that it constituted "a revolutionary movement inaugurated by those of foreign blood, or American blood."

Liliuokalani was fifty-two years old when the chief justice of Hawaii's Supreme Court, Albert Judd, administered the oath that made her queen on January 29, 1891. After the ceremony, Judd took her aside and offered a piece of private advice. "Should any members of your cabinet propose anything to you," he counseled, "say yes." Had she heeded this warning, had she accepted the role of a figurehead and allowed the haole to continue running Hawaii, she might never have been overthrown.

Some of the new queen's enemies were contemptible quick-buck profiteers without the slightest interest in the land or the people around them. Others, however, had lived on the islands for years or had been born there. Some loved Hawaii and considered themselves true patriots. Lorrin Thurston was one of these.

All four of Thurston's grandparents had come to Hawaii as missionaries. He attended schools—one of which expelled him as an "incorrigible" rebel—that also had Hawaiian students. Unlike some of his haole friends, he became fluent in the Hawaiian language and even assumed a Hawaiian name, Kakina, that he used in signing letters and documents throughout his life. While still a teenager he immersed himself in politics, skipping school one day in 1874 to watch the bitterly contested election of King Kalakaua, which erupted into rioting. For the rest of his life, he was drawn to the center of great events.

Thurston never graduated from high school but found work as a law clerk and as a supervisor and bookkeeper at Wailuku Sugar Company. With the money he earned, he put himself through Columbia University Law School, in New York, and then returned to Honolulu to practice law in partnership with his friend William Smith. Soon he became a leader in the fight to undermine the Hawaiian monarchy. Imbued as he was with the idea that only whites could rule the islands efficiently, he was able to consider this a form of patriotism.

At the beginning of 1892, Thurston founded the Annexation Club, with the declared goal of bringing Hawaii into the United States. At its first meeting, he was chosen as its leader. Soon afterward, he persuaded the club to send him to Washington to drum up support for its cause.

Thurston carried a letter of introduction from John L. Stevens, the American minister in Honolulu. He presented his case for annexation so convincingly to Secretary of the Navy Benjamin Tracy that Tracy took him to the White House to meet President Benjamin Harrison.

> Mr. Tracy told me to wait in an outer room while he spoke with the President. After about a half-hour, the secretary re-appeared and beckoned me to accompany him outdoors. Then he spoke: "I have explained fully to the President what you have said to me, and have this to say to you: the President does not think he should see you, but he authorizes me to say that, if conditions in Hawaii compel you people to act as you have indicated, and you come to Washington with an annexation proposition, you will find an extremely sympathetic administration here." That was all I wanted to know.

Thurston brought home the news his fellow conspirators most wished to hear: the United States was on their side. This was no surprise to Stevens. Before leaving Washington to assume his post, he had discussed the annexation question at length with Secretary of State James G. Blaine, and knew him to be an ardent supporter. The American naval commander at Honolulu, Felix McCurley, promised him that the navy would "fully cooperate and sustain him in any action he may take." These assurances left him with no doubt that both the State Department and the navy wished him to do whatever was necessary to overthrow Hawaii's monarchy.

A few months after Thurston returned to Honolulu, he received an extraordinary letter from the representative he had left behind in Washington, a well-connected court clerk named Archibald Hopkins. It said the Harrison administration wished to offer the queen a bribe. "I am authorized to inform you," the letter said, "that the United States Government will pay to Queen Liliuokalani and those connected with her, the sum of two hundred and fifty thousand dollars, for the assignment to the United States of the Sovereignty of Hawaii." Thurston replied that there was unfortunately "no probability" of the queen's accepting the offer, since she was "in an independent frame of mind . . . of a stubborn headstrong disposition, jealous of royal prerogatives and desirous of extending rather than giving up any of the power and privileges which she now possesses."

Thurston and his comrades wished above all for good government, which to them meant rule by the white minority. The census of 1890 found that there were 40,612 native Hawaiians on the archipelago; 27,391 Chinese and Japanese laborers; and a grand total of just 6,220 Americans, Britons, Germans, French, Norwegians, and Hawaiian-born whites. Given these numbers, it was natural that the haole would want nothing to do with democracy. For decades they had effectively controlled the islands, and by imposing the "bayonet constitution," they had formalized their power. They had no desire to surrender it by adopting a system under which each resident of the islands would have an equal vote.

QUEEN LILIUOKALANI SPENT THE MORNING OF JANUARY 14, 1893, PRESIDING over an elaborate ceremony that marked the end of the annual legislative session. She entered the assembly hall wearing a lavender silk gown and a diamond coronet, attended by ministers, chamberlains, court ladies, and a retinue of guards carrying traditional feather-topped poles called *kahili*. With what one witness called "great dignity," she read her speech thanking the legislators for their work and bidding them farewell.

By the time the queen returned to Iolani Palace, the seat of Hawaiian royalty, something unusual was happening there. Several dozen formally dressed Hawaiians, members of a group called the Hawaiian Patriotic Association, had assembled in a show of support the queen had evidently orchestrated. She received them in her Throne Room. One held a copy of the new constitution curbing haole power and begged her to promulgate it. With a flourish she agreed, and then withdrew to an adjoining room to which she had summoned her cabinet.

The moment Lorrin Thurston learned that the queen was trying to proclaim a new constitution, he swung into action. By early afternoon he and a group of comrades had corralled her four cabinet ministers, who he found "in a blue funk as to their course." His advice to them was as radical as it was subversive: they should declare the queen in rebellion, proclaim her throne vacant, and turn power over to what he liked to call "the intelligent part of the community."

It was a daring plan, but how could the rebels prevent native Hawaiians, including the queen's own Household Guards, from rising up to defend their monarch? The answer lay offshore. Resting at anchor near Pearl Harbor was the *Boston,* a 3,000-ton cruiser that was one of the most modern warships in United States Navy. She cut an imposing figure, with two towering masts, two smokestacks, a battery of cannon on each side, and the American flag flying from her bow. Nearly two hundred sailors and marines were aboard. If the American minister called them to shore, they would make an ideal protection force for the new regime.

Late that afternoon, Thurston summoned several dozen comrades to the Fort Street law office of William Smith, his closest friend and collaborator. There he proposed that his new protégé Henry Cooper, a recent arrival from Indiana, be empowered to name a "Committee of Safety" that would "devise ways and means of dealing with the situation." All agreed. Cooper picked thirteen men from the crowd, including himself and Thurston. All were active members of the Annexation Club. Nine were American by birth or ancestry. No native Hawaiian was among them.

Thurston's book of memoirs contains a foldout page with individual photos of each member of the Committee of Safety. They look to have been an impressive group. Each one is formally dressed. Most appear young (Thurston himself was thirty-five). All have whiskers, each set designed differently, from Smith's elegant handlebar mustache to Thurston's neatly cropped black beard and Cooper's longer, fuller one. None is smiling. They might have been the chamber of commerce in a small American city, or a delegation from the mainland visiting Hawaii on an inspection tour.

After Cooper finished naming the Committee of Safety, he asked the rest of the crowd to leave so that the group could hold its first meeting. As soon as the door was closed, Thurston spoke. "I move that it is the sense of this meeting that the solution of the present situation is annexation to the United States," he said simply. His motion was adopted without dissent.

The revolutionaries were eager for confrontation, but the queen, their target, proved less so. While Thurston was marshaling his forces, she was at the palace, listening to arguments that her proposed constitution was too radical. Finally she yielded. At mid-afternoon she emerged from the cabinet room and faced her expectant supporters.

"I was ready, and expected to proclaim a new constitution today," she told them from a balcony. "But behold, I have met with obstacles that prevented it. Return to your homes peaceably and quietly. . . . I am obliged to postpone the granting of a new constitution for a few days."

Rather than placating the revolutionaries, this statement further inflamed them. By suggesting that she would resume her campaign for a new constitution in "a few days," or even "sometime," as the Hawaiian phrase she used could also have been translated, the queen made clear that she had not given up her effort to restore native Hawaiian political power. As long as she was on her throne, the haole would be insecure.

That evening Thurston invited the men he trusted most to his wood-frame home for what he called "a sub-meeting." In all there were six, including William Castle, son of the missionary-turned-planter Samuel Castle and the country's largest landowner. All knew that troops aboard the *Boston* held the key to their victory. They also knew that Stevens, who had the power to bring those troops ashore at any moment, strongly supported their cause. Now, they decided, was the time to call upon him. This would be the call that sealed Hawaii's fate.

When the "sub-meeting" broke up, five of the six guests took their leave and walked back to their homes. Thurston's friend and coconspirator William Smith stayed behind. After a short private discussion, the two of them decided that despite the late hour, they should visit Stevens immediately, tell him of their plans, and appeal for his decisive help.

Stevens had just returned from a ten-day cruise aboard the *Boston* and must have been surprised to hear a knock on his door that night. He knew the two men and their business, though, and welcomed them. According to the later report of a presidential commission, "They disclosed to him all their plans."

They feared arrest and punishment. He promised them protection. They needed the troops on shore to overawe the queen's supporters and the Government. This he agreed to, and did furnish. They had few arms and no trained soldiers. They did not mean to fight. It was arranged between them and the American Minister that the proclamation dethroning the queen and organizing a provisional government should be read from the Government building, and he would follow it with speedy recognition. All this was to be done with American troops, provided with small arms and artillery, across a narrow street within a stone's throw.

On the next morning, Sunday, January 15, Thurston rose at dawn. He still hoped to bring the queen's cabinet ministers into his plot, and at six-thirty he met with the two he considered most favorable, Interior Minister John Colburn and Attorney General Arthur Peterson. He told them that he and his comrades had decided they could not "sit over a volcano" indefinitely and were now determined to overthrow the queen. Would these two eminent gentlemen join the rebellion?

Both were taken aback and said they would need time to consider such a bold offer. Thurston left unhappily, warning the men not to tell the other two ministers what he had revealed about his plans. They did so anyway.

From that unpleasant meeting, Thurston proceeded to William Castle's two-story clapboard manse, where the Committee of Safety was waiting. He reported his failure to bring cabinet ministers into the plot but said he was still certain of success. The revolution, he told his comrades, must be proclaimed at a public meeting the next day. They agreed, and then decided to take care of one formality. Once the queen was overthrown, Hawaii would need a temporary leader to steer it into the United States. Thurston, the tireless incendiary who had orchestrated this revolution, was the obvious choice.

At that moment, Thurston made a characteristically shrewd decision. His long and virulent campaign against the monarchy had made him perhaps the most hated man in Hawaii. He was sharply opinionated, hot-tempered, and highly undiplomatic, and he knew it. So he thanked his friends for their nomination but said he should not accept it because he was "too radical" and had "too many business arrangements." He would look for someone better.

Excitement crackled through Hawaii's haole community on Monday morning. The Committee of Safety gathered at Castle's home to complete plans for that afternoon's mass meeting. It was in the midst of its work when, to everyone's surprise, Charles Wilson, the queen's police chief and supposed paramour, suddenly appeared at the door. He called Thurston outside.

"I know what you fellows are up to, and I want you to quit and go home," he said. Thurston shook his head.

"We are not going home, Charlie," he replied. "Things have advanced too far."

Wilson said he could personally guarantee that the queen would never again proclaim a new constitution, "even if I have to lock her up in a room to keep her from doing it." Thurston remained unmoved.

"It's no use, Charlie," he said. "We will not take any further chances."

Wilson curtly told Thurston that he and the rest should consider themselves warned. Then he withdrew, walked briskly to the palace, and burst into the cabinet room. He bluntly told the ministers that they had only one hope of saving their government and the monarchy. They must order the immediate arrest of every conspirator.

That was too drastic a step for the four ministers, whose loyalty was divided, to say the least. They feared the wrath of Stevens and the United States. Wilson cursed them as "damned cowards," but they were already sensing how this drama would end.

Thurston and the other conspirators had taken Wilson's warning seriously. Moments after he left, they decided it was time to call in American troops. They wrote an appeal to Stevens that was less than eloquent but compelling nonetheless.

We the undersigned, citizens and residents of Honolulu, respectfully represent that, in view of the recent public events in this Kingdom, culminating in the revolutionary acts of Queen Liliuokalani on Saturday last, the public safety is menaced and lives and property are in peril, and we appeal to you and the United States forces at your command for assistance.

The Queen, with the aid of armed forces, and accompanied by threats of violence and bloodshed from those with whom she was acting, attempted to proclaim a new constitution; and while prevented for the time being from accomplishing her object, declared publicly that she would only defer her action.

This conduct and action was upon an occasion and under circumstances which have created general alarm and terror. We are unable to protect ourselves without aid, and therefore pray for the protection of the United States forces.

Thirteen men, the ones who composed the Committee of Safety, signed this appeal. All were white, and all but two owned stock in sugar plantations or other enterprises in the country. Among them were some of Hawaii's richest men, including William Castle and the shipping magnate William Wilder.

After dispatching their appeal to Stevens, the insurgents went their separate ways, agreeing to meet after lunch at the Honolulu armory, where their mass meeting was to be held. On the streets they saw copies of an official proclamation that had been posted around town. It was a pledge from the queen that, in the future, she would seek to change the constitution "only by methods provided in the constitution itself."

This concession came too late to placate the more than one thousand people who converged on the armory at two o'clock that afternoon. Nearly all were from what one historian called the "male white foreign element," and none were in the mood for compromise. Wilder ran the meeting, and Henry Baldwin, one of Hawaii's most powerful sugar barons, was among the speakers.

To no one's surprise, Thurston was the dominant figure at this rally. As a boisterous audience listened, he read a resolution declaring that the queen had acted "illegally and unconstitutionally" by pursuing policies that were "revolutionary and treasonable in character." It concluded by authorizing the Committee of Safety to "devise such ways and means as may be necessary to secure the permanent maintenance of law and order and the protection of life, liberty and property in Hawaii."

"I say, gentlemen, that now and here is the time to act!" Thurston thundered, and the crowd erupted in cheers. "The man who has not the spirit to rise after the menace to our liberties has no right to keep them. Has the tropical sun cooled and thinned our blood, or have we flowing in our veins the warm, rich blood which makes men love liberty and die for it? I move the adoption of the resolution!"

All of that afternoon's speakers denounced the queen for her attempt to impose a new constitution. None, however, called for her overthrow. Thurston later explained that he did not consider that necessary, since "there was a unanimous understanding that dethronement and abrogation were intended." He also had to worry that if he and his friends openly called for insurrection, even the pusillanimous cabinet might be moved to order their arrest. Insurrection was what he was planning, though, and the crowd's unanimous adoption of his resolution steeled his resolve.

That mass meeting was not the only one held in Honolulu on the afternoon of January 16. As it was under way, several hundred supporters of the queen gathered at nearby Palace Square for a rally of their own. Few had any idea of how advanced the antiroyalist plot was. Their speeches were cautious and for the most part polite, although one speaker did declare, "Any man that would speak against a woman, especially a queen, is an animal and a fit companion for a hog."

The queen's supporters dispersed after their Palace Square rally, but the rebels who had met at the armory did not rest. At four o'clock, the thirteen members of the Committee of Safety gathered at Smith's home to plot their next move. After some discussion, they decided they needed at least one more day to organize themselves. This meant Stevens would have to delay landing troops. Thurston and Smith went immediately to the American legation to ask him to do so. To their surprise, he refused.

"Gentlemen," he told them, "the troops of the *Boston* land this afternoon at five o'clock, whether you are ready or not."

Stevens had much in common with Thurston and the other revolutionaries whose victory he was about to secure. He was born in Maine in 1820, the same year the first group of missionaries arrived in Hawaii, and as a young man had been a preacher. Later he struck up a friendship with Blaine, then an ambitious local politician and editor of the *Kennebec Journal*. Blaine was an ardent supporter of Hawaiian annexation, and wrote an editorial urging it in the first issue of the *Journal* that he edited. Stevens embraced the cause with equal fervor.

In the years after the Civil War, Blaine began making his mark in politics. He was elected to Congress, became Speaker of the House, and in 1884 was the Republican candidate for president, losing to Grover Cleveland. Five years later, President Benjamin Harrison named him secretary of state. One of Blaine's first acts was to appoint Stevens as minister to Hawaii.

The chain of command for the Hawaiian revolution was thus fixed. Secretary of State Blaine gave the go-ahead. He sent Stevens to Honolulu to make the necessary arrangements. Once there, Stevens found Thurston ready to act. Together they planned and carried out the rebellion.

On the afternoon of January 16, 1893, Stevens sat down at his desk and wrote a brief, fateful note to Captain Gilbert Wiltse, the extravagantly mustachioed commander of the *Boston*. Its single sentence is a dry classic of diplomatic mendacity, full of motifs that Americans would hear often in the century to come.

In view of the existing critical circumstances in Honolulu, indicating an inadequate legal force, I request you to land marines and sailors from the ship under your command for the protection of the United States legation and the United States consulate, and to secure the safety of American life and property.

At five o'clock that evening, 162 American marines and sailors landed at a pier at the foot of Nuuana Avenue in Honolulu. They comprised an artillery company, a company of marines, and two companies of infantrymen. Each soldier had a rifle slung around his neck and wore an ammunition belt with sixty extra cartridges. The artillerymen hauled Gatling guns and small cannon.

Thurston watched from the pier as the soldiers disembarked and followed them for several blocks. On his way back to his office, he ran into a plantation manager named W. H. Rickard, who held a seat in the legislature and strongly supported the queen. Rickard was in a rage.

"Damn you, Thurston!" he shouted, shaking his fist. "You did this!"

"Did what?"

"Had these troops landed!"

"You credit me with considerable influence, to be able to direct the United States troops," Thurston replied. "I had no more to do with their coming ashore than you did, and I have no more idea of what they are going to do than you have."

Thurston was too modest. He and Stevens were working closely together. They were not in constant touch during those January days and did not tell each other of their hour-by-hour plans, but that was not necessary. Each understood what the other was doing and gave the other crucial support. Neither could have carried out the revolution alone. Their partnership made it possible.

Hawaiians who peered from behind doors or stopped in their tracks to stare as American soldiers marched through the sandy streets that day must have been baffled. Few had ever seen a Western-style military formation, and even fewer had any idea why the soldiers had landed. Only when they saw members of the Committee of Safety cheering the advancing force did most of them realize that it was hostile to the monarchy. The cabinet gathered for an emergency meeting, and soon afterward Foreign Minister Samuel Parker sent a plaintive appeal to Stevens.

> As the situation is one that does not call for interference on the part of the U.S. Government, my colleagues and myself would most respectfully request of Your Excellency the authority upon which this action was taken. I would also add that any protection that might have been considered necessary for the American Legation or for American interests in this city would have been cheerfully furnished by Her Majesty's Government.

Stevens did not reply to this message. He was out surveying possible campsites for the American soldiers, finally settling on a building called Arion Hall. This would not have been a good place from which to guard Americans, since few lived or worked nearby. It had, however, the convenient asset of being next to Government House and within easy cannon range of Iolani Palace.

As the soldiers set up camp, the Committee of Safety was celebrating at the home of one of its members, the Tasmanian-born Henry Waterhouse. This was the committee's moment of triumph, and every member realized it. The landing of American troops guaranteed their victory. All that was needed to complete the revolutionary charade was for them to proclaim a new government and for Stevens to recognize it. American soldiers would discourage any resistance from the queen or her partisans.

This meeting at Waterhouse's home was remarkable for two reasons. First, by odd coincidence, three of the most important conspirators— the impassioned lawyer Thurston, the sugar baron Castle, and the shipping magnate Wilder—had taken ill and were unable to attend. Second, and perhaps not unrelated, this meeting marked the emergence of the man who would dominate Hawaii for the next period of its history. He was Sanford Dole, a grandson of missionaries, Williams College graduate, and respected Supreme Court judge. Several years later, Dole would help his cousin's son, James, to begin building the fruit company that bears their family name.

Although Dole was not at Waterhouse's home that evening and was not a member of the Annexation Club, he had attended Thurston's "submeeting" two nights earlier, so he knew what was afoot. When Committee of Safety members began musing about whom they should choose to run Hawaii after their revolution, someone mentioned his name. This "met with the immediate approval of the entire group," one participant later said. An emissary went to fetch the white-bearded jurist.

Mrs. Dole and I were sitting in our parlor when a man who lives in Kaneohe came over from Mr. Waterhouse's and said they wanted me to head this affair. I said "No." I said "Why will not Thurston take it?" I was told he was sick abed from having worked day and night on this matter since it was initiated. I agreed to go over. . . .

A messenger was sent over to Minister Stevens's house to inquire if it was correct that he was in sympathy with us—and he was, I gathered.

I came home to sleep over the offer, but my sleep was fitful and greatly disturbed. I would sleep and then wake up with this matter on my mind, and passed a very unpleasant night.

Early the next morning, Tuesday, January 17, Dole called on the bedridden Thurston. They talked for a few minutes about Hawaii's future. Dole said he had not yet decided whether to accept leadership of the new government. He did, however, agree to deliver a letter that Thurston had written to Stevens. It informed Stevens that the new government would be proclaimed that afternoon, and asked that he recognize it promptly.

After returning home, Dole sat alone for a long time, gazing from his veranda over the palm trees and the warm ocean beyond. Finally he decided to accept the provisional presidency of a new Republic of Hawaii. He regarded it, he later wrote, as "a position I would fill possibly for a few months" while arrangements were made for Hawaii's annexation to the United States.

Dole's first act as part of the rebellion was to visit its patron. He handed Stevens the letter Thurston had given him. Stevens read it, then looked up and said to Dole, "I think you have a great opportunity."

From the American legation, Dole proceeded to Smith's law office, where the conspirators were gathered. He told them he was ready to lead their incoming government, and they cheered him for it. With his ingrained sense of propriety, he then went to Government House and wrote out his resignation from the Supreme Court. Only after finishing did he realize that there was no longer any authority to whom he could submit it.

The queen's police chief, Charles Wilson, had not yet reconciled himself to the death of the monarchy. He ordered the Household Guards to prepare for action, and for a short while it seemed possible that combat might break out. Cabinet ministers had at their disposal about 550 soldiers and police officers, most of them armed with rifles, and fourteen artillery pieces. Whether to send them into hostile action was a decision none of them had ever imagined making. They were desperate for someone to tell them what to do. With no one else to consult, they summoned the handful of foreign ambassadors resident in Honolulu. All turned up except Stevens, who pleaded illness. All counseled against resistance.

That morning, the revolution's only drops of blood were shed. One of the conspirators, John Good, had spent several hours collecting weapons and ammunition. As he drove his heavily laden wagon past the corner of Fort and King Streets, a police officer tried to stop him. He pulled out his pistol and fired, wounding the officer in his shoulder, and then proceeded on his way.

In a last-minute effort to fend off the inevitable, the queen ordered her entire cabinet to ride immediately to see Stevens. He agreed to receive only one of the four ministers, Attorney General Peterson, who told him that the cabinet was still the official government of Hawaii. Stevens was not impressed. He sent Peterson off with a warning that if the "insurgents were attacked or arrested by the queen's forces, the United States troops would intervene."

That made unmistakably clear that American soldiers had landed not to preserve peace but to assure a rebel victory. It sealed the monarchy's doom. All that remained was to make the act official, and shortly after two o'clock that afternoon, the rebels did so. They assembled in front of Government House, the official seat of political power in Hawaii, and one of them, Henry Cooper, who had arrived on the islands barely two years before, stepped forward. In his hand he held a proclamation that Thurston had dictated from his sickbed that morning. As about sixty American soldiers stood nearby, he read it to a small crowd.

Its essence came first: "The Hawaiian monarchical system of government is hereby abrogated." Other clauses established a provisional government "to exist until terms of union with the United States of America have been negotiated and agreed upon"; named Sanford Dole to head it; and decreed that all functionaries of the old government could keep their jobs except six: Wilson, the four cabinet ministers, and Queen Liliuokalani.

The few dozen spectators raised a cheer. When it subsided, Dole and the three men who constituted his new "executive council" walked into Government House. At the suite where cabinet ministers usually worked, they found only a few clerks. The ministers had adjourned to the nearby police station and were busily preparing yet another appeal to Stevens. At this late moment, they still hoped their executioner might suddenly come to their rescue. Short of ordering armed resistance, there was nothing else they could do.

"Certain treasonable persons at present occupy the Government building in Honolulu," the ministers wrote to Stevens in what turned out to be their last piece of official correspondence. "Her Majesty's cabinet asks respectfully, has your country recognized said Provisional

Government, and if not, Her Majesty's Government under the above existing circumstances respectfully requests the assistance of your Government in preserving the peace of the country."

As cabinet ministers were composing this letter, Dole and his comrades were already working at Government House, busily dispatching commissions, letters, and proclamations. American troops stood on guard outside. Then, at around four-thirty, a messenger arrived with the document that certified the conspirators' triumph. It was a one-sentence proclamation from Stevens:

> A Provisional Government having been duly constituted in the place of the recent Government of Queen Liliuokalani, and said Provisional Government being in possession of the Government Building, the Archives and the Treasury and is in control of the capital of the Hawaiian Islands, I hereby recognize said Provisional Government as the *de facto* Government of the Hawaiian Islands.

Neither the queen nor her cabinet had yet yielded or even been asked to do so. One of the conspirators, Samuel Damon, a former adviser to the queen who was still on good terms with her, decided he should be the one to make the demand. He walked the short distance to the police station, where he found cabinet ministers arguing about what to do next. For several minutes they besieged him with protests. He replied by telling them very simply what had happened and what it meant. The United States had recognized the new regime; the old one must surrender.

Cabinet ministers may have felt at least fleeting pangs of anguish, but with an American gunboat lying in the harbor and 162 American soldiers ashore, they knew the day was lost. They agreed to accompany Damon to break the news to the queen. "It was pressed upon her by the ministers and other persons at that conference that it was useless for her to make any contest, because it was one with the United States," one chronicler later wrote. She dismissed the delegation, took up her pen, and wrote an astute, carefully worded statement. It was a surrender but not an abdication, and made clear that she was stepping down only under American pressure.

> I, Liliuokalani, by the Grace of God under the Constitution of the Kingdom, Queen, do hereby solemnly protest against any and all acts done against myself and the constitutional Government of the Hawaiian Kingdom by

certain persons claiming to have established a provisional government of and for this Kingdom.

That I yield to the superior force of the United States of America, whose minister plenipotentiary, John L. Stevens, has caused the United States troops to land at Honolulu and declared that he would support the said provisional government.

Now, to avoid any collision of armed forces and perhaps the loss of life, I do under this protest, and impelled by said force, yield my authority until such time as the Government of the United States shall, upon the facts being presented to it, undo the action of its representatives and reinstate me in the authority which I claim as the constitutional sovereign of the Hawaiian Islands.

After signing this document, the queen ordered her cabinet ministers to give up the police station and the military barracks. The Committee of Safety took possession of them without incident. Dole sent a letter to Stevens expressing his "deep appreciation" for the quick recognition of his government.

Thurston overthrew the Hawaiian monarchy with a core group of fewer than thirty men. They may have thought they made the Hawaiian revolution, and in a sense they did. Without the presence of Stevens or another like-minded American minister, however, they might never have even attempted it. A different kind of minister would have reprimanded the rebels in Hawaii rather than offer them military support. That would have rendered their enterprise all but hopeless.

Although Stevens was an unabashed partisan, he was no rogue agent. He had been sent to Hawaii to promote annexation, and the men who sent him, President Harrison and Secretary of State Blaine, knew precisely what that must entail. It was true, as his critics would later claim, that Stevens acted without explicit orders from Washington. He certainly overstepped his authority when he brought troops ashore, especially since he knew that the "general alarm and terror" of which the Committee of Safety had complained was a fiction. Still, he was doing what the president and the secretary of state wanted. He used his power and theirs to depose the Hawaiian monarchy. That made him the first American to direct the overthrow of a foreign government.

Summary:
- U.S. deception
- Three C's
- Cuba robbed of Independence

2

Bound for Goo-Goo Land

U.S. racism

The euphoria that gripped Cubans in the last days of 1898 was almost beyond imagination. Their country had been racked by rebellion for thirty years, the last few filled with terrible suffering. That summer, as their uprising reached a crescendo, American troops had arrived to help them deliver the death blow that ended three centuries of Spanish rule. Now, with the victory finally won, Cuban patriots and their American comrades were preparing for the biggest party in the island's history.

Leaders of "revolutionary patriotic committees" in Havana planned a full week of festivities, to begin on New Year's Day. There would be grand balls, boat races, fireworks, public speeches, and a gala dinner in honor of the victorious rebel commanders. Thousands of Cuban soldiers would march through the streets to receive the cheers of a grateful nation.

Just as the celebration was to begin, however, the newly named American military governor of Cuba, General John Brooke, made a stunning announcement. He forbade the entire program. Not only would there be no parade of Cuban soldiers, but any who tried to enter Havana would be turned back. Furthermore, the general declared, the United States did not recognize the rebel army and wished it to disband.

This abrupt turnaround outraged Cuban patriots, especially the thousands who had fought so long and tenaciously for independence. The United States snatched their great prize, independence, away from them at the last moment. As years passed, they and their descendants would watch in mounting frustration as their new overlord used various means, including the imposition of tyrants, to keep control of Cuba.

Cubans were among the first people to feel the effect of the profound changes that reshaped the American psyche at the end of the nineteenth

Independence

century. This was the moment when, with remarkable suddenness, Americans ceased to be satisfied with holding territory on the North American mainland. They became consumed with a grand new idea, that of a United States whose influence extended around the world. In the words of the historian Louis Pérez, 1898 was "a watershed year, a moment in which outcomes were both defining and decisive, at once an end and a beginning: that special conjuncture of historical circumstances that often serves to delineate one historical epoch from another."

Territorial expansion was nothing new to Americans. They had been pushing westward ever since the first settlers arrived at Jamestown and Plymouth. In the process they appropriated a great continent, killing or displacing nearly all of its native inhabitants. During the 1840s, in their first burst of imperial war, they seized half of Mexico. Many came to believe that the United States had a "manifest destiny" to occupy and settle all the land bounded by Canada, the Gulf of Mexico, and the Atlantic and Pacific Oceans. The idea of going farther, though, was something quite new.

In the months after the 1893 revolution in Hawaii, that country's new leaders sought annexation to the United States, but President Grover Cleveland—who had succeeded Benjamin Harrison in March of that year—would not hear of it. He was quite right when he declared that most Americans rejected the seizure of faraway lands "as not only opposed to our national policy, but as a perversion of our national mission." Five years later, this consensus evaporated. Almost overnight, it was replaced by a national clamor for overseas expansion. This was the quickest and most profound reversal of public opinion in the history of American foreign policy.

The foundation for this remarkable turnaround was laid by a handful of visionary writers and intellectuals. In 1893 one of them, Frederick Jackson Turner, published one of the most provocative essays ever written by an American historian. He used as his point of departure the national census of 1890, which famously concluded that there was no longer a frontier in the United States. That "closed the first period of American history," Turner declared, and left the country with a stark choice. It could either declare itself satisfied with its present size, something it had never done before, or seek territory beyond North America. In his paper and subsequent articles, Turner left his readers with no doubt as to which he believed would be the wiser choice.

For nearly three centuries the dominant fact in American life has been expansion. With the settlement of the Pacific Coast and the occupation of the free lands, this movement has come to a check. That these energies of expansion will no longer operate would be a rash prediction; and the demands for a vigorous foreign policy, for an inter-oceanic canal, for a revival of our power upon the seas, and for the extension of American influence to outlying islands and adjoining countries, are indications that the movement will continue.

The philosopher-sailor who translated calls like this into a plan of action was Captain Alfred Thayer Mahan, director of the fledgling Naval War College. His book *The Influence of Sea Power upon History* argued that no nation had ever become great without control of foreign markets and access to the natural resources of foreign countries. To achieve that control, he asserted, a nation must maintain a navy powerful enough to protect its merchant fleet and force uncooperative countries to open themselves to trade and investment. A navy with such ambition needed a network of supply bases around the world. Applying these arguments to the United States, Mahan urged that it not only speedily build a canal across Central America but also establish bases in the Caribbean, the Pacific, and wherever else it wished to trade.

"Whether they will or no, Americans must now begin to look outward," Mahan wrote. "The growing production of the country demands it."

Mahan was the toast of Washington during the 1890s. He appeared before congressional committees and developed close friendships with powerful politicians. Senator Henry Cabot Lodge of Massachusetts, a leading expansionist, considered his writings to be secular scripture. Theodore Roosevelt wrote a glowing review of his book and corresponded with him on questions of sea power and the annexation of distant islands. These three—Lodge in Congress, Roosevelt in the executive branch, and Mahan in the minds of men—became the Holy Trinity of American expansionism.

They and others of like mind laid out their case in different ways. Some argued that the United States had to take new territories in order to prevent European powers, or perhaps even Japan, from taking them. Others stressed the missionary aspect of colonialism, the obligation of more "advanced" races to civilize the world. Military commanders realized that a more forceful American military posture would give them greater power and bigger budgets. The most persuasive of these arguments, though, always came back to a single, essential point.

By the end of the nineteenth century, farms and factories in the United States were producing considerably more goods than Americans could consume. For the nation to continue its rise to wealth, it needed foreign markets. They could not be found in Europe, where governments, like that of the United States, protected domestic industries behind high tariff walls. Americans had to look to faraway countries, weak countries, countries that had large markets and rich resources but had not yet fallen under the sway of any great power.

This search for influence abroad gripped the United States in 1898. Spreading democracy, Christianizing heathen nations, building a strong navy, establishing military bases around the world, and bringing foreign governments under American control were never ends in themselves. They were ways for the United States to assure itself access to the markets, resources, and investment potential of distant lands.

Although the American economy grew tremendously during the last quarter of the nineteenth century, much of the country's fabulous new wealth enriched only a few thousand captains of industry. Conditions for most ordinary people were steadily deteriorating. By 1893, one of every six American workers was unemployed, and many of the rest lived on subsistence wages. Plummeting agricultural prices in the 1890s killed off a whole generation of small farmers. Strikes and labor riots broke out from New York to Chicago to California. Socialist and anarchist movements began attracting broad followings. In 1894, Secretary of State Walter Gresham, reflecting a widespread fear, said he saw "symptoms of revolution" spreading across the country.

Many business and political leaders concluded that the only way the American economy could expand quickly enough to deal with these threats was to find new markets abroad. Among them was President Cleveland's Treasury secretary, John Carlisle, who warned in his annual report for 1894 that "the prosperity of our people depends largely on their ability to sell their surplus products in foreign markets at remunerative prices." Senator Albert Beveridge of Indiana came to the same conclusion. "American factories are making more than the American people can use; American soil is producing more than they can consume," he asserted. "Fate has written our policy for us. The trade of the world must and shall be ours."

. . .

CUBA, THE LARGEST ISLAND IN THE CARIBBEAN AND THE LAST GREAT BASTION of what had once been a vast Spanish empire in the Americas, was in turmoil during the second half of the nineteenth century. Patriots there fought a ten-year war of independence that ended with an inconclusive truce in 1878, and rebelled again in 1879–80. Their third offensive broke out in 1895. Its chief organizer was an extravagantly gifted lawyer, diplomat, poet, and essayist, José Martí, who from his New York exile managed to unite a host of factions, both within Cuba and in émigré communities. His success persuaded two celebrated commanders from the first war, Máximo Gómez and Antonio Maceo, to come out of retirement and take up arms again. After careful planning, the three of them landed on the island in the spring of 1895 and launched a new rebellion. Martí, who insisted on riding at the head of a military column, was killed in one of the rebels' first skirmishes. His comrades posted his last, unfinished letter on a pine board at their campground. In it he urged his compatriots not only to free their country from Spain but also "to prevent, by the independence of Cuba, the United States from spreading over the West Indies and falling, with that added weight, upon other lands of our America."

The rebel army made steady progress, and the Spanish commander, General Valeriano Weyler, adopted radical tactics to blunt its advance. He ordered his troops to force huge numbers of Cubans into fortified camps, where thousands died, and declared much of the countryside a free-fire zone. Rebels responded by burning farms, slaughtering herds of cattle, and destroying sugar mills. Soon much of the population was starving, bitterly angry, and more passionate than ever in its support for independence.

In the spring of 1897, William McKinley, a Republican who was supported by midwestern business interests, succeeded the anti-imperialist Democrat Grover Cleveland as president of the United States. Like most Americans, McKinley had long considered Spanish rule to be a blight on Cuba. The prospect of the Cubans governing themselves, however, alarmed him even more. He worried that an independent Cuba would become too assertive and not do Washington's bidding.

McKinley had reason to worry. Cuban rebel leaders were promising that once in power, they would launch sweeping social reforms, starting with land redistribution. That struck fear into the hearts of American businessmen, who had more than $50 million invested on the island, most of it in agriculture. Early in 1898, McKinley decided it was time to send both sides in the conflict a strong message. He ordered the battleship *Maine* to leave its place in the Atlantic Fleet and head for Havana.

Officially the *Maine* was simply making a "friendly visit," but no one in Cuba took that explanation seriously. All realized that she was serving as a "gunboat calling card," a symbol of America's determination to control the course of events in the Caribbean. For three weeks she lay quietly at anchor in Havana. Then, on the night of February 15, 1898, she was torn apart by a tremendous explosion. More than 250 American sailors perished. News of the disaster electrified the United States. All assumed that Spain was responsible, and when the navy issued a report blaming the disaster on "an external explosion," their assumptions turned to certainty.

Many Americans already felt a passionate hatred for Spanish colonialism and a romantic attachment to the idea of "Cuba Libre." Their emotions had been fired by a series of wildly sensational newspaper reports that together constitute one of the most shameful episodes in the history of the American press. William Randolph Hearst, the owner of the *New York Journal* and a string of other newspapers across the country, had been attracting readers for months with vivid denunciations of Spanish colonialists. Like countless others who have sought to set the United States on the path to war, he knew that he needed a villain, an individual on whom he could focus the public's outrage. The king of Spain was at that moment a fourteen-year-old boy, and the regent, his mother, was an Austrian princess, so neither of them would do. Hearst settled on General Weyler, and published a series of bloodcurdling stories that made him the personification of evil.

"Weyler, the brute, the devastator of haciendas, and the outrager of women . . . is pitiless, cold, an exterminator of men," ran one such account. "There is nothing to prevent his carnal, animal brain from running riot with itself in inventing tortures and infamies of bloody debauchery."

The moment Hearst heard about the sinking of the *Maine,* he recognized it as a great opportunity. For weeks after the explosion, he filled page after page with mendacious "scoops," fabricated interviews with unnamed government officials, and declarations that the battleship had been "destroyed by treachery" and "split in two by an enemy's secret infernal machine." The *Journal's* daily circulation doubled in four weeks. Other newspapers joined the frenzy, and their campaign brought Americans to near-hysteria.

With such intense emotion surging through the United States, it was easy for McKinley to turn aside repeated offers from the new Spanish prime minister, Práxedes Sagasta, to resolve the Cuban conflict peacefully. Sagasta was a modernizing Liberal who understood that his country's colonial policies had brought its empire to the brink of collapse. Immediately after taking office in 1897, he replaced the hated Weyler, and then tried to placate the rebels by offering them home rule. The rebels, sensing that victory was at hand, rejected his offer. That made Sagasta all the more eager to sue for peace, and several times during the spring of 1898 he offered to negotiate a settlement with the United States. Dismissing these overtures as insincere, McKinley and his supporters said that they had lost patience with Spain and were determined to resolve the Cuban situation by force of arms.

Behind their tough talk lay an obvious fact. Negotiations would most likely have led to an independent Cuba where neither the United States nor any other country would have military bases. This was hardly the outcome McKinley wanted, and it would have horrified expansionists like Roosevelt, Lodge, and Mahan. Lodge went so far as to warn McKinley that if he did not intervene, he would kill Republican chances in that year's election.

"If the war in Cuba drags on through the summer with nothing done," he told the president, "we shall go down to the greatest defeat ever known."

Years later, the historian Samuel Eliot Morison surveyed Spain's efforts to resolve the Cuban crisis peacefully and concluded, "Any president with a backbone would have seized this opportunity for an honorable solution." Such a solution, however, would have denied the United States the prizes it sought. They could be won only by conquest. McKinley understood this, and on April 11 he asked Congress to authorize "forcible intervention" in Cuba.

This step alarmed Cuban revolutionary leaders. They had long believed that, in General Maceo's words, it would be "better to rise or fall without help than to contract debts of gratitude with such a powerful neighbor." The rebels' legal counsel in New York, Horatio Rubens, warned that American intervention would be taken as "nothing less than a declaration of war by the United States against the Cuban revolution" and vowed that rebel forces would resist any American attempt to take the island "with force of arms, as bitterly and tenaciously as we have fought the armies of Spain."

Protests like these had a great effect in Washington, where the cry of "Cuba Libre" still stirred many hearts. Members of Congress were reluctant to vote for McKinley's war resolution as long as the Cuban people opposed it. They had refused to annex Hawaii after it became clear that most Hawaiians were against the idea. Now, five years later, Americans were showing the same reluctance. Many were uncomfortable with the idea of sending soldiers to aid a movement that did not want American help. To secure congressional support for intervention in Cuba, McKinley agreed to accept an extraordinary amendment offered by Senator Henry Teller of Colorado. It began by declaring that "the people of the island of Cuba are, and of right ought to be, free and independent" and ended with a solemn pledge: "The United States hereby disclaims any disposition or intention to exercise sovereignty, jurisdiction, or control over said island except for the pacification thereof, and asserts its determination, when that is accomplished, to leave the government and control of the island to its people." The Senate approved it unanimously.

That promise, which came to be known as the Teller Amendment, calmed the rebels' fears. "It is true that they have not entered into an accord with our government," wrote one of their leaders, General Calixto García, "but they have recognized our right to be free, and that is enough for me."

On April 25, Congress declared that a state of war existed between the United States and Spain. Members of the House of Representatives celebrated their vote by breaking into rousing choruses of "Dixie" and "The Battle Hymn of the Republic" as they left the chamber. "A spirit of wild jingoism seems to have taken possession of this usually conservative body," McKinley's secretary wrote in his diary.

A nation that was still recovering from the bitter divisions of the Civil War finally had a cause everyone could embrace. President McKinley called for 125,000 military volunteers, and more than twice that number poured into recruiting stations. The New York Journal suggested that heroic athletes like the baseball star Cap Anson and the boxing champion "Gentleman" Jim Corbett be recruited to lead an elite unit. Not to be outdone, the rival New York World published an article by Buffalo Bill Cody headlined, "How I Could Drive the Spaniards from Cuba with Thirty Thousand Braves!" Theodore Roosevelt announced that he would quit his post as assistant secretary of the navy to raise and lead a fighting unit.

"It was a war entered without misgivings and in the noblest frame of mind," the military historian Walter Millis wrote thirty years later. "Seldom can history have recorded a plainer case of military aggression; yet seldom has a war been started in so profound a conviction of its righteousness."

Events moved quickly in the weeks that followed. Roosevelt ordered Commodore George Dewey to proceed to Manila Bay, in the Philippines, and destroy the Spanish fleet that had been deployed there. This Dewey did with astonishing ease in a single day, May 1, after giving his famous command "You may fire when you are ready, Gridley."

Six weeks later, American soldiers landed near Santiago on Cuba's southeastern coast. They fought three one-day battles, the most famous being the one in which Roosevelt, dressed in a uniform he had ordered from Brooks Brothers, led a charge up Kettle Hill, later called San Juan Hill. On July 3, American cruisers destroyed the few decrepit Spanish naval vessels anchored at Santiago. Spanish forces soon ended their resistance, and the Cuban and American commanders, Generals Calixto García and William Shafter, prepared to accept their formal surrender. Before the ceremony, though, Shafter astonished García by sending him a message saying he could not participate in the ceremony or even enter Santiago. That was the first hint that the United States would not keep the promise Congress had made when it passed the Teller Amendment.

On August 12, barely two months after the American landing, diplomats representing Spain and the United States met at the White House and signed a "protocol of peace" that ended the war. Just 385 Americans had been killed in action, barely more than Sioux Indians had killed at Little Big Horn in the country's last major military engagement, twenty-two years before. About two thousand more died later of wounds and disease, but even that number was less than had fallen in single afternoons during intense battles of the Civil War. It had been, in the words of the American statesman John Hay, "a splendid little war."

With victory won, the time had come for the United States to begin its withdrawal and, in the words of the Teller Amendment, "leave the government and control of the island to its people." Instead it did the opposite.

In the United States, enthusiasm for Cuban independence faded quickly. Whitelaw Reid, the publisher of the *New York Tribune* and the journalist closest to President McKinley, proclaimed the "absolute necessity of controlling Cuba for our own defense," and rejected the Teller Amendment as "a self-denying ordinance possible only in a moment of national hysteria." Senator Beveridge said it was not binding because Congress had approved it "in a moment of impulsive but mistaken generosity." The *New York Times* asserted that Americans had a "higher obligation" than strict fidelity to ill-advised promises, and must become "permanent possessors of Cuba if the Cubans prove to be altogether incapable of self-government."

These pillars of American democracy were arguing quite explicitly that the United States was not obligated to keep promises embodied in law if those promises were later deemed to have been unwisely made. Over the next year, they and others justified this remarkable argument through a series of propositions. All were calculated to soothe the public conscience, and all were largely or completely false.

The first of these propositions was that American fighters, not Cubans, had expelled the Spanish from Cuba. Newspaper reporters told their credulous readers that when the U.S. Army arrived, it found the Cuban rebel force "in desperate straits," "threatened with collapse," and "bogged down in a bitter stalemate." Quite the opposite was true. After three years of continual fighting, Cuban rebels had won control of most of the island, forced the hungry and disease-plagued Spanish army to withdraw into guarded enclaves, and made plans to attack Santiago and other cities. They were headed toward victory when the Americans landed.

The second myth that Americans were led to embrace was that Cuban revolutionaries were cowardly laggards who had watched in bewildered admiration while Americans defeated the Spanish army. "This ally has done little but stay in the rear," one newspaper correspondent reported from the front. Another found that the Cubans "made very weak allies." A third wrote that the rebel army "did little or no fighting" and "has borne no testimony to its desire to free Cuba."

This was another piece of self-deception, but understandable. Few American correspondents had been in Cuba to watch as rebels built their power over a period of years, won broad popular support, and waged a highly successful guerrilla war. To most of these journalists, the war began only when American forces landed in the spring of 1898. None understood that Cuban units had secured the beaches where

American soldiers landed near Santiago; even the American naval commander there, Admiral William Sampson, said afterward that the absence of Spanish troops on the beaches "remains a mystery." Other Cubans served as scouts and intelligence agents for the Americans, although they indignantly refused repeated demands that they work as porters and laborers.

To most Americans, war consisted of set-piece battles in which armies faced off. They loved reading about charges like the one at San Juan Hill, in which few Cubans participated. The long war of attrition that Cubans had waged unfolded far from the view of American officers and correspondents. Most of them did not realize that this campaign played a decisive role in the victory of 1898.

Once Americans convinced themselves that Cubans were cowards who had no idea of how to organize an army, it was easy for them to conclude that Cuba was incapable of ruling itself. The American press never focused on the revolutionary leaders, some of whom were highly educated, experienced, and sophisticated. Instead they portrayed the rebel force as an ignorant rabble composed largely of blacks who were barely removed from savagery. As a result, McKinley and his allies in government and business had no trouble portraying them as equal to the Hawaiians in ignorance and stupidity. *Reflects Rudyard Racism*

"Self-government!" General Shafter snorted when a reporter asked him about it. "Why, these people are no more fit for self-government than gunpowder is for hell."

Within days of the Spanish surrender, American officials began telling the Cubans that they should forget the promise of independence embodied in the Teller Amendment. President McKinley declared that the United States would rule Cuba under "the law of belligerent right over conquered territory." Attorney General John Griggs told the vice president of Cuba's provisional government that the U.S. Army in Havana was an "invading army that would carry with it American sovereignty wherever it went."

The confusion many Cubans felt as they heard these statements turned to indignant anger when General Brooke refused to allow their liberating army to participate in the celebration planned for the first days of 1899. Many were dumbfounded. "None of us thought that [American intervention] would be followed by a military occupation of the country by our allies, who treat us as a people incapable of acting for ourselves, and who have reduced us to obedience, to submission,

Self-government

and to a tutelage imposed by force of circumstances," General Máximo Gómez wrote. "This cannot be our fate after years of struggle."

Most Americans had little regard for Cubans, so it was natural that they would reject such protests. Many went even further. They were angry that Cubans had not fallen on their knees to thank the United States for liberating them. News correspondents reported that instead of embracing American soldiers, the Cubans seemed "sour," "sullen," "conceited," "vain and jealous." One wrote of his astonishment to find that they were not "filled with gratitude towards us." None seemed willing or able to understand how logical it was for Cubans to feel this way. They took the Cubans' resentment as further proof of their ignorance and immaturity.

Cuban patriots had for years promised that after independence, they would stabilize their country by promoting social justice. Americans wanted something quite different. "The people ask me what we mean by stable government in Cuba," the new military governor, General Leonard Wood, wrote in a report to Washington soon after he assumed office in 1900. "I tell them that when money can be borrowed at a reasonable rate of interest and when capital is willing to invest in the island, a condition of stability will have been reached." In a note to President McKinley, he was even more succinct: "When people ask me what I mean by stable government, I tell them, 'Money at six percent.'"

On July 25, 1900, General Wood published an order calling for the election of delegates to a Cuban constitutional convention. Fewer than one-third of the qualified voters turned out, and even they refused to support many of the candidates the Americans sponsored. General Wood described the thirty-one delegates as "about ten absolutely first class men and about fifteen men of doubtful qualifications and character, and about six of the worst rascals and fakirs in Cuba."

That autumn, Secretary of War Elihu Root, who had been a leading corporate attorney in New York, and Senator Orville Platt of Connecticut, chairman of the Senate Committee on Relations with Cuba, wrote the law that would shape Cuba's future. The Platt Amendment, as it came to be known, is a crucial document in the history of American foreign policy. It gave the United States a way to control Cuba without running it directly, by maintaining a submissive local regime. Washington would go on to apply this system in many parts of the Caribbean and Central America, where to this day it is known as *plattismo*.

Under the Platt Amendment, the United States agreed to end its occupation of Cuba as soon as the Cubans accepted a constitution with provisions giving the United States the right to maintain military bases in Cuba; the right to veto any treaty between Cuba and any other country; the right to supervise the Cuban treasury; and "the right to intervene for the preservation of Cuban independence [or] the maintenance of a government adequate for the protection of life, property and individual liberty." In essence, the Platt Amendment gave Cubans permission to rule themselves as long as they allowed the United States to veto any decision they made.

Members of Congress could not avoid realizing that by passing the Platt Amendment, they would be reneging on the pledge they had made to Cuba less than three years before. Each had to ask himself a painful question that the *New York Evening Post* framed in a pithy editorial: "Given a solemn and unmistakable promise of independence to Cuba, how can I lie out of it and still go to church to thank God that I am not as other men are?" Senators resolved this dilemma without evident difficulty. On February 27, 1901, they approved the Platt Amendment by a vote of forty-three to twenty. Republicans cast all the affirmative votes. Later the House of Representatives joined in approval, also on a party-line vote. President McKinley signed the amendment into law on March 2. That plunged Cuba into what one historian called "a storm of excitement."

Havana was in turmoil on the night of March 2. A torchlight procession delivered a petition of protest to Wood at the Governor's Palace, and another crowd of demonstrators sought out the convention delegates and urged them to stand firm in their opposition to American demands. Similar demonstrations occurred on the following night. Outside the capital, municipal governments throughout the island poured out a flood of protest messages and resolutions, while public meetings were epidemic. On the night of March 5, speakers told a procession in Santiago that if the United States held to its demands, the Cubans must go to war once more.

Cuban delegates to the constitutional convention had to decide whether to accept the Platt Amendment. American officials assured them that the United States wished no direct influence over Cuba's internal affairs, and also warned them that if they did not accept the Platt Amendment, Congress would impose even harsher terms. After long debate, much of it conducted behind closed doors, the Cuban delegates agreed, by a vote of fifteen to fourteen, to do what the United States wished. A year later, in an election the Americans supervised, Tomás Estrada Palma, who had lived for years in the town of Central Valley, New York, was chosen as the first president of the Republic of Cuba. General Wood, the military governor, wrote in a private letter what every sentient Cuban and American knew: "There is, of course, little or no independence left Cuba under the Platt Amendment."

THE PUERTO RICAN POET LOLA RODRÍGUEZ DE TIÓ, WHO SPENT YEARS IN Cuba, once described these islands as "two wings of the same bird." Expansionists in the United States agreed. As Theodore Roosevelt was preparing to sail for Cuba in the spring of 1898, he sent Senator Henry Cabot Lodge a letter warning, "Do not make peace until we get Porto Rico." Lodge told him not to worry.

"Porto Rico is not forgotten and we mean to have it," he assured his friend. "Unless I am utterly and profoundly mistaken, the Administration is now fully committed to the large policy we both desire."

The island of Puerto Rico, which is less than one-tenth the size of Cuba, never erupted in armed rebellion against Spain. Like Cuba, though, it produced a remarkable group of revolutionary intellectuals who embodied the nationalism that seized many colonial hearts in the second half of the nineteenth century. For years Spain resisted their calls for self-rule, but that changed when the reform-minded Práxedes Sagasta became prime minister in 1897. Soon after taking office, Sagasta offered autonomy to both Cuba and Puerto Rico. Cuban rebels, with years of fighting behind them and thousands of men under arms, were bent on military victory and scorned his offer. Puerto Ricans, however, instantly accepted.

"Porto Ricans are generally jubilant over the news received from Spain concerning political autonomy," the American consul Philip Hanna wrote in a dispatch. "The natives generally believe that Spain will grant them a form of home rule as will be in every way satisfactory to them."

Spain's autonomy decree gave Puerto Ricans the right to elect a House of Representatives with wide-ranging powers, including authority to name a cabinet that would govern the island. They went to the polls on March 27, 1898. Most voted for the Liberal Fusion Party of Luis Muñoz Rivera, editor of the crusading newspaper *La Democracia* and a passionate leader of the autonomy movement.

The home-rule government had not yet taken office when, in the predawn hours of May 12, a fleet of seven American warships took up positions facing San Juan, the Puerto Rican capital. At first light, the fleet's commander, Admiral Sampson, ordered his flagship, the *Iowa*, to open fire on Spanish positions. A desultory artillery duel followed. The Americans fired 1,362 shells and killed about a dozen people. Spanish defenders replied with 441 shells and several volleys of infantry fire, managing to kill one American soldier. After three and a half hours, the guns fell silent. In military terms this was a minor engagement, but it sent an unmistakable message. Puerto Rico would not be able to avoid being caught up in the Spanish-American War.

For the next two months, American ships maintained a mostly effective blockade aimed at preventing the Spanish from sending supplies or reinforcements to their troops in Puerto Rico. The Spanish, though, were too focused on Cuba to pay much attention to events on the smaller island. So were the Americans. Hoping to take advantage of this situation, members of Puerto Rico's new House of Representatives convened for their first session, on July 17. On that same day, the new cabinet, headed by Muñoz Rivera, began to function. It would hold power for just eight days.

At 8:45 on the morning of July 25, a detachment of marines and sailors from the American gunboat *Gloucester* waded ashore near Guánica, on Puerto Rico's southwestern coast. After a bit of shooting in which they suffered no casualties, they secured the town and raised the American flag over its customs house. The moment that flag began to flutter in the tropical breeze, the United States effectively took control of Puerto Rico. Every institution of Spanish rule, including the autonomous government, quickly withered away.

Some Puerto Ricans looked forward to the prospect of American rule. They hoped for a period of nation building that might last twenty years or so, followed by—depending on their political persuasion—independence or annexation to the United States. Many were inspired by a generously worded proclamation that the American commander, General Nelson Miles, issued at the end of July:

> We have not come to make war upon the people of a country that for centuries has been oppressed, but, on the contrary, to bring you protection. . . . This is not a war of devastation, but one to give to all within the control of its military and naval forces the advantages and blessings of enlightened civilization.

The war in Puerto Rico was a sideshow, almost completely overshadowed by the conflict in Cuba. American casualties were astonishingly light, just 9 dead and 46 wounded. The Spanish and Puerto Ricans lost a total of about 450 soldiers and civilians dead, wounded, or captured. One of the most prominent American correspondents who covered the war, Richard Harding Davis, later described it as "a picnic" and "a *fête des fleurs*."

At the Paris peace conference of December 1898, where the terms of final surrender were fixed, Spain tried to retain Puerto Rico, arguing that the United States had never before challenged its sovereignty there. The Spanish even offered to give the United States territory elsewhere if they could keep Puerto Rico. President McKinley rejected all such suggestions. In private instructions to American negotiators, he said he had decided that Puerto Rico was "to become the territory of the United States." The Spanish, defeated and weak, had no choice but to accept.

On October 18, at a formal ceremony on the balcony of the governor's palace in San Juan, Spanish commanders transferred sovereignty over Puerto Rico to the United States. "It was all a quiet affair," the *New York Evening Post* reported. "There was no excitement, and but little enthusiasm. An hour after its close, the streets had assumed their wanted appearance. There was little to show that anything important had taken place, that by this brief ceremony Spain's power on the island of Puerto Rico had ended forever."

NO AMERICAN ALIVE IN 1898 COULD HAVE HAD ANY DOUBT ABOUT WHY THE United States had gone to war with Spain. The conflict was fought to resolve a single question: Who would control Cuba? Conditions in Cuba led to the war, Cuba was the battleground, and Cuba was the prize. But when American and Spanish diplomats met in Paris to negotiate a treaty ending the war, they had to consider the fate of another land, one that was very large, unknown to Americans, and far distant from their shores.

Cuba had exerted a hold on the American imagination for many years, at least since Thomas Jefferson wrote of his hope that it would one day become part of the United States. The Philippine Islands were quite another matter. Few Americans had the faintest idea of where they were. Nonetheless, as a result of Commodore Dewey's victory at

Manila, the United States suddenly exercised power over them. No one had planned this. President McKinley had to decide what the United States should do with the vast archipelago.

McKinley was known above all for his inscrutability. He gave almost all the people he met the impression that he agreed with them, and rarely allowed even his closest advisers to know what he was thinking. Historians have described him as an "enigma" whose inner mind was "well concealed" and who "obscured his views by a fog of phraseology, conventional or oracular."

At first, McKinley seemed to want only enough territory in the Philippines to build a naval base at Manila. Then he considered the idea of granting the islands independence, perhaps under an international guarantee. In the end, less worldly considerations dictated his decision.

McKinley was a devout Christian living in an era of religious revivalism. He would later tell a group of Methodist missionaries that while he was wrestling with the Philippines question, he fell to his knees in the White House on several evenings "and prayed Almighty God for light and guidance."

"One night late, it came to me this way," he said. "There was nothing left for us to do but to take them all, and to educate the Filipinos and uplift them and Christianize them, and by God's grace do the very best we could for them, as our fellow men for whom Christ also died."

With that, the momentous decision was made. Historians still wonder why McKinley made it. He was deeply religious, and may truly have felt moved by divine revelation. In a speech to the delegation he sent to negotiate in Paris, he gave another explanation, saying he was acting to seize "the commercial opportunity, to which American statesmanship cannot be indifferent." What is certain is that McKinley, in the words of one historian, "knew the Filipinos not at all, and would misjudge their response with tragic persistence." He himself admitted that when he heard news of Dewey's victory at Manila, he "could not have told where those darned islands were within two thousand miles." His fervor to "Christianize" the Filipinos, most of whom were already practicing Catholics, suggested his ignorance of conditions on the islands. He certainly had no idea that they were in the throes of the first anticolonial revolution in the modern history of Asia.

"The episode marked a pivotal point in the American experience," Stanley Karnow wrote in his history of the Philippines. "For the first time, U.S. soldiers fought overseas. And, for the first time, America was to acquire territory beyond its shores—the former colony itself becoming colonialist."

On May 1, 1898, three weeks after destroying the Spanish fleet, Dewey welcomed the Filipino guerrilla leader Emilio Aguinaldo aboard his flagship, the *Olympia*. Their versions of what transpired are contradictory. Aguinaldo said they agreed to fight the Spanish together and then establish an independent Republic of the Philippines. Dewey swore that he made no such commitment. Neither man spoke much of the other's language and no interpreter was present, so the confusion is understandable. Whatever the truth, when Aguinaldo declared the independence of the Philippines, on June 12, neither Dewey nor any other representative of the United States turned up at the ceremony.

That snub led Aguinaldo and other Filipino leaders to fear that the United States would not recognize their country's independence. General Thomas Anderson, a Civil War veteran who was the first commander of American troops in the Philippines, sought to reassure them. "I desire to have amicable relations with you," he wrote to Aguinaldo on July 4, "and to have you and your people cooperate with us in military operations against the Spanish forces."

General Anderson may have been sincere, but as he was writing his letter to Aguinaldo, policy in Washington was changing. President McKinley, obeying what he took to be the word of God, had decided that the United States should assume ownership not simply of an enclave at Manila but of the entire Philippine archipelago. He directed his negotiators in Paris to offer the Spanish $20 million for it. Spain was in no position to refuse, and on December 10, American and Spanish diplomats signed what became known as the Treaty of Paris. It gave the United States possession of Cuba, Puerto Rico, and the distant Philippine archipelago, which had more than seven thousand islands and a population of seven million.

On December 21, McKinley issued an "executive letter" proclaiming American sovereignty over the Philippines. Rebels there were already proceeding along their own path. They had elected a constituent assembly that produced a constitution, and under its provisions the Republic of the Philippines was proclaimed on January 23, 1899, with Aguinaldo as its first president. Twelve days later, this new nation declared war against United States forces on the islands. McKinley took no notice. To him the Filipinos were what the historian Richard Welch called "a disorganized and helpless people."

Sovereignty

McKinley was well aware of Aguinaldo's insurgents and their claims. It is probable that he still underestimated the extent of territorial control exercised by Aguinaldo's forces, but in McKinley's opinion it was unimportant how much territory the insurgent government claimed. . . . McKinley could not believe that Aguinaldo's insurgents would be so stupid as to resist the power and benevolence of the United States. McKinley seems to have entertained the self-contradictory notions that Aguinaldo was an evil, self-seeking bandit chieftain and that he could be as easily managed as an office-seeker in Canton, Ohio.

The Treaty of Paris gave the United States sovereignty over the Philippines, but it could not come into force until the Senate ratified it. The debate was long and heated. Opponents denounced the treaty as an imperialist grab of a distant land that shamed American ideals and overextended American power. Senator George Frisbie Hoar of Massachusetts warned that it would turn the United States into "a vulgar, commonplace empire founded upon physical force, controlling subject races and vassal states, in which one class must forever rule and the other classes must forever obey." Supporters countered with three arguments: that it would be ludicrous to recognize Filipino independence since there was no such thing as a Filipino nation; that it was America's duty to civilize the backward Filipinos; and that possession of the archipelago would bring incalculable commercial and strategic advantages.

As this debate was reaching its climax, in what the *New York World* called "an amazing coincidence," news came that Filipino insurgents had attacked American positions in Manila. It later turned out that there had indeed been a skirmish but that an American private had fired the first shot. That was not clear at the time, however, and probably would not have mattered anyway. Several senators declared that they now felt obligated to vote for the treaty as a sign of support for beleaguered American soldiers on the other side of the globe. "We come as ministering angels, not as despots," Senator Knute Nelson of Minnesota assured his colleagues. Evidently convinced of that, the Senate ratified the Treaty of Paris by a margin of fifty-seven to twenty-seven, barely more than the required two-thirds majority.

President McKinley may well have believed that God wished the United States to "uplift" and "Christianize" the Filipino people. Speeches by senators during the treaty debate, along with many articles in the press, however, offered a more tangible rationale for taking the Philippines.

Businessmen had become fascinated with the prospect of selling goods in China, which, after losing a war with Japan in 1895, had become weak and incapable of resisting intervention. They saw a magnificent confluence of circumstances, as this vast land became available for exploitation at the same time they were casting desperately about for new markets.

"We could not turn [the Philippines] over to France or Germany, our commercial rivals in the Orient," McKinley told Congress in his message asking ratification of the Treaty of Paris. "That would be bad business and discreditable."

When the United States assumed sovereignty over the Philippines, it inherited Spain's confrontation with the rebel army. Soldiers of the United States had never before fought outside North America. Nor, with the arguable exception of the Indian wars, had they ever fought against an army defending its country's independence. They had no idea of what they would be facing in their campaign against the "goo-goos," as they called the Filipinos, but they launched their war with supreme self-confidence.

It began in February 1899, with a pitched battle for Manila. From the beginning, there was little doubt about how it would end. The insurgents had the advantage of numbers, but by every other standard the Americans were clearly superior. Aguinaldo and his troops were crippled by a lack of weaponry, enforced by an effective American naval blockade. American soldiers landed in waves, by the tens of thousands, eager to fight against an enemy of whose motivations they were blissfully unaware. In letters home, they told friends and relatives that they had come "to blow every nigger to nigger heaven" and vowed to fight "until the niggers are killed off like Indians."

Faced with these handicaps, the guerrillas turned to tactics unlike any the Americans had ever seen. They laid snares and booby traps, slit throats, set fires, administered poisons, and mutilated prisoners. The Americans, some of whose officers were veteran Indian fighters, responded in kind. When two companies under the command of General Lloyd Wheaton were ambushed southeast of Manila, Wheaton ordered every town and village within twelve miles to be destroyed and their inhabitants killed.

During the first half of the Philippine War, American commanders imposed censorship on foreign correspondents to assure that news of episodes like this did not reach the home audience. Only after censorship was lifted in 1901 were Americans able to learn how the war was being waged. Newspapers began carrying reports like one filed early in 1901 by a correspondent from the *Philadelphia Ledger.*

> Our present war is no bloodless, fake, opera bouffe engagement. Our men have been relentless; have killed to exterminate men, women, children, prisoners and captives, active insurgents and suspected people, from lads of ten and up, an idea prevailing that the Filipino, as such, was little better than a dog, noisome reptile in some instances, whose best disposition was the rubbish heap. Our soldiers have pumped salt water into men to "make them talk," have taken prisoner people who held up their hands and peacefully surrendered, and an hour later, without an atom of evidence to show that they were even *insurrectos,* stood them on a bridge and shot them down one by one, to drop into the water below and float down as an example to those who found their bullet-riddled corpses.

The turning point in this war may have come on the afternoon of March 23, 1901, when a thirty-six-year-old brigadier general named Frederick Funston staged one of the boldest counterguerrilla operations in American military history. Funston, who had won the Medal of Honor in Cuba three years earlier, was commanding a district on the island of Luzon when he received news, extracted from a captured courier, that Aguinaldo was encamped at a village in his district. He came up with the idea of using a group of Filipino scouts to help him penetrate the village and capture Aguinaldo. The scouts were from the Macabebe ethnic group, which considered itself a rival of the Tagalogs, to which Aguinaldo and many other rebels belonged.

General Funston and four other officers set out on their mission with seventy-nine Macabebe scouts. Their plan was for the scouts to pose as rebels and tell Aguinaldo that they were bringing him a group of American prisoners. When the group was about ten miles from Aguinaldo's hideout, he sent word that the Americans should be kept away. He did invite the "rebels" to come, though, and as his honor guard was welcoming them, they suddenly began firing.

"Stop all the foolishness!" Aguinaldo shouted from inside his headquarters. "Don't waste ammunition!"

One of the scouts turned, burst into Aguinaldo's office, and, with pistol drawn, told him, "You are our prisoners. We are not insurgents. We are Americans! Surrender or be killed!"

Aguinaldo and his officers were too stunned to respond. Within minutes, they had been subdued and disarmed. General Funston appeared soon afterward and introduced himself to the rebel leader.

"Is this not some joke?" Aguinaldo asked.

It was not. Aguinaldo was arrested and brought to Manila, which Funston later said "went wild with excitement." Americans back home were thrilled with their new hero. Their satisfaction deepened when, less than a month after Aguinaldo's capture, he issued a proclamation accepting American sovereignty and urging his comrades to give up their fight.

Several thousand did, leading the American commander in the Philippines, General Arthur MacArthur, to proclaim the rebellion "almost entirely suppressed." He spoke too soon. Rebels who were still in the field fought with intensifying ferocity. In September 1901, a band of them overran an American position on the island of Samar with a brutality that set off some of the harshest countermeasures ever ordered by officers of the United States.

The episode began with what seemed like a routine landing of infantrymen at a beach near the village of Balangiga. Some seemed to realize that they were in uncertain territory. As they approached the shore, one lieutenant gazed ahead and told his comrades, "We are bound for goo-goo land now."

The Americans occupied Balangiga for several weeks, subduing it, according to later testimony, through imprisonment, torture, and rape. At dawn on the morning of September 28, they rose as usual to the sound of reveille. A few remained on sentry duty while the rest ate breakfast. The town's police chief strolled up to one of the sentries, said a few pleasant words, and then suddenly produced a long knife and stabbed him. Immediately the church bells began ringing. Scores of rebels who had infiltrated the town poured out of their hiding places. They fiercely set upon the unarmed Americans, stabbing and hacking them to death. Within minutes the campground was awash in blood. Some Americans managed to escape in boats, and made their way to a base thirty miles up the coast. Of the seventy-four men who had been posted in Balangiga, only twenty survived, most with multiple stab wounds.

News of the "Balangiga massacre" was quickly flashed back to the United States. It stunned a nation that was only beginning to realize what kind of war was being fought in the Philippines. American commanders on the islands were just as shocked, but they were in a position to react, and react they did. They ordered Colonel Jacob Smith, who had participated in the Wounded Knee massacre in the Dakota Territory a decade before, to proceed to Samar and do whatever was necessary to subdue the rebels. Smith arrived, took charge of the remaining garrisons, and ordered his men to kill everyone over the age of ten and turn the island's interior into "a howling wilderness."

"I want no prisoners," he told them. "I wish you to kill and burn. The more you kill and the more you burn, the better you will please me."

American soldiers carried out these orders with gusto. They started by razing Balangiga, and then rampaged through the countryside. Knowing that the assailants at Balangiga had disguised themselves as civilians, they took little care to discriminate between combatants and noncombatants. Fueled by a passion to avenge their comrades, they killed hundreds of people, burned crops, slaughtered cattle, and destroyed dozens of settlements.

During one long and amazingly ill-conceived march through the Samar jungle, eleven marines perished from a combination of starvation and exposure. Their captain, delirious and only intermittently conscious, became convinced that their Filipino porters had contributed to their deaths by withholding potatoes, salt, and other supplies. He singled out eleven of them, one for each dead marine, and had them shot.

Americans had used harsh tactics since the beginning of the Philippine War, but the summary execution of eleven Filipinos who were working for them, and who had committed no apparent crime, was too much for commanders to ignore. They ordered the offending officer court-martialed on charges of murder. He was eventually acquitted, but the case set off an explosion of outrage in the United States.

Until this episode, many Americans had believed that their soldiers were different from others, operating on a higher moral plane because their cause was good. After Balangiga, however, a flood of revelations forced them out of their innocence. Newspaper reporters sought out returned veterans and from their accounts learned that American soldiers in the Philippines had resorted to all manner of torture. The most notorious was the "water cure," in which sections of bamboo were forced down the throats of prisoners and then used to fill the prisoners' stomachs with dirty water until they swelled in torment. Soldiers would jump on the prisoner's stomach to force the water out, often repeating the process until the victim either informed or died. This technique was so widely reported in the United States that the *Cleveland Plain Dealer* even published a joke about it.

MA: What's the sound of running water out there, Willie?
WILLIE: It's only us boys, Ma. We've been trying the Philippine water cure on Bobby Snow, an' now we're pouring him out.

Others took the matter more seriously. "We have actually come to do the thing we went to war to banish," the *Baltimore American* lamented. The *Indianapolis News* concluded that the United States had adopted "the methods of barbarism," and the *New York Post* declared that American troops "have been pursuing a policy of wholesale and deliberate murder." David Starr Jordan, the president of Stanford University, declared that Filipinos had done no more than rebel against "alien control" and that therefore "it was our fault and ours alone that this war began." The revered Harvard professor William James said that Americans were guilty of "murdering another culture" and concluded one of his speeches by declaring, "God damn the U.S. for its vile conduct in the Philippines!" Mark Twain suggested that the time had come to redesign the American flag with "the white stripes painted black and the stars replaced by skull and crossbones."

This spasm of recrimination continued for several months, but soon a countercampaign began. Defenders of American policy, who at first were too overwhelmed by the onslaught of horrific revelations to respond, finally found their voice. Extreme conditions, they insisted, had forced soldiers to act as they did. The *New York Times* argued that "brave and loyal officers" had reacted understandably to the "cruel, treacherous, murderous" Filipinos. The *St. Louis Globe-Democrat* said that American soldiers had done nothing in the Philippines that they had not done during the Civil War and that "in view of the provocation received and the peculiar nature of the task to be performed, the transgressions have been extremely slight." The *Providence Journal* urged its readers to accept "the wisdom of fighting fire with fire."

A second theme that echoed through the press was that any atrocities committed in the Philippines had been aberrations. They were "deplorable," the *St. Paul Pioneer Press* conceded, but had "no bearing on fundamental questions of national policy." The *New York Tribune* said only a few soldiers were guilty and "the penalty must fall not upon the policy, but upon those men."

Teddy in office

By the time this debate reached its crescendo, in the early months of 1902, President McKinley had been assassinated and replaced in office by Theodore Roosevelt. To Roosevelt fell the task of defending the honor of the troops he loved, and he embraced it even though he had never been enthusiastic about the Philippine operation. He enlisted his close friend and ally Henry Cabot Lodge to lead the defense. In a long and eloquent speech on the Senate floor, Lodge conceded that there had been cases "of water cure, of menaces of shooting unless information was given up, of rough and cruel treatment applied to secure information." But Americans who lived "in sheltered homes far from the sound and trials of war," he warned, could not understand the challenges of bringing law to a "semi-civilized people with all the tendencies and characteristics of Asiatics."

"Let us, oh, let us be just, at least to our own," Lodge begged the Senate.

At Roosevelt's suggestion, Lodge arranged for the Senate to hold hearings into charges of American misconduct in the Philippines. It was a clever move. Lodge himself ran the hearings, and he carefully limited their scope. There was much testimony about operational tactics, but no exploration of the broader policy that lay behind them. The committee did not even issue a final report. One historian described its work as "less a whitewash than an exercise in sleight-of-hand."

Resistance ended

On July 4, 1902, soon after the investigating committee ended its work, President Roosevelt declared the Philippines pacified. He was justified in doing so. The important guerrilla leaders had been killed or captured and resistance had all but ceased. It had been a far more costly operation than anyone had predicted at the outset. In three and a half torturous years of war, 4,374 American soldiers were killed, more than ten times the toll in Cuba. About sixteen thousand guerrillas and at least twenty thousand civilians were also killed. Filipinos remember those years as some of the bloodiest in their history. Americans quickly forgot that the war ever happened.

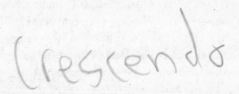

Crescendo

3

From a Whorehouse to a White House

A postage stamp led the United States to overthrow the most formidable leader Nicaragua ever had. It set off a chain of events that reverberate to this day, making it probably the most influential stamp in history. Had it never been issued, Nicaragua might have emerged long ago as a peaceful, prosperous country. Instead it is chronically poor and unstable, a cauldron of rivalries and a stage for repeated American interventions.

To the casual eye, this stamp looks unremarkable. It is printed in purple and depicts a steaming volcano at the edge of a lake. Around the edges are the words "Nicaragua," "Correos" "10 Centavos," and, in tiny letters at the bottom, "American Bank Note Company NY." When it was issued in 1900, Nicaragua was in the midst of a modernizing revolution. Today it is a poignant reminder of what might have been.

During the last decades of the nineteenth century, the ideals of social and political reform swept across Central America. Visionary leaders, inspired by European philosophers and nation builders, sought to wipe away the feudal systems that had frozen their countries into immobility. One of them, President José Santos Zelaya of Nicaragua, took his nationalist principles so seriously that the United States felt compelled to overthrow him.

Portraits of Zelaya, like the one that today adorns Nicaragua's twenty-cordoba note, show him to have had a forceful countenance, with an elegantly twirled mustache and piercing eyes that seem to blaze with impatient energy. As a young man, he displayed such promise that his father, an army colonel and coffee farmer, arranged to send him to school in Europe. After graduating, he returned home with his Belgian wife and joined the Liberal Party, which represented the ideals of secularism and radical reform. In 1893, as the long-ruling Conservatives were consumed by factional conflict, he and a group of Liberal comrades organized a revolt that brought them down with remarkable ease. Within a few months, he emerged as the country's new leader.

Zelaya was six weeks short of his fortieth birthday when he was sworn in as president of Nicaragua. He proclaimed a revolutionary program and set out to shake his country from its long slumber. He built roads, ports, railways, government buildings, and more than 140 schools; paved the streets of Managua, lined them with street lamps, and imported the country's first automobile; legalized civil marriage and divorce; and even founded the nation's first baseball league, which included a team called "Youth" and another called "The Insurgency." He encouraged business, especially the nascent coffee industry. In foreign affairs, he promoted a union of the five small Central American countries and fervently embraced the grand project that had thrust Nicaragua onto the world stage: the interoceanic canal.

Every American president since Ulysses S. Grant had pushed for the canal project. In 1876 a government commission studied possible routes and concluded that the one across Nicaragua "possesses, both for the construction and maintenance of a canal, greater advantage, and offers fewer difficulties from engineering, commercial and economic points of view, than any one of the other routes." Slowly the project gained momentum. In 1889 a private company chartered by Congress began dredging near Nicaragua's Atlantic coast. It was undercapitalized and went broke shortly before Zelaya came to power.

One group of men cheered this failure. They were members of a Paris-based syndicate that owned a great swath of land across Panama, where French engineers had tried and failed to build a canal. These men stood to become very rich if they could find a buyer for their land. The only possible customer was the United States government, but it was pursuing the Nicaragua route. Persuading Washington to change course would require a highly sophisticated lobbying campaign. To direct it, the syndicate hired a gifted New York lawyer who understood better than anyone else of his generation how to bend government to the will of business.

As American corporations began expanding to enormous size in the late nineteenth century, they encountered a host of organizational and political problems. Many turned for help to William Nelson Cromwell. In appearance Cromwell was almost eccentric, with light blue eyes, a fair complexion, and long locks of snow-white hair. Behind that odd facade lay a brilliantly sharpened mind. Cromwell's business triumphs were legendary.

"He can smile as sweetly as a society belle," one newspaper correspondent wrote, "and at the same time deal a blow at a business foe that ties him in a hopeless tangle of financial knots."

As both a master of corporate law and a consummate Washington lobbyist, Cromwell was an ideal partner for the French canal syndicate. In 1898 the chief of the syndicate, Philippe Bunau-Varilla, hired him and gave him a daunting assignment: arrange for the United States to build its canal across Panama instead of Nicaragua.

Cromwell's first tactic was to obstruct the slow but steady progress that was being made toward a resumption of work in Nicaragua. This he did repeatedly, with much help from friends in Congress and the State Department. Then, in 1901, the assassination of President McKinley brought Theodore Roosevelt, an ardent believer in sea power, to office.

Roosevelt was determined to have the canal built quickly, no matter where. Early in 1902, he asked Congress to appropriate $140 million for a canal across Nicaragua. Cromwell had managed to win several influential figures to his side, including Senator Mark Hanna, a senior leader of the Republican Party. To cement their alliance, he made a $60,000 contribution to the Republicans, charging it off to the canal company as a business expense. Even these friends, however, were not strong enough to defeat the Nicaragua bill. On January 9 the House of Representatives approved it by the daunting margin of 308 to 2.

Cromwell had managed to postpone this debate for years. Now that it was at hand, his cause looked doomed. He could win only if fate was somehow to intervene. It did, in the form of the American Bank Note Company.

Like a number of other small countries, Nicaragua had hired this reputable New York firm to manufacture its postage stamps. The company's designers produced stamps that showed Nicaragua's most notable geographical landmarks. Among them was a series depicting the majestic Momotombo volcano, complete with a plume of smoke spiraling from its crater. One day in Washington, an astute lobbyist for the French canal syndicate noticed one of these stamps on a letter sent from Nicaragua. It gave him an inspiration that changed the course of history.

By coincidence, 1902 was a year of extraordinary volcanic activity in the Caribbean. In May a devastating eruption killed thirty thousand people on the island of Martinique. Soon afterward there was another eruption, on St. Vincent. American newspapers were full of horrifying stories about the destructive power of volcanoes, and for several months the public mind was seized by a kind of volcano hysteria. Cromwell realized that he could take great advantage of this happenstance.

First he planted in the *New York Sun* a small item, later shown to have been false or highly exaggerated, reporting that the Momotombo volcano had erupted and set off seismic shocks. Then he rounded up a sheaf of Momotombo stamps, had them pasted onto sheets of paper bearing the title "An official witness to the volcanic activity of Nicaragua," and sent one to each senator. The leaflets conveyed an obvious message: it would be madness to build a canal in a country so geologically unstable that it used the image of a smoking volcano on its postage stamps.

Few people in Washington knew that Momotombo is nearly dormant, that it lies more than one hundred miles from the proposed canal route, and that the decision to portray it on a stamp had been made not in Nicaragua but by designers in New York. As the stamps were passed around Washington, the ministers of Nicaragua and Costa Rica, who were directing what they thought would be a fairly easy campaign to secure approval of the Nicaragua route, suddenly found themselves overwhelmed. When debate over the canal bill began in the Senate, Mark Hanna delivered a passionate speech favoring the Panama route, illustrating it with a frightening though highly fanciful map purporting to show zones of seismic danger in Central America. His speech and behind-the-scenes lobbying, closely coordinated with Cromwell's parallel efforts, produced the desired result. On June 19, 1902, three days after senators received the Momotombo stamps, they voted for the Panama route by a margin of forty-two to thirty-four. Soon afterward the House reversed itself and also accepted that route. For his lobbying services, Cromwell collected a fee of $800,000.

The Momotombo stamp was not the only factor in the vote. It came against the backdrop of a political feud between the chairman of the Senate Foreign Relations Committee, John T. Morgan of Alabama, a leading advocate of the Nicaragua route, and Senator Hanna, who chose the Panama side partly as a way to undermine Morgan. Some senators were influenced by a last-minute report from the Isthmian Canal Commission, concluding that there were advantages to the Panama route. Others saw it as a good financial deal after the canal company reduced its asking price from $109 million to $40 million. Transcripts of the debate, however, show that senators had a highly exaggerated view of the danger volcanoes could pose to a Nicaraguan canal. The transcripts, as well as later statements by members of Congress, leave no doubt that the Momotombo stamp and the resulting fear of volcanic eruption in Nicaragua played a decisive role in the vote for Panama.

Senator Morgan complained after the vote that a "corrupt and influential" pro-Panama lobby had unscrupulously misled his colleagues. He was right, but the issue had been decided. On June 29, President Roosevelt signed the law authorizing construction of a canal across Panama. Today a block of the Momotombo stamps is prominently displayed at the Interoceanic Canal Museum there.

During the years when it appeared that the canal was going to be built across Nicaragua, American officials got along well with President Zelaya. In 1898 the American minister in Managua wrote in a dispatch that Zelaya "has given the people of Nicaragua as good a government as they will permit him) . . . . Foreigners who attend to their own business, and do not meddle with politics which does not concern them, are fully protected." Two years later, Secretary of State John Hay praised Zelaya's "ability, high character and integrity." The American consul at San Juan del Norte, which was to be the Caribbean terminus of the canal, called him "the ablest and strongest man in Central America" and reported that he "is very popular with the masses, and is giving them an excellent government."

After Congress chose the Panama route, this admiration quickly turned to disdain. American officials who had once viewed Zelaya's campaign to promote Central American unity as noble began to see it as destabilizing. His efforts to regulate American companies, once thought of as symbols of his self-confident nationalism, started to look defiant.

"To the State Department, Nicaragua was no longer a country that needed to be coddled or cared for in preparation for future usefulness," the American historian John Ellis Findling later wrote. "Rather, it was now a country that needed to be watched carefully and kept in line."

President Roosevelt plunged into the canal project with unrestrained vigor. Before he could build anything in the Republic of Panama, however, he had to resolve one remaining problem. There was no such thing as a Republic of Panama. Panama was a province of Colombia, and Colombian leaders were reluctant to surrender sovereignty over the proposed canal zone—although they suggested they might reconsider if the United States offered more money.

"I feel there are two alternatives," Roosevelt wrote to Secretary of

State Hay. "(1) To take up Nicaragua; (2) in some shape or way to interfere when it becomes necessary so as to secure the Panama route without further dealing with the foolish and homicidal corruptionists in Bogotá." After brief reflection, he chose the second option.

The United States had little experience in fomenting revolutions. It did, however, have one model. A decade earlier, the American diplomat John L. Stevens had devised a simple plan that allowed a handful of people with little popular support to overthrow the government of Hawaii. Roosevelt decided to adapt that plan for Panama. He would encourage Panamanian "revolutionaries" to proclaim independence from Colombia, quickly give them diplomatic recognition, and then use American troops to prevent the Colombian army from reestablishing control.

On November 2, 1903, the commander of the American gunboat *Nashville,* anchored at Colón on Panama's Caribbean coast, received an order from Washington to "prevent the landing of any armed forces with hostile intent, either government or insurgent." He was puzzled, because no revolution had broken out. The next day, one did. A hastily assembled group of rebels announced in the provincial capital, Panama City, that they were declaring Panama independent.

There was no army post in Panama City, but there was a large one in Colón, and its commander reacted immediately to news of the rebellion. He assembled a five-hundred-man force, marched it across town to the railroad station, and demanded a train to take it to Panama City. The American manager of the Colón railroad station falsely told him that only a single car was available. Undaunted, the commander boarded with his staff officers, evidently confident that he could crush the rebels even without a large force. He had fallen into a trap. Americans telegraphed ahead and arranged for him and his officers to be arrested as they stepped off the train.

A second American warship, the *Dixie,* docked at Colón on November 5 and put four hundred marines ashore. The next day the United States formally recognized the rebels as leaders of a new Republic of Panama. Eight more warships quickly appeared in the waters off Colón, forming a blockade that made it impossible for Colombian vessels to reach the breakaway province. One historian called it "as brazen—and successful—an act of gunboat diplomacy as the world has ever seen."

Even Roosevelt himself seemed ambivalent about what he had done. At first he sought to deny it. "I did not foment a revolution on the isthmus," he protested to one interviewer. Soon afterward he asserted that Colombia's "utterly incompetent" leaders had foolishly lost Panama by refusing to approve the canal treaty "in spite of the plainest warnings." He was evidently not persuaded by his own words, because at his next cabinet meeting he asked Attorney General Philander Knox to come up with a legal argument he could use to justify the operation.

"Oh, Mr. President," Knox replied, "do not let so great an achievement suffer from any taint of legality."

"Have I answered the charges?" Roosevelt asked anxiously. "Have I?"

"You certainly have, Mr. President," Secretary of War Elihu Root wryly answered. "You have shown that you were accused of seduction, and you have conclusively proved that you were guilty of rape."

In Nicaragua, President Zelaya took these events with remarkable equanimity. He never showed any anger at losing the canal, or any outrage at the American-sponsored "revolution" that cut a nearby nation in two. Instead, just a few weeks after the uprising, he received an envoy from the Republic of Panama, gave a dinner party in his honor, and recognized his government. He had good reason for all this, as John Ellis Findling explained.

> Zelaya's complacency toward the loss of the canal route can be explained by two major factors new in isthmian affairs. First, the years 1902 and 1903 were peaceful ones for Central America, and Zelaya used the time to begin quietly shaping a new Central American union under his leadership. . . . Second, [he] had begun to grant large and potentially lucrative concessions to American and Nicaraguan businessmen. A United States canal would probably have interfered with this economic policy.

Like idealists and utopians up to the present day, Zelaya dreamed of reestablishing the united Central America that existed from 1821 to 1838. In 1902 he called the presidents of the other four Central American countries—Guatemala, El Salvador, Honduras, and Costa Rica—to a conference at which he hoped to launch the process of reunification. It produced a series of fine-sounding accords, but soon the isthmus fell back into its age-old conflict between Conservatives and Liberals. Zelaya began trying to impose his will, first by applying political pressure and then by sending military expeditions into Honduras and El Salvador.

Once construction of the Panama Canal started, American officials took an exceedingly dim view of adventures like these. Yet Zelaya's periodic military forays, upsetting as they were to some in Washington, would probably not have been enough to lead the United States to decree his overthrow. Nor would his failure to observe the niceties of democracy at home. To these two transgressions, however, he added a third, which tipped the balance against him. He continually clashed with American companies operating in his country.

Among all of Zelaya's accomplishments, none stands above his unification of the Nicaraguan nation. Through his efforts, the British, who had long controlled the thriving ports on Nicaragua's eastern coast and the tropical wilderness around them, finally gave up their pretensions there. After they were gone, American businessmen moved in. More than a dozen bought concessions from Zelaya's government that allowed them exclusive logging, mining, or other rights in specified areas. Several later turned against him and appealed to the State Department for help.

Among the most pugnacious of these was George D. Emery, a Boston lumber merchant. In 1894, Emery bought a concession to harvest mahogany, cedar, and other fine woods from a forest in eastern Nicaragua. Within a few years he had become the prime supplier of mahogany to the Pullman Palace Car Company and other discriminating customers. He employed more than 1,500 Nicaraguan laborers, paid the government $40,000 per year in concession fees, and represented $2 million in American investment.

Emery's concession agreement required him to do two things: build a rail line through his forest preserve, and plant two trees for every one he cut down. He did neither. When the government began insisting, he demanded that the State Department defend him against Zelaya's "molestation and oppressive extractions."

President Roosevelt paid little attention to the complaints of businessmen like Emery, and the question of whether he would have moved to crush Zelaya has intrigued Nicaraguan historians for years. Roosevelt is often thought of as one of the founders of American imperialism. His colorful exploits in Cuba, his oft-quoted declaration that the United States should keep a "big stick" handy for use in world affairs, and his willingness to stage a sham revolution in Panama all argue for that view. It would be incomplete, however. Roosevelt was eager to resolve troubles with foreign nations peacefully when possible, and he took great pride in the fact that during his presidency, the United States never started a conflict in which a single life was lost. He had no sympathy for idle ruling classes like those that had long dominated Central America. In José Santos Zelaya, a man of restless intellect, impatient energy, and reformist zeal, he may even have seen a reflection of himself. As late as 1908, he was still addressing the Nicaraguan leader as his "great and good friend."

Nevertheless, Roosevelt was indirectly responsible for Zelaya's overthrow, because he propounded the principle that justified it. Since 1823, U.S. policy in the Western Hemisphere had been shaped by the Monroe Doctrine, a unilateral declaration that the United States would not tolerate any attempt by European powers to influence the course of events in the Americas. Once work began on the Panama Canal, Roosevelt decided to go further. In 1904 he proclaimed the "Roosevelt Corollary" to the Monroe Doctrine, which asserted the right of the United States to intervene in any country in the Western Hemisphere that it judged to be in need of intervention.

> If a nation shows that it knows how to act with reasonable efficiency and decency in social and political matters, if it keeps order and pays its obligations, it need fear no interference from the United States. Chronic wrongdoing, or an impotence which results in a general loosening of the ties of civilized society, may in America, as elsewhere, ultimately require intervention by some civilized nation, and in the Western Hemisphere the adherence of the United States to the Monroe Doctrine may force the U.S., however reluctantly, in flagrant cases of such wrongdoing or impotence, to the exercise of an international peace power.

Roosevelt left the presidency in March 1909. His successor, William Howard Taft, was closer to big business, and chose Philander Knox, a highly successful corporate lawyer and former attorney general, to be secretary of state. Knox had spent years representing major American corporations, most notably Carnegie Steel, and had worked closely with William Nelson Cromwell to organize the company that became United States Steel. One of his most cherished clients was the Philadelphia-based La Luz and Los Angeles Mining Company, which held a lucrative gold mining concession in eastern Nicaragua. Besides his professional relationship with La Luz, Knox was politically and socially close to the Fletcher family of Philadelphia, which owned it.

The Fletchers protected their company in an unusually effective way. Gilmore Fletcher managed it. His brother, Henry Fletcher, worked at the

State Department, holding a series of influential positions and ultimately rising to undersecretary. Both detested Zelaya, especially after he
began threatening, in 1908, to cancel the La Luz concession.

Encouraged by the Fletcher brothers, Knox looked eagerly for a way to
force Zelaya from power. He thought he might have one when the lumber baron George Emery approached him. Emery was demanding that
the Nicaraguan government compensate him for losses he said he had
incurred in Nicaragua, and Knox seized on his case. He sent a brusque
note to the Nicaraguan minister in Washington, warning him that his
country's "unnecessary, unwarranted and dilatory" delay in settling this
claim threatened the "good will" that existed between Managua and
Washington. Much to Knox's surprise and perhaps disappointment,
Zelaya met all his demands and quickly accepted the settlement Emery
proposed. Under its provisions, Emery gave up his concession and
received $640,000 in compensation.

Soon afterward, Knox's anger flared again when Zelaya signed an
agreement to borrow £1.25 million from European banks to finance his
dream project, a coast-to-coast railroad. Knox had nothing against the
railroad, but he understood perfectly well that by borrowing money
from European rather than American banks, Zelaya was trying to make
his country less dependent on the United States. This he could not
abide. He asked the British and French governments to quash the loan,
but they politely refused. In the summer of 1909, it was successfully
floated in London and Paris.

For several years, Knox and others in Washington had been spreading rumors that Zelaya was secretly negotiating with European or Japanese interests to build a canal across his country that would compete
with the one the United States was building in Panama. Those rumors
were false, but Zelaya did not deny that the canal idea intrigued him.
Nor did he hide his conviction that it was to Nicaragua's advantage to
have friends other than the United States. He was a fervent nationalist
with outsized ambitions for himself and his country. Once he ordered a
Peruvian citizen deported from Nicaragua, and when the Peruvian
threatened to appeal to his government, Zelaya replied, "Appeal by all
means! When I ridicule the United States, laugh at Germany and spit on
England, what do you suppose I care for your beggarly Peru?"

Knox found all this quite intolerable. In the summer of 1909, he
began orchestrating a campaign designed to turn American public opinion against Zelaya. He seized on several minor incidents in Nicaragua,

including one in which an American tobacco merchant was briefly jailed, to paint the Nicaraguan regime as brutal and oppressive. He sent diplomats to Nicaragua whom he knew to be strongly anti-Zelaya, and passed their lurid reports to friends in the press. Soon American newspapers were screaming that Zelaya had imposed a "reign of terror" in Nicaragua and become "the menace of Central America." As their sensationalist campaign reached a peak, President Taft gravely announced that the United States would no longer "tolerate and deal with such a medieval despot."

With this declaration, the United States pronounced Zelaya's political death sentence. American businessmen in Bluefields, the main town on the Caribbean coast, rushed to carry out the execution. With tacit approval from the American consul, William Moffett, with whom they shared their plans at every stage, they formed a conspiracy with the ambitious provincial governor, General Juan José Estrada. On October 10, 1909, Estrada declared himself president of Nicaragua and appealed to the United States for diplomatic recognition.

This revolution was extraordinarily well financed. The chief accountant for the La Luz mining company, Adolfo Díaz, a bespectacled clerk from a modest Conservative family, served as its treasurer. American companies operating in and around Bluefields sent him large sums of money. The cost of the revolution has been variously estimated at between $63,000 and $2 million.

Estrada used much of the money to raise and equip a militia. It did not prove a great fighting force, though, and his proclaimed march on Managua quickly bogged down in the jungle. Zelaya sent troops to crush it. Knox, watching from Washington, was stymied. His revolution had broken out, but it was quickly collapsing. He needed a pretext to intervene. To his great good fortune, Zelaya gave him one.

Estrada's call for rebel fighters, like every call for fighters in Central America, had attracted dozens of American adventurers, mercenaries, and gunslingers. Some were miners looking for excitement. Others worked for American-owned companies in Bluefields or other coastal towns. A handful sailed down from New Orleans. Two would go down in Nicaraguan history.

Lee Roy Cannon was a Virginian who had been a rubber planter in Nicaragua, a police officer in El Salvador, and a mercenary in Honduras. He had retired to Guatemala, but apparently retirement did not suit

Loyalty

him. When Estrada offered him the rank of colonel in Nicaragua's rebel army, he accepted.

Cannon's closest comrade was another veteran of Central American wars, Leonard Groce, a Texan who had taken leave from his job as the supervisor of mining properties for La Luz. The two men carried out several operations together. After one of them, both were captured. They confessed to having laid a mine in the San Juan River with the intention of blowing up the *Diamante*, a naval vessel that was carrying five hundred government soldiers to suppress their uprising. Both were summarily convicted of "the crime of rebellion" and sentenced to die. Zelaya rejected their pleas for clemency, and early on the morning of November 17, 1909, they were put to death by firing squad.

As soon as news of these executions reached Washington, Knox seized on it. He fired off an angry note to the Nicaraguan foreign minister declaring that the United States would "not for one moment tolerate such treatment of American citizens." Then he issued an official legal opinion holding that because Estrada's rebellion had given his men the "stature" of belligerents, Cannon and Groce had been entitled to prisoner-of-war status. That made Zelaya a war criminal.

Knox tried to persuade Guatemala, El Salvador, and Costa Rica to send armies into Nicaragua to topple Zelaya, but all three demurred. That left the secretary of state and President Taft to decide whether the United States should act alone. They had no trouble making up their minds. On December 1, Knox wrote the Nicaraguan minister in Washington an extraordinary letter demanding that Zelaya's government be replaced by "one entirely disassociated from the present intolerable conditions." Nicaraguan schoolchildren study it to this day.

Huge issue in History

> It is notorious that President Zelaya has almost continually kept Central America in tension or turmoil. . . . It is equally a matter of common knowledge that under the regime of President Zelaya, republican institutions have ceased in Nicaragua to exist except in name, that public opinion and the press have been throttled, and that prison has been the reward of any tendency to real patriotism. . . .
>
> Two Americans who, this government is now convinced, were officers connected with the revolutionary forces, and therefore entitled to be dealt with according to the enlightened practice of civilized nations, have been killed by direct order of President Zelaya. Their execution is

said to have been preceded by barbarous cruelties. The consulate at Managua is now officially reported to have been menaced. . . .

The government of the United States is convinced that the revolution represents the will of a majority of the Nicaraguan people more than does the government of President Zelaya. . . . In these circumstances, the President no longer feels for the government of President Zelaya that respect and confidence which would make it appropriate hereafter to maintain with it regular diplomatic relations.

There was no mistaking the seriousness of this message. "We are stricken to the heart, we are paralyzed," the Nicaraguan minister said after receiving it. Zelaya was also taken aback. He appealed to Mexico and Costa Rica, whose leaders were on good terms with the Taft administration, to intercede on his behalf, but they refused. Then he proposed that a commission made up of Mexicans and Americans come to Nicaragua to investigate the Cannon and Groce cases, and promised to resign if it found him guilty of any wrongdoing. Taft replied by ordering warships to approach both Nicaraguan coasts, and the marines to assemble in Panama.

The Knox Note, as it came to be known, made clear that the United States would not rest until Zelaya was gone. Given the American military forces arrayed against him, he had no alternative but to comply. On December 16, 1909, he submitted his resignation. In his farewell speech to the National Assembly, he said he hoped his departure would produce peace "and above all, the suspension of the hostility shown by the United States, to which I wish to give no pretext that will allow it to continue intervening in any way with the destiny of this country." A few days later he boarded a ship at the Pacific port of Corinto and sailed into exile.

The new president, José Madríz, a distinguished Liberal jurist, made suppressing the rebellion his first priority. He dispatched an infantry force to Bluefields, and also ordered the purchase of a New Orleans–based steamship, the *Venus,* and her refitting for military use. By the time the *Venus* arrived off the coast of Bluefields, in mid-May 1910, the infantry was already there. Government commanders demanded that Estrada's rebels surrender or face simultaneous attack from land and sea.

Before a shot could be fired, the United States intervened. William Moffett, the American consul, sent the commander of the *Venus* a note telling him that out of concern for the lives of Americans in and around

Bluefields, he had declared the area a "neutral zone." Following the example of John L. Stevens, the American diplomat who had ordered government troops in Hawaii not to attack or arrest rebels, Moffett ordered the commander not to fire at any onshore position and not to interfere with commercial shipping. This meant that the *Venus* could neither attack the rebels nor stop ships that were bringing them arms. It also assured the rebels of a continuing source of income from customs revenue.

When Moffett wrote the note, he had no military power to enforce it. A few days later, two American warships, the *Paducah* and the *Dubuque*, appeared at Bluefields and disgorged several companies of marines. Their commander was Major Smedley Butler, a master of counterinsurgency who, at the age of twenty-eight, was already a veteran of the Spanish-American War, the Philippine conflict, and the Panama intervention of 1903. Butler's men took control of Bluefields without resistance. After quickly assessing the situation there, he concluded that the rebels had no chance of withstanding an army attack.

"Unless something drastic was done, the revolution would fail," Butler wrote later. "It didn't take a ton of bricks to make me see daylight. It was plain that Washington would like to see the revolutionists come out on top."

To help that happen, Butler devised a simple formula. He wrote a letter to the Nicaraguan army commanders poised outside Bluefields, telling them that while they were of course free to attack whenever they wished, he must insist that they not use firearms. Stray bullets, he explained, "might accidentally hit American citizens."

"How are we to take the town if we can't shoot?" the commanders demanded in reply. "And won't you also disarm the revolutionaries defending the town?"

"There is no danger of the defenders killing American troops," Butler told them smoothly, "because they will be shooting outwards, but your troops will be firing towards us."

Nicaraguan soldiers encamped outside Bluefields were thus forbidden to assault the rebels there. They withdrew and marched to the town of Rama, about twenty-five miles up the coast. Butler led a handful of marines after them.

We sent an American beachcomber on ahead to Rama to be sure there would be another American life to protect, and then re-enacted the farce at Bluefields. We forbade shooting by the government forces, and they finally melted away, convinced of the hopelessness of opposing the revolutionists backed by the Marines. The revolution ended then and there.

President Madríz, who had devoted his life to jurisprudence, believed he could negotiate with the United States on the basis of legality. He did not anticipate that American leaders would intervene so directly against his government. When they did, he proposed a series of compromises. American diplomats rejected all of them, insisting that Nicaragua must have a government free of "Zelayist influence." There was nothing more to be said or done. At the end of August, Madríz resigned from office and followed Zelaya into exile.

With the seat of power vacant, General Estrada was able to march unopposed to Managua. While still under way, he sent a telegram to Secretary of State Knox assuring American leaders of "the warm regard entertained for them by the victorious party of the revolution." He entered the capital and was sworn in as president on August 21, 1910.

"On that day," *New York Times* correspondent Harold Denny later wrote, "began the American rule of Nicaragua, political and economic."

The day was more significant than Denny could have known. It may now be recognized as the opening of an era. This was the first time the United States government had explicitly orchestrated the overthrow of a foreign leader. In Hawaii, an American diplomat had managed the revolution, but without specific instructions from Washington. In Cuba, Puerto Rico, and the Philippines, American "regime change" operations were part of a larger war. The overthrow of President Zelaya in Nicaragua was the first real American coup.

ON A DECEMBER EVENING IN 1910, BARELY A YEAR AFTER ZELAYA FELL, FOUR dapper figures stepped out of their New Orleans hotel to sample the fleshy delights of Storyville, one of the world's most celebrated concentrations of bordellos, jazz clubs, and gambling halls. Music spilled onto the streets. Women flashed meretricious smiles and more at men wearing silk suits and diamond stickpins. It was a fine place for four adventurers to spend their last night in the United States before setting out to overthrow a government.

As the four strolled through Storyville, United States Secret Service agents followed at a respectful distance. The agents had been watching them for days. It was common knowledge that these four men were plotting a revolution in Honduras, and the Secret Service, which was responsible for enforcing neutrality laws, wanted to make sure they did not launch it from American soil.

The best known of the four conspirators was Lee Christmas, a flamboyant soldier of fortune who had fought in almost every Central American war and revolution of the past quarter century. Christmas, who styled himself a general, wore a tasseled uniform made especially for him by a Paris tailor. He was as famous in the United States as he was in Central America. Sunday supplements competed to publish breathless accounts of his exploits. One of them, in the *New York Times*, called him "a Dumas hero in real life" and "the most spectacular figure in Central America today."

Business, specifically the business of revolution, brought Christmas to New Orleans at the end of 1910. The most ambitious and successful banana planter in Central America, Sam Zemurray, had hired him to overthrow the Honduran government, and he had come to New Orleans to organize the plot. This he had done. Now he needed to slip away from the Secret Service so he could sail off to Honduras and start fighting.

That night in Storyville, Christmas was accompanied by his three most important coconspirators. One was a notorious New Orleans gangster, George "Machine Gun" Molony, whom Christmas trusted to shoot his way into or out of any situation they might encounter in Honduras. The other two were Hondurans: Manuel Bonilla, the man Zemurray had chosen to be the country's next president, and Bonilla's chief aide, Florian Dávadi. Trapped in New Orleans as they were, these four decided to make the best of their situation. That led them to the sumptuous May Evans bordello on Basin Street.

As the four conspirators disappeared into the warm embrace for which May Evans was famous, Secret Service agents took up posts nearby. It must have been frustrating duty. The agents huddled against the raw wind that chills New Orleans in midwinter, while the men they were watching caroused the night away inside. Finally, at two o'clock in the morning, they called it a night.

"It's nothing but a drunken brawl in the District," they reported to their supervisor before heading home.

Christmas was immediately told that the agents had walked away from their posts. He jumped from his bed, quickly dressed, grabbed Bonilla and their two companions, and raced toward their car.

"Well, *compadre*," he told Bonilla as they sped away, "this is the first time I've ever heard of anybody going from a whorehouse to a White House!"

The four men raced to Bayou St. John, where Sam Zemurray's private yacht was docked, climbed aboard, and then sailed across Lake Pontchartrain and the Mississippi Sound to his hideaway on Ship Island. Their patron was waiting for them. He had cases of rifles and ammunition hidden on the island, and under cover of the winter darkness, the men ferried them to the *Hornet,* a surplus navy ship they had bought for the operation. Before dawn they set sail for Honduras.

Deposing Zelaya's government in Nicaragua had required the combined efforts of the State Department, the navy, the marines, and President Taft. In Honduras, Zemurray set out to do the job himself. No American businessman ever held a foreign nation's destiny so completely in his hands.

"Sam the Banana Man" was one of the most colorful figures in the history of American capitalism. In New Orleans he is remembered as a philanthropist who donated $1 million to Tulane University and paid to build a hospital for black women. Agronomists still admire his contributions to the science of banana cultivation. Some Jews consider him an exemplary figure of their Diaspora, an immigrant from Eastern Europe who arrived at Ellis Island as a penniless youth and rose to great wealth and power. In Honduras, people know him as the man who overthrew their government and took over their country.

It is safe to presume that no one in Kishinev, today the capital of Moldova, had ever seen a banana when Samuel Zmuri was born there in 1877. Nor had most people in Alabama, where the renamed Sam Zemurray landed with relatives when he was fifteen years old. He found work as a dock laborer in Mobile. There he watched sailors dump bunches of overripe bananas into the sea. He came up with the idea of buying them and sending them quickly to inland towns. Business boomed. By the time Zemurray was twenty-one, he was worth more than $100,000.

After selling other people's bananas for more than a decade, Zemurray decided to try growing his own. He borrowed half a million dollars, some of it at usurious interest rates of up to 50 percent, and bought fifteen thousand acres of land in Honduras. Once again he was brilliantly successful, easily paying off his loans and becoming a major force in the banana trade. His only problem was the Honduran government.

Like many other American businessmen in Central America, Zemurray considered his land a private fiefdom. He resented having to pay taxes and abide by Honduran laws and regulations. That put him in conflict with President Miguel Dávila, who not only insisted that foreign businesses submit to taxation but was campaigning to limit the amount of land foreigners could own in Honduras.

Dávila was a Liberal who had been a protégé of the deposed Nicaraguan leader José Santos Zelaya. When Zelaya fell, he lost a vital political and military ally. Among those who realized this was Sam Zemurray. He decided that Dávila was now ripe to be overthrown, and with typical resolve set out to do the overthrowing himself.

The first thing Zemurray needed was a pretender, someone who could take over the Honduran presidency and run the country on his behalf. Bonilla, a conspiracy-minded former general who had once before seized the presidency, was an ideal candidate. Since being overthrown, Bonilla had been living in British Honduras (present-day Belize) and dreaming of a return to power. He had the ambition, but not the means. In the spring of 1910, he described his situation quite simply.

"I am in need of the indispensable elements," he wrote to a friend. "Without the decided assistance of *El Amigo,* I do not rise in arms against General Dávila."

El Amigo was, of course, the most powerful man in Honduras, Sam Zemurray. It was inevitable that he and Bonilla would join forces. *"El Amigo* had no other Honduran *político* who, once installed in power, would be so understanding about the banana men's problems," according to one history of the period. "Zemurray would unlikely stop his intrigues until the effective exercise of power in Honduras was in the hands of a leader or faction sympathetic to his banana business."

Although Zemurray and Bonilla made a fine pair, they could not launch a revolution on their own. Zemurray had the money, and Bonilla made a reasonable front man, but neither had the skills to assemble and lead a reliable fighting force. Both knew who could. Lee Christmas, who had served as director of the Honduran police during Bonilla's presidency, was the hemisphere's most famous soldier of fortune. No one was better suited to the job of overthrowing a Central American government. Zemurray approached him with a generous offer, and he quickly accepted.

At the end of 1910, Christmas, Bonilla, and Zemurray met in New Orleans to make their plan. They made no attempt to hide what they were doing. Christmas set about recruiting among the eager crowd of ne'er-do-wells who hung around New Orleans waiting for just such a chance. Zemurray, meanwhile, arranged to buy the *Hornet*.

Secret Service agents realized full well that the *Hornet* was to be used in an attempt to overthrow the Honduran government. They told her new owners that she would be forbidden to sail unless federal inspectors certified that she was transporting no weaponry. Zemurray invited inspectors aboard, and they found her to be carrying only large amounts of food, two hundred tons of coal, and twenty men. That meant they could not detain her, and on December 22, the conspirators set sail from Algiers Point.

Rather than head for Honduras, though, the *Hornet* hovered just outside the American three-mile limit. The plan was for her to wait there until Christmas and the other conspirators could shake off their Secret Service detail. On the night of December 23 in Storyville, they did. Early the next morning, the *Hornet,* newly laden with rifles, ammunition, and George Molony's cherished Hotchkiss machine gun, sailed into action.

On New Year's Eve the *Hornet* approached the Honduran island of Roatán and quickly captured it, with the defending government force surrendering after firing just one shot. Christmas and Molony left their men there to celebrate. They took a launch to the nearby island of Utila, dragged the local commander out of bed, and told him he was deposed. Then they forced him to run in circles around his cabin, dressed only in underwear, and shout "Viva Bonilla!"

Two American gunboats, the *Tacoma* and the *Marietta,* were cruising nearby. Their commanders were uncertain whether to seize the *Hornet*. They knew they should act according to Washington's wishes, and were awaiting orders.

The United States had a special interest in Honduras at this moment. Under a series of Liberal presidents, Honduras had fallen into the habit of borrowing money from European banks. President Taft and Secretary of State Knox disapproved of this practice, just as they had disapproved of Zelaya's railroad loan in 1909. They asked President Dávila to transfer his debt by accepting a $30 million loan from the American banking firm of J. P. Morgan, most of which would be used to pay off the European creditors. To guarantee repayment, J. P. Morgan would take over the Honduran customs service and oversee its Treasury, in effect turning the country into a protectorate.

This proposal put President Dávila in an impossible position. He knew that if he accepted the loan, many of his fellow Liberals would erupt in anger. If he rejected it, the Americans were certain to punish him.

As Dávila wrestled with his dilemma, rebels aboard the *Hornet* sailed to the port of Trujillo and seized it. When news of this reached the Honduran minister in Washington, he decided that it was time for him to sign the treaty authorizing the Morgan loan. He marched to the State Department and did so. That confused matters, and the news led Captain George Cooper, commander of the *Marietta*, to place the *Hornet* under military guard. He warned the insurgents on board not to launch further attacks, and when a group of them did anyway, he ordered the vessel seized for violating American neutrality laws.

Despite this apparent unpleasantness, Christmas remained on friendly terms with Captain Cooper. On January 17, the two men met aboard the *Marietta*. "He informed me," Cooper reported in a dispatch to Washington, "that the State Department was well aware of all the plans of the revolutionists before they began, and that they were practically encouraged."

This was clear diplomatic code. Cooper was asking the State Department if it did indeed support the revolution. When he received no reply contradicting Christmas's claim, he logically came to accept it as true. He was correct.

Officials in Washington were ambivalent when the Honduran revolution broke out, but they soon concluded that its success would benefit the United States. They considered Dávila untrustworthy because of his well-known Liberal sympathies and feared that, if allowed to remain in office, he would become a dangerous symbol of independence who might inspire nationalists elsewhere in Central America. His doubts about the Morgan loan confirmed his lack of deference to American power. Bonilla, on the other hand, was eager to lead Honduras into what would necessarily be a highly unequal partnership with the United States. It was an easy call.

Christmas brought his men ashore from their confiscated ship and led them toward La Ceiba, the main town on the coast. When they arrived there, they found that Captain Cooper had done them a great favor. He had sent a message to the local army commander, General Francisco Guerrero, declaring La Ceiba a "neutral zone" that was "off limits" to any fighting. Guerrero, forbidden to defend his positions, resolved to attack the insurgents outside town.

The battle of La Ceiba, fought on January 25, 1911, was one of the fiercest of that era. Hundreds of men fought on each side. "Machine Gun" Molony lived up to his name by proving highly adept with his Hotchkiss, even using it to capture the defenders' single Krupp artillery piece. In the end, the insurgents triumphed. Among the dead was General Guerrero, who was shot off his horse while urging his men to the front.

In the Honduran capital, Tegucigalpa, President Dávila knew that the fall of La Ceiba was very bad news. Hoping to salvage something from the disaster, he called the American minister to his office and said he was "ready to deliver the presidency to any person designated by the United States." To prove his good faith, he asked the National Assembly to approve the Morgan loan treaty. By a vote of thirty-two to four, it indignantly refused and instead passed a resolution declaring the treaty unconstitutional and "an offense against Honduras."

"Honduras had escaped the grasp of bankers," one historian later wrote, "only to fall into the clutches of the banana men."

The vote against the Morgan loan sealed President Dávila's fate. A few days later, the United States issued an order forbidding any more fighting in Honduras, meaning that Dávila could no longer use his army. Stripped of the most elemental power of self-defense, he resigned the presidency. He was defeated not by Lee Christmas but by a fiat issued in Washington.

Over the next few weeks, Christmas and an American diplomat, Thomas Dawson, met several times aboard the *Marietta* to decide the future of Honduras. They came up with a formula under which a provisional president would hold office for a year and then resign in favor of Bonilla. It worked as planned, and Bonilla assumed the presidency in February 1912. As he took the oath of office in Tegucigalpa, seventy-five United States Marines guarded the wharf that American fruit companies used in Puerto Cortés, to ensure that nationalists would not destroy it in protest.

An American prosecutor in New Orleans later indicted both Bonilla and Christmas for violating neutrality laws, but the cases never came to trial. President Taft personally ordered the charges against Bonilla dropped. The prosecutor, understanding this message, soon did the same for Christmas.

President Bonilla handsomely rewarded the man who had placed him in power. Soon after taking office, he awarded Zemurray 10,000 hectares of banana land—about 24,700 acres—near the north coast. Later he added 10,000 hectares near the Guatemalan border. Then he gave Zemurray a unique permit allowing his businesses to import whatever they needed duty-free. Finally, he authorized Zemurray to raise a $500,000 loan in the name of the Honduran government, and use the money to repay himself for what he claimed to have spent organizing the revolution.

With assets like these, it is no wonder that Zemurray soon became known as "the uncrowned king of Central America." He was certainly the king of Honduras. After Bonilla's death in 1913, he controlled a string of presidents. In 1925 he secured exclusive lumbering rights to a region covering one-tenth of Honduran territory. Later he merged his enterprises with United Fruit and took over as the firm's managing director. Under his leadership, United Fruit became inextricably interwoven with the fabric of Central American life. According to one study, it "throttled competitors, dominated governments, manacled railroads, ruined planters, choked cooperatives, domineered over workers, fought organized labor and exploited consumers." Four decades later, this uniquely powerful company would help overthrow another Central American government.

4

A Break in the History of the World

The most powerful fleet of warships ever to sail under one flag lined up for a glorious procession off the coast of Virginia on the cool, cloudy morning of December 16, 1907. Thousands of people cheered from the shore and from small boats. Many waved American flags. Only a handful of them, though, knew where this fleet was going.

As a band played "The Girl I Left Behind Me," sixteen battleships sailed slowly past the presidential yacht *Mayflower* at four-hundred-yard intervals. Together they carried fourteen thousand soldiers and marines, along with nearly a quarter of a million tons of armament. All were painted white, with gilded scrollwork adorning their bows. President Theodore Roosevelt, as fervent an advocate of sea power as ever occupied the White House, could barely contain his excitement.

"Did you ever see such a fleet?" he asked his guests aboard the *Mayflower,* flashing his famous grin. "And such a day? It ought to make us all feel proud!"

Roosevelt had spent much of his presidency pushing for the construction of the ships. He wanted to show them off to the world, but no war was brewing to which they could be dispatched. With typical flair, he decided to assemble them into one spectacular fleet and send it on a long voyage. The Great White Fleet, as it came to be known, would sail south from Virginia, call at ports in the Caribbean, proceed along both coasts of South America, and finally dock in California.

The fleet represented fearsome martial power, but it was more than simply a weapon of war. It symbolized the self-confidence and sense of limitless possibility that gripped the American imagination in the first decade of the twentieth century. Roosevelt thought it a fine idea to show the flag in Trinidad, Brazil, Chile, Peru, and Mexico. Even that itinerary, however, was not ambitious enough for him. He was the first president whose conception of American power was truly global, and the Great White Fleet was his way of proclaiming it.

A few hours after the fleet passed out of Hampton Roads, its commander, Admiral Robley Evans, summoned his officers and gave them startling news. Their route would not be as announced. Roosevelt had given him the real plan, to be kept secret until they sailed. The fleet would indeed sail around South America to California, but it would not stop there. It was to cross the Pacific Ocean, enter and cross the Indian Ocean, pass through the Suez Canal, sail across the Mediterranean, pass Gibraltar, and then cross the Atlantic to dock back in Virginia. This would be a tour not around a continent but around the world.

When the plan became public, Roosevelt's critics howled in protest. Sending such an enormous fleet of warships on such an ambitious trip was highly provocative, they charged, not to mention dangerous and expensive. Senator Eugene Hale of Maine, chairman of the Naval Appropriations Committee, threatened to withhold the necessary funds. Roosevelt replied curtly that he already had all the money he needed.

"Try and get it back!" he dared Hale.

For the next fourteen months, Americans breathlessly followed the progress of the Great White Fleet. After a few sailors were involved in a barroom brawl in Rio de Janeiro, newspaper correspondents began portraying it as skirting constantly on the edge of danger. In fact, the opposite was true. The fleet's officers and men were welcomed warmly wherever they called.

In South America they were feted with banquets, parades, gala balls, and sporting contests, and a Peruvian composer even wrote a rousing march for them, "The White Squadron." At Pearl Harbor, they spent six days enjoying luaus, regattas, and other tropical pleasures. In Auckland, New Zealand, Maori dancers performed for them. A quarter of a million people greeted them in Sydney. From Australia they sailed to Manila, capital of the American-owned Philippines, but because of a cholera epidemic they were confined to their ships. Then it was on to Japan, which American strategists had already identified as an emerging rival in the Pacific; to China; back to the Philippines; westward to Ceylon (modern-day Sri Lanka); and, finally, through the Suez Canal and across the Atlantic to home.

The fleet arrived back at its Virginia base on George Washington's birthday, February 22, 1909. A huge crowd turned out despite steady rain. As the giant ships maneuvered into their berths, a military band played "There's No Place like Home." President Roosevelt, who had only two weeks remaining in his term, was of course on hand. He later wrote that sponsoring this extraordinary voyage was "the most important service I rendered for peace."

That is debatable, but the Great White Fleet's world tour did have profound effects. It gave the navy invaluable experience in the logistics of long-distance deployment. For naval architects, it provided a host of insights that led to the development of the next generation of warships. In every country where the fleet called, it left government leaders and ordinary people with a new appreciation of American power. Most important, it was an ingeniously theatrical form of saber rattling, a proclamation that the United States was now a major force in world affairs. No one who saw the Great White Fleet could have doubted either this nation's power or its ambition.

HISTORIC SHIFTS IN WORLD POLITICS OFTEN HAPPEN SLOWLY AND ARE HARDLY even noticeable until years later. That was not the case with the emergence of the United States as a world power. It happened quite suddenly in the spring and summer of 1898.

Until then, most Americans had seemed satisfied with a nation whose reach extended only across their own continent. Their leaders had passed up several chances to seize Hawaii. They could have grabbed Cuba when revolution first broke out there in 1868 but did not even consider it. Nor did they try to take the Dominican Republic in the 1870s, when it seemed to be available for annexation.

In 1898 the United States definitively embraced what Senator Henry Cabot Lodge called "the large policy." Historians have given it various names: expansionism, imperialism, neocolonialism. Whatever it is called, it represents the will of Americans to extend their global reach.

"How stupendous a change in the world these six months have brought," the British diplomat and historian James Bryce marveled in the autumn of 1898. "Six months ago you no more thought of annexing the Philippine Isles and Porto Rico than you think of annexing Spitzbergen today."

Some Americans did, in fact, entertain ambitions that reached almost that far. Henry Cabot Lodge was among several members of Congress who urged the annexation of Canada. Roosevelt mused about attacking Spain, and picked out Cádiz and Barcelona as possible targets. Portuguese leaders feared that American troops might seize the Azores.

Several times before the United States emerged as a world power in 1898, it had used its military might to force other countries to accept its goods. Commodore Matthew Perry led gunboats to Japan in 1854 and, in their shadow, induced the Japanese to sign a treaty opening their ports to American traders. In 1882 a naval force dispatched by President Chester A. Arthur did the same in Korea. Only at the end of the century, though, did the American economy reach a level of productivity that made these impositions a central feature of United States foreign policy.

"Here, then, is the new *realpolitik*," proclaimed the eminent historian Charles Beard. "A free opportunity for expansion in foreign markets is indispensable to the prosperity of American business. Modern diplomacy is commercial. Its chief concern is with the promotion of economic interests abroad."

Outsiders watched the emergence of this new America with a combination of awe and fear. Among the most astonished were European newspaper correspondents who were posted in the United States during 1898. One wrote in the London *Times* that he had witnessed nothing less than "a break in the history of the world." Another, in the *Manchester Guardian*, reported that nearly every American had come to embrace the expansionist idea, while the few critics "are simply laughed at for their pains."

Some of these journalists were unsettled by what they saw. "Love for the impossible, the manic passion for what has never been dared before, penetrates your nerves after an hour, makes your eyes shine and your hands shake, and you run," wrote *La Stampa*'s New York correspondent. *Le Temps* said the United States, formerly "as democratic as any society can be," had become "a state already closer to the other states of the old world, that arms itself like them and aggrandizes itself like them." The *Frankfurter Zeitung* warned Americans against "the disastrous consequences of their exuberance" but realized that they would not listen.

Americans have never worried too much about diplomatic questions. Wild as their land is wild, they have their own opinions, their own politics and their own diplomatic code. Economically and psychologically, they have all that is needed for this. They go forward on the road they believe they must travel and do not care at all what Europe says.

For at least a century, many people in the United States had believed it was their "manifest destiny" to dominate North America. Most cheered when, in 1898, they were told that this destiny was now global and entitled them to influence and dominate lands beyond their own shores. An outspoken band of idealists, however, denounced this change of national course as a mean-spirited betrayal of the American tradition. Among these protesters were university presidents, writers, several titans of industry including Andrew Carnegie, clergymen, labor leaders, and politicians of both parties, including former president Grover Cleveland. They condemned America's interventions abroad, especially the war against nationalist guerrillas in the Philippines, and urged Americans to allow other nations the right to self-determination that they themselves so deeply cherished. One of these critics, E. L. Godkin, the crusading editor of *The Nation,* lamented that by new standards, no one was considered a "true-blue American" who harbored "doubts of the ability of the United States to thrash other nations; or who fails to acknowledge the right of the United States to occupy such territories, canals, isthmuses or peninsulas as they may think it is desirable to have, or who speaks disrespectfully of the Monroe Doctrine, or who doubts the need of a large navy, or who admires European society, or who likes to go to Europe, or who fails, in case he has to go, to make comparisons unfavorable to Europe."

This kind of talk drove expansionists to distraction. Theodore Roosevelt denounced Godkin as "a malignant and dishonest liar." The anti-imperialists as a group, he wrote in a letter to his friend Lodge, were "futile sentimentalists of the international arbitration type" who exhibited "a flabby type of character which eats away at the great fighting features of our race." On another occasion he described them as "simply unhung traitors."

In the end, the anti-imperialists failed not because they were too radical but because they were not radical enough. The United States was changing with amazing speed. Railroads and telegraph lines brought Americans closer to each other than they had ever been. Giant factories sprung up and absorbed wave after wave of European immigrants. The pace of life palpably quickened, especially in cities, which had begun to establish their dominance over national life. All of this appalled many of the anti-imperialists. They were elderly traditionalists who wanted the United States to remain the inwardly focused country it had always been. Their calls for American restraint, and their lamentations on the evils of modernity, did not resonate in a country brimming with ambition, energy, and a sense of unlimited possibility.

The first wave of American "regime change" operations, which lasted from 1893 to 1911, was propelled largely by the search for resources, markets, and commercial opportunities. Not all of the early imperialists, however, were the tools of big business. Roosevelt, Lodge, and Captain Alfred Thayer Mahan were moved by what they considered to be the transcendent imperatives of history. Expanding, they believed, was simply what great nations did. In their minds, promoting commerce and defending national security fused into what one historian has called "an aggressive national egoism and a romantic attachment to national power." They considered themselves nothing less than instruments of destiny and Providence.

The missionary instinct was already deeply ingrained in the American psyche. From the time John Winthrop proclaimed his dream of building a "city upon a hill" to which the world would look for inspiration, Americans have considered themselves a special people. At the end of the nineteenth century, many came to believe they had a duty to civilize needy savages and rescue exploited masses from oppression. Rudyard Kipling encouraged their missionary spirit with a famous poem published in *McClure's Magazine* as the debate over annexing the Philippines began.

> Take up the White Man's burden
> Send forth the best ye breed,
> Go bind your sons to exile
> To serve your captives' need;
> To wait in heavy harness
> On fluttered folk and wild,
> Your new-caught sullen peoples,
> Half-devil and half-child.

Americans have a profoundly compassionate side. Many not only appreciate the freedom and prosperity with which they have been blessed but fervently wish to share their good fortune with others. Time and again, they have proved willing to support foreign interventions that are presented as missions to rescue less fortunate people.

When President McKinley said he was going to war in Cuba to stop "oppression at our very doors," Americans cheered. They did so again a decade later, when the Taft administration declared that it was deposing the government of Nicaragua in order to impose "republican institutions" and promote "real patriotism." Since then, every time the United States has set out to overthrow a foreign government, its leaders have insisted that they are acting not to expand American power but to help people who are suffering.

This paternalism was often mixed with racism. Many Americans considered Latin Americans and Pacific islanders to be "colored" natives in need of guidance from whites. In a nation whose black population was systematically repressed, and where racial prejudice was widespread, this view helped many people accept the need for the United States to dominate foreign countries.

Speeches justifying American expansionism on the grounds of the white race's presumed superiority were staples of political discourse in the 1890s. Senator Albert Beveridge of Indiana described expansion as part of a natural process, "the disappearance of debased civilizations and decaying races before the higher civilization of the nobler and more virile types of man." Representative Charles Cochrane of Mississippi spoke of "the onward march of the indomitable race that founded this Republic" and predicted "the conquest of the world by the Aryan races." When he finished this speech, the House burst into applause.

It was logical that the rhetoric of imperialism would be heavily tinged with racism. What is more interesting is that anti-imperialists also used racist arguments. Many of them believed the United States should not seize foreign territories because doing so would increase the number of nonwhite people within its borders. Ultimately, they feared, these territories might have to be allowed to send representatives to Congress. One of the anti-imperialists, Representative Champ Clark of Missouri, rose to warn vividly of the horrors that would bring.

How can we endure our shame when a Chinese senator from Hawaii, with his pigtail hanging down his back, with his pagan joss in his hand, shall rise from his curule chair and in pidgin English proceed to chop logic with George Frisbie Hoar or Henry Cabot Lodge? *O tempora! O mores!* . . .

Mr. Speaker, should [you] preside here twenty years hence, it may be that you will have a polyglot House, and it will be your painful duty to recognize "the gentleman from Patagonia," "the gentleman from Cuba," "the gentleman from Santo Domingo," "the gentleman from Korea," "the gentleman from Hong Kong," "the gentleman from Fiji," "the gentleman from Greenland," or, with fear and trembling, "the gentleman from the Cannibal Islands," who will gaze upon you with watering mouth and gleaming teeth.

WITHIN DAYS AFTER THE OVERTHROW OF THE HAWAIIAN MONARCHY, ON January 17, 1893, many American newspapers were condemning it. The *New York Evening Post* called it "a revolution on a strictly cash basis." To the *New York Times,* it was "a business operation purely." Other papers reported it under headlines like "Minister Stevens Helped Overthrow Liliuokalani" and "The Warship *Boston* Cut a Big Figure in Hawaiian Revolution."

As these articles were appearing, Hawaii's new leaders were securing their power. President Sanford Dole and his "advisory council" declared martial law, suspended the right of habeas corpus, and ordered the creation of a National Guard. Then, evidently worried that even those steps might not be enough to safeguard their infant regime, they arranged for John L. Stevens, the American diplomat who made their revolution possible, to raise the Stars and Stripes over Government House in Honolulu and proclaim that in the name of the United States, he was assuming "protection of the Hawaiian Islands."

"A company of United States Marines was stationed at the government building, and a force of sailors was given the C. R. Bishop residence and ground," Dole wrote later. "Under this protectorate, matters quieted down."

A few days later, Lorrin Thurston, chief organizer of the Hawaiian revolution, arrived in Washington with four other "annexation commissioners." They brought with them a draft of a treaty providing for the "full, complete and perpetual political union between the United States of America and the Hawaiian Islands." Before the Senate could vote on it, however, a most unwelcome Hawaiian turned up in Washington: the deposed queen. In a written statement to Secretary of State John Watson Foster, who had replaced the ailing James G. Blaine, she asserted that the rebellion in her country "would not have lasted an hour" without the support of American troops and that the new government had "neither the moral nor the physical support of the masses of the Hawaiian people."

These accusations reinforced the doubts many Americans had about annexing Hawaii, and with the end of its session approaching, the Senate decided not to vote on the annexation treaty. Thurston and his disappointed comrades had to leave Washington without their prize. On March 4, 1893, Grover Cleveland was inaugurated for his second, nonconsecutive term as president. Cleveland was a Democrat and a declared anti-imperialist. Five days after taking office, he withdrew the treaty.

On July 4, 1894, the archipelago's new leaders responded to this rebuff by proclaiming a Republic of Hawaii, with Sanford Dole as president. Under its constitution, most legislators would be appointed rather than elected, and only men with savings and property would be eligible for public office. This all but excluded native Hawaiians from the government of their land, and a few months later, a group of them staged an abortive uprising. The former queen was among those arrested. On the sixth day of her imprisonment, a delegation of officials visited her and induced her to sign a document of abdication. She later said she had signed it to save other defendants from execution, but a military tribunal sentenced five of them to death anyway. The sentences were not carried out, however, and within a couple of years all the plotters were freed. Liliuokalani herself was sentenced to five years in prison, and freed after two.

In 1897, Cleveland was succeeded by William McKinley, a probusiness Republican who sympathized with the imperial idea. A delegation from the Hawaiian government visited him soon after his inauguration. One of its members, William Smith, wrote later that hearing him after years of listening to Cleveland was "like the difference between daylight and darkness."

McKinley soon announced his support for the annexation of Hawaii, and the lobbying began anew. President Dole himself came to Washington to help lead it. No one paid him much attention, but as he was starting to lose hope, the atmosphere in Washington suddenly changed. In the spring of 1898, in quick succession, the *Maine* was destroyed at Havana, the United States went to war with Spain, and Commodore Dewey wiped out the Spanish fleet in the Philippines. Annexationists found themselves with a new and hugely persuasive argument: Hawaii would be the base Americans needed in their emerging campaign to project power in Asia.

"The annexation of the Hawaiian Islands, for the first time in our history, is presented to us as a war necessity," Representative De Alva S. Alexander of New York gravely declared. "Today we need the Hawaiian Islands much more than they ever needed us."

Many of his colleagues quickly came to agree. In short order, seized by the fever that transformed the United States in the summer of 1898, both houses of Congress approved the annexation treaty. McKinley signed it on July 7, and with his signature, Hawaii became a territory of the United States.

"There is little doubt that Hawaii was annexed because of the Spanish War," William Adam Russ wrote at the end of his two-volume history of the period. "The chain of circumstances which explains that event goes like this: the United States fought Spain in defense of Cuban rights; in order to defeat Spain it was thought necessary to conquer the Philippines; in order to win the Philippines a halfway stop was needed to serve as a coaling station. In other words, Hawaiian annexation came about when the United States needed the islands for its newly conceived empire."

Two generations later, following a world war that the United States entered after an attack on Pearl Harbor, many members of Congress were reluctant to grant statehood to Hawaii, partly because of its racial composition and partly because of its distance from the mainland. After Congress voted to admit Alaska in 1958, those arguments became impossible to sustain. On March 11, 1959, the Senate voted to make Hawaii the fiftieth state, and the House of Representatives followed the next day. Three months later, Hawaiians went to the polls in a plebiscite and voted for statehood by a seventeen-to-one margin. Of the 240 electoral precincts, only one, the small island of Niihau, almost all of whose residents were native Hawaiians, voted no.

Native Hawaiians will probably never again constitute even a large minority of the population in the land of their ancestors. According to the 2000 census, fewer than 10 percent of the people living in the archipelago fall into the category "Native Hawaiian and Other Pacific Islander." Nonetheless, during the last decades of the twentieth century, many Hawaiians began to look more closely at their heritage. A movement for "Hawaiian sovereignty" emerged and won considerable support—partly because it never defined specifically what "sovereignty" should be. Few Hawaiians went so far as to advocate separation from the United States, but a surprising number, including some leading politicians, came to believe that Hawaii should be granted some form of autonomy that would recognize the uniqueness of its history and the way it became part of the Union.

In 1993, one hundred years after the American-backed revolution that brought down Hawaii's monarchy, this movement achieved a remarkable success. Its leaders persuaded the United States Senate and the House of Representatives to pass a resolution declaring that Congress "apologizes to Native Hawaiians on behalf of the people of the United States for the overthrow of the Hawaiian Kingdom on January 17, 1893," and for the subsequent "deprivation of the rights of Native Hawaiians to self-determination."

The entire Hawaiian congressional delegation came to the Oval Office to watch President Bill Clinton sign the resolution, on November 22, 1993. "One hundred years ago, a powerful country helped overthrow a legal government," Senator Daniel Akaka asserted. "We've finally come to the point where this has been acknowledged by the United States."

Supporters of this resolution were not the only ones who considered its passage to be a profoundly important event. While it was being debated, several opponents warned that if passed, it could have far-reaching effects. According to one of the dissenters, Senator Slade Gorton of Washington, "the logical consequence of this resolution would be independence." Some Hawaiians dared to hope that he would one day be proven right.

Most people on the islands, however, are pleased with the way their history has turned out. They enjoy the prosperity and freedom that comes with American citizenship, and especially with statehood. Their experience suggests that when the United States assumes real responsibility for territories it seizes, it can lead them toward stability and happiness. In Hawaii, it did that slowly and often reluctantly. The revolution of 1893 and the annexation that followed undermined a culture and ended the life of a nation. Compared to what such operations have brought to other countries, though, this one ended well.

ALTHOUGH THE ANNEXATION OF HAWAII PROVOKED INTENSE DEBATE IN THE United States, it was ultimately accomplished with the stroke of a pen. No force in Hawaii had the slightest hope of challenging it. That was not the case in Cuba.

The Republic of Cuba came into existence on May 20, 1902. Its early years were marked by sporadic uprisings and attacks on American property. After a protest against electoral fraud in 1906, American troops landed and placed the country under direct military rule. They stayed for three years. When they left, President William Howard Taft warned

Cubans that although the United States did not wish to annex their country, it was "absolutely out of the question that the island should continue to be independent" if its citizens persisted in their "insurrectionary habit."

Opposition movements matured during the rule of Gerardo Machado in the 1920s and 1930s. All of Latin America was being swept by winds of nationalism and anti-Yankee sentiment, and they blew especially strongly in Cuba, which had strong trade unions, a core of radical writers and thinkers, and a long tradition of resistance to foreign power. The greatest beneficiary was the Communist Party. Founded in 1925 and quickly banned by Machado, it took advantage of its position as an outlawed enemy of the dictator, and by 1930 was the dominant force in Cuba's labor movement. During this period, Communists managed to persuade many Cubans that they were the nation's truest patriots.

After Franklin Roosevelt became president of the United States in 1933, he decided that the Machado dictatorship had become an embarrassment and encouraged the Cuban army to rebel. It did so, and out of the ensuing turmoil emerged a sergeant named Fulgencio Batista. By the mid-1930s he was master of Cuba, and he shaped its fate for most of the next quarter century.

Batista broke diplomatic relations with the Soviet Union, cracked down on the Communist Party, and invited American military advisers to train his army. He later encouraged American investors, including prominent gangsters, to build what became a spectacularly lucrative tourism industry based on prostitution and casino gambling. His most lasting legacy, however, may have been his cancellation of the congressional election that was to have been held in 1952. Among the candidates was Fidel Castro, a charismatic young lawyer and former student leader. Castro might have gone on to a career in electoral politics, but after Batista's coup made that impossible, he turned to revolution.

For an astonishingly long time, American policy makers deluded themselves into believing that all was well in Cuba. In 1957 the National Security Council reported that Cuban-American relations faced "no critical problems or difficulties." A year later Allen Dulles, director of the Central Intelligence Agency, told a congressional hearing that there was no likelihood of Soviet influence growing anywhere in Latin America. Blithe assurances like these suggest the shock that many Americans, especially those in Washington, felt when Batista fled the country on January 1, 1959, a few steps ahead of Castro's rebels.

The day after Batista's flight, Castro descended from his mountain stronghold to Santiago, the city that the Americans had prevented General Calixto García from entering at the end of the Spanish-American War. In the central plaza, which is named for Carlos Manuel de Céspedes, another nineteenth-century rebel leader, Castro made his first speech as leader of the victorious revolution. He said nothing about his political plans but made a solemn promise. It was one that would have puzzled most Americans, but it thrilled the Cuban soul.

> This time the revolution will not be frustrated! This time, fortunately for Cuba, the revolution will achieve its true objective. It will not be like 1898, when the Americans came and made themselves masters of the country.

The Cuban revolution, and especially Castro's turn toward anti-Yankee radicalism, baffled most Americans. Few had any idea of how the United States had treated Cuba in the past, so naturally they could not understand why Cubans wished so fervently to break out of the American orbit. Many were astonished, just as their grandparents had been in 1898, to learn that "liberated" Cubans were ungrateful to the United States. President Dwight Eisenhower was among the baffled:

> Here is a country that, you would believe on the basis of our history, would be one of our real friends. The whole history . . . would seem to make it a puzzling matter to figure out just exactly why the Cubans and the Cuban government would be so unhappy when, after all, their principal market is here, their best market. You would think they would want good relationships. I don't know exactly what the difficulty is.

Castro's government confiscated foreign corporations, banned capitalist enterprise, and steered Cuba into a close alliance with the Soviet Union. In 1961, exiles sponsored by the CIA invaded Cuba in an attempt to depose him but failed miserably. Eighteen months later, after the Soviets deployed offensive missiles in Cuba, Soviet and American leaders brought their countries to the brink of nuclear combat in the most terrifying showdown of the Cold War. Successive American presidents vowed to bring Castro down, and at several points the CIA tried to kill him. He not only survived but devoted much of his life to undermining United States interests from Nicaragua to Angola. That made him an icon of anti-Americanism and a hero to millions around the world.

Castro was a pure product of American policy toward Cuba. If the United States had not crushed Cuba's drive to independence in the early twentieth century, if it had not supported a series of repressive dictators there, and if it had not stood by while the 1952 election was canceled, a figure like Castro would almost certainly not have emerged. His regime is the quintessential result of a "regime change" operation gone wrong, one that comes back to haunt the country that sponsored it.

IN PUERTO RICO, 450 MILES EAST OF CUBA, AMERICAN OCCUPATION TROOPS declared the second anniversary of their takeover to be a national holiday. On that day, July 25, 1900, there would be banquets, speeches, band concerts, and a military parade. For the Americans, still caught up in the excitement of their country's sudden rise to world power, it seemed a wonderful moment to celebrate. They had, after all, acquired at almost no cost a lovely little island ideally situated to guard vital Caribbean trade routes.

Puerto Ricans were in a more somber mood. On the eve of the celebration, Luis Muñoz Rivera, Puerto Rico's most distinguished political figure, sat down despondently to write his view of what the invasion had wrought.

> The North American government found in Puerto Rico a degree of autonomy larger than that of Canada. It should have respected and enlarged it, but only wanted to and did destroy it. . . . Because of that, and other things about which we shall remain silent, we shall not celebrate our 25th of July. Because we thought that an era of liberty was dawning and instead we are witnessing a spectacle of terrible assimilation . . . because none of the promises were kept, and because our present condition is that of serfs attached to conquered territory.

The first decades of American colonial rule in Puerto Rico were an unhappy time. They began with an act of Congress, the Foraker Act, that established the rules by which the island would be governed. It vested absolute power in a governor appointed by the president of the United States. There would be an elected, thirty-five-member House of Delegates, but its decisions were subject to veto by either the governor or Congress. The only Puerto Rican who testified at a congressional hearing on the act was Julio Henna, a veteran civil rights campaigner.

"No liberty, no rights, no protection," Henna said in an eloquent summary of its provisions. "We are Mr. Nobody from Nowhere."

During the early years of the twentieth century, four American corporations gobbled up most of Puerto Rico's best land. On it they planted sugar, a crop suited to large-scale farming. The big losers were families who grew coffee, which is known as the "poor man's crop" because it can be cultivated on small plots. By 1930, sugar accounted for 60 percent of the country's exports, while coffee, once the island's principal crop, had fallen to just 1 percent.

With little access to land, ordinary Puerto Ricans became steadily poorer. One study found that while 17 percent of them were unemployed at the time of the American invasion, 30 percent were unemployed a quarter century later. One-third were illiterate. Malaria, intestinal diseases, and malnutrition were facts of everyday life, and most people had no access to even rudimentary medical care. Life expectancy was forty-six years. Running water and electricity were rare luxuries. The annual per capita income was $230. Politics, in one historian's words, was dominated by a coalition of "profit-hungry foreign corporations, a colonial state steeped in paternalism and distrustful of the capabilities of the subjects under its rule, and a complacent local political leadership wanting to protect their class prerogatives."

Part of what made Puerto Rico's condition so vexing was the permanent uncertainty about its political status. It was never set on the path toward statehood, as Hawaii was, or toward the independence that was ultimately bestowed on the Philippines. Congress granted American citizenship to Puerto Ricans in 1917, and in 1948 gave them the right to elect their own governor. Four years later, they voted in a referendum to accept the unique status of a "free associated state"—part of the United States, but not a state itself. At a glittering ceremony on July 25, 1952, exactly fifty-four years after marines landed on the beach at Guánica, the Puerto Rican flag was raised to fly alongside the American flag over the Capitol building in San Juan.

The governor who presided over that ceremony was Luis Muñoz Marín, son of Luis Muñoz Rivera, whose dream of self-rule the United States had crushed at the dawn of the century. Rarely does the son of a brilliant political leader turn out to match his father in energy and vision, but Muñoz Marín did. He began his long political career as an advocate of independence for Puerto Rico, but in the years after World War II, he concluded that the eternal debate over political status was consuming so much political and emotional energy that little was left for resolving the island's dire problems. He also believed that in the newly complex Cold War world, keeping a small island within a larger nation made sense. In his speeches and writings, he urged Puerto Ricans to accept realities dictated from Washington and work within them to improve their lives.

Beginning in the late 1940s, political leaders in Washington came to realize that ruling an impoverished colony in the Caribbean made the United States look bad. This sentiment became more urgent when Cuba turned to Communism after 1959 and the Caribbean found itself caught up in the Cold War. Americans began allowing Puerto Rico steadily increasing control over its own affairs. As the island started to flower, not just economically but also intellectually, Puerto Rico became a center of democratic thought and action. Its national life finally began to fulfill the dreams its patriotic sons and daughters had harbored for generations.

Despite more than a century of overt and covert efforts to turn them into "real Americans," Puerto Ricans cling to their heritage with remarkable ferocity. Spanish is still their language of choice. They send their own team to the Olympic Games, and overwhelmingly oppose any effort to merge it with the United States team. Whether on the island or in New York and the other American cities where more than two million Puerto Ricans live, they are passionate about their native food, music, and traditions. Even in the heart of the melting pot, they have not melted. When they speak of "my country," most mean Puerto Rico, not the United States.

Election results and public opinion surveys suggest that many Puerto Ricans, perhaps even most, are satisfied with the political limbo in which they live. Their many frustrations are easy to understand, but so is their unwillingness to embrace the unknown implications of either statehood or independence. They have carved out a space in the global cartography that may be indistinct but has considerable advantages. It guarantees that they will not fall into the troubles that afflict their island neighbors—Haiti, the Dominican Republic, Cuba, and Jamaica— while allowing them free entry into the mainland, a steady flow of subsidies from Washington, and the right to maintain a good measure of their traditional identity.

Most Puerto Ricans understand that the United States, despite all its misdeeds over a century of colonial mastery, harbors no ambition to oppress them. Almost all wish to maintain their friendly ties to the mainland, although they disagree vigorously on how to do so—by continuing the island's "associated" status, by joining the Union as the fifty-first state, or by becoming an independent country.

As colonial experiments go, American rule over Puerto Rico has been relatively benign. It did not produce the violent backlash that emerged in countries like Cuba, Nicaragua, and the Philippines. This is due mainly to the fact that the United States agreed to take direct political responsibility for governing Puerto Rico, rather than ruling it through local clients.

A reasonable case can be made for the proposition that Puerto Rico would be better off today if the United States had not seized it in 1898. Given the realities of that history, however, it has emerged in better shape than most lands whose governments the United States overthrew. A happy end to this long story, in the form of a resolution to the question of the island's political status, is at least possible. That would take away from Americans the stigma of ruling another people, a role for which they are psychologically and spiritually unsuited. It would also give them a welcome chance to believe that their toppling of foreign regimes need not always end badly.

OF ALL THE NATIONS WHOSE DESTINY THE UNITED STATES CAME TO MASTER IN the early years of the twentieth century, the Philippines was by far the largest, most distant, and most complex. When it became an American possession, it had a population of over seven million, larger than that of Hawaii, Cuba, Puerto Rico, Nicaragua, and Honduras combined. Americans knew less about its seven thousand islands than they knew about the moon.

"'Tis not more than two months since ye larned whether they were islands or canned goods," the satirist Finley Peter Dunne wrote as the United States took over the Philippines.

The United States ruled the Philippines through an American governor and an advisory legislature, the lower house of which was elected. In the first election, held in 1907, 3 percent of the adult population voted. The overwhelming winner was the Nationalist Party, whose platform called for "complete, absolute and immediate independence."

Americans ignored this demand for decades. As the world changed, however, many came to agree that independence for the Philippines might be a good idea. It would relieve the United States of the opprobrium reserved for colonizers and—given the extreme closeness of relations between the two lands—would still allow the United States to maintain considerable power over the archipelago. In 1934, Congress approved a proposal to grant independence within ten years. It could not be carried out because World War II intervened but came to fruition a year after the war ended.

On July 4, 1946, the United States formally relinquished power over the Philippines. Soon afterward, General Eisenhower recommended that the United States withdraw from its military bases there, the largest of which were Subic Bay Naval Station and Clark Air Base. He recognized their strategic value but concluded that it was outweighed by the anti-Americanism their presence would certainly provoke. Sadly, his superiors were not as far-sighted, and his recommendation was ignored. A few months after the independence ceremony, the new Filipino government signed an agreement leasing these bases to the United States for ninety-nine years.

Over the years that followed, Subic Bay and Clark grew to become cities unto themselves. Thousands of American soldiers were based at each one, and tens of thousands of Filipinos worked in their commissaries, warehouses, and repair shops. A vast network of bars, bordellos, and massage parlors thrived outside the bases' perimeters. Just as Eisenhower predicted, these bases became a vivid symbol of American power and a focal point of nationalist anger. Filipino leaders, however, were eager to please their American patrons and did not want to lose the $200 million that the bases brought into the islands' economy each year.

In 1965, President Lyndon Johnson began a major escalation of the American war effort in Vietnam, giving Subic Bay and Clark a greater strategic importance than ever. In that same year, an ambitious politician named Ferdinand Marcos was elected president of the Philippines. The combination of these two factors—the bases' growing importance and the emergence of Marcos—shaped the next quarter century of Philippine history.

During Marcos's two four-year terms as president, dissatisfaction with his callous indifference to the injustices of Filipino life set off a series of armed rebellions. In 1971 he declared that since only a strong government could contain the growing insurgencies that his misrule provoked, he had no choice but to impose martial law. He closed Congress, suspended the constitution, canceled the forthcoming presidential election, and ordered the arrest of thirty thousand opposition figures. For the next fourteen years, he ran one of the most corrupt regimes in Asia. Through a maze of government-protected cartels and monopolies, he and his comrades stole billions of dollars. The country, which had been progressing slowly toward prosperity and freedom, slid backward into repression and poverty.

None of the American presidents who dealt with Marcos during his period of absolute power held him in much esteem. His personal and political style repelled Richard Nixon. Jimmy Carter could not abide the campaigns of torture, rape, and murder by which he maintained his regime. Ronald Reagan, who had a warm spot for anti-Communist dictators, heard complaints about him from American businessmen who could no longer make money in the Philippines because the ruling clique was taking it all. Despite these reservations, however, the United States maintained its friendship with Marcos until the end. It gave his regime billions of dollars in military aid, much of which he spent on violent campaigns against both rebel insurgencies and peaceful opposition movements. The reason was clear. Clark Air Base and Subic Bay Naval Station had become foundations of American military power in Asia, and the United States was willing to do whatever was necessary to hold on to them.

One of the few concessions the United States managed to wrest from Marcos was the release from prison of Benigno Aquino, the main opposition leader. Aquino came to the United States for medical treatment, and, before long, began casting his eyes back on his homeland. On August 20, 1983, against the advice of some of his friends, he returned to Manila. As his plane descended, he slipped into the lavatory to put on a bulletproof vest. It did not help. Seconds after he stepped into the airport, a military squad blocked his way. One of its members fired a shot into the back of Aquino's head, and he fell dead.

"I point an accusing finger straight at the United States," declared Raúl Manglapus, an anti-Communist moderate who was one of the country's leading political figures. "Their support made murder and repression possible."

The assassination of Aquino proved too much for Filipinos to bear. Under the banner "People Power," they rose up against Marcos in one of the most remarkable peaceful revolutions in Asian history. Hoping to weaken it, the dictator called a presidential election for February 7, 1986. Aquino's widow, Corazon, ran against him. The official tally gave victory to Marcos, but no one believed it. Protests escalated, and even powerful military officers began endorsing them. Only the United States remained at Marcos's side.

"I don't know anything more important than those bases," President Reagan explained at a news conference.

Within a few days, however, even American officials had to recognize that their old ally was lost. Soon afterward, he realized it himself. On February 25, he and his wife flew on an American helicopter to Clark Air Base, and then on to Guam. From there they made their way to Hawaii, where the deposed tyrant died three years later.

Corazon Aquino, who became president after Marcos fled, returned to her people the civil rights and public freedoms Marcos had taken from them. Her government failed to make substantial progress toward resolving the country's huge social and economic problems, but restoring democracy was not its only achievement. It also negotiated an epochal agreement with the United States that led to the closing of American military bases in the Philippines. The last American soldiers left Clark and Subic Bay at the end of 1992.

The story of Washington's rule over the Philippines, first direct and then indirect, is above all one of lost opportunity. Americans waged a horrific war to subdue the islands at the beginning of the twentieth century, but once they won, their brutality ended. They did not impose murderous tyrants the way they did in much of Central America and the Caribbean. The parliamentary election they organized in 1907, although hardly democratic by modern standards, was the first of its kind in Asia. In the years that followed, they treated their Asian subjects no worse than the British did, perhaps better than the Dutch treated Indonesians, and certainly better than the Japanese treated people in the countries they occupied during World War II. When France was fighting to hold on to Indochina in the 1950s, the United States had already granted independence to the Philippines.

During their decades of power in the Philippines, however, Americans never sought to promote the kind of social progress that might have led the country toward long-term stability. As in other parts of the world, Washington's fear of radicalism led it to support an oligarchy that was more interested in stealing money than in developing the country. The United States did bequeath to the Filipinos a form of democracy, but when the archipelago was finally allowed to go its own way, in the 1990s, it was as poor as it was unstable.

What would have happened if the United States had not seized the Philippines at the beginning of the twentieth century? Another colonial power might have done so, and perhaps found itself caught in the trap that the Dutch faced in Indonesia, or the French in Indochina. Alternately, Filipinos might have been able to maintain their independence. That could have led them to a happier twentieth century. Even if it did not, it would have spared the United States the blame, justified or not, that many Filipinos and others around the world assign to it for the troubles the Philippines now faces.

NEARLY A DECADE PASSED BETWEEN THE TIME THE UNITED STATES SUBDUED the Philippines and its next "regime change" operation. During that time, it adjusted its approach. President Taft adopted a policy he called "dollar diplomacy," under which the United States brought countries into its orbit through commercial rather than military means. He assured foreign leaders that they had nothing to fear as long as they allowed free rein to American businesses and sought loans only from American banks. The first to reject those conditions was President José Santos Zelaya of Nicaragua.

Nicaraguans remember Zelaya as a visionary who dared to imagine that his small, isolated country could reach greatness. His sins—impatience, egotism, an autocratic temperament, and a tendency to mix public funds with his own—were and are common traits among leaders in Central America and beyond. Few others, however, have matched his reformist passion or his genuine concern for the downtrodden.

Zelaya wandered the world unhappily in the years after his overthrow. He ended up in New York, and in 1918 he died in his apartment at 3905 Broadway. Although he never returned to his homeland, his memory and, more important, the memory of how the United States had pushed him out of power burned in the hearts of Nicaraguans. That made it impossible for his successor, General Estrada, to consolidate power. Estrada was finally forced to resign, and his faint-hearted vice president, Adolfo Díaz, the former chief accountant of the La Luz mining company, succeeded him.

The ascension of this weak and pliable figure to the presidency marked final victory for President Taft and Secretary of State Knox. Knox quickly arranged for two New York banking houses, Brown Brothers and J. and W. Seligman, to lend Nicaragua $15 million and take over the country's customs agency to guarantee repayment. By 1912, Americans were also running the country's national bank, steamship line, and railway.

Nicaraguans never accepted their country's role as a protectorate of the United States. At the end of 1912, Benjamin Zeledón, a fervent admirer of Zelaya, launched a futile but heroic rebellion. He died while fighting the United States Marines. Among those who saw his body being dragged to a cemetery near Masaya was a teenager named Augusto César Sandino. It was a decisive moment.

"Zeledón's death," Sandino later wrote, "gave me the key to understanding our country's situation in the face of Yankee piracy."

Fourteen years later, with United States Marines still occupying his country, Sandino launched a rebellion of his own. At first the State Department sought to dismiss his guerrillas as a "comparatively small body" made up of "lawless elements" and "ordinary bandits." That view became steadily harder to sustain, and finally, in 1933, President Herbert Hoover decided the United States had shed enough blood in Nicaragua and ordered the marines home.

With the Americans gone, Sandino agreed to talk peace. He traveled to Managua under a guarantee of safe conduct, and in remarkably short order agreed to end his rebellion and rejoin the country's normal political life. That settled the matter for everyone except the ambitious young commander of the American-created National Guard, General Anastasio Somoza García. He correctly saw Sandino as a threat to his ambitions and arranged for him to be assassinated. Soon afterward, General Somoza seized the presidency for himself.

Shortly before Sandino was killed, he prophesized that he "would not live much longer," but said that was fine because "there are young people who will continue my fight." He was quite right. In 1956 an idealistic young poet assassinated President Somoza. Soon afterward, a group called the Sandinista National Liberation Front, named for Sandino, launched a rebellion against the dynastic Somoza dictatorship. It seized power in 1979, formed an alliance with Fidel Castro's Cuba, and proclaimed a nationalist program that directly challenged American power. President Ronald Reagan responded by sponsoring another round of war in Nicaragua's mountains and jungles. This turned Nicaragua into a bloody battlefield of the Cold War. Thousands of Nicaraguans died in a conflict that was in part a proxy fight between the United States and Cuba. American-sponsored rebels did not achieve their main goal, the overthrow of the Sandinista regime, but in 1990, two years after the war ended, Nicaraguans voted the Sandinistas out of office. The country remained deeply polarized, however, and one of the poorest in the Western Hemisphere.

In few countries is it possible to trace the development of anti-American sentiment as clearly as in Nicaragua. A century of trouble between the two nations, which led to the death of thousands and great suffering for generations of Nicaraguans, began when the United States deposed President Zelaya in 1909. Benjamin Zeledón took up arms to avenge him. Zeledón's death inspired the young Sandino, who, in turn, inspired the modern Sandinista Front.

For all his faults, Zelaya was the greatest statesman Nicaragua ever produced. If the United States had found a way to deal with him, it might have avoided the disasters that followed. Instead, it crushed a leader who embraced capitalist principles more fully than any other Central American of his era.

That terrible miscalculation drew the United States into a century of interventions in Nicaragua. They took a heavy toll in blood and treasure, profoundly damaged America's image in the world, and helped keep generations of Nicaraguans in misery. Nicaragua still competes with Haiti to lead the Western Hemisphere in much that is undesirable, including rates of poverty, unemployment, infant mortality, and deaths from curable diseases.

Not all of Nicaragua's misfortune can be attributed to a single cause. At the dawn of the twentieth century, though, it was headed toward a very different future from the one that unfolded. If Nicaragua had been left to develop in its own way, it might have become prosperous, democratic, and a stabilizing force in Central America. Instead it is just the opposite.

SAM ZEMURRAY LIKED TO DESCRIBE HONDURAS, WHICH LIES JUST ACROSS Nicaragua's northern border, as a country where "a mule costs more than a congressman." He bought plenty of both, and a string of pliable presidents as well. In the years after the coup he sponsored in 1911, his Cuyamel Fruit Company and two others—Standard Fruit and United Fruit—came to own almost all the fertile land in the country. They also owned and operated its ports, electric power plants, sugar mills, and largest bank.

In exchange for these concessions, the fruit companies promised to build a rail network that would tie the country together. They never did. The only lines they built were the ones they needed, connecting their plantations to Caribbean ports. The *Life Pictorial Atlas of the World,* published in 1961, devoted exactly one sentence to Honduras: "A great banana exporter, Honduras has 1,000 miles of railroad, 900 of which belong to U.S. fruit companies."

Strikes, political protests, uprisings, and attempted coups racked Honduras for decades. To suppress them, the country's presidents maintained a strong army that absorbed more than half of the national budget. When the army could not do the job, it called in the United States Marines.

The suffocating control that Americans maintained over Honduras prevented the emergence of a local business class. In Guatemala, El Salvador, Nicaragua, and Costa Rica, coffee planters slowly accumulated capital, invested in banks and other commercial enterprises, and went on to assert civic and political power. That never happened in Honduras. The only option available to energetic or ambitious Hondurans was to work for one of the banana companies. These companies were triumphs of the American free market, but they used their power to prevent capitalism from emerging in Honduras.

In 1958 the Liberal Party, which Sam Zemurray's coup had forced from office nearly half a century before, finally returned to power. Its leader, Ramón Villeda Morales, took over a country in which United Fruit was the biggest company, the biggest landowner, and the biggest private employer. He called it "the country of the seventies—seventy percent illiteracy, seventy percent illegitimacy, seventy percent rural populations, seventy percent avoidable deaths."

Villeda tried to pass a land reform law, but was forced to withdraw it under intense pressure from United Fruit. When his term was about to expire in 1963, the Liberal candidate who was nominated to succeed him vowed to revive the law, and also to curb the power of the army. That combination disturbed some powerful Hondurans. Ten days before the election, the army staged a coup, installed General Oswaldo López Arellano in the presidency, dissolved Congress, and suspended the constitution. Military officers ruled Honduras for the next eighteen years. During this period, the fruit companies' grip on the country weakened as plant diseases ravaged several of their plantations and banana production in other nations increased.

In 1975 the Securities and Exchange Commission discovered that

General López Arellano had received $1.25 million in secret payments from United Brands, the conglomerate that had absorbed United Fruit. The army reacted by removing López Arellano from the presidency and replacing him with another officer. At the New York headquarters of United Brands, the scandal had a more dramatic impact. Eli Black, the company's president and board chairman, became the focus of a federal investigation. On the morning of February 3, 1975, he smashed a hole in the window of his office on the forty-fourth floor of the Pan Am building and jumped through it.

Honduras held its next election in 1981, and Roberto Suazo Cordova, a country doctor and veteran political infighter, emerged as president. True power, however, remained with the military, specifically with the highly ambitious army commander General Gustavo Álvarez. That suited the United States, because Álvarez was a fierce anti-Communist who detested the Sandinista movement that had recently come to power in neighboring Nicaragua. When the Reagan administration asked him to turn Honduras into a base for anti-Sandinista rebels, known as contras, he eagerly agreed. Soon hundreds of contras were operating from camps along the Nicaraguan border, and thousands of American soldiers were flying in and out of the ballooning Aguacate air base nearby. From 1980 to 1984, annual United States military aid to Honduras increased from $4 million to $77 million. Once again, it had surrendered its national sovereignty to Americans.

Rivals forced General Álvarez from power in 1984 but did not dismantle his repressive machine. It had two purposes: supporting the contras and repressing dissent within Honduras. To achieve this latter goal, the army established a secret squad called Battalion 3-16, trained and supported by the CIA, that maintained clandestine torture chambers and carried out kidnappings and killings. The most powerful figure in the country during this period was the American ambassador, John Negroponte, who studiously ignored all pleas that he try to curb the regime's excesses.

While the contra war raged, progress toward democracy in Honduras was impossible and citizens faced a frightening form of government-sponsored terror. The war had another effect, which did not become clear until years later. Thousands of poor Honduran families, submerged in grinding poverty and fearful of the military, fled the country during the 1980s. Many ended up in Los Angeles. There, large numbers of Honduran teenagers joined violent street gangs. In the 1990s many of these youths were deported back to Honduras, where they faced the same lack of opportunity that had forced their parents to flee. Soon they established in their homeland a replica of the bloody gang culture they had absorbed in Los Angeles.

These awful turns in Honduran national life were in part the result of United States intervention, and they symbolize the unimaginable consequences that "regime change" operations can have. At the beginning of the twentieth century, Americans deposed a government in Honduras in order to give banana companies freedom to make money there. For decades, these companies imposed governments that crushed every attempt at national development. In the 1980s, when democracy finally seemed ready to emerge in Honduras, the United States prevented it from flowering because it threatened the anti-Sandinista project that was Washington's obsession. That was the period when Honduran children turned up by the thousands in Los Angeles, where many of them fell into the criminality they later brought home. Honduras, a miserably poor country where the average person earns less than $3,000 a year, was unprepared for this plague. It sank into a tragedy more brutal than any it had ever known.

No one can know what might have happened in Honduras if the United States had never intervened there. Two facts, however, are indisputable. First, the United States has been the overwhelming force in Honduran life for more than a century. Second, Honduras today faces a nightmare of poverty, violence, and instability. Hondurans bear part of the blame for this heartrending situation, but Americans cannot escape their share.

THE SHATTERING EVENTS OF 1898 ESTABLISHED THE UNITED STATES AS A world power. In the first years of the twentieth century, it began flexing its newfound political muscle. The first region to feel the effect was the Caribbean Basin. Once the United States resolved to build an interoceanic canal, it felt the need to control events in nearby countries. "The inevitable effect of our building the canal," Secretary of War Elihu Root asserted in 1906, "must be to require us to police the surrounding premises."

Most of the nations in these "surrounding premises" were still searching for their modern identities. Viewed from the United States, they seemed chronically unstable or in turmoil. Americans came to believe that by establishing "order" in these unhappy lands, they could achieve two wonderful results simultaneously. They would bring economic benefit to themselves while at the same time civilizing and modernizing nations that seemed primitive and crying out for guidance. Caught up in the all-encompassing idea of their country's "manifest destiny," they convinced themselves that American influence abroad could only be positive and that anyone who rejected it must be bad.

"All that this country desires is that the other republics on this continent shall be happy and prosperous," Theodore Roosevelt declared, "and they cannot be happy and prosperous unless they maintain order within their boundaries and behave with a just regard for their obligations toward outsiders."

The "outsiders" toward whom Latin Americans were supposed to behave properly were businessmen from the United States. Countries that allowed them free rein were considered progressive and friendly. Those that did not were turned into pariah states and targets for intervention.

The first burst of American expansionism was over by the time President Taft left office at the beginning of 1913. By then, the United States owned Puerto Rico and the Philippines, and had turned Cuba, Nicaragua, and Honduras into official or unofficial protectorates. Through a series of political and military maneuvers, it had come to dominate the Caribbean Basin. It had also annexed two uninhabited but strategically located Pacific atolls, Wake and Midway, as well as Guam and the islands that became known as American Samoa. In each of these places, it established naval bases that became valuable assets as it began projecting power around the world.

"The tendency of modern times is toward consolidation," Senator Lodge asserted. "Small states are of the past, and have no future."

The leaders of those small states, like José Santos Zelaya in Nicaragua and Miguel Dávila in Honduras, found that powerful figures in Washington considered their independence deeply threatening. Their overthrows marked the end of a period during which Central America was moving toward profound social reform. They dreamed of transforming their feudal societies into modern capitalist states, but American intervention aborted their grand project.

Expansion presented the United States with a dilemma that has confronted many colonial powers. If it allowed democracy to flower in the countries it controlled, those nations would begin acting in accordance with their own interests rather than the interests of the United States, and American influence over them would diminish. Establishing that influence, though, was the reason the United States had intervened in those countries in the first place. Americans had to choose between permitting them to become democracies or maintaining power over them. It was an easy choice.

If the United States had been more far-sighted, it might have found a way to embrace and influence reformers in Cuba, Puerto Rico, the Philippines, Nicaragua, and Honduras. That could have produced a fairer social order in those countries, with two results. First, it would have improved the lives of many who have instead lived and died in poverty. Second, it would have eased festering social conflicts that periodically exploded into violence and dragged the United States into new rounds of intervention.

Nationalists reflexively rebel against governments they perceive as lackeys of foreign power. In the twentieth century, many of these rebels were men and women inspired by American history, American principles, and the rhetoric of American democracy. They were critical of the United States, however, and wished to reduce or eliminate the power it wielded over their countries. Their defiance made them anathema to American leaders, who crushed them time after time.

The course the United States followed brought enormous power and wealth but slowly poisoned the political climate in the affected countries. Over a period of decades, many of their citizens concluded that democratic opposition movements had no chance of success because the United States opposed them so firmly. That led them to begin embracing more radical alternatives. If the elections of 1952 in Cuba had not been canceled, and if candidates like the young Fidel Castro had been allowed to finish their campaigns for public office and use democratic institutions to modernize Cuba, a Communist regime might never have emerged there. If the United States had not resolutely supported dictators in Nicaragua, it would not have been confronted with the leftist Sandinista movement of the 1980s.

In the quarter century before 1898, much of the world suffered through a series of economic crises. The United States was not exempt, passing through depressions or financial panics in the mid-1870s, mid-1880s, and early 1890s. Political leaders saw overseas expansion as the ideal way to end this destructive cycle. They believed it would answer the urgent questions raised by two epochal developments that changed the United States at the end of the nineteenth century: the closing of its frontier and the greatly increased production of its farms and factories. Successive presidents embraced the "open door" policy, which they described as a way of bringing all nations into a global trading system. It might better have been called "kick in the door," because in reality it was a policy of forcing foreign nations to buy American products, share their resources with the United States, and grant privileges to American businesses, whether they wanted to or not.

American leaders clamored for this policy because, they said, the country desperately needed a way to resolve its "glut" of overproduction. This glut, however, was largely illusory. While wealthy Americans were lamenting it, huge numbers of ordinary people were living in conditions of severe deprivation. The surplus production from farms and factories could have been used to lift millions out of poverty, but this would have required a form of wealth redistribution that was repugnant to powerful Americans. Instead they looked abroad.

By embracing the "open door" policy, the United States managed to export many of its social problems. The emergence of markets abroad put Americans to work, but it distorted the economies of poor countries in ways that greatly increased their poverty. As American companies accumulated vast sugar and fruit plantations in the Pacific, Central America, and the Caribbean, they forced countless small farmers off their land. Many became contract laborers who worked only when Americans needed them, and naturally came to resent the United States. At the same time, American companies flooded these countries with manufactured goods, preventing the development of local industry.

The first American "regime change" operations had effects that rippled across the country and around the world. Within the United States, they brought together a nation that was still divided by the legacy of the Civil War; secured the power of the sensationalist press, especially its most ardent exponent, William Randolph Hearst; and convinced most Americans that their country was destined for global leadership. They also robbed Americans of an important measure of their innocence. The scandal over torture and murder in the Philippines, for example, might have led Americans to rethink their country's worldwide ambitions, but it did not. Instead, they came to accept the idea that their soldiers might have to commit atrocities in order to subdue insurgents and win wars. Loud protests followed revelations of the abuses Americans had committed in the Philippines but, in the end, those protests faded away. They were drowned out by voices insisting that any abuses must have been aberrations and that to dwell on them would show weakness and a lack of patriotism.

American presidents justified these first "regime change" operations by insisting that they wanted only to liberate oppressed peoples, but in fact all these interventions were carried out mainly for economic reasons. The United States annexed Hawaii and the Philippines because they were ideal stepping-stones to the East Asia trade; took Puerto Rico to protect trade routes and establish a naval base; and deposed the presidents of Nicaragua and Honduras because they refused to allow American companies to operate freely in their countries. In none of these places was Washington prepared for either the challenges of rule or the anger of nationalists.

Why did Americans support policies that brought suffering to people in foreign lands? There are two reasons, so intertwined that they became one. The essential reason is that American control of faraway places came to be seen as vital to the material prosperity of the United States. This explanation, however, is wrapped inside another one: the deep-seated belief of most Americans that their country is a force for good in the world. Thus, by extension, even the destructive missions the United States embarks on to impose its authority are tolerable. Generations of American political and business leaders have recognized the power of the noble idea of American exceptionalism. When they intervene abroad for selfish or ignoble reasons, they always insist that in the end, their actions will benefit not only the United States but also the citizens of the country in which they are intervening—and, by extension, the causes of peace and justice in the world.

Two other facts of geopolitical life emerge from the history that Americans made between 1893 and 1913. One is the decisive role that presidents of the United States play in shaping the course of world events. There is no limit to the number of "what if" scenarios to which this evident fact can give rise. If the anti-imperialist Grover Cleveland had not lost the election of 1888 to Benjamin Harrison (Cleveland won the popular vote but lost in the Electoral College), the United States would certainly not have supported a revolution against the monarchy in Hawaii. If someone other than William McKinley had been president in 1898, he might have decided to set Cuba and the Philippines on the path to independence after the Spanish-American War. If the strongly probusiness William Howard Taft had not won the presidency in 1908 and named the corporate lawyer Philander Knox as secretary of state, Washington might not have insisted on crushing the Zelaya government in Nicaragua and, with it, the hope for modernization in Central

America. Since presidents can so decisively shape the fate of foreign nations, it is no wonder that non-Americans sometimes wish they could vote in American elections.

A second fact that jumps from the history of this era is the absolute lack of interest the United States showed in the opinions of the people whose lands it seized. American leaders knew full well that most Hawaiians opposed the annexation of their country but proceeded with it anyway. No representative of Cuba, the Philippines, or Puerto Rico was present at the negotiations in Paris that ended the Spanish-American War and sealed their countries' fates. In Nicaragua and Honduras, even American diplomats conceded in their dispatches to Washington that the Liberal reform project was far more popular than the oligarchic regimes the United States imposed. The idea that the victorious power should listen to public opinion in these countries would have struck most Americans as absurd. They believed Latin Americans and Asians to be as they were portrayed in editorial cartoons: ragged children, usually nonwhite, who had no more idea of what was good for them than a block of stone.

Although much has been written about the profound changes that 1898 brought to the United States and about the decisive impact that year had on former Spanish colonies, less attention has been focused on the impact in Spain itself. There, the great defeat was for many years described simply as *el catástrofe*. It marked the end of an empire that had survived for more than four centuries and had played a decisive role in world history. Inevitably, the collapse of that empire led to a period of recrimination and self-doubt. It also, however, produced a group of brilliant poets, novelists, and philosophers who became known as the Generation of '98, and who together constituted probably the most important intellectual movement in Spanish history. These figures, among them Ramón del Valle-Inclán, Miguel de Unamuno, and José Ortega y Gasset, proclaimed a cultural and spiritual rebirth for their country in the wake of its loss. Their belief that a nation can achieve greatness within itself, rather than through empire, helped lay the foundation for the Spanish Republic that came to life in the 1930s and, more successfully, for the vibrant Spain that emerged at the end of the twentieth century. Some have even seen in Spain's resurgence a model for the way countries can not only survive the loss of empire but emerge from it to become stabilizing forces in the world they once sought to dominate.

PART TWO

Covert Action

5

Despotism and Godless Terrorism

On the Austin campus of the University of Texas, a great library houses a collection of objects that have set off shattering revolutions. Among them are the world's first photograph, which was printed on a pewter plate in 1826; a Gutenberg Bible, one of five in the United States; and a copy of the first book printed in English. Waves of history radiate from these objects. They inspire awe, set off complex emotions, and tug at the mystic chords of memory.

One of the most extraordinary objects in this collection does not seem to belong in a library at all. It is a reconstruction of the home office that John Foster Dulles used during his term as secretary of state, from 1953 to 1958. His family donated the entire office, complete with furniture, wall panels, carpets, bookcases, and books. Visitors may view the framed photos Dulles kept on his desk, his silver tea set, his collection of fine jade, and a display of gifts he received from foreign dignitaries. The library considers this room to be a historical artifact. So it is.

On most days, Dulles worked at the State Department until late afternoon. At about six o'clock he was driven to the White House, where he and President Dwight Eisenhower would, in Eisenhower's words, "try to analyze the broader aspects of the world drama we saw unfolding." Then, if he had no pressing diplomatic engagement, Dulles came home to this room. He would pour himself a glass of Old Overholt rye, sit down in his favorite armchair, and peer into the fireplace. Often he absentmindedly stirred his drink with his index finger. Sometimes he would read a detective novel. At other times, he reflected silently on the challenges of power.

Although the precise topics Dulles thought about as he sat in this room are unrecorded, the experience of seeing it is strongly evocative.

Quite probably, Dulles considered the overthrow of foreign governments. In this armchair, before this fireplace, with these curtains behind him, he shaped the fate of millions around the world, including generations yet unborn.

If ever a man was born to international privilege, it was John Foster Dulles. His family traced its ancestry to Charlemagne. As a boy he thrived under the special encouragement of his grandfather and namesake, the lawyer-diplomat John Watson Foster, who had been a treaty negotiator, minister to Russia and Spain, and secretary of state under President Benjamin Harrison. (In this last capacity, he worked with Lorrin Thurston in 1893 on the unsuccessful campaign to annex Hawaii.) Young Dulles often stayed at his grandfather's manse in Washington. Foster took him to dinner parties at the White House, and allowed him to join in long conversations with distinguished guests who called at his home, among them President William Howard Taft, former president Grover Cleveland, and future president Woodrow Wilson.

Besides being a diplomat, Foster was one of the first high-level international lawyers in Washington. He negotiated loans to foreign governments, served as counsel to the Mexican and Chinese legations, and undertook diplomatic missions for Presidents Cleveland, William McKinley, and Theodore Roosevelt. Perhaps most important, he influenced his grandson to follow in his footsteps.

In order to spend as much time as possible with his grandfather, Dulles attended law school at George Washington University. That made it difficult for him to find a job at any of the major New York firms, which preferred to hire Ivy League graduates. His doting grandfather stepped in to help. As a young man in Indiana, Foster had worked with a lawyer named Algernon Sullivan, who later moved to New York and formed a partnership with William Nelson Cromwell, the silver-haired legal genius who persuaded Congress to build the Central American canal across Panama instead of Nicaragua. Sullivan was no longer living, so Foster approached his surviving partner.

"Isn't the memory of an old association enough to give this young man a chance?" he asked Cromwell.

Few power brokers would refuse such an appeal from a former secretary of state. Dulles was hired as a clerk at the firm of Sullivan & Cromwell, with a monthly salary of $50. Unlike other clerks, he was able to live well, since his grandfather allowed him to draw on the $20,000 that had been set aside as the young man's inheritance. He needed that help only for a short time. Propelled by his sharp legal mind and network of connections, Dulles rose through the firm more quickly than anyone ever had. By 1927, sixteen years after being hired, he was its sole managing partner and one of the highest-paid lawyers in the world.

Dulles's web of international contacts grew spectacularly during this period. In the spring of 1915, President Wilson named Dulles's uncle, Robert Lansing, to succeed William Jennings Bryan as secretary of state. Lansing arranged for the young lawyer to receive a string of diplomatic assignments. By the time he reached his mid-thirties, Dulles was on easy terms with some of the world's richest and most powerful men. From them he absorbed what one of his biographers, the historian Ronald Pruessen, called a "rather simplistic" view of the world.

> Dulles may have been a world watcher, but his thoughts always demonstrated the angular vision that came with a perch in a Wall Street tower. . . . The way he saw the world, in particular—the kinds of problems he identified and the kinds of concerns that led him to identify them—had been shaped by a lifetime of experiences. . . . Day-to-day work with [corporate] clients, spread out over forty years, strongly affected his perspective on international affairs and helped shape the frame of reference from which he operated long before he was secretary of state. It helped him develop a particular interest in the commercial and financial facets of international relations and a particular attentiveness to what he thought were the economic imperatives of American foreign policy. . . . Economic preoccupations were often a dominant and initiating force in his world view and thought.

The list of Dulles's clients at Sullivan & Cromwell is nothing less than a guide to the biggest multinational corporations of early-twentieth-century America. Some were companies that Cromwell had brought to the firm years before, like the Cuban Cane Sugar Corporation and International Railways of Central America. Others were American banking houses, among them Brown Brothers and J. and W. Seligman, which were then effectively governing Nicaragua, and foreign houses like Credit Lyonnais and Dresdner Bank. Dulles arranged loans to governments across Latin America, Europe, and the Middle East; sued the Soviet Union on behalf of American insurance companies; organized a worldwide takeover campaign for the American Bank Note Company, which had printed the fateful Nicaraguan stamp showing a volcano in fictitious eruption; and negotiated utility concessions in Mexico and Panama for the American & Foreign Power Company. His clients built ports in Brazil, dug mines in Peru, and drilled for oil in Colombia. They ranged from International Nickel Company, one of the world's largest resource cartels, to the National Railroad Company of Haiti, which owned a single sixty-five-mile stretch of track north of Port-au-Prince.

Dulles was especially interested in Germany, which he visited regularly during the 1920s and 1930s. According to the most exhaustive book about Sullivan & Cromwell, the firm "thrived on its cartels and collusion with the new Nazi regime," and Dulles spent much of 1934 "publicly supporting Hitler," leaving his partners "shocked that he could so easily disregard law and international treaties to justify Nazi repression." When asked during this period how he dealt with German clients who were Jewish, he replied that he had simply decided "to keep away from them." Finally, facing a revolt by his partners, he agreed in 1935 to close the firm's Berlin office, later backdating the decision to a year earlier.

Soon after World War II ended, Dulles found in Communism the evil he had been so slow to find in Nazism. His epiphany came when he read Stalin's *Problems of Leninism,* which he found gripping. Several times he compared it to Hitler's *Mein Kampf* as a blueprint for world domination.

In the spring of 1949, Governor Thomas E. Dewey of New York appointed Dulles to fill a vacant seat in the United States Senate. When Dulles ran for a full term that November, he decked his campaign car with a banner proclaiming him "Enemy of the Reds!" His patrician style and evident unfamiliarity with the lives of ordinary people, however, made him an unappealing candidate, and he lost to Herbert Lehman, a liberal Democrat. This experience convinced him that if he wished to exert political influence, he should pursue appointive rather than elective office.

Law and politics were not Dulles's only passions. Throughout his life he was also moved by deep Christian faith. It was an integral part of his character, and from it grew the intensity of his anti-Communist zeal. He cannot be understood apart from it.

Dulles's paternal grandfather was a missionary who spent years preaching in India. The young man's father was pastor of the First Presbyterian Church in Watertown, New York, on the shore of Lake Ontario. As a child, Dulles attended three church services on Sunday and several others on weekdays. Every week he was expected to memorize two verses from a hymn and ten verses from Psalms or the New Testament.

His mother wanted him to follow the family tradition by becoming a clergyman, and not until arriving at Princeton did he consider other options. In later life he was an elder of the Presbyterian Church and a member of Union Theological Seminary's board of directors. After his death he was described as "the only religious leader, lay or clerical, ever to become Secretary of State."

Dulles believed that the heritage of the United States, which he described as "in its essentials a religious heritage," placed Americans under a special obligation. He felt what he called "a deep sense of mission," a conviction that "those who found a good way of life had a duty to help others to find the same way." Like his father, he was a born preacher; like his grandfather, a missionary. When the 1950s dawned, he was looking for a way to channel his "Christian insight and Christian inspiration" into the fight against "the evil methods and designs of Soviet Communism."

The best way to do that, Dulles quite reasonably concluded, was to become secretary of state. He thought he had the job in 1948, when his old friend Thomas Dewey seemed poised to take the presidency from Harry Truman, but voters frustrated his ambition by giving Truman an upset victory. Determined to try again, he spent the next several years expanding his network of Republican contacts and publishing articles about Communism and the Soviet threat.

In the spring of 1952, Eisenhower declared his candidacy for the Republican presidential nomination. He had spent his adult life in the army, far from the refined circles in which Dulles moved. A mutual friend, General Lucius Clay, suggested that Dulles fly to Paris to meet Eisenhower, who was then serving as supreme commander of the North Atlantic Treaty Organization. Dulles found this a fine idea, and arranged to give a speech in Paris as a way of disguising the true purpose of his trip. He and Eisenhower met for two long conversations. The general was much impressed. He relied on Dulles throughout his presidential campaign and soon after the election named him secretary of state.

Dulles was then sixty-five years old. He had been shaped by three powerful influences: a uniquely privileged upbringing, a long career advising the world's richest corporations, and a profound religious faith. His deepest values, beliefs, and instincts were those of the international elite in which he had spent his life. One of his biographers wrote that he was "out of touch with the rough and tumble of humanity" because "his whole background was superior, sheltered, successful, safe."

At the State Department, as at Sullivan & Cromwell, Dulles was famous for his solitary style of decision making. It was said that he carried the department in his hat, and that even his assistant secretaries did not know what he was planning. He shaped important policies without consulting anyone inside or outside the State Department. The diplomat and historian Townsend Hoopes called him "a compulsive oversimplifier" whose "mind was fundamentally shrewd and practical, but quite narrow in range, seeking always immediate and tangible results."

> Dulles was an intellectual loner—a man who relied not merely in the last resort, but almost exclusively, in large matters and small, on his own counsel. His views on important matters were developed by an apparently elaborate, structured and wholly internalized process. . . . The resulting conclusion thus stood at the end of a long chain of logic and, when finally arrived at, was not easily reversed.

By nature Dulles was stiff and confrontational. He conveyed an absolute certainty about his course that many took for arrogance. One biographer wrote that he "scarcely knew the meaning of compromise, and insofar as he understood it, he despised it." He believed that a secretary of state should not be a conciliator but rather, in Eisenhower's words, "a sort of international prosecuting attorney."

In the take-no-prisoners style he had honed at Sullivan & Cromwell, Dulles wished neither to meet, accommodate, or negotiate with the enemy. He resolutely opposed the idea of cultural exchanges between the United States and any country under Communist rule. For years he sought to prevent American newspapers from sending correspondents to China. He steadfastly counseled Eisenhower against holding summit meetings with Soviet leaders. "Indeed," one biographer has written, "evidence of America-Soviet agreement on any issue troubled him, for he judged it could only be a ruse designed to cause the free world to 'let down its guard.'"

> Dulles, as a lawyer, had been trained in adversarial terms; interests, for him, could at times appear to be whatever was necessary to overwhelm the opponent. Moreover, he had been much impressed by Arnold Toynbee's suggestion that without some kind of external challenge, civilizations withered and died. It was not too difficult, then, for threats and interests to merge in Dulles's mind: to conclude that the United States

might actually have an interest in being threatened, if through that process Americans could be goaded into doing what was necessary to preserve their way of life.

When Eisenhower and Dulles took office, at the beginning of 1953, the main fact of international political life was the spread of Communism. The Soviet Union had imposed its rule on much of Eastern Europe, successfully tested an atomic bomb, and attempted to starve West Berlin into submission with a sixteen-month blockade. A Communist army had seized power in China, and another had tried to do so in Greece. Communist parties in France and Italy were strong and growing. Thousands of Americans had been killed fighting Communist forces in Korea. Senator Joseph McCarthy of Wisconsin shocked many Americans with charges that Communists had even infiltrated the United States Army and State Department. The United States was gripped by a fear of encirclement, a terrible sense that it was losing the postwar battle of ideologies.

During the 1952 presidential campaign, Dulles made a series of speeches accusing the Truman administration of weakness in the face of Communist advances. He promised that a Republican White House would "roll back" Communism by securing the "liberation" of nations that had fallen victim to its "despotism and godless terrorism." As soon as the election was won, he began searching for a place where the United States could strike a blow against this scourge. Before he had even taken office, like a messenger from heaven, a senior British intelligence officer arrived in Washington carrying a proposal that perfectly fit Dulles's needs.

BRITAIN WAS AT THAT MOMENT FACING A GRAVE CHALLENGE. ITS ABILITY TO project military power, fuel its industries, and give its citizens a high standard of living depended largely on the oil it extracted from Iran. Since 1901 a single corporation, the Anglo-Iranian Oil Company, principally owned by the British government, had held a monopoly on the extraction, refining, and sale of Iranian oil. Anglo-Iranian's grossly unequal contract, negotiated with a corrupt monarch, required it to pay Iran just 16 percent of the money it earned from selling the country's oil. It probably paid even less than that, but the truth was never known, since no outsider was permitted to audit its books. Anglo-Iranian made more profit in 1950 alone than it had paid Iran in royalties over the previous half century.

In the years after World War II, the currents of nationalism and anticolonialism surged across Asia, Africa, and Latin America. They carried an outspokenly idealistic Iranian, Mohammad Mossadegh, to power in the spring of 1951. Prime Minister Mossadegh embodied the cause that had become his country's obsession. He was determined to expel the Anglo-Iranian Oil Company, nationalize the oil industry, and use the money it generated to develop Iran.

Mossadegh, a European-educated aristocrat who was sixty-nine years old when he came to power, believed passionately in two causes: nationalism and democracy. In Iran, nationalism meant taking control of the country's oil resources. Democracy meant concentrating political power in the elected parliament and prime minister, rather than in the monarch, Mohammad Reza Shah. With the former project, Mossadegh turned Britain into an enemy, and with the latter he alienated the shah.

In the spring of 1951, both houses of the Iranian parliament voted unanimously to nationalize the oil industry. It was an epochal moment, and the entire nation celebrated. "All of Iran's misery, wretchedness, lawlessness and corruption over the last fifty years has been caused by oil and the extortions of the oil company," one radio commentator declared.

Under the nationalization law, Iran agreed to compensate Britain for the money it had spent building its wells and refinery, although any impartial arbitrator would probably have concluded that given the amount of profit the British had made in Iran over the years, Iran's debt would be less than nil. Mossadegh loved to point out that the British had themselves recently nationalized their coal and steel industries. He insisted that he was only trying to do what the British had done: turn their nation's wealth to its own benefit, and make reforms in order to prevent people from resorting to revolution. British diplomats in the Middle East were, of course, unmoved by this argument.

"We English have had hundreds of years of experience on how to treat the natives," one of them scoffed. "Socialism is all right back home, but out here you have to be the master."

Mossadegh's rise to power and parliament's vote to nationalize the oil industry thrilled Iranians but outraged British leaders. The idea that a backward country like Iran could rise up and deal them such a blow was so stunning as to be incomprehensible. They scornfully rejected suggestions that they offer to split their profits with Iran on a fifty-fifty basis, as American companies were doing in nearby countries. Instead they vowed to resist.

"Persian oil is of vital importance to our economy," Foreign Secretary Herbert Morrison declared. "We regard it as essential to do everything possible to prevent the Persians from getting away with a breach of their contractual obligations."

Over the next year, the British did just that. At various points they considered bribing Mossadegh, assassinating him, and launching a military invasion of Iran, a plan they might have carried out if President Truman and Secretary of State Dean Acheson had not become almost apoplectic on learning of it. The British sabotaged their own installations at Abadan in the hopes of convincing Mossadegh that he could not possibly run the oil industry without them; blockaded Iranian ports so no tankers could enter or leave; and appealed unsuccessfully to the United Nations Security Council and the International Court of Justice. Finally, they concluded that only one option was left. They resolved to organize a coup.

Britain had dominated Iran for generations, and during that time had suborned a variety of military officers, journalists, religious leaders, and others who could help overthrow a government if the need arose. Officials in London ordered their agents in Tehran to set a plot in motion. Before the British could strike their blow, however, Mossadegh discovered what they were planning. He did the only thing he could have done to protect himself and his government. On October 16, 1952, he ordered the British embassy shut and all its employees sent out of the country. Among them were the intelligence agents who were organizing the coup.

This left the British disarmed. Their covert operatives had been expelled from Iran, Truman's opposition made an invasion impossible, and world organizations refused to intervene. The British government faced the disorienting prospect of losing its most valuable foreign asset to a backward country led by a man they considered, according to various diplomatic cables, "wild," "fanatical," "absurd," "gangster-like" "completely unscrupulous," and "clearly imbalanced."

Modern Iran has produced few figures of Mossadegh's stature. On his mother's side he was descended from Persian royalty. His father came from a distinguished clan and was Iran's finance minister for more than twenty years. He studied in France and Switzerland, and became the first Iranian to win a doctorate in law from a European university. By the time he was elected prime minister, he had a lifetime of political experience behind him.

Mossadegh was also a highly emotional man. Tears rolled down his cheeks when he delivered speeches about Iran's poverty and misery. Several times he collapsed while addressing parliament, leading *Newsweek* to call him a "fainting fanatic." He suffered from many ailments, some physical and others of unknown cause, and had a disarming habit of receiving guests while lying in bed. His scrupulous honesty and intense parsimony—he used to peel two-ply tissues apart before using them—made him highly unusual in Middle Eastern politics and greatly endeared him to his people. In January 1952, *Time* named him man of the year, choosing him over Winston Churchill, Douglas MacArthur, Harry Truman, and Dwight Eisenhower. It called him an "obstinate opportunist" but also "the Iranian George Washington" and "the most world-renowned man his ancient race had produced for centuries."

Barely two weeks after Mossadegh shut the British embassy in Tehran, Americans went to the polls and elected Eisenhower as president. Soon after that, Eisenhower announced that Dulles would be his secretary of state. Suddenly the gloom that had enveloped the British government began to lift.

At that moment the chief of CIA operations in the Middle East, Kermit Roosevelt, happened to be passing through London on his way home from a visit to Iran. He met with several of his British counterparts, and they presented him with an extraordinary proposal. They wanted the CIA to carry out the coup in Iran that they themselves could no longer execute, and had already drawn up what Roosevelt called "a plan of battle."

> What they had in mind was nothing less than the overthrow of Mossadegh. Furthermore, they saw no point in wasting time by delay. They wanted to start immediately. I had to explain that the project would require considerable clearance from my government and that I was not entirely sure what the results would be. As I told my British colleagues, we had, I felt sure, no chance to win approval from the outgoing administration of Truman and Acheson. The new Republicans, however, might be quite different.

British officials were so impatient to set the coup in motion that they decided to propose it at once, without even waiting for Eisenhower to be inaugurated. They sent one of their top intelligence agents, Christopher Montague Woodhouse, to Washington to present their case to Dulles. Woodhouse and other British officials realized that their argument— Mossadegh must be overthrown because he was nationalizing a British oil company—would not stir the Americans to action. They had to find another one. It took no deep thought to decide what it should be. Woodhouse told the Americans that Mossadegh was leading Iran toward Communism.

Under normal circumstances, this would be a difficult case to make. There was a Communist party in Iran, known as Tudeh, and like every other party in the country, it supported the oil nationalization project. Mossadegh, a convinced democrat, allowed Tudeh to function freely but never embraced its program. In fact, he abhorred Communist doctrine and rigorously excluded Communists from his government. The American diplomat in Tehran assigned to monitor Tudeh recognized all this, and reported to Washington that the party was "well-organized but not very powerful." Years later, an Iranian-American scholar conducted an exhaustive study of Tudeh's position in 1953, and concluded that "the type of coordinated cooperation and mutual reliance the Americans feared existed between Mossadegh and the Tudeh could not have existed."

> The perceived Tudeh threat, as feared by the perpetrators of the coup, was not real. The party had neither the numbers, nor the popularity, nor a plan to take over state power with any hope of holding on to it. . . . This decision [to stage the coup] seems to have had little to do with on-the-ground realities and much to do with the ideological imperatives of the period: the Cold War.

Woodhouse gave Dulles the idea that he could portray Mossadegh's overthrow as a "rollback" of Communism. The State Department, however, did not have the capacity to overthrow governments. For that, Dulles would have to enlist the CIA. It was still a new agency, created in 1947 to replace the wartime Office of Strategic Services. Truman had used the CIA to gather intelligence and also to carry out covert operations, such as supporting anti-Communist political parties in Europe. Never, though, had he or Secretary of State Acheson ordered the CIA—or any other agency—to overthrow a foreign government.

Dulles had no such reservations. Two factors made him especially eager to use the CIA in this way. The first was the lack of alternatives. Long gone were the days when an American president could send troops to invade and seize a faraway land. A new world power, the Soviet Union, counterbalanced the United States and severely restricted its freedom to overthrow governments. An American invasion could set off a confrontation between superpowers that might spiral into nuclear holocaust. In the CIA, Dulles thought he might have the tool he needed, a way to shift the balance of world power without resorting to military force.

Calling on the CIA had another great attraction for Dulles. He knew he would work in perfect harmony with its director, because the director was his younger brother, Allen. This was the first and only time in American history that siblings ran the overt and covert arms of foreign policy. They worked seamlessly together, combining the diplomatic resources of the State Department with the CIA's growing skill at clandestine operations.

Before the coup could be set in motion, the Dulles brothers needed President Eisenhower's approval. It was not an easy sell. At a meeting of the National Security Council on March 4, 1953, Eisenhower wondered aloud why it wasn't possible "to get some of the people in these downtrodden countries to like us instead of hating us." Secretary of State Dulles conceded that Mossadegh was no Communist but insisted that "if he were to be assassinated or removed from power, a political vacuum might occur in Iran and the communists might easily take over." If that happened, he warned, "not only would the free world be deprived of the enormous assets represented by Iranian oil production and reserves, but . . . in short order the other areas of the Middle East, with some sixty percent of the world's oil reserves, would fall into Communist hands."

Dulles had two lifelong obsessions: fighting Communism and protecting the rights of multinational corporations. In his mind they were, as the historian James A. Bill has written, "interrelated and mutually reinforcing."

There is little doubt that petroleum considerations were involved in the American decision to assist in the overthrow of the Mossadegh government. . . . Although many have argued for America's disinterest in Iranian oil, given the conditions of glut that prevailed, Middle Eastern history demonstrates that the United States had always sought such

access, glut or no glut. . . . Concerns about communism and the avail-
ability of petroleum were interlocked. Together, they drove America to a
policy of direct intervention.

After the National Security Council meeting in March, planning for a
coup began in earnest. Allen Dulles, in consultation with his British
counterparts, chose a retired general named Fazlollah Zahedi as titular
leader of the coup. Then he sent $1 million to the CIA station in Tehran
for use "in any way that would bring about the fall of Mossadegh." John
Foster Dulles directed the American ambassador in Tehran, Loy Hender-
son, to contact Iranians who might be interested in helping to carry out
the coup.

Two secret agents, Donald Wilber of the CIA and Norman Darbyshire
of the British Secret Intelligence Service, spent several weeks that spring
in Cyprus devising a plan for the coup. It was unlike any plan that either
country, or any country, had made before. With the cold calculation of
the surgeon, these agents plotted to cut Mossadegh away from his people.

Under their plan, the Americans would spend $150,000 to bribe jour-
nalists, editors, Islamic preachers, and other opinion leaders to "create,
extend and enhance public hostility and distrust and fear of Mossadegh
and his government." Then they would hire thugs to carry out "staged
attacks" on religious figures and other respected Iranians, making it
seem that Mossadegh had ordered them. Meanwhile, General Zahedi
would be given a sum of money, later fixed at $135,000, to "win addi-
tional friends" and "influence key people." The plan budgeted another
$11,000 per week, a great sum at that time, to bribe members of the Iran-
ian parliament. On "coup day," thousands of paid demonstrators would
converge on parliament to demand that it dismiss Mossadegh. Parliament would respond with a "quasi-legal" vote to do so. If Mossadegh
resisted, military units loyal to General Zahedi would arrest him.

"So this is how we get rid of that madman Mossadegh!" Secretary of
State Dulles exclaimed happily when he was handed a copy of the plan.

Not everyone embraced the idea. Several CIA officers opposed it, and
one of them, Roger Goiran, chief of the CIA station in Tehran, went so
far as to quit. Neither of the State Department's principal Iran experts
was even informed about the plot until it was about to be sprung. That
was just as well, since State Department archives were bulging with dispatches from Henry Grady, who had been Truman's ambassador in Iran,
reporting that Mossadegh "has the backing of 95 to 98 percent of the

people of this country," and from Grady's boss, Undersecretary of State George McGhee, who considered Mossadegh "a conservative" and "a patriotic Iranian nationalist" with "no reason to be attracted to socialism or communism."

None of this made the slightest impact on Dulles. His deepest instinct, rather than any cool assessment of facts, told him that overthrowing Mossadegh was a good idea. Never did he consult with anyone who believed differently.

The American press played an important supporting role in Operation Ajax, as the Iran coup was code-named. A few newspapers and magazines published favorable articles about Mossadegh, but they were the exceptions. The *New York Times* regularly referred to him as a dictator. Other papers compared him to Hitler and Stalin. *Newsweek* reported that, with his help, Communists were "taking over" Iran. *Time* called his election "one of the worst calamities to the anti-communist world since the Red conquest of China."

To direct its coup against Mossadegh, the CIA had to send a senior agent on what would necessarily be a dangerous clandestine mission to Tehran. Allen Dulles had just the man in Kermit Roosevelt, the thirty-seven-year-old Harvard graduate who was the agency's top Middle East expert. By a quirk of history, he was the grandson of President Theodore Roosevelt, who half a century earlier had helped bring the United States into the "regime change" era.

Roosevelt slipped into Iran at a remote border crossing on July 19, 1953, and immediately set about his subversive work. It took him just a few days to set Iran aflame. Using a network of Iranian agents and spending lavish amounts of money, he created an entirely artificial wave of anti-Mossadegh protest. Members of parliament withdrew their support from Mossadegh and denounced him with wild charges. Religious leaders gave sermons calling him an atheist, a Jew, and an infidel. Newspapers were filled with articles and cartoons depicting him as everything from a homosexual to an agent of British imperialism. He realized that some unseen hand was directing this campaign, but because he had such an ingrained and perhaps exaggerated faith in democracy, he did nothing to repress it.

"Mossadegh's avowed commitment to promoting and respecting political and civil rights and liberties, and allowing the due process of law to take its course, greatly benefited his enemies," the historian Fakhreddin Azimi wrote years later.

At the beginning of August, though, Mossadegh did take one step to upset the CIA's plan. He learned that foreign intelligence agents were bribing members of parliament to support a no-confidence motion against him, and to thwart them, he called a national referendum on a proposition that would allow him to dissolve parliament and call new elections. On this occasion he shaded his democratic principles, using separate ballot boxes for "yes" and "no" voters. The result was over-whelmingly favorable. His enemies denounced him, but he had won a round. Bribed members of parliament could not carry out the CIA's plan to remove him through a "quasi-legal" vote, since there no longer was a parliament.

Roosevelt quickly came up with an alternative plan. He would arrange for Mohammad Reza Shah to sign royal decrees, or *firmans*, dismissing Mossadegh from office and appointing General Zahedi as the new prime minister. This course could also be described as "quasi-legal," since under Iranian law, only parliament had the right to elect and dismiss prime ministers. Roosevelt realized that Mossadegh, who among other things was the country's best-educated legal scholar, would reject the *firman* and refuse to step down. He had a plan for that, too. A squad of royalist soldiers would deliver the *firman,* and when Mossadegh rejected it the soldiers would arrest him.

The great obstacle to this plan turned out to be the shah. He hated Mossadegh, who was turning him into little more than a figurehead, but was terrified of risking his throne by joining a plot. In a series of meetings held late at night in the backseat of a car parked near the royal palace, Roosevelt tried and failed to persuade the shah to join the coup. Slowly he increased the pressure. First he arranged to fly the shah's strong-willed twin sister, Ashraf, home from the French Riviera to appeal to him; she agreed to do so after receiving a sum of money and, according to one account, a mink coat. When that approach failed, Roosevelt sent two of his Iranian agents to assure the shah that the plot was a good one and certain to succeed. Still the shah vacillated. Finally, Roosevelt summoned General Norman Schwarzkopf, a dashing figure who had spent years in Iran running an elite military unit—and whose son would lead the Desert Storm invasion of Iraq four decades later—to close the deal.

The shah received Schwarzkopf in a ballroom at the palace, but at first refused to speak. Through gestures, he let his guest know that he feared that microphones were hidden in the walls or ceiling. Finally the two men pulled a table into the center of the room and climbed on top of it. In what must have been unusually forceful whispers, Schwarzkopf made clear that the power of both Britain and the United States lay behind this plot, and that the shah had no choice other than to cooperate. Slowly the shah gave in. The next day he told Roosevelt he would sign the *firmans*, but only on condition that immediately afterward, he could fly to his retreat on the Caspian Sea.

"If by any horrible chance things go wrong, the Empress and I will take our plane straight to Baghdad," he explained.

That was not exactly a resounding commitment to the coup, but it was good enough for Roosevelt. He secured the *firmans* and, on the afternoon of August 14, gave the one dismissing Mossadegh to an officer who was part of the plot, Colonel Nematollah Nassiri, commander of the Imperial Guard. Late that night, Nassiri led a squad of men to Mossadegh's house. There he told the gatekeeper that he needed to see the prime minister immediately.

Then, much to Nassiri's surprise, a company of loyalist soldiers emerged from the shadows, surrounded him, and took him prisoner. Mossadegh had discovered the plot in time. The man who was supposed to arrest him was himself arrested.

At dawn the next morning, Radio Tehran broadcast the triumphant news that the government had crushed an attempted coup by the shah and "foreign elements." The shah heard this news at his Caspian retreat, and reacted just as he had promised. With Empress Soraya at his side, he jumped into his Beechcraft and flew to Baghdad. There he boarded a commercial flight to Rome. When an American reporter asked him if he expected to return to Iran, he replied, "Probably, but not in the immediate future."

Roosevelt, however, was not so easily discouraged. He had built up a far-reaching network of Iranian agents and had paid them a great deal of money. Many of them, especially those in the police and the army, had not yet had a chance to show what they could do. Sitting in his bunker beneath the American embassy, he considered his options. Returning home was the obvious one. He even received a cable from his CIA superiors urging that he do so. Instead of obeying, he summoned two of his top Iranian operatives and told them he was determined to make another stab at Mossadegh.

These two agents had excellent relations with Tehran's street gangs, and Roosevelt told them he now wished to use those gangs to set off riots around the city. To his dismay, they replied that they could no longer help him because the risk of arrest had become too great. This was a potentially fatal blow to Roosevelt's new plan. He responded in the best tradition of secret agents. First he offered the two agents $50,000 to continue working with him. They remained unmoved. Then he added the second part of his deal: if the men refused, he would kill them. That changed their minds. They left the embassy compound with a briefcase full of cash and a renewed willingness to help.

That week, a plague of violence descended on Tehran. Gangs of thugs ran wildly through the streets, breaking shop windows, firing guns into mosques, beating passersby, and shouting "Long Live Mossadegh and Communism!" Other thugs, claiming allegiance to the self-exiled shah, attacked the first ones. Leaders of both factions were actually working for Roosevelt. He wanted to create the impression that the country was degenerating into chaos, and he succeeded magnificently.

Mossadegh's supporters tried to organize demonstrations on his behalf, but once again his democratic instincts led him to react naively. He disdained the politics of the street, and ordered leaders of political parties loyal to him not to join the fighting. Then he sent police units to restore order, not realizing that many of their commanders were secretly on Roosevelt's payroll. Several joined the rioters they were supposed to suppress.

Leaders of the Tudeh party, who had several hundred militants at their command, made a last-minute offer to Mossadegh. They had no weapons, but if he would give them some, they would attack the mobs that were trying to destroy his regime. The old man was horrified.

"If ever I agree to arm a political party," he told one Tudeh leader angrily, "may God sever my right arm!"

Roosevelt chose Wednesday, August 19, as the climactic day. On that morning, thousands of demonstrators rampaged through the streets, demanding Mossadegh's resignation. They seized Radio Tehran and set fire to the offices of a progovernment newspaper. At midday, military and police units whose commanders Roosevelt had bribed joined the fray, storming the foreign ministry, the central police station, and the headquarters of the army's general staff.

As Tehran fell into violent anarchy, Roosevelt calmly emerged from the embassy compound and drove to a safe house where he had stashed General Zahedi. It was time for the general to play his role as Iran's designated savior. He did so with gusto, riding with a group of his jubilant supporters to Radio Tehran and proclaiming to the nation that he was "the lawful prime minister by the Shah's orders." From there he proceeded to his temporary headquarters at the Officers' Club, where a throng of ecstatic admirers was waiting.

The day's final battle was for control of Mossadegh's house. Attackers tried for two hours to storm it but were met with withering machine-gun volleys from inside. Men fell by the dozen. The tide finally turned when a column of tanks appeared, sent by a commander who was part of the plot. The tanks fired shell after shell into the house. Finally resistance from inside ceased. A platoon of soldiers gingerly moved in. Defenders had fled over a back wall, taking their deposed leader with them. The crowd outside surged into his house, looting it and then setting it afire.

No one was more amazed by this sudden turn of events than the shah. He was dining at his Rome hotel when news correspondents burst in to tell him the news of Mossadegh's overthrow. For several moments he was unable to speak.

"Can it be true?" he finally asked.

In the days that followed, the shah returned home and reclaimed the Peacock Throne he had so hastily abandoned. Mossadegh surrendered and was placed under arrest. General Zahedi became Iran's new prime minister.

Before leaving Tehran, Roosevelt paid a farewell call on the shah. This time they met inside the palace, not furtively in a car outside. A servant brought vodka, and the shah offered a toast.

"I owe my throne to God, my people, my army—and to you," he said.

Roosevelt and the shah spoke for a few minutes, but there was little to say. Then General Zahedi, the new prime minister, arrived to join them. These three men were among the few who had any idea of the real story behind that week's tumultuous events. All knew they had changed the course of Iranian history.

"We were all smiles now," Roosevelt wrote afterward. "Warmth and friendship filled the room."

6

Get Rid of This Stinker

The most heavily attended funeral in Guatemalan history was for a man who had been dead twenty-four years. More than 100,000 people filled the streets of Guatemala City and jammed the cemetery. Many threw red carnations at the cortege and chanted, "Jacobo! Jacobo!" Some, especially those old enough to remember the statesman they were burying, were overcome with emotion.

"All I know is that there was no persecution during his government," said a seventy-seven-year-old man in the crowd who struggled to hold back his tears. "Afterwards, people began dying."

Jacobo Arbenz Guzmán was the second of two presidents who governed Guatemala during the country's "democratic spring," which lasted from 1944 to 1954. For decades after the CIA overthrew him and chased him from his homeland, it was dangerous to speak well of Arbenz or lament his fate. He died alone and forgotten. Only when his remains were finally brought home to Guatemala and buried, on October 20, 1995, did his people have a chance to honor him. They did so with a fervor born of unspeakable suffering.

Arbenz took office in 1951, the same year another nationalist, Mohammad Mossadegh, became prime minister of Iran. Each assumed leadership of a wretchedly poor nation that was just beginning to enjoy the blessings of democracy. Each challenged the power of a giant foreign-owned company. The company howled in protest, and charged that the government was Communistic. Secretary of State John Foster Dulles agreed.

Few private companies have ever been as closely interwoven with the United States government as United Fruit was during the mid-1950s. Dulles had, for decades, been one of its principal legal counselors. His brother, Allen, the CIA director, had also done legal work for the company and owned a substantial block of its stock. John Moors Cabot, the assistant secretary of state for inter-American affairs, was a large shareholder. So was his brother, Thomas Dudley Cabot, the director of international security affairs in the State Department, who had been United Fruit's president. General Robert Cutler, head of the National Security Council, was its former chairman of the board. John J. McCloy, the president of the International Bank for Reconstruction and Development, was a former board member. Both undersecretary of state Walter Bedell Smith and Robert Hill, the American ambassador to Costa Rica, would join the board after leaving government service.

During the first half of the twentieth century, United Fruit made great profits in Guatemala because it was able to operate without interference from the Guatemalan government. It simply claimed good farmland, arranged for legal title through one-sided deals with dictators, and then operated plantations on its own terms, free of such annoyances as taxes or labor regulations. As long as that system prevailed, men like John Foster Dulles considered Guatemala a "friendly" and "stable" country. When a new kind of government emerged there and began to challenge the company, they disapproved.

For thirteen years during the 1930s and 1940s, United Fruit thrived in Guatemala under the patronage of Jorge Ubico, a classically outsized Latin American *caudillo*. According to one historian, Ubico "called anyone a Communist whose social, economic and political ideologies were more progressive than his own" and "trusted only the army, wealthy indigenous landowners and foreign corporations." The most important of those corporations was United Fruit, which provided tens of thousands of full- and part-time jobs in Guatemala. Ubico showered United Fruit with concession agreements, including one in 1936 that his agents negotiated personally with Dulles. It gave the company a ninety-nine-year lease on a vast tract of land along the rich Pacific plain at Tiquisate, and guaranteed it an exemption from all taxes for the duration of the lease.

Guatemalans became restive as Ubico's harsh rule wore on. An emerging middle class, inspired by the democratic rhetoric of World War II and the examples of reformist presidents Lázaro Cárdenas in Mexico and Franklin D. Roosevelt in the United States, began agitating for change. During the summer and fall of 1944, thousands of demonstrators, led by schoolteachers, launched a wave of street protests. As they reached a peak, young officers staged a lightning uprising and toppled the old regime. Guatemala's own "October Revolution" was won at the cost of fewer than one hundred lives.

A few months later, Guatemalans went to the polls in their country's first democratic election. By an overwhelming margin, they chose a visionary young schoolteacher, Juan José Arévalo, as their president. In his inaugural address, delivered to an expectant nation on March 15, 1945, Arevalo cited Roosevelt as his inspiration, and vowed to follow his example.

> There has in the past been a fundamental lack of sympathy for the working man, and the faintest cry for justice was avoided and punished as if one were trying to eradicate the beginnings of a frightful epidemic. Now we are going to begin a period of sympathy for the man who works in the fields, in the shops, on the military bases, in small businesses. . . . We are going to add justice and humanity to order, because order based on injustice and humiliation is good for nothing.

President Arévalo laid a solid foundation for Guatemala's new democracy, and did much to bring his country into the modern age. During his six-year term, the National Assembly established the country's first social security system, guaranteed the rights of trade unions, fixed a forty-eight-hour workweek, and even levied a modest tax on large landholders. Each of these measures represented a challenge to United Fruit. The company had been setting its own rules in Guatemala for more than half a century, and did not look favorably on the surge of nationalism that Arévalo embodied. It resisted him every way it could.

Arévalo's term ended on March 15, 1951. As thousands watched, he handed the presidential sash over to his elected successor, Jacobo Arbenz. It was the first peaceful transfer of power in Guatemalan history. Arévalo, though, was not in a celebratory mood. In his farewell speech, he lamented that he had not been able to do more for his people:

> The banana magnates, co-nationals of Roosevelt, rebelled against the audacity of a Central American president who gave to his fellow citizens a legal equality with the honorable families of exporters. . . . It was then that the schoolteacher, ingenuous and romantic, from the presidency of his country, discovered how perishable, frail and slippery the brilliant international doctrines of democracy and freedom were. It was then, with the deepest despondency and pain, that I felt, with consequent

indignation, the pressure of that anonymous force that rules, without laws or morals, international relations and the relationships of men.

The incoming president was destined to feel that pressure even more intensely. Arbenz was a thirty-seven-year-old colonel who had helped lead the 1944 uprising against Ubico, but he was by no means a typical Guatemalan army officer. His father was a pharmacist who had emigrated from Switzerland and had committed suicide while Jacobo was still a boy. That ended his hope of becoming a scientist or an engineer, but a friend in the tight-knit Swiss community arranged for him to be given a place at the Military Academy. There he compiled a brilliant academic record and excelled at boxing and polo. He was also strikingly good-looking, blue-eyed and fair-haired but with a Latin profile. At a Central American athletic competition, he met a young Salvadoran woman, María Cristina Vilanova, who, despite her upper-class background, was a passionate leftist. After their marriage, she encouraged him to develop a social conscience and political ambition. He showed both in his inaugural address, setting out "three fundamental objectives" for his presidency:

> to convert our country from a dependent nation with a semi-colonial economy into an economically independent country; to convert Guatemala from a country bound by a predominantly feudal economy into a modern capitalist state; and to make this transformation in a way that will raise the standard of living of the great mass of our people to the highest level.

This was a sweeping agenda, and as soon as President Arbenz began to press it, he found himself at odds with all three of the American companies that dominated Guatemala's economy. First he announced plans to build a publicly owned electric system, which would break a highly lucrative monopoly held by Electric Bond & Share. Then he turned his attention to International Railways of Central America, which owned nearly all the country's rail lines, including the sole link between the capital and the Atlantic port of Puerto Barrios—most of which it also owned. Arbenz proposed to build a new deepwater port, open to all, with a highway connection to the capital. Then, confronting the cruelly unbalanced system of land ownership that was and is at the root of poverty in Guatemala, he won passage of a landmark law that threatened United Fruit itself.

The Agrarian Reform Law, which the National Assembly passed on June 17, 1952, was the crowning achievement of Guatemala's democratic revolution. Under its provisions, the government could seize and redistribute all uncultivated land on estates larger than 672 acres, compensating owners according to the land's declared tax value. This was a direct challenge to United Fruit, which owned more than 550,000 acres, about one-fifth of the country's arable land, but cultivated less than 15 percent of it. The company said it needed these vast, fertile tracts for future contingencies. To citizens of a country where hundreds of thousands went hungry for want of land, this seemed grossly unjust.

The three interlocking companies most affected by Arbenz's reforms had controlled Guatemala for decades. United Fruit was by far the country's largest landowner and largest private employer. It held 46 percent of the stock in International Railways of Central America, thereby securing freight service and access to Puerto Barrios at highly favorable rates. Electric Bond & Share supplied power for the railways and banana plantations. Together, the three companies had more than $100 million invested in Guatemala. Arbenz subjected them to a host of new regulations, and many of their executives and stockholders came to detest him. So did the New York lawyer who represented all three of them, John Foster Dulles.

Early in 1953, the Guatemalan government seized 234,000 uncultivated acres of United Fruit's 295,000-acre plantation at Tiquisate. It offered compensation of $1.185 million, the value the company had declared for tax purposes. United Fruit executives rejected the offer, asserting that no one took self-assessed valuations seriously. They demanded $19 million.

Most Guatemalans considered land redistribution a welcome step in a nation where democracy was beginning to bloom. It looked quite different from Washington. Many old friends of United Fruit had assumed influential positions in the Eisenhower administration just as the Guatemalan government was seizing the company's land. They considered these seizures not only illegal and outrageous but proof of Communist influence. Since Guatemala is the traditional leader in Central America, they also worried that any reforms allowed to succeed there would quickly spread to other countries. In their minds, defending

United Fruit and defeating Central American Communism fused into a single goal. They could achieve it only by overthrowing Arbenz.

United Fruit rose to its mythical status in Guatemala under the leadership of Sam Zemurray, the visionary "Banana Man" who had organized the overthrow of President Miguel Dávila of Honduras in 1911 and gone on to become one of the most powerful figures in Central America. Soon after Guatemala turned democratic, in 1944, Zemurray sensed that its reformist government would give the company trouble. The stakes were high, and he wanted to be sure that American public opinion was with him. He decided to hire an outside public relations expert. The new man was Edward Bernays, a nephew of Sigmund Freud and the dominant figure in his young profession.

Bernays was one of the first masters of modern mass psychology. He liked to describe himself as the "father of public relations," and no one disagreed. His specialty was what he called "the conscious and intelligent manipulation of the organized habits and opinions of the masses." He proposed to Zemurray that United Fruit launch a campaign to blacken the image of Guatemala's government. That, he argued, could decisively weaken it and perhaps set off events that would trigger its collapse.

"I have the feeling that Guatemala might respond to pitiless publicity in this country," Bernays surmised.

Never before had an American corporation waged a propaganda campaign in the United States aimed at undermining the president of a foreign country. Zemurray was reluctant to make United Fruit the first. Then, in the spring of 1951, Bernays sent him a message with alarming news. The reformist leader of faraway Iran, Mohammad Mossadegh, had just done the unthinkable by nationalizing the Anglo-Iranian Oil Company. "Guatemala might follow suit," Bernays wrote in his note.

That was all Zemurray needed to hear. He authorized Bernays to launch his campaign, and the results soon began to show. First were a series of articles in the *New York Times,* portraying Guatemala as falling victim to "reds"; they appeared after Bernays visited *Times* publisher Arthur Hays Sulzberger. Next came reports in leading magazines, most of them written, like the *Times* series, with helpful advice from Bernays. Then Bernays began organizing press junkets to Guatemala. They produced glowing dispatches about United Fruit and terrifying ones about the emergence of Marxist dictatorship in Guatemala.

Prominent members of Congress echoed these themes. Most outspoken among them was a Massachusetts senator with a familiar name, Henry Cabot Lodge, scion of two families that United Fruit had helped make rich. In the same chamber where his grandfather and namesake had helped secure American control of Cuba and the Philippines more than half a century before, Lodge delivered vituperative speeches depicting Guatemalan leaders as crypto-Communists. Meanwhile, in the House of Representatives, the majority leader and future speaker, John McCormack—also from Massachusetts, where United Fruit had sustained generations of prosperity—rose regularly to deliver chilling warnings that Guatemala's democratic leaders had become "subservient to the Kremlin's design for world conquest" and were turning their country into "a Soviet beachhead."

This rhetoric reached a new peak after the Agrarian Reform Law was passed. Powerful officials in Washington, products of the international business world and utterly ignorant of the realities of Guatemalan life, considered the idea of land redistribution to be inherently Marxist. "Products of the Cold War ethos," the historian Richard Immerman has written, "they believed it axiomatic that no government would take such a radical measure against a United States business if it were not dominated by communists."

Guatemala's communist party was actually a modest affair. Even at its peak it had only a few hundred active members, no mass base, and no support in the foreign ministry or army. Communists never held more than four seats in the sixty-one-member National Assembly. None sat in Arbenz's cabinet, although two gifted young Communist firebrands, one the leader of a labor federation and the other a charismatic peasant organizer, were among his closest advisers.

Arbenz was a leftist and intrigued by Marxist ideas. Often he irritated the United States with symbolic gestures, like allowing an official newspaper to charge that American forces were using germ warfare in Korea, or permitting the National Assembly to observe a minute of silence when Stalin died in 1953. He may have considered these incidents trivial. Officials in Washington, however, seized on them as proof that he had become an enemy.

If the first American error in assessing Arbenz was to believe that he was leading Guatemala toward Communism, the second was to assume that he was doing so as part of a master plan drafted in Moscow. Secretary of State Dulles in particular had not the slightest doubt that the Soviet Union was actively working to shape events in Guatemala. The fact that the Soviets had no military, economic, or even diplomatic relations with Guatemala, that no delegation of Guatemalans had ever visited Moscow, and that a study by the State Department itself had found the few Guatemalan Communists to be "indigenous to the area" interested him not at all. In the spring of 1954, he told a South American diplomat that although it was "impossible to produce evidence clearly tying the Guatemalan government to Moscow," American leaders were acting against that government "based on our deep conviction that such a tie must exist."

No evidence ever emerged to support that "deep conviction." Not in the vast archive of files the CIA captured after its coup, nor in any other document or testimony that has surfaced since, is there any indication that Soviet leaders were even slightly interested in Guatemala during the 1950s. Dulles could not have fathomed that. He was convinced to the point of theological certainty that the Soviets were behind every challenge to American power in the world. So was the rest of the Eisenhower administration. It believed, as one historian has put it, "that it was dealing not with misguided, irresponsible nationalists, but with ruthless agents of international communism."

Dulles and his colleagues came into office determined to rid themselves of the troublesome regime in Guatemala, but without a clear idea of how to do so. Kermit Roosevelt's triumph in Iran showed them the way. They decided to design a Guatemalan version of Operation Ajax. To reflect their confidence, they code-named it Operation Success.

On December 3, 1953, the CIA authorized an initial $3 million to set the plot in motion. It would start with a propaganda campaign, proceed through a wave of destabilizing violence, and culminate in an attack staged to look like a domestic uprising. This operation, though, would be much larger in scale than the one in Iran. Allen Dulles's idea was to find a suitable opposition leader among Guatemalan exiles; equip him with a militia that could pose as a full-scale rebel army; hire American pilots to bomb Guatemala City; and then, with the country in chaos, have the American ambassador tell military commanders that peace would return only if they deposed Arbenz.

The ambassador that Secretary of State Dulles chose for this job was John Peurifoy, a West Point dropout from South Carolina who had failed the foreign service examination and, eager to work in government, took a job as an elevator operator at the Capitol. He made friends easily and with the help of home-state connections landed a job at the

State Department. In 1950 he became ambassador to Greece, where he showed himself to be a flamboyant figure, happiest when driving fast cars or denouncing leftists. His passion for the latter attracted Dulles's attention, and at the end of 1953 he was named the new United States ambassador to Guatemala. The *New York Times* speculated that this choice would mean "a change in the asserted passivity with which the United States has watched the growth of Communist influence."

On the evening of December 16, Peurifoy had his first and only meeting with Arbenz. It lasted for six hours, over an extended dinner at Arbenz's official residence. When Arbenz began to discourse on United Fruit's abuses, Peurifoy interrupted to say that the real problem in Guatemala was "commie influence." The next day he sent Dulles a curt assessment of the man they had targeted: "If he is not a communist, he will certainly do until one comes along."

"Normal approaches will not work in Guatemala," Peurifoy added ominously. "The candle is burning slowly and surely, and it is only a matter of time before the large American interests will be forced out entirely."

These were just the words Dulles wanted to hear. He brought the cable to Eisenhower, who read it gravely. By the time he finished, according to his own account, he had decided to give Operation Success his final approval.

Eisenhower's order set the CIA off on its second plot against a foreign government. It was run autonomously within the agency, meaning that its coordinator, Colonel Al Haney, a former college football star who had run CIA guerrillas behind enemy lines in Korea, could report directly to Allen Dulles. Haney established a clandestine headquarters at a military airfield in Opa-Locka, Florida, on the outskirts of Miami; a transshipment post for weapons at France Field in the Panama Canal Zone; and a network of remote airstrips in Honduras and Nicaragua, both of which were ruled by dictators who fervently wished to see Arbenz overthrown. Allen Dulles found all of this "brilliant," but Colonel J. C. King, the head of Western Hemisphere operations for the CIA's directorate of plans, which carries out covert action, spoke up to dissent. King had no use for nationalists like Arbenz, but he worried about the long-term impact of Haney's ambitious plan.

"He'll be starting a civil war in the middle of Central America!" King protested.

Allen Dulles responded by inviting both King and Haney to his

Georgetown estate, Highlands. Over cocktails, he told them they had no more reason to argue. The president and secretary of state had ordered that Arbenz be overthrown. It was the CIA's job to carry out that order.

"Go to it, my boy," Dulles said as he slapped his hands on Haney's broad shoulders. "You've got the green light."

Operation Success was now fully approved in Washington, and fully funded—with $4.5 million, more than the CIA had ever spent on a covert operation. It lacked only one essential element: a Guatemalan to play the role of rebel leader. After several false starts, the CIA settled on a former army officer, Carlos Castillo Armas, who had led an abortive uprising in 1950 and had become a familiar figure in Guatemalan exile circles. Agents found him in Honduras, flew him to Opa-Locka, told him they were working with United Fruit on an anti-Arbenz project, and proposed that he become its putative leader. He accepted immediately.

During the spring of 1954, Castillo Armas waited in Honduras while the CIA hired fighters, requisitioned planes, prepared bases, and secured the cooperation of Honduran and Nicaraguan officials. The CIA station on the fourth floor of the American embassy in Guatemala City buzzed with activity. So did the operational base at Opa-Locka.

One of the agents assigned to Operation Success, Howard Hunt, who later became notorious for his role in the Watergate burglary, came up with the idea of using the Roman Catholic clergy to turn Guatemalans against Arbenz. Catholic priests and bishops in Guatemala, as in other Latin American countries, were closely aligned with the ruling class, and they loathed reformers like Arbenz. Hunt visited the most powerful Catholic prelate in the United States, Francis Cardinal Spellman of New York, and asked him if he could bring his Guatemalan counterparts into the coup plot. Spellman assured him that would be no problem. Soon, as Hunt later recalled, CIA agents "were writing scripts or leaflets for the Guatemalan clergy, the Catholic clergy, and this information was going out in [pastoral letters] across the country and in radio broadcasts." The most important of these pastoral letters, read in every Catholic church in Guatemala on April 9, warned the faithful that a demonic force called Communism was trying to destroy their homeland and called on them to "rise as a single man against this enemy of God and country."

While the CIA was busily laying the groundwork for a coup in Guatemala, Secretary of State Dulles intensified his diplomatic campaign.

In March he traveled to Caracas, Venezuela, for a meeting of the Organization of American States. Some foreign ministers came to Caracas with hopes of discussing economic development, but Dulles insisted that their "major interest" must be Communism. He introduced a resolution declaring that if a country in the Western Hemisphere fell under the control of "the international communist movement," any other nation in the hemisphere would be legally justified in taking "appropriate action." Guatemala's representative, Foreign Minister Guillermo Toriello, called this resolution "merely a pretext for intervention in our internal affairs."

> The plan of national liberation being carried out with firmness by my government has necessarily affected the privileges of foreign enterprises that are impeding the progress and economic development of the country. . . . They wanted to find a ready expedient to maintain the economic dependence of the American Republics and suppress the legitimate desires of their peoples, cataloguing as "communism" every manifestation of nationalism or economic independence, any desire for social progress, any intellectual curiosity, and any interest in liberal and progressive reforms.

More than a few delegates sympathized with this view, but Dulles was determined to win passage of his resolution. He remained in Caracas for two weeks, sitting through long meetings during which he fended off no fewer than fifty amendments. Finally and inevitably, he was successful. Sixteen countries supported the "Declaration of Caracas." Only Guatemala opposed it, with Mexico and Argentina abstaining.

This outcome was a great success for the United States, and it deeply shook Arbenz. The Dulles brothers agreed to intensify their pressure on him until the time seemed right to strike him down. Before they could do so, he made an unexpected misstep that delighted them.

Until Guatemala turned to democracy, in 1944, the United States had been its main arms supplier. After the transition, the Americans stopped sending weaponry. They also pressured Denmark, Mexico, Cuba, Argentina, and Switzerland to back out of arms deals with Guatemala. When the CIA began arming Guatemalan exiles, Arbenz became alarmed at the poor state of his defenses. He looked urgently for a country that would sell him weapons, and finally found one. On May 15,

1954, a freighter called the *Alfhelm* docked at Puerto Barrios and workers began unloading crates labeled "Optical and Laboratory Equipment." Inside were arms and ammunition from Czechoslovakia.

Czech arms makers had demanded payment in cash, and most of the weaponry they shipped turned out to be obsolete, impractical, or nonfunctional. Still, they could not have sold weapons to Guatemala without approval from Moscow. The symbolism of the *Alfhelm* shipment was overwhelming. A vessel loaded with Soviet-bloc arms had landed in Guatemala. To Representative McCormack, this was "like an atom bomb planted in the rear of our backyard." Secretary of State Dulles declared it proof of "communist infiltration."

"That is the problem," he told reporters in Washington, "not United Fruit."

From that moment, it became almost impossible for anyone in Washington to defend Arbenz. Some might have tried if they had known what the State Department and CIA were intending to do. The coup in Guatemala, though, like the one in Iran, was conceived in great secrecy. No one outside a handful of men knew about the plan, so no one could object, warn, or protest. This attraction of covert "regime change" operations was not lost on the Dulles brothers.

Some doubts about the administration's policy toward Guatemala did emerge, publicly and privately, but they were easily brushed aside. One came on the pages of the *New York Times,* where the reporter Sydney Gruson wrote several articles after the *Alfhelm* incident suggesting that Guatemalans were rallying around their government and that they were caught up not in Communism but in "fervent nationalism." This was not what United Fruit and the Eisenhower administration wished Americans to hear. Allen Dulles arranged a dinner with his friend Julius Adler, the business manager of the *Times,* and complained. Adler passed the complaint on to *Times* publisher Arthur Hays Sulzberger. A few days later, Gruson's boss pulled him out of Guatemala.

Allen Dulles also had to deal with a problem at his CIA station in Guatemala. The station chief, Birch O'Neill, did not like the idea of a coup. Like his counterpart in Tehran a year before, Roger Goiran, he warned that it would not work out well in the long run. Dulles responded by transferring O'Neill out of the country.

As Allen Dulles was removing these potential obstacles, his brother faced dissent from several State Department officials. One of them, Louis Halle, a member of the policy planning staff, circulated a lengthy memorandum asserting that Guatemala was in desperate need of social reform, that its government was "nationalist and anti-Yanqui" but not pro-Communist, and that the entire crisis was of United Fruit's making. Another official, Deputy Undersecretary of State Robert Murphy, found out about Operation Success by accident and fired off an angry note to Dulles telling him that the idea was "wrong" and would probably be "very expensive over the long term."

"To resort to this action confesses the bankruptcy of our political policy vis-à-vis that country," Murphy wrote.

Secretary of State Dulles had long since made up his mind to overthrow Arbenz, and did not bother to reply to dissenters in his ranks. News of their protests, though, filtered through higher echelons of the State Department. Ambassador Peurifoy was concerned enough to ask his superiors if there had been a change in plans. In a return cable, Raymond Leddy, the State Department's policy director for Central America, assured him that Operation Success was still on.

"We are on the road to settling this problem," Leddy wrote. "There is a 100 percent determination, from top down, to get rid of this stinker and not to stop until that is done."

Haney's operation was already in full swing. He had recruited a mini-army of nearly five hundred Guatemalan exiles, American soldiers of fortune, and assorted Central American mercenaries and had sent them to camps in Nicaragua, Honduras, and Florida, where they were being given rudimentary training. His clandestine "Voice of Liberation" radio station, supposedly transmitting from "somewhere in Guatemala" but actually based in Opa-Locka, was broadcasting a stream of false reports about popular unrest and military rebellions. It was time for Haney to send his handpicked "liberator," Colonel Castillo Armas, into action.

Soon after dawn on June 18, Castillo Armas summoned his men, packed them into jeeps and trucks, and led them northward in his command car, a battered old station wagon. They crossed the Honduran border without incident. Then, following the orders his CIA handlers had given him, Castillo Armas led his motorcade six miles into Guatemalan territory. There he stopped. This was the invasion.

Arbenz placed his army and police on alert but, on the advice of Foreign Minister Toriello, did not send troops to the border area. Toriello hoped to resolve this matter diplomatically. He wanted to show the world that foreign-sponsored troops were on Guatemalan territory, and did not want any government soldiers there to muddy the issue.

By mid-morning, Toriello was writing an urgent appeal to the United Nations Security Council. He asked the council to meet immediately and condemn an invasion of Guatemala launched "at the instigation of certain foreign monopolies." While he wrote, the "Voice of Liberation" was broadcasting breathless reports of Castillo Armas's supposed swift progress through the countryside. Two CIA planes buzzed low over the main military barracks in Guatemala City, firing machine-gun rounds and dropping a fragmentation bomb that set off a series of loud explosions. Ambassador Peurifoy, one of the few people in the country who knew exactly what was happening, heard them in his embassy office. He looked out his window, saw smoke billowing up from the barracks, and dashed off a gleeful cable to Dulles.

"Looks like this is it," he wrote.

The air raids continued for several days. One plane shot up the airport in Guatemala City. Others hit fuel tanks and military posts across the country. They led to several injuries and some property damage, but their purpose was not military. Like the bogus radio broadcasts, they were aimed at creating the impression that a war was under way. Each time a plane strafed another town, Guatemalans became more insecure, confused, and fearful—and more willing to believe what they heard on the "Voice of Liberation."

Secretary of State Dulles was receiving almost hour-by-hour reports on these events, from his brother and from Ambassador Peurifoy. His position, however, required him to dissemble in public. On the afternoon of June 19, the State Department issued a disingenuous statement saying it had news of "serious uprisings" and "outbreaks of violence" in Guatemala. Then it declared the lie that was at the heart of Operation Success.

"The department has no evidence that indicates this is anything other than a revolt of Guatemalans against the government," it said.

Arbenz knew that was untrue. He had come to realize that the United States was behind this rebellion, which meant that he could not defeat it with armed force. This realization drove him first to drink, and then to a decision to address his country by radio. In his speech he declared that "the arch-traitor Castillo Armas" was leading a "United Fruit Company expeditionary force" against his government.

Our crime is having enacted an agrarian reform which affected the interests of the United Fruit Company. Our crime is wanting to have our own route to the Atlantic, our own electric power and our own docks and ports. Our crime is our patriotic wish to advance, to progress, to win an economic independence that would match our political independence. . . .

It is completely untrue that communists are taking over the government. . . . We have imposed no terror. It is, on the contrary, the Guatemalan friends of Mr. Foster Dulles who wish to spread terror among our people, attacking women and children by surprise with impunity from pirate airplanes.

In the days after that speech, things began looking better for Arbenz. The army remained loyal to him, and his popularity among ordinary Guatemalans was unbroken. At a meeting of the Security Council in New York, France introduced a resolution calling for an end to "any action likely to cause bloodshed" in Guatemala and directing all countries to refrain from "rendering assistance to any such action." Castillo Armas was making no military progress. Most important, the air raids, which had driven much of the country to near-panic, were tapering off because one of the CIA's four P-47 Thunderbolts had been shot out of action and a second had crashed.

From his command post at Opa-Locka, Al Haney sent an urgent cable to Allen Dulles. It said that Operation Success was on the verge of collapse and would probably fail without more air support. Dulles went immediately to the White House to ask President Eisenhower for permission to dispatch two more planes. Eisenhower readily agreed. Later he told one of his aides that he had seen no realistic alternative.

"If at any time you take the route of violence or support of violence," he said, "then you commit yourself to carrying it through, and it's too late to have second thoughts."

Arbenz, who of course knew nothing of this, pressed his diplomatic offensive. He dispatched Toriello to New York, and there the foreign minister urged the Security Council to send an investigating team to Guatemala immediately. This was exactly what the Americans wished to prevent. The new United States ambassador to the United Nations— none other than former senator Henry Cabot Lodge—worked feverishly behind the scenes, and in a pivotal decision on June 25, the Security Council voted not to investigate what was happening in Guatemala.

While Lodge was holding the diplomatic fort, Haney sent his two new planes into action. His first round of raids had been for psychological effect, but now they took a more serious turn. For three days and nights, the planes strafed military bases, shot up fuel tanks, and dropped incendiary bombs on ammunition dumps. These attacks spread alarm and led hundreds of people to flee from their homes. On the day of the Security Council vote, in a last-minute appeal that was poignant almost to the point of pathos, Toriello sent a long cable to Dulles.

> I regret to inform your Excellency that a savage attack with TNT bombs took place yesterday on the civilian population of Chiquimula, as well as the strafing of that city and the cities of Gualán and Zacapa. . . . Guatemala appeals urgently to your Excellency to communicate to you this painful situation, and asks that your enlightened government, always respectful of the human rights of which it has been the standard-bearer, be good enough to intercede with the Security Council.

Dulles ignored this appeal. He could afford to, because events were now turning his way. No outsider had discovered the great ruse of Operation Success. Most Guatemalans believed what the "Voice of Liberation" told them: that Castillo Armas was leading a rebel army through the countryside, that many Guatemalan soldiers had risen up to join him, and that the government was powerless to stop the juggernaut.

As the bombing campaign intensified, Arbenz began to lose his grip. At one point he considered calling the peasantry to armed resistance, but his military commanders would not hear of it. He was out of options. At midday on Sunday, June 27, he sent Toriello to the American embassy to arrange the terms of his surrender.

Ambassador Peurifoy, who had taken to wearing a flight suit and brandishing a pistol, told Toriello that if there was a "clean sweep" at the National Palace, he might be able to persuade "insurgent forces" to end their campaign. A few hours later, the army chief of staff, Colonel Carlos Enrique Díaz, invited Peurifoy to his home. When Peurifoy arrived, the four other senior Guatemalan military commanders were also there. Díaz began by complaining bitterly about what the United States was doing in his country. Peurifoy, by his own account, "replied sharply that if he had brought me to his house to make accusations against my government, I would leave immediately." That reminded the Guatemalans who was in the stronger position. They reluctantly agreed to confront Arbenz and demand his resignation, but indignantly told Peurifoy that under no circumstances would they negotiate with Castillo Armas or bring him into a new government.

At four o'clock that afternoon, the commanders called on Arbenz. They told him they had constituted themselves as a military junta and were deposing him. He had no choice but to agree. His friends promised him two things: that they would never deal with Castillo Armas, and that they would allow him to deliver a farewell message over the radio. At nine-fifteen in the evening, Arbenz addressed his people for the last time.

Workers, peasants, patriots, my friends, people of Guatemala: Guatemala is enduring a most difficult trial. For fifteen days a cruel war against Guatemala has been underway. The United Fruit Company, in collaboration with the governing circles of the United States, is responsible for what is happening to us. . . .

I have not violated my faith in democratic liberties, in the independence of Guatemala and in all the good that is the future of humanity. . . . I have always said to you that we would fight regardless of the cost, but the cost should not include the destruction of our country and the sending of our riches abroad. And this could happen if we do not eliminate the pretext that our powerful enemy has raised.

A government different from mine, but always inspired by our October Revolution, is preferable to twenty years of fascist bloody tyranny under the rule of the bands that Castillo Armas has brought into the country.

After Arbenz finished his broadcast, he left the studio and walked forlornly to the Mexican embassy, where he asked for and was granted political asylum. Colonel Díaz took the microphone. He officially accepted the reins of power, and then promised Guatemalans, "The struggle against mercenary invaders will not abate." Ambassador Peurifoy's jaw tightened as he listened over the radio. When Díaz was finished, the ambassador slammed his hand onto his desk.

"OK," he spat, "now I'll have to crack down on that s.o.b."

The broadcast also upset the two principal CIA operatives in Guatemala, station chief John Doherty and agent Enno Hobbing, who had been sent from Washington to help oversee Operation Success. As soon as it was over, they agreed that their work was not yet complete. They decided to depose Díaz that very night and replace him with an officer they knew and trusted, Colonel Elfegio Monzón.

Doherty and Hobbing drove to Monzón's home, gave him the good news that he was about to become president, and packed him into their backseat. Together the three drove to Díaz's headquarters. It was midnight when they arrived.

Díaz, who had been in power for only a few hours, feared the worst. He began by trying to defend Arbenz's reforms, but Hobbing cut him off.

"Let me explain something to you," he said. "You made a big mistake when you took over the government."

There was a long moment of silence as Díaz absorbed this message. Then Hobbing spoke again. "Colonel," he told Díaz, "you're just not convenient for the requirements of American foreign policy."

"But I talked to your ambassador!" Díaz protested.

"Well, Colonel, there is diplomacy and then there is reality. Our ambassador represents diplomacy. I represent reality. And the reality is we don't want you."

"Can I hear it from the ambassador?" Díaz asked plaintively.

It was four o'clock in the morning when an irritated Peurifoy arrived at Díaz's headquarters. They had a tense meeting. Díaz insisted that he would not resign without a guarantee that Guatemala would not be turned over to Castillo Armas. Peurifoy refused to give it. Finally he stormed out. Back at the embassy at dawn, he composed a pithy cable to Haney.

"We have been double-crossed," it said. "BOMB!"

That afternoon, at a clandestine airstrip in Honduras, a CIA pilot named Jerry DeLarm stepped into the cockpit of a P-47. Accompanied by a fighter escort, he headed to Guatemala City. There he dropped two bombs on the parade ground of the main military base and several more on the government radio station.

Reality was closing in on Colonel Díaz. He summoned Peurifoy in the predawn hours of Tuesday, June 29, but as soon as they started talking he was called into a side room to consult with other officers. A few minutes later he emerged, with a tommy gun pointed at his ribs. Beside him was Colonel Monzón.

"My colleague Díaz has decided to resign," Monzón said suavely. "I am replacing him."

Monzón formed a three-man junta and, a few days later, flew to El Salvador for negotiations with Castillo Armas. They met under Ambassador Peurifoy's supervision. His influence brought them to a speedy agreement. Within a few days, the two subsidiary members of the junta, reportedly encouraged by payments of $100,000 apiece, accepted diplomatic posts abroad. On July 5, Monzón followed them into retirement. Castillo Armas replaced him and proclaimed himself president of Guatemala. Soon afterward, Secretary of State Dulles addressed Americans by radio and told them that a great victory over Communism had been won.

> The Guatemalan government and Communist agents throughout the world have persistently attempted to obscure the real issue—that of Communist imperialism—by claiming that the U.S. is only interested in protecting American business. We regret that there have been disputes between the Guatemalan government and the United Fruit Company. . . . But this issue is relatively unimportant. . . . Led by Colonel Castillo Armas, patriots arose in Guatemala to challenge the Communist leadership and to change it. Thus the situation is being cured by the Guatemalans themselves.

Dulles knew he was being untruthful when he asserted that "Guatemalans themselves" were responsible for overthrowing Arbenz, but he did not realize that the other claim he made in his victory proclamation was also false. He truly believed that Arbenz was a tool of "Communist imperialism" rather than what he actually was: an idealistic, reform-minded nationalist who bore Americans no ill will. By overthrowing him, the United States crushed a democratic experiment that held great promise for Latin America. As in Iran a year earlier, it deposed a regime that embraced fundamental American ideals but that had committed the sin of seeking to retake control of its own natural resources.

7

Not the Preferred Way to Commit Suicide

News agencies never sleep, so it was no surprise that Malcolm Browne, the Associated Press correspondent in Saigon, was still at work when his office telephone rang late on the evening of June 10, 1963. The caller was Thich Duc Nghiep, a Buddhist monk Browne had come to know while covering the escalating conflict between Buddhists and the Catholic-dominated government of South Vietnam. He told Browne that anyone who appeared at the Xa Loi Pagoda the next morning would witness "an important event."

That evening, the monk called several other foreign correspondents with the same message. Only Browne took him seriously. He had written extensively about the spreading Buddhist rebellion and sensed that it would shape Vietnam's future. Before dawn the next morning, he and his Vietnamese assistant set out for the pagoda. They found it packed with monks in saffron-colored robes and nuns in gray ones. The air inside was hot, thick, and heavily sweet with incense. Smoke spiraled upward from a hundred braziers. Holy men and women lost themselves in ancient chants.

Browne took a place. One of the nuns approached him, and as she poured him tea, he could see tears streaming down her face. A few minutes later, Thich Duc Nghiep caught sight of him and approached. He had a simple suggestion: do not leave "until events have run their course."

For half an hour Browne sat amid this scene. Suddenly, at a signal, the monks and nuns stopped their chanting, rose, solemnly filed out of the pagoda, and formed a column outside. They assembled behind an old Austin sedan carrying five monks and followed it through the streets. Where Phan Dinh Phung intersected with one of the city's major avenues, Le Van Duyet, the procession stopped. Marchers formed a circle to block off all approaches.

Three monks emerged from the car, one elderly and the others supporting him. The younger ones placed a square cushion on the pavement in the center of the intersection and helped the older one settle into the archetypal lotus position. As he fingered his oak beads and murmured the sacred words *nam mo amita Buddha,* "return to Buddha," they fetched a gasoline tank from the car and splashed a pink gas-and-diesel mixture over him. After they stepped away, he produced a box of matches, lit one, and dropped it onto his lap. Instantly he was consumed by fire.

> As the breeze whipped the flames from his face, I could see that although his eyes were closed, his features were contorted with agony. But throughout his ordeal he never uttered a sound or changed his position, even as the smell of burning flesh filled the air. A horrified moan arose from the crowd, and the ragged chanting of some of the monks was interrupted by screams and cries of anguish. Two monks unfurled a large cloth banner reading (in English), "A Buddhist Priest Burns for Buddhist Demands."

Stunned by what he was seeing, Browne reflexively shot picture after picture. After a few minutes, a fire truck and several police cars with shrieking sirens appeared, but demonstrators lay in front of them and clung to their wheels so they could not reach the pyre. Soon the flames began to subside. When they died out, several monks appeared with a wooden coffin and tried to lift the dead man's body into it. His limbs had become rigid. As the coffin was carried back to Xa Loi Pagoda, both arms spilled out. One was still smoking.

Browne's photos of the burning monk stunned people around the world. The day after they were taken, a visitor to the Oval Office noticed that President John F. Kennedy had a set of them on his desk. They seemed to symbolize the unraveling of South Vietnam and the impotence of its president, Ngo Dinh Diem. Over the next few months, these images helped push the Kennedy administration toward a momentous decision. Diem had lost the administration's confidence and would be overthrown.

THE VERDANT LAND OF VIETNAM, CURVING LIKE A DRAGON'S TAIL ALONG THE sinuous coast of Indochina, became a French colony in the nineteenth century. Generations of French families built lives there, carving rubber plantations out of the jungle and turning Saigon, the capital, into an exotic colonial outpost. In the turbulent years after World War II, nationalist and anticolonialist passion erupted in Vietnam just as it erupted in lands as distant as Iran and Guatemala. Many foreign leaders failed to recognize its power. The most self-destructively myopic were the Americans. Their blindness would lead the United States to the greatest military defeat in its history.

Japan had occupied and controlled Vietnam during the world war. An army of partisans, the Vietminh, waged guerrilla war against the occupiers, using weapons (and smoking cigarettes) dropped to them by the Americans. After the Japanese surrender, the partisan leader, Ho Chi Minh, a frail-looking figure in his fifties with a thin beard, decided that the time was right to declare his country's independence. On September 2, 1945, before a large crowd in the northern city of Hanoi, he delivered a speech that any American would have found familiar.

"All men are created equal," he proclaimed. "They are endowed by their creator with certain inalienable rights. Among these are life, liberty and the pursuit of happiness."

Ho looked instinctively to the United States, partly because he had what one historian called "a lifelong admiration for Americans" and partly because he had few other allies. France, determined to resume its position as Vietnam's ruling power, refused to recognize his new government. Britain, which feared the example that a Vietminh takeover would have in its own colonies, also opposed him. Communist leaders in China and the Soviet Union feared his nationalism. It was logical for him to turn to Washington for help.

Ho's efforts to attract American support, which included sending letters to President Harry Truman and General George Marshall, proved fruitless. The French settled back into their old role in Vietnam. Slowly Ho came to realize that if he wanted to make his country's independence real, the Vietminh would have to fight another war, this time against French colonialists. That war was reaching its climax when Dwight Eisenhower assumed the presidency in 1953.

By then, the French had been worn down by years of fighting against Vietnamese guerrillas. They concluded, with great pain, that they must give up their splendid colony and sue for peace. Early in 1954, French and Vietminh negotiators met in Geneva. Negotiators from China, the Soviet Union, Britain, and the United States were also there. Secretary of

State Dulles headed the American delegation. A figure of at least equal stature, Zhou Enlai, represented Communist China. Dulles considered the Chinese regime no less than demonic, and when a reporter asked him if he would consider meeting with Zhou, he replied icily.

"Not unless our automobiles collide," he said.

Dulles came to Geneva hoping to prevent an agreement. He had little success, and left after a week. Soon afterward, the remaining negotiators agreed to a temporary partition of Vietnam along the seventeenth parallel. Communists would control the north and have a capital in Hanoi. Former allies of the French would establish a separate government in the south, with their capital in Saigon. There would be nationwide elections in two years, after which north and south would be reunited. In the meantime, no outside power was to send weapons or soldiers into either part of Vietnam.

France ended its rule over Vietnam with a suitably muted ceremony. On October 9, 1954, under a rainy sky, a small group of soldiers assembled around a flagpole at Mangin Athletic Stadium in Hanoi and lowered the Tricolor. A bugler played plaintive notes. There were no songs or speeches. In its misbegotten eight-year war, France lost a staggering 44,967 dead and another 79,560 wounded.

Few people in Hanoi noticed the ceremony. They were too busy preparing to welcome their triumphant Vietminh. The day after the French withdrew, thirty thousand guerrilla fighters marched into the city. Their victory was not yet complete, because Vietnam had been divided, but the division was to last only two years. Ho Chi Minh had inflicted a stunning defeat on a far richer and seemingly more powerful enemy. He was the country's most popular figure. Many Vietnamese assumed that in the 1956 election, he would be chosen to lead their country.

Dulles had done everything he could to keep the French at their posts in Vietnam, but they were determined to leave. That did not mean, however, that he had to sit idly by while Vietnamese voters elected a Communist to lead their reunified country. He never considered the possibility of seeking an accommodation with Ho. Instead he set out to undermine the Geneva agreement by making the country's division permanent.

To direct this ambitious project, Dulles chose Colonel Edward Landsdale, the most accomplished American counterinsurgency expert of that era. Landsdale had won a great victory by crushing guerrillas in the Philippines, working in partnership with an English-speaking Filipino leader, Ramon Magsaysay, who he plucked from obscurity, lavishly financed, maneuvered up through the political ranks, and finally installed as president. He needed the same kind of partner for his Vietnam project. One was waiting.

Ngo Dinh Diem was a devout Catholic who came from a long line of Vietnamese mandarins. He had studied public administration and, while still in his thirties, served as interior minister in one of Emperor Bao Dai's pro-French cabinets. Later he came to favor independence, but because of his intense anti-Communism he refused to join the Vietminh. In 1950 he traveled to the United States, where he spent two years living an ascetic life at Maryknoll seminaries in Lakewood, New Jersey, and Ossining, New York. He also made valuable political contacts. Through the intercession of the militantly anti-Communist Francis Cardinal Spellman, he met State Department officials and influential members of Congress. Spellman made a special point of introducing him to Catholic politicians, among them Senator John F. Kennedy of Massachusetts.

When the Americans had to find a Vietnamese to do their bidding in Saigon, Diem was one of the few they knew. He was then a portly fifty-three-year-old bachelor and lay celibate living at a Benedictine monastery in Belgium. Neither Dulles nor Landsdale had ever met him, but Landsdale vouched for his anti-Communist credentials, and that was all Dulles needed to hear. France had no better candidate to suggest. Nor did the pliant Emperor Bao Dai, who was then living in Cannes. A few months before the French withdrawal, Diem was duly anointed. He flew from Paris to Saigon, and took office as prime minister on the propitious day Asians call "double seven," the seventh day of the seventh month, July 7, 1954.

Landsdale gave Diem a few days to settle in, and then went to meet him at the lavish Gia Long Palace, formerly the French governor's residence. Walking down one of its corridors, he ran into what he later described as "a plump man in a white suit," and asked where he could find Prime Minister Diem.

"I am Diem," the man replied.

That was the beginning of a long, doomed partnership. Landsdale took Diem under his wing, and within a few months rescued him from two attempted coups, one of which he suppressed by bribing rebel leaders with $12 million of the CIA's money. Then he launched the anti-Communist campaign Dulles had sent him to wage.

Landsdale's tactics ranged from sabotaging city buses in Hanoi to paying soothsayers to predict doom under the Communists. One of his biggest projects was helping to set off an exodus of hundreds of thousands of Catholics from North to South, urging them to flee with a campaign that included radio messages proclaiming, "Christ has gone to the South" and "Virgin Mary has departed from the North." None of this provoked the rebellion Landsdale expected, and with each passing day, the nationwide election drew closer. Everyone realized that it would carry Ho, the country's founder, to the presidency of a united Vietnam. Eisenhower guessed that "possibly eighty percent of the population" would vote for him. This presented the Americans with a serious dilemma. When an aide brought Secretary of State Dulles a cable from Diem suggesting a way out, he read it immediately.

"He sat very quietly," recalled Paul Kattenburg, the State Department desk officer for Vietnam. "We all sat very quietly. I can recall distinctly the clock ticking away on his wall, and his breathing heavily as he read through the paper—turning to us, the few of us who were there at that meeting, and saying, 'I don't believe Diem wants to hold elections, and I believe we should support him in this.'"

VIETNAM WAS SUPPOSED TO BE DIVIDED FOR TWO YEARS ONLY. THAT changed after Diem and Dulles decided not to hold the scheduled 1956 election. With no election, there could be no reunification. Instead, two new nations emerged: North Vietnam and South Vietnam.

At the end of 1955, after a referendum that he won with a reported 98.2 percent of the vote, Diem deposed Bao Dai and made himself chief of state. He used his new power to impose a constitution that gave him sweeping authority. While Ho ruled North Vietnam in traditional Communist fashion, through a politburo made up of trusted comrades, Diem shaped a politburo of his own, made up of close relatives. They ruled the country as a family.

Diem's eldest brother, Ngo Dinh Can, held no official post but ruled central Vietnam like a feudal warlord. Another brother, Ngo Dinh Thuc, was a Catholic archbishop and also an avaricious investor who had made a fortune in rubber, timber, and real estate. A third, Ngo Dinh Luyen, became ambassador to Britain. Most important and visible of all were the president's fourth brother, Ngo Dinh Nhu, and Nhu's flamboyant wife. Nhu, an avid admirer of Machiavelli who was sometimes called the "Vietnamese Rasputin," was President Diem's closest adviser and alter ego. Madame Nhu, a sharp-tongued defender of the regime, liked to say she did not fear death because "I love power, and in the next life I have a chance to be even more powerful than I am."

America's determination to defend an independent South Vietnam led Ho and his comrades to launch their third anticolonial war. In 1960 they proclaimed a military campaign aimed at "the elimination of the U.S. imperialists and the Ngo Dinh Diem clique." A few months later, leaders of a dozen dissident political and religious groups in the South announced the formation of a new coalition, the National Liberation Front, that would confront Diem politically while guerrillas, now called Vietcong, waged war on the battlefield.

No one in Washington considered the formation of the National Liberation Front to be anything other than a Communist propaganda stunt. That was a lamentable error. The NLF, a fairly broad coalition of left-leaning political parties, urban intellectuals, and middle-class professionals, developed a strong following in many provinces. During its first two or three years of existence, and to a certain degree even later, after it became directly allied with North Vietnam, it had interests different from those of the Communists. Americans never sought to probe those differences or open any channel of contact to anti-Diem civilians.

Secretary of State Dulles fell ill, retired, and died in 1958. After that, President Eisenhower seemed to lose interest in Vietnam. On January 19, 1961, the day before he left office, he briefed President-elect Kennedy on world trouble spots. There was plenty to talk about. The pro-American regime in Laos was collapsing. An anticolonial rebellion was raging in Algeria, and another seemed about to break out in the Congo. The CIA was training a secret army to invade Cuba in the hope of deposing Fidel Castro's new regime. Tensions were rising in Berlin. It took several months, though, for Kennedy to realize the oddest aspect of that meeting.

"You know," he marveled to an aide, "Eisenhower never mentioned it, never uttered the word 'Vietnam.'"

During Kennedy's presidency, the number of American soldiers in South Vietnam rose from 865 to 16,500. Kennedy sent jet fighters, helicopters, heavy artillery, and all manner of other weaponry, none of which turned the tide of battle. In fact, as the journalist and historian Stanley Karnow later wrote, American aid "paradoxically sapped the Diem regime."

The aid, overwhelmingly military, confirmed Diem's conviction that he was waging a conventional conflict, and it stiffened his resistance to political, economic and social reforms. Moreover, his battalions became more and more reluctant to confront the Vietcong squarely, relying instead on American air strikes and artillery shells to do their job for them. This suited Diem, who instructed his officers to avoid casualties. Their primary role, in his view, was not to fight the Vietcong but to protect him against possible coups.

One of the first special envoys Kennedy sent to Vietnam—there would be a steady stream—was Vice President Lyndon Johnson, who flew to Saigon in May 1961. Johnson came back a believer in the "domino theory," convinced that if the Communists were allowed to take South Vietnam, they would soon push their war to "the beaches of Waikiki." In one of his speeches, he went so far as to praise Diem as "the Churchill of Southeast Asia," although when Karnow asked him afterward if he really believed that, he demurred.

"Shit," he replied, "Diem's the only boy we got out there."

With that succinct line, Johnson crystallized United States policy in Vietnam during the late 1950s and early 1960s. Diem was the American surrogate. Lacking a popular base, plucked from a religious group that represented only 10 percent of his country's population, surrounded by a venal family and uninterested in the daily work of government, he was chosen because no one else fit American requirements. As in so many other countries, the Americans looked in South Vietnam for a leader who would be a crowd-pleasing nationalist and also do what Washington wished, only to discover that they could not have both.

Diem became increasingly uncomfortable with the growing American role in his country. More than once he complained to the United States ambassador in Saigon, Frederick Nolting, that American troops were only intensifying the conflict by provoking strong responses from the North. Still the troops, called "advisers" as a way of maintaining the fiction that they were not fighting, poured in. Between 1961 and 1963, they engaged in hundreds of firefights, and American planes flew thousands of bombing sorties against Vietcong positions. During that same period, 108 Americans were killed, and the United States lost twenty-three aircraft.

Diem complained about "all these soldiers I never asked to come here." During an inspection tour of Cam Ranh Bay, he pointed to the harbor and told his aides, "The Americans want a base there, but I shall never accept that." When Ambassador Nolting, following a script written in Washington, told him that the United States wished to "share in the decision making process in the political, economic and military fields," he replied, "Vietnam does not want to be a protectorate." People started calling him a reluctant protégé, a client who refused to behave like a client, a puppet who pulled his own strings. The worst came when his brother and chief adviser, Ngo Dinh Nhu, suggested that perhaps the time had come to negotiate with the Vietcong.

"I am anti-communist from the point of view of doctrine, but I am not anti-communist from the point of view of politics or humanity," Nhu told a television interviewer in the spring of 1963. "I consider the communists as brothers, lost sheep. I am not for an assault against the communists because we are a small country, and we only want to live in peace."

The final act in the drama of Diem's rule was unfolding. On May 8, Buddhists gathered in Hue to mark the 2,527th birthday of the Buddha. The local strongman, Ngo Dinh Can—who was also the president's brother—decided to enforce an old decree prohibiting the celebrants from flying the traditional blue-red-saffron Buddhist flag, even though only a few days earlier the city had been aflutter with Catholic banners to mark the 25th anniversary of Archbishop Ngo Dinh Thuc's ordination. Buddhists began a series of protests. Police fired on one of them, killing a woman and eight children.

Buddhist leaders reacted by launching a nationwide campaign against Diem. They distributed leaflets, met with foreign journalists, and staged rallies and hunger strikes. People flocked to their cause, often for reasons that had little to do with religion. They were have-nots rebelling against the rich, ordinary people defying authoritarian power, and, in the words of *New York Times* correspondent David Halberstam, "twentieth-century Asians protesting against older Asians molded from a mandarin past."

When Diem did not respond to this campaign, Buddhist leaders announced that monks might commit suicide as a way of showing the depth of their anger. Diem dismissed this threat. So did many Americans in Vietnam, including some news correspondents. One who did not was Malcolm Browne.

The monk who burned himself to death on the morning of June 11 was named Thich Quang Duc. He was sixty-seven years old, had been a monk for nearly half a century, and was revered as a bodhisattva, a being on the path to enlightenment who chooses to forgo it in order to help others become enlightened. In a statement that his comrades distributed after his death, he made a "respectful" plea to Diem to show "charity and compassion" to all religions. The ruling family's most outspoken member, Madame Nhu, replied by ridiculing the spectacle of what she called a "barbecue."

"Let them burn," she said. "We shall clap our hands."

NO ONE IN WASHINGTON TOOK THE SUICIDE SO LIGHTLY. IT WAS PART OF A steady flow of bad news from Vietnam that President Kennedy and his aides were forced to confront during the spring and summer of 1963. Vietcong guerrillas had established control over 20 percent of South Vietnam and moved freely in an area twice that large. The South Vietnamese army was proving reluctant to fight. Official corruption, fed by ballooning American aid programs, was rampant. Diem was losing popularity. To keep order, he was forced to rule with increasing repression, much of it directed by his brother and chief adviser, Ngo Dinh Nhu.

One of Kennedy's first decisions after the monk's suicide was to replace Ambassador Nolting, a courtly Virginian who had become close to Diem. He considered naming Landsdale, but there is an unwritten rule against appointing CIA officers as ambassadors, and he dropped the idea. Instead he chose an entirely different figure, one of his oldest political rivals, Henry Cabot Lodge, an aristocratic pillar of the Republican establishment.

Lodge had represented Massachusetts in the Senate until 1952, when he lost his seat to Kennedy. After his defeat, Secretary of State Dulles arranged for him to be named ambassador to the United Nations, where he had played a supporting role in the overthrow of Jacobo Arbenz in Guatemala. In 1960, Lodge was Richard Nixon's running mate on the Republican ticket that Kennedy and Lyndon Johnson defeated. His prominence, his diplomatic experience, his strong political base in Washington, and his mastery of the French language made him a logical choice for the Vietnam post. So did his Republican pedigree. Kennedy and his aides knew that the Saigon post was full of risks and liked the idea of having a Republican to blame if things went wrong.

Lodge found South Vietnam in turmoil when he arrived on Friday evening, August 23, 1963. Growing unrest, including the self-immolation of four more Buddhist monks, had led President Diem to place the country under martial law. Police squads had swooped down on Buddhist pagodas and arrested hundreds of monks, among them the country's eighty-year-old Buddhist patriarch. In Hue they fought a pitched eight-hour street battle against Buddhist protesters.

That weekend in Washington, in an appalling display of confusion and missed signals, the Kennedy administration stumbled into a "regime change" operation destined to end in blood. It was the culmination of weeks of debate over how to deal with Diem. Some in the administration believed that he was still the best hope for South Vietnam. Others had given up on him and conjured his demise.

On Saturday, August 24, all three of Diem's most powerful supporters in Washington were out of town. Secretary of State Dean Rusk was attending a Yankees game in New York, Secretary of Defense Robert McNamara was vacationing in Wyoming, and President Kennedy was at his home on Cape Cod. That left the American foreign policy apparatus in the hands of three lower-ranking officials, all of whom wanted Diem overthrown.

The most eager of these was Assistant Secretary of State Roger Hilsman, the administration's chief East Asia specialist. Hilsman, who had been a commando in Burma during World War II, considered himself an expert on both counterinsurgency and the politics of Indochina. On that Saturday, he drafted a fateful cable to Lodge. It directed Lodge to tell Diem directly that the United States "cannot tolerate a situation in which power lies in Nhu's hands" and to demand that Diem sever all political ties to his brother. If Diem "remains obdurate and refuses," the cable said, "we must face the possibility that Diem himself cannot be preserved."

"Concurrently with above," it concluded, "Ambassador and country teams should urgently examine all possible replacement leadership and make detailed plans as to how we might bring about Diem's replacement if this becomes necessary."

That afternoon, Hilsman and one of his chief allies, Undersecretary of State Averell Harriman, sought out George Ball, who was acting head of the State Department in Rusk's absence. They found him on the ninth green of the Falls Road Golf Course in Maryland. Ball was the third member of the State Department's anti-Diem troika. He liked Hilsman's cable and agreed to telephone Kennedy and recommend that it be sent.

For reasons that remain unclear, Kennedy did not focus on the seriousness of this cable. He may have been distracted by his weekend pursuits. Ball phrased his appeal in terms that he knew would reassure the president. Kennedy made only one minor change in the message, and then approved it.

"If Rusk and Gilpatrick agree, George, then go ahead," he said.

Neither Rusk nor Deputy Secretary of Defense Roswell Gilpatrick had yet been consulted, but Ball did not mention that. After hanging up, he called Rusk in New York and told him he was preparing to send a cable to Saigon that President Kennedy had already approved. Rusk, as was his habit, told them that anything the President approved was fine with him. He even strengthened their cable with a new sentence: "You may also tell appropriate military commanders we will give them direct support in any interim period of breakdown of central government mechanism."

According to State Department protocol, a cable of this importance had to be approved not simply by the president and secretary of state but also by the secretary of defense, the director of the CIA, and the chairman of the Joint Chiefs of Staff. All were out of reach on that Saturday evening, so Ball checked with their deputies instead. Officials at that level are not wont to veto presidential directives, and none tried to do so.

Once the anti-Diem group had secured these approvals, they needed only Kennedy's final go-ahead. Michael Forrestal, a member of the National Security Council, called him to obtain it. To his surprise, he found the president suddenly hesitant. He had been having second thoughts.

"Are you sure you are all right?" Kennedy asked.

Forrestal managed to reassure him, and that was that. At 9:43 that evening, a clerk at the State Department dispatched the cable. The debate that should have taken place beforehand broke out on Monday morning.

An angry Kennedy summoned his foreign policy advisers to the White House and began by sternly reprimanding Hilsman, Harriman, Ball, and Forrestal for what he called their "impulsiveness." General Maxwell Taylor, chairman of the Joint Chiefs, was just as upset. He said he would never have approved the cable, and accused those who drafted it of staging "an aggressive end run" that would have been possible only on a weekend. Vice President Johnson, Secretary of Defense McNamara, and CIA director John McCone all warned that overthrowing Diem would create more problems than it would solve. The argument stretched on over four days of meetings, leaving Kennedy angry and frustrated.

"My God!" he exclaimed to a friend that week. "My government is coming apart!"

In Saigon, Ambassador Lodge was enthusiastically preparing the way for "regime change." He sent signals to dissident generals and dispatched a series of cables to Washington urging quick action against Diem. In one, dated August 29, he warned that if the United States did not "move promptly," South Vietnam might soon fall into the hands of "pro-communist or at least neutralist politicians."

We are launched on a course from which there is no respectable turning back: the overthrow of the Diem government. There is no turning back because U.S. prestige is already publicly committed to this end in large measure, and will become more so as the facts leak out. In a more fundamental sense, there is no turning back because there is no possibility, in my view, that the war can be won under a Diem administration.

That cable evidently impressed Kennedy. A few days after receiving it, he sat on the lawn of his Cape Cod retreat for a television interview with Walter Cronkite of CBS. When Cronkite asked him if he thought the Diem government could win the war, he gave an answer that was also a signal to Saigon.

"With changes in policies and personnel, I think it can," Kennedy said. "If it doesn't make those changes, I would think that the chances of winning it would not be very good."

When Diem and Nhu heard this, they understood that their regime was in danger. They looked for a new strategy. Nhu decided to propose a rapprochement with the North. Soon after he did, the National Liberation Front said it was willing to join a coalition government in the South; United Nations Secretary General U Thant called for "neutralization" of the South and Vietnam's eventual reunification; President Charles de Gaulle of France endorsed the idea; and the French ambassador in Saigon began working secretly with a Polish colleague to arrange contacts between the governments of North and South Vietnam—although not secretly enough to prevent the CIA from learning what they were doing.

The Kennedy administration was choosing between two awful alternatives: supporting a corrupt and unpopular government that was losing the war, or endorsing a coup to overthrow that government. From the vantage point of history, it is reasonable to ask why no one suggested the obvious third option. The United States could simply have washed its hands of the crisis and left it for the Vietnamese to resolve. That would probably have led to the establishment of Communist or pro-Communist rule over the entire country, but that is what ultimately happened anyway. A withdrawal at this point would have saved hundreds of thousands of lives, avoided the devastation of Vietnam, and spared the United States its greatest national trauma since the Civil War. Why did no one suggest it?

In fact, the idea did surface several times. Paul Kattenburg, who had become chairman of the administration's Vietnam Interdepartmental Working Group, returned from a trip to Saigon in late August with a very gloomy view. He concluded that the Vietnamese had become steadily more nationalistic and would never accept a foreign-backed regime in Saigon. At a National Security Council meeting on August 31, he suggested that the time had come "for us to make the decision to get out honorably." His comrades promptly slapped him down.

"We will not pull out until the war is won," Rusk told him, curtly and to general approval.

Kattenburg had spoken the unspeakable, and was rewarded for his heresy with a diplomatic post in Guyana. A few weeks later, though, no less a figure than Attorney General Robert Kennedy wondered aloud at a White House meeting whether an eventual Communist victory in Vietnam "could be resisted with any government." If not, he suggested, perhaps it was "time to get out of Vietnam completely."

Others at the meeting considered this idea so weird as to be almost beyond response. Robert Kennedy might have been able to press his argument if he had thought it through more carefully and prepared a serious case, but he had not. After he spoke, one person at the meeting later recalled, his suggestion "hovered for a moment then died away, a hopelessly alien thought in a field of unexamined assumptions and entrenched convictions."

In Saigon, Lodge was pressing ahead with his plans for a coup. He had decided that, as he wrote in one cable to Washington, "the United States must not appear publicly in the matter." That meant he would need a clandestine envoy to the plotters. For this delicate job he chose Lucien Conein, a bluff and broad-shouldered CIA agent with years of experience in covert action.

Conein, who used the code name "Black Luigi," was a larger-than-life figure and self-described "expert liar." Reporters described him as a character "sprung to life from a pulp adventure," a lover of life who "never saw a mirror he didn't like" and was "eccentric, boisterous, often uncontrollable yet deeply sensitive and thoroughly professional." When President Kennedy first saw his name and asked who he was, McNamara replied, "He's a Lawrence of Arabia type." Ambassador Lodge called him "the indispensable man." Never was he more so than during the autumn of 1963.

The general who seemed best able to pull off a successful coup was Duong Van Minh, the most prominent and popular officer in the country and President Diem's nominal military adviser. "Big Minh," as the Americans called him, was a blunt-spoken veteran of the French colonial army. Diem came to mistrust him, and, by 1963, he had no troops under his command. That left him with plenty of time for his two passions, playing tennis and cultivating orchids. It also disposed him toward plotting.

On August 29, Conein approached General Minh and broached the subject of a coup. The two men spoke for more than an hour. Minh allowed that something could be happening or made to happen, but would say no more. He knew that the Americans were divided among themselves, and feared that if he spoke too freely, someone might leak his plans to Diem. All he needed from Conein was approval to proceed. If the United States wanted Diem overthrown, he said, it should send restive generals a concrete signal.

Conein passed this request up the chain of command, and a few days later the Kennedy administration gave "Big Minh" the signal he wanted. It suspended a $14 million loan to South Vietnam that was to pay for two high-profile development projects, a waterworks and an electric plant. Minh was satisfied and designated his most trusted coconspirator, General Tran Van Don, acting chief of the South Vietnamese general staff, as his liaison with Conein. Don was a French-born aristocrat, a graduate of the French military academy, and something of an intellectual. He and Conein had been friends for nearly twenty years. As the coup plot took shape in September and October, they were in regular touch. To avoid arousing suspicion, they usually met in the office of a Saigon dentist.

"Whatever else happened," Conein recalled later, "I certainly had a lot of work done on my teeth."

The political climate in Saigon rose steadily that autumn. Nhu intensified his criticism of United States policy, at one point scorning Lodge as a "man of no morality." He continued to drop hints about a possible peace overture to the Communists, saying that "the Americans have done everything to push me into their arms." In a farcical election on September 27, Nhu and his wife were reelected to the rubber-stamp parliament, with identical winning percentages of 99 percent. A week later, another Buddhist monk burned himself to death, the first such suicide since the summer.

Lodge faced one unexpected problem within his embassy. He had made clear from the day he arrived that he wanted his staff to speak with a single voice. At the beginning of October, he started hearing that the chief of the CIA station at his embassy, John "Jocko" Richardson, was having doubts about the coup plot. Richardson maintained ties with Nhu, and because of his position and background—he had directed spectacularly successful anti-Nazi operations in World War II and been a highly effective station chief in the Philippines—his views carried considerable weight in Washington. With these assets, Lodge realized, he could tip the already precarious balance within the Kennedy administration and force cancellation of the coup. At the beginning of October he managed to have Richardson transferred out of Vietnam and replaced by a more enthusiastic agent.

At four-twenty on Tuesday afternoon, October 29, President Kennedy gathered fifteen of his senior foreign policy and national security advisers at the White House for a final meeting about the imminent coup. Years later, a tape of that meeting surfaced. The transcript is deeply disheartening, a textbook example of how not to shape policy. Kennedy's men presented differing views, as would be expected. What was remarkable about this meeting, though, was that so many of the participants expressed serious doubts about the coup. Even more bizarre, neither Kennedy nor anyone else responded to these warnings. No one suggested that if there was so much dissent, maybe the coup should be suspended or canceled. There was no call for a vote, or even any systematic discussion of what repercussions a coup might have. Once the Americans signaled to their Vietnamese friends that they wished Diem overthrown, the project took on a life on its own.

With Hilsman not attending the meeting, the job of arguing for the coup fell to Harriman. He made the case with remarkable restraint, saying only that he did not believe Diem had "the leadership to carry his country through to victory." That was the sum total of the pro-coup

case. On the other side were four of the administration's most senior figures: Attorney General Kennedy, General Taylor, CIA director McCone,
and Secretary of State Rusk. Another dissident, General Paul Harkins,
chief of the American military mission in Saigon, expressed his doubts
in a cable that President Kennedy read aloud at the meeting. One after
another, they anguished over what was about to happen.

ROBERT KENNEDY: I may be a minority, but I don't see that this makes any
sense on the face of it. . . . We're putting the whole future of the country and, really, Southeast Asia, in the hands of somebody we don't
know very well. . . . Maybe it's going to be successful, but I don't think
there's anybody, any reports that I've seen, [indicating] that anybody
has a plan to show where this is going.

TAYLOR: I must say that I agree with the Attorney General at present [and]
would be willing to step further . . . first because you'll have a completely inexperienced government, and secondly because the provincial chiefs, who are so essential to the conduct of the field, will all be
changed, and it's taken us over a year now to develop any truly effective work in that area.

MCCONE: Our opinion is somewhat the same as General Taylor
expressed. . . . A successful coup, in our opinion—I feel very definitely
that's right—would create a period of political confusion, interregnum,
and would seriously affect the war for a period of time which is not
possible to estimate. It might be disastrous.

RUSK: I don't think we ought to put our faith in anybody on the Vietnamese side at this point. . . . I'm skeptical about the likelihood that
the Vietnamese are going to play completely honest with us. . . . I
don't think they owe us that, or think they do, and they're not going
to play with Westerners on that basis. So I think there are problems
here [that] are pretty far-reaching.

HARKINS: I'm not opposed to change, no indeed, but I am inclined to feel
that at this time, the change should be in methods of governing rather
than complete change of personnel. I have seen no batting order proposed by any of the coup groups. I think we should take a hard look at
any proposed list before we make any decisions.

Even the president himself expressed doubts about the project. "If we
miscalculate, we could lose overnight our position in Southeast Asia,"

he mused at one point. Then, speaking of Lodge, he said, "Looks to be his ass. He's for a coup. He's for it, for what he thinks are very good reasons. I say he's much stronger for it than we are here."

After everyone present had spoken his piece, there might have been one logical response. Someone, ideally the president, might have said: We are about to do something hugely important in Vietnam, but what has been said at this meeting raises serious doubts about it. This is our last chance to stop the coup. Should we?

Instead of demanding that his aides give him their precise recommendations, however, Kennedy allowed this meeting to dissolve inconclusively. The miasma of doubt that filled the room remained amorphous and unfocused. No one ever presented a coherent, systematic argument against the coup, nor did Kennedy ever ask to hear one.

"Let's put it all [on] Cabot," he said. "Then you're talking an end to this thing."

With that cryptic, perhaps flippant comment, the coup was finally approved. "What is remarkable about the discussion on October 29, 1963, is that a broad array of top officials voiced doubts about the coup, including JFK himself, without any actual effect on the course of events," the historian and archivist John Prados marveled in his introduction to the published transcript. "President Kennedy does not announce a clear decision, but the group proceeds as if the United States does support the coup."

GENERAL DON HAD PROMISED TO GIVE LODGE FORTY-EIGHT HOURS' NOTICE before striking his blow, but as the date approached, he and the other plotters decided that would be too risky. All he would tell Conein was that he would move before November 2. The precise moment, as it turned out, was chosen by accident.

Early on Friday morning, November 1, the pro-Diem commander of the South Vietnamese navy, Captain Ho Tan Quyen, played a round of tennis with other officers at the Officers' Club in Saigon. It was his thirty-sixth birthday, and his comrades invited him to a meal in celebration. He declined, saying he had to return home to attend to his children, but his deputy persuaded him to change his mind. They set out for a nearby restaurant. Along the way, Captain Quyen's deputy, who was part of the coup plot, shot him dead. This was not part of the plan, but the moment General Minh learned of it, he knew there was no turning back. He had spent several weeks making clandestine contacts within the military and had a variety of infantry, cavalry, and air force units at his disposal. Now he ordered them into action.

As soon as General Don received his orders, he called Conein and asked him to come immediately to the headquarters of the South Vietnamese general staff, and bring with him all the cash he had available. Conein arrived with three million piastres, the equivalent of about $42,000, for food and other expenses; the plotters had not wished to arouse suspicion by raising money in advance. He also brought a radio that put him in direct touch with other CIA officers and, through them, with senior officials in Washington. His first message—"nine, nine, nine, nine, nine"—was a coded confirmation that the coup had begun.

General Don hurriedly summoned all military commanders in the Saigon area to a luncheon at the Officers' Club. When they had assembled, he told them a coup was under way. Each was asked to declare, on tape, his support. Most did. The others were arrested.

As this extraordinary luncheon was taking place, rebel units were fanning through the city. They seized the airport, the police station, two radio stations, the naval headquarters, and the post office complex. Some units were sent to block highways along which loyal troops might arrive from the provinces.

Rebel officers decided to guarantee Diem and Nhu free passage out of the country if they would surrender immediately, but when they telephoned Gia Long Palace, neither would come to the phone. Diem had survived coups before, and thought he could resist this one as well. His first response was to call General Minh for help. Only when he was told that Minh was leading the uprising did he realize its seriousness. He reached General Don, and said he was prepared to announce reforms and name a new cabinet.

"It is too late now," Don replied. "All the troops are moving on the capital."

Diem finally decided to call Ambassador Lodge. The ambassador knew exactly what was happening but pretended he did not. Their conversation was strained to the point of surrealism.

"Some units have made a rebellion," Diem began, "and I want to know: what is the attitude of the United States?"

"I do not feel well enough informed to tell you," Lodge replied disingenuously. "I have heard the shooting, but am not acquainted with all the facts. Also, it is 4:30 AM in Washington, and the U.S. government cannot possibly have a view."

"But you must have some general idea," Diem insisted. "After all, I am a chief of state. I have tried to do my duty. I want to do now what duty and good sense require. I believe in duty above all."

"You have certainly done your duty. As I told you only this morning, I admire your courage and your great contributions to your country. No one can take away from you the credit for all you have done. Now I am worried about your physical safety. I have a report that those in charge of the current activity offer you and your brother safe conduct out of the country if you resign. Had you heard this?"

"No," Diem said. Then he paused for several moments, slowly grasping that Lodge was aligned with the plotters.

"You have my telephone number," he finally said.

"Yes," said Lodge. "If I can do anything for your physical safety, please call me."

At four o'clock the next morning, rebel troops launched their assault on the palace. They fired cannon and machine guns, and were met with return fire from loyal troops inside. After two hours, as dawn broke, a white flag appeared from a palace window. A rebel captain led a squad toward the building to accept Diem's surrender, but, as he approached, a shot rang out from inside and he fell dead. At that outrage, his men stormed the palace. They found neither Diem nor Nhu.

The two brothers had fled to Cholon, the Chinese section of Saigon, and found refuge with a Chinese businessman there. He took them to a clubhouse of the Republican Youth, one of Nhu's strong-arm organizations, and then called the Taiwanese embassy to ask if diplomats there would grant the two leaders asylum. The diplomats refused.

Diem finally realized that the end was at hand. He called General Don and said he was ready to surrender at the Cha Tam Catholic church in Cholon. What he did not know was that several hours earlier, the coup plotters had met to decide his fate. "To kill weeds, you must pull them up at the roots," one of them told the others. No vote was taken, but the consensus was clear.

General Minh chose a squad of trusted men for the job of picking up Diem and Nhu. One of them was his bodyguard, Captain Nguyen Van Nhung, an accomplished assassin. The squad commandeered two jeeps and an M-113 armored troop carrier. As it was setting off, General Minh flashed a hand signal to Captain Nhung. He held up two fingers of his right hand: dispatch them both.

In short order, the convoy reached Cholon and found the church where Diem and Nhu were waiting. The two brothers were ordered into the M-113. Nhu protested.

"You use such a vehicle to drive the President?" he asked indignantly.

No one listened. Both men's hands were tied behind their backs, and they were shoved inside. The convoy sped back toward general staff headquarters.

When it arrived, the door to the M-113 opened and Captain Nhung emerged. Inside, the bodies of Diem and Nhu, riddled with bullets, lay in a pool of blood. Nhu had been stabbed as well as shot. The commander of the squad that captured them, General Mai Huu Xuan, marched directly to Minh, saluted, and reported in French, *"Mission accomplie."* That startled General Don.

"Why are they dead?" Don asked.

"And what does it matter that they are dead?" Minh replied.

Conein was not present when the bodies arrived. Eager to see what was happening in the city, he had taken a drive toward his home. Moments after arriving there, he received a telephone call summoning him to the embassy. There he was given an order that came directly from President Kennedy: find Diem.

At ten-thirty that Saturday morning, Conein arrived back at military headquarters. He found General Minh sitting in the Officers' Club. Without hesitating, he asked where Diem and Nhu were.

"They committed suicide," Minh said smoothly. "They were in the Catholic Church in Cholon, and they committed suicide."

Conein had left this headquarters only a couple of hours earlier, with the impression that the two brothers would be placed under arrest. He was shocked to hear that they were dead.

"Look," he told Minh, "you're a Buddhist, I'm a Catholic. If they committed suicide at that church and the priest holds Mass tonight, that story won't hold water. Where are they?"

"Their bodies are behind general staff headquarters. Do you want to see them?"

"No."

"Why not?"

"Well, if by chance one of a million of the people believe you, that they committed suicide in church, and I see that they have not committed suicide and I know differently, then if it ever leaks out, I am in trouble."

It was a wise move. Conein suspected the truth, and realized that he would be confronted with it if he saw the corpses. Now he could honestly say he had no information other than what the generals had told him. That is what he wrote in his cable to Kennedy.

The president was at a meeting in the Cabinet Room of the White House when Michael Forrestal rushed in with the report that Diem and Nhu were dead. He was stunned. Apparently he had never considered the possibility that the coup might end this way. A head of state who had been an American ally for years, a man Kennedy had personally known and supported, and a fellow Catholic on top of it all, was dead in the wake of an American-backed coup.

"Kennedy leaped to his feet and rushed from the room with a look of shock and dismay on his face which I had never seen before," General Taylor later recalled. "He had always insisted Diem must never suffer more than exile, and had been led to believe or had persuaded himself that a change in government could be carried out without bloodshed."

The CIA soon obtained a set of photos showing the mangled bodies of Diem and his brother, with their hands still tied behind their backs. At a White House staff meeting on the morning of November 4, the president's national security adviser, McGeorge Bundy, warned that the pictures would undoubtedly be on the world's front pages within a day or two. People would draw the obvious conclusion.

"This is not the preferred way to commit suicide," Bundy dryly observed.

Kennedy was disconsolate. The killings in Saigon, Forrestal later said, "troubled him really deeply . . . bothered him as a moral and religious matter, shook his confidence in the kind of advice he was getting from Vietnam." According to the historian Ellen Hammer, he was "shaken and depressed" to realize that "the first Catholic ever to become a Vietnamese chief of state was dead, assassinated as a direct result of a policy authorized by the first American Catholic president." At one point an aide tried to console him by reminding him that Diem and Nhu had been tyrants.

"No," he replied. "They were in a difficult position. They did the best they could for their country."

8

We're Going to Smash Him

Starting at breakfast and ending before dinner on September 15, 1970, a handful of business executives and government officials in Washington did something no Americans had ever done before. In a rapid-fire series of meetings, amid grave warnings about threats to national security, they resolved to overthrow a government that had not yet even taken power. Their victim was to be Salvador Allende Gossens, the incoming president of Chile.

By some standards Chile would seem an odd place for the United States to launch such a risky and violent plot. It is a small country, far from American shores, and has never posed the slightest military threat to the United States. Henry Kissinger once famously dismissed Chile as "a dagger pointed at the heart of Antarctica." Yet when Allende won the presidential election there on September 4, 1970, he set off panic in the corridors of American power. He was a lifelong anti-imperialist and admirer of Fidel Castro who had vowed to nationalize the American-owned companies that dominated his country's economy.

Because Allende did not win a majority of votes cast in the presidential election—36.3 percent in a three-way race—his victory had to be confirmed by the Chilean Congress. In past cases like this, Congress had chosen the first-place finisher, and it seemed certain to do so again. Agustín Edwards, one of Chile's richest men and owner of its largest newspaper, *El Mecurio,* could not abide that possibility. He went to the American embassy in Santiago, the Chilean capital, and put a blunt question to Ambassador Edward Korry.

"Will the U.S. do anything militarily, directly or indirectly?" he asked.

"No," Korry told him simply.

That was not the answer Edwards wanted to hear. He decided to appeal over Korry's head, to more powerful officials in Washington. Their interests, he could sense, coincided with his own.

Edwards was personally, professionally, and ideologically close to most of the leading American executives with interests in Chile. Through them, he had access to the highest circles of the Nixon administration. President Nixon had repeatedly declared his determination to protect American business interests abroad, fight Communism, and suppress challenges to United States hegemony in the Western Hemisphere. Edwards flew to Washington to tell the president that he could do all three in Chile.

On September 9, as Edwards was packing his bags in Santiago, directors of the International Telephone & Telegraph Corporation held their monthly meeting in New York. ITT was one of the world's largest conglomerates. It had large holdings in Chile and faced the same threat that hung over Edwards's business empire. Its prized asset, the Chilean telephone system, was high on Allende's list for nationalization.

During that ITT board meeting, Harold Geneen, the company's chief operating officer and one of the best-known businessmen in the world, took one of the board members aside to make an audacious proposition. "What he told me," the board member later testified, "was that he was prepared to put as much as a million dollars in support of any plan that was adopted by the government for the purpose of bringing about a coalition of the opposition to Allende."

That board member was none other than John McCone, the former CIA director. McCone had joined ITT less than a year after leaving the CIA but remained a consultant to the agency, meaning that he was simultaneously on both payrolls. This unique arrangement made him the ideal link between ITT and the top levels of the United States government.

McCone was able to see Kissinger, the president's national security adviser, immediately to convey Geneen's million-dollar offer. Although Kissinger did not accept it, he was impressed with how seriously ITT was taking the Chile problem. Later McCone also presented his case to his successor and former deputy at the CIA, Richard Helms.

A covert campaign in Chile could not be launched without an order from the president. Edwards undertook to secure that order. As his intermediary, he chose his old friend and business partner Donald Kendall, chairman of the board and chief executive officer of Pepsi-Cola.

He stayed at Kendall's house in Connecticut and told him that Chile was about to fall under Communist rule.

Pepsi-Cola lubricated these relationships. Kendall had hired Nixon to be the company's international legal counsel in the mid-1960s, when Nixon was in the political wilderness, and later became one of his biggest campaign contributors. Edwards, among his many other business ventures, was the principal Pepsi distributor in Chile. All three thrived where international business overlapped with geopolitics.

On September 14, Kendall brought his father to the White House to meet President Nixon. During a break in the socializing, he took Nixon aside and repeated what Edwards had told him about Chile. Nixon focused intensely on his warnings. From that moment, he never wavered in his determination to bring Allende down.

"He had been triggered into action," Kissinger later wrote.

Immediately after hearing from Kendall, Nixon sent him to meet with Kissinger and Attorney General John Mitchell. Kendall urged them to hear what Edwards had to say, and they agreed to meet with him the next morning. Their breakfast conversation would prove to be among the more far-reaching in the history of U.S.–Latin American relations. Edwards painted a dark picture of what was happening in his homeland. He predicted that if Allende was allowed to take office, he would nationalize the Chilean economy, force American businesses out, and steer Chile into the Soviet-Cuban orbit.

Kissinger listened attentively. As soon as the meeting was over, he called Helms and asked him to meet with Edwards to glean "whatever insight he might have" on ways of stopping Allende. Later in the morning, Kissinger met with another powerful figure eager to protect large interests in Chile, his friend and patron David Rockefeller of Chase Manhattan Bank.

At three o'clock that afternoon, Kissinger, Mitchell, and Helms came to the Oval Office to receive Nixon's marching orders. Their meeting lasted only thirteen minutes. Nixon was so explicit that no more time was needed. Under Chilean law, Congress had to certify Allende's election within fifty days after the election. Nixon wanted that somehow to be prevented.

No tape or transcript of this meeting is known to exist. One official who was present, however, later told the *New York Times* that Nixon gave the impression of being "extremely anxious" for quick results. Another described him as "frantic." As the president spoke, Helms scribbled a page of notes that has become a classic document in the history of diplomacy and covert action.

- 1 in 10 chance perhaps, but save Chile!
- worth spending
- not concerned risks involved
- no involvement of embassy
- $10,000,000 available, more if necessary
- full-time job—best men we have
- game plan
- make economy scream
- · 48 hours for plan of action

CHILEANS LIKE TO SAY THAT THEIRS IS "NOT ONE OF THOSE TROPICAL countries." It is part of South America, but its history is proof that geography does not always determine destiny. It has suffered through less anarchy, civil war, and repression than almost any other country in the hemisphere. In the 139 years after its first constitution took effect in 1833, its democratic order was interrupted only three times. Two-thirds of the way through the twentieth century, Chile was well on its way to modernity, with a high literacy rate, a relatively large middle class, and a strong civil society. The democratic approach to life and politics was as deeply woven into the national psyche as anywhere in Latin America.

Most countries whose governments Americans have overthrown possess a valuable resource. Chile is no exception. It is the world's leading producer of copper, which for thousands of years has been one of the world's most prized commodities. Copper shaped the development of the human race, and with the dawn of the electrical age, it became more important than ever because of its excellent conductivity. It is a vital material in motors, generators, dynamos, cables, and wires, and is in everyday use in objects from lamps to doorknobs to teakettles.

At the beginning of the twentieth century, American businesses became interested in Chilean copper. In 1905 the Braden Copper Company, which would later be absorbed into Kennecott Copper Corporation, began mining at El Teniente, a mountain of ore set in the Andes about one hundred miles southeast of Santiago. Seven years later a forerunner of the Anaconda Copper Mining Company began operations at Chuquicamata, in the northern desert.

These two American-owned companies, Kennecott and Anaconda, grew into the twin titans of the world copper business. By midcentury, El Teniente was the largest underground copper mine in the world, and Chuquicamata was the largest open-pit mine. Kennecott's operations in Chile earned an after-tax profit of about $20 million per year. Anaconda's brought in $30 million. Together these two companies accounted for most of Chile's export earnings and a third of its tax revenues. That gave them overwhelming influence over Chilean political as well as economic life.

Besides mining companies and consumer-products companies like Pepsi-Cola, one other American firm, International Telephone and Telegraph, played a major role in Chile. In 1930, when ITT was a cutting-edge telecommunications firm, it bought a majority share of the British-owned Chile Telephone Company, and with it control over the country's burgeoning telephone and telegraph systems. That proved to be one of the best investments it ever made, producing a steady stream of profit that by the early 1960s exceeded $10 million annually.

By that time, change was sweeping across Latin America. Cuban guerrillas overthrew the Batista dictatorship and imposed a radical social and political program. Other dictators fell in Peru, Colombia, Venezuela, and Argentina. A restive young generation cast about for new political ideas.

In 1961, seeking to respond to this challenge, President Kennedy created the Alliance for Progress, a hemispheric organization committed to "comprehensive" social and political change. He asked his aides to look for a country that could be the first Alliance for Progress showcase. It had to be one where a basic political and physical infrastructure was already in place and where people had demonstrated a desire for peaceful change. Chile, with its strong private sector and democratic tradition, was the obvious choice. Kennedy hoped that there, he could show the world that the capitalist model of third-world development worked better than the Marxist one. During the 1960s, Chile received more than $1.2 billion in aid from the Alliance for Progress and directly from the United States, more per capita than any other country in the hemisphere.

At first this attention from Washington brought Chile nothing more than money. Beginning in 1964, it brought something else. That was the year the CIA set out on a decadelong campaign of intervention and destabilization that ultimately tore Chile away from its democratic roots.

The CIA began sending money and other forms of support to

Chilean newspapers, student groups, trade unions, and political parties in the early 1960s. It concentrated its support on the center-left Christian Democratic Party, whose leader, Eduardo Frei, was an ebullient reformer in exactly the right mold to fit Washington's fancy. His good looks and media-conscious style even led reporters and columnists to call him the "Chilean Kennedy." When he ran for president in 1964, his American friends rallied to his side. They did so not just because they liked him but also because they fervently wished to block the Socialist candidate, Allende, who was becoming a nightmare figure for some in Washington.

Allende was the classic bourgeois revolutionary. Although born into privilege, he was a passionate advocate of radical social change. His militancy grew from a combination of Marxist gospel and the realities of life he saw around him. Despite Chile's relatively prosperous position among South American nations, millions of its people lived in desperate poverty, and this genuinely moved Allende. Equally outrageous to him was the fact that foreign companies controlled his country's all-important copper industry.

Horn-rimmed eyeglasses, tweedy jackets, and a slightly raffish mustache gave Allende the air of a college professor or Left Bank intellectual. He was a sophisticate and something of a dandy, a connoisseur of art, wine, and female beauty. His socialist convictions had not prevented him from becoming a pillar of the political establishment. He was also a third-generation Mason—not common for Marxists—and mixed easily with the Chilean elite. In private he could be world-weary, cynical, and even depressive.

The CIA covertly spent $3 million to ensure that Frei would defeat Allende in the 1964 election, paying more than half the cost of his campaign. He won easily. Over the next four years the CIA spent $2 million on covert projects aimed at supporting Frei, along with $175,000 in covert aid to twenty-two candidates who ran for Congress in 1965, nine of whom were elected. It also subsidized an anti-Communist women's group, supported a breakaway faction of the Socialist Party, paid for political organizing campaigns in slums outside Santiago, sponsored dissident groups within the Communist-dominated labor movement, endowed a news wire service and a right-wing weekly newspaper, and regularly placed editorials in *El Mercurio*.

The United States also intensified its long effort to cultivate friends in the Chilean military. Between 1950 and 1969, nearly four thousand

Chilean officers were trained at American military bases, most at the U.S. Army School of the Americas in the Panama Canal Zone, where students learned a rigorous counterinsurgency doctrine that equated Marxism with treason. Chile also received $163 million in American military aid during this period, more than any other country in the hemisphere except Brazil.

All of this overt and covert aid gave the United States a deep stake in Chile. It led some officials to believe that, as in Vietnam, they had purchased the right to guide the course of Chilean politics. Edward Korry, who became the ambassador in 1967, went so far as to assert that the United States had assumed a "fiduciary responsibility" for this country, whose capital was five thousand miles from Washington.

United States policy toward Chile, and indeed toward all of Latin America, changed dramatically after Richard Nixon assumed the presidency in January 1969. Nixon disdained the Alliance for Progress, partly because of its association with Kennedy and partly because he considered it a dangerous triumph of idealism over reality. He feared that by promoting reform, especially land redistribution, it would undermine right-wing governments that were friendly to the United States. Rather than encourage Latin America's "democratic left," as Kennedy and Johnson had tried to do, he would support its business elite and military.

"I will never agree with the policy of downgrading the military in Latin America," Nixon told one meeting of the National Security Council. "They are power centers subject to our influence. The others, the intellectuals, are not subject to our influence."

In 1970, Allende ran for president not as the candidate of his own Socialist Party, which was too weak to win on its own, but at the head of a leftist coalition called Popular Unity. The challenge of keeping him out of power came to obsess the American embassy in Santiago. Early in 1970, Ambassador Korry and his CIA station chief, Henry Hecksher, asked the Nixon administration for permission to embark on a covert "spoiling" campaign to block him. They addressed their request to the "40 Committee," named after the number of the presidential directive that created it, which was composed of the country's top national security officials. Kissinger effectively ran the committee; when he proposed an action, the others approved. His old friend David Rockefeller, whose Chase Manhattan Bank had multibillion-dollar interests in South America, urged him to press ahead with the "spoiling" campaign.

As the Chilean election approached, Rockefeller recalled in his memoir, he made a telephone call that helped push the Nixon administration onto its anti-Allende course.

> In March 1970, well before the election, my friend Agustín (Doonie) Edwards, publisher of *El Mercurio,* Chile's leading newspaper, told me Allende was a Soviet dupe who would destroy Chile's fragile economy and extend Communist influence in the region. If Allende won, Doonie warned, Chile would become another Cuba, a satellite of the Soviet Union. He insisted that the United States must prevent Allende's election. Doonie's concerns were so intense that I put him in touch with Henry Kissinger.

Kissinger would be more directly responsible for what happened in Chile than any other American, with the possible exception of Nixon himself. For three years, during which he dealt with a host of crises around the world, he never lost interest in Chile. That was because Nixon pressed him relentlessly, and also because the anti-Allende project fit perfectly with his view of the world and of America's place in it.

From his background as a refugee from Nazi Germany, Kissinger took the lesson that a statesman's transcendent goal must always be to establish and maintain stability among nations. He wrote his doctoral dissertation on Prince Metternich, the nineteenth-century Austrian diplomat who was one of the modern world's master practitioners of big-power diplomacy. Once in office, he applied some of Metternich's ideas. He projected American power through regional allies like Iran, Zaire, and Indonesia, and turned a blind eye as dictators in those countries oppressed and looted with abandon. One of his longtime associates, Lawrence Eagleburger, concluded that he was guided by principles that "are antithetical to the American experience."

"Americans tend to want to pursue a set of moral principles," Eagleburger asserted. "Henry does not have an intrinsic feel for the American political system, and he does not start with the same values and assumptions."

During his long career, Kissinger, like many statesmen of his generation, had paid almost no attention to Latin America. In the spring of 1969, he visited the Chilean embassy in Washington and bluntly told the ambassador, "I am not interested in, nor do I know anything about, the southern portion of the world from the Pyrenees on down." A year later, he heard from Edwards and everything changed.

On March 25, 1970, the "40 Committee" approved the "spoiling" campaign against Allende with a budget of $135,000, later increased to $390,000. It was a smaller-scale version of the multimillion-dollar effort the CIA had launched to prevent Allende from winning in 1964. Agents dusted off many of the same tactics, from planting propaganda in the press to supporting anti-Communist "civic action" groups. Some printed and distributed posters showing Soviet tanks on the streets of Prague. Others opened tendentious news agencies, sowed discord within Popular Unity, and produced anti-Allende books, pamphlets, and leaflets.

As the presidential campaign intensified in Chile, Harold Geneen, the ITT chairman, decided to try to influence its outcome. He asked McCone to arrange for him to meet William Broe, the CIA's chief of covert operations in the Western Hemisphere. They met in the ITT suite at the Sheraton Carlton Hotel in Washington on July 16. Geneen said his company wanted to use the CIA as a conduit to pass money to the campaign of Jorge Alessandri, the rightist presidential candidate. Broe suggested that the company make its contribution directly, and with help from CIA officers in Santiago, it did. ITT covertly donated $350,000 to the Alessandri campaign and arranged for other American businesses to donate another $350,000.

Although the CIA's "spoiling" campaign and the large contributions that American companies made to Alessandri may have had some effect, it was not enough. On September 4, 1970, Chilean voters went to the polls and gave Allende his victory by plurality. Such outcomes were not unusual in Chile's multiparty political system, and Congress had a long-established tradition of choosing the first-place finisher as president. That was what President Nixon, on the afternoon of September 15, ordered Kissinger and Helms to prevent.

"The president came down very hard that he wanted something done, and he didn't much care how, and that he was prepared to make money available," Helms later testified. "This was a pretty all-inclusive order. . . . If I ever carried a marshal's baton in my knapsack out of the Oval Office, it was that day."

NIXON ORDERED THE CIA TO PRODUCE AN ANTI-ALLENDE PLAN WITHIN forty-eight hours, so Helms had no time to waste. Early the next morning, September 16, 1970, he met with his covert action specialists. He told them, according to one participant, "that President Nixon had decided that an Allende regime in Chile was unacceptable to the United States"; that Nixon had "asked the Agency to prevent Allende from coming to power or to unseat him"; and that, in a break from normal practice, "the Agency is to carry out this mission without coordination from the Department of State or Defense."

The next day, while Helms and his operatives were working to design this covert operation, Kissinger told a group of newspaper editors in Chicago that if Allende was allowed to take power, he would establish "some sort of Communist government" that would cause "massive problems" for the United States. He returned to Washington that afternoon and at eight-thirty the next morning convened a meeting of the 40 Committee to hear the CIA's proposal. As Helms outlined it, the anti-Allende operation would have two parts. The first, called Track I, was aimed at blocking Allende by "legal" means. It was immediately implemented, and led to the placement of dozens of articles in the Chilean press warning of disaster if Allende became president. Its principal focus was the outgoing president, Eduardo Frei. The CIA hoped that its press campaign, together with private mailings to Frei and orchestrated pressure on him from political confidants, would lead him to call on Congress to break with Chilean tradition and deny the presidency to the candidate who had won the most popular votes.

This approach failed, largely because President Frei was, as one CIA cable put it, a "too gentle soul" and unwilling to support the disruption of his country's political system. Within a few weeks, Track I became subsumed in a far more ambitious project the CIA called Track II, which aimed explicitly at fomenting a military coup. Plotters at CIA headquarters in Langley, Virginia, directed their agents in Santiago to begin "probing for military possibilities to thwart Allende" and to look for ways of "strengthening the resolve of the Chilean military to act against Allende."

"Contact the military and let them know USG [the United States government] wants a military solution and that we will support them now and later," one cable said. "In sum, we want you to sponsor a military move which can take place, to the extent possible, in a climate of economic and political uncertainty."

To create that climate, the Americans needed to push Chile toward chaos. Kissinger set out to do so, using all of the considerable resources at his command. He justified this effort with what became one of his most-quoted maxims. "I don't see why we need to stand by and watch a country go Communist due to the irresponsibility of its own people," he told his fellow plotters.

As this project was taking shape, several diplomats and CIA officers who learned of it expressed serious doubts. A National Security Study Memorandum produced at Kissinger's direction concluded that "the U.S. has no vital national interests within Chile" and "the world military balance of power would not be significantly altered by an Allende government." Henry Hecksher, chief of the CIA station in Santiago, who had worked on the covert campaign to deny the election to Allende, reported that with the election now over, he would "not consider any kind of intervention in the constitutional processes desirable." Another CIA officer wrote in a memo that Allende was not likely to take orders from Moscow or Havana and that plotting against him would be "repeating the errors we made in 1959 and 1960 when we drove Fidel Castro into the Soviet camp." Assistant Secretary of State Charles Meyer predicted that covert action against Allende would "further tarnish America's image in Latin America." Kissinger's chief adviser on Latin America, Viron Vaky, warned him that the consequences of striking against Allende "could be disastrous."

> What we propose is patently a violation of our own principles and policy tenets. Moralism aside, this has practical operational consequences. . . .
> If these principles have any meaning, we normally depart from them only to meet the gravest threat to us, e.g. to our survival. Is Allende a mortal threat to the U.S.? It is hard to argue this.

These doubters did not realize how fiercely determined Nixon and Kissinger were to block Allende. Their warnings had no effect on the coup plotters in Washington. One of them, David Atlee Phillips, was out to overthrow his second Latin American government.

Phillips, who had run the highly successful "Voice of Liberation" radio campaign during the 1954 coup against President Jacobo Arbenz of Guatemala, became codirector of the CIA's newly formed Chile Task Force. His partner was William Broe. The two of them were in almost hourly contact with the CIA station in Santiago, under what one official later called "constant, constant pressure" from the White House.

As the American plot against Allende began to take shape, Phillips and Broe sent a lengthy cable to their agents in Santiago. It directed

The first foreign leader to be overthrown with the collaboration of American officials was Queen Liliuokalani of
Hawaii.

A few dozen sugar planters and descendants of missionaries, led by the firebrand
lawyer Lorrin Thurston *(left)*, staged Hawaii's modest "revolution" in 1893. The
queen's forces could not suppress it because the American minister in Honolulu,
John L. Stevens *(right)*, immediately recognized the insurgent regime and called
American soldiers ashore to defend it.

President William McKinley *(left)* and his successor, Theodore Roosevelt, presided over the first burst of American expansionism. Roosevelt called his critics "futile sentimentalists of the international arbitration type" who exhibited "a flabby type of character which eats away at the great fighting features of our race."

I'LL SAVE YOU!

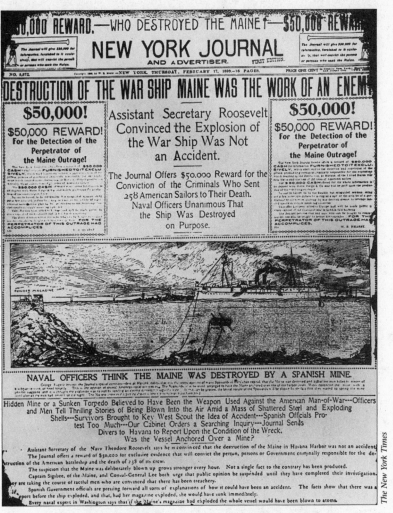

More than 250 American soldiers and sailors were killed when the warship *Maine* exploded in Havana harbor on February 15, 1898. Most Americans, inflamed by a wave of sensationalist newspaper reports, blamed Spain for the explosion. President McKinley seized on this passion to declare the war against Spain that turned Cuba into an American protectorate. Historians now believe the *Maine* was destroyed not by hostile action, but by an accident inside the ship.

American soldiers won the Spanish-American War in a single day of heavy combat, July 1, 1898. One of the decisive battles was for the town of El Caney, near the Cuban port of Santiago.

In Puerto Rico, Americans crushed the elected government of Luis Muñoz Rivera. He later condemned the American takeover "because none of the promises were kept, and because our present condition is that of serfs attached to conquered territory."

The Cuban nationalist leader Jose Martí inspired his country's revolution against Spain, but also wished "to prevent, by the independence of Cuba, the United States from spreading over the West Indies and falling, with that added weight, upon other lands of our America."

After the United States seized the Philippines in 1898, Emilio Aguinaldo led thousands of poorly armed rebels in a resistance war.

Senator Henry Cabot Lodge defended the use of harsh tactics, including torture, against Filipinos and other "semi-civilized people."

American troops fought rebels in the Philippines for three and a half years. More than 4,000 Americans and 35,000 Filipinos were killed.

President José Santos Zelaya was the most formidable leader Nicaragua ever had. His attempts to regulate American mining and lumber companies, and his insistence on seeking loans from European rather than American banks, led the United States to overthrow him in 1909.

The American commander who directed this operation, Major Smedley Butler, later wrote that he "helped pacify Nicaragua for the international banking house of Brown Brothers."

Soon after Zelaya was overthrown, the United States helped place Adolfo Díaz, chief accountant for the American-owned La Luz Mining Company, in the Nicaraguan presidency. He allowed American advisers, like the two standing behind him in this photo, to guide his government.

In 1911 President Miguel Dávila of Honduras *(above)*, was overthrown in an operation staged jointly by the United States Navy and a band of rebels led by the flamboyant American mercenary Lee Christmas *(right)*.

Central America's most powerful banana planter, Sam Zemurray, financed the Honduran revolution and was rewarded with vast tracts of the country's most fertile land.

During the Cold War, American leaders used the CIA to depose elected governments. The first two of these operations, in Iran and Guatemala, were carried out on orders from President Dwight Eisenhower *(left)* and his secretary of state, John Foster Dulles.

Allen Dulles, the secretary of state's younger brother, was director of the CIA.

The CIA staged its first coup in Iran, where Prime Minister Mohammad Mossadegh had nationalized his country's oil industry. Mobs paid by the CIA rampaged through Tehran in the summer of 1953.

After the coup, Mossadegh was arrested, placed on trial, and found guilty of treason. He spent three years in prison and the rest of his life under house arrest.

The CIA placed Mohammed Reza Shah back on the Peacock Throne. His repressive rule set off the Islamic revolution of 1979.

President Jacobo Arbenz of Guatemala promoted a land reform program that benefited thousands of impoverished peasants. It outraged the United Fruit Company, which Secretary of State Dulles had represented during his years as a corporate lawyer.

American officials portrayed Arbenz as a tool of the Soviets. In 1954 CIA pilots bombed targets in Guatemala, among them Fort Matamoros, an important military base in the capital.

CIA pilots also dropped leaflets like this one, which says: "Fight for God, Fatherland, Freedom, Work, Truth, Justice. Fight against Communist atheism, Communist interventionism, Communist oppression, Communist poverty, Communist lies, Communist police."

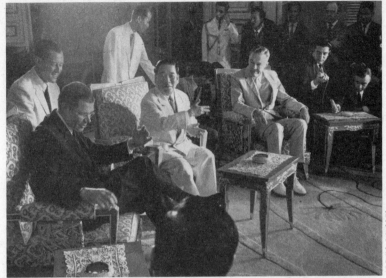

American officials played a key role in making Ngo Dinh Diem president of South Vietnam. In September 1963, Secretary of Defense Robert McNamara *(left)* and United States Ambassador Henry Cabot Lodge *(right)* assured Diem of continued American support. Lodge was named after his grandfather, who had strongly promoted the extension of United States power overseas.

Diem refused to promise the Americans that he would not negotiate with communist-led insurgents. Six weeks after his meeting with McNamara and Lodge, he was overthrown and killed.

On December 4, 1972, President Salvador Allende of Chile told the United Nations General Assembly that his country would "no longer tolerate the subordination implied by having more than eighty percent of its exports in the hands of a small group of large foreign companies."

Nine months after his appearance at the U.N., Allende was overthrown in a coup. He spent his final hours at La Moneda, the presidential palace, which was bombed by rebel planes.

Secretary of State Henry Kissinger, who played an important role in promoting the Chilean coup, met afterward with the country's new leader, General Augusto Pinochet.

Courtesy Ronald Reagan Library

President Ronald Reagan was playing golf in Augusta, Georgia, when political violence broke out on the Caribbean island of Grenada. His national security adviser, Robert McFarlane *(left)*, and Secretary of State George Shultz awoke him before dawn on October 22, 1983, to discuss the crisis. He quickly decided to send troops to depose the new regime.

The New York Times

The upheaval in Grenada began when a militant faction ordered the imprisonment and execution of Prime Minister Maurice Bishop.

American soldiers found little resistance on the tiny island, and quickly arrested members of the clique that had ordered Bishop's death.

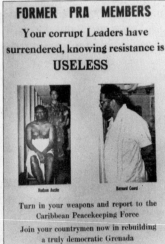

FORMER PRA MEMBERS
Your corrupt Leaders have surrendered, knowing resistance is
USELESS

Hudson Austin   Bernard Coard

Turn in your weapons and report to the Caribbean Peacekeeping Force
Join your countrymen now in rebuilding a truly democratic Grenada

George Tames/The New York Times

AP/Wide World Photos

General Manuel Antonio Noriega of Panama was on the CIA payroll for nearly thirty years. Despite his deep involvement in the drug trade, many American leaders considered him a valuable ally. Vice President George H. W. Bush met with him in 1983.

Alan Riding/The New York Times

Noriega's nemesis was a crusading doctor, Hugo Spadafora. Soon after Spadafora began denouncing Noriega as a corrupt and violent drug trafficker, he was captured, brought to a Panamanian military base, and tortured to death.

AP/Wide World Photos

In 1989, after Bush became president, he turned against Noriega and ordered American troops to invade Panama and overthrow him. During the invasion, large areas of the capital were devastated.

The guerrilla commander Abdul Haq *(right)* was among the few secular, pro-Western warlords in Afghanistan, but he was also fiercely independent. Because he told Americans that he would never "be your puppet," the CIA refused to support him.

After terrorists directed from Afghanistan attacked the United States on September 11, 2001, President George W. Bush resolved to overthrow the Taliban regime there. Rather than send American troops, he subcontracted this war to fighters from an Afghan militia, the Northern Alliance.

Corbis

American troops who invaded Iraq in 2003 met almost no resistance as they sped across the desert toward Baghdad. After the Americans deposed dictator Saddam Hussein and seized his palace complexes, their victory seemed complete.

Iraqi News Agency

United States Marine Corps

Iraq soon erupted in violence. Insurgents killed thousands of American soldiers, and drew them into a bitter campaign that cost tens of thousands of Iraqi lives and left towns like Fallujah in ruins.

them to use three tools—"economic warfare," "political warfare," and "psychological warfare"—to create a "coup climate" and a "pretext or flash point for action."

> Sensitize feeling within and without Chile that election of Allende is a nefarious development for Chile, Latin America, and the world. . . . Surface ineluctable conclusion that military coup is the only answer. . . . Key is psych war within Chile. The station should employ every stratagem, every ploy, however bizarre, to create this internal resistance. Prop war should become sharper and more provocative. . . . Public and provocative rallies should be held, growing in size and intensity until the Communists must react. . . . If we are successful in heightening tension through the three main lines noted above, the pretext will, in all probability, present itself.

Agents in Santiago understood this message perfectly well. "You have asked us to provoke chaos in Chile," Hecksher cabled back to headquarters. "We provide you with formula for chaos, which is unlikely to be bloodless."

Over the next several weeks, the political climate in Chile became increasingly tense. Newspapers and radio stations, including several that the CIA was subsidizing, denounced Allende and warned graphically of the horrors his government would surely bring. A fascist-oriented group, Fatherland and Liberty, which had received $38,500 from the CIA, staged a rally in Santiago. CIA agents quietly contacted nearly two dozen Chilean military officers, and those who seemed open to the idea of staging a coup, according to a later report of the United States Congress, "were given assurances of strong support at the highest levels of the U.S. government both before and after the coup."

A centerpiece of this operation, which bore the CIA cryptonym FUBELT, apparently a reference to the tightening of a belt around Chile, was the disruption of Chile's economy. Helms wrote in a memo to Kissinger that since "a suddenly disastrous economic situation would be the most logical pretext for a military move," the United States should work to create "at least a mini-crisis." It had many ways to do so. In cables to Washington, Ambassador Korry suggested that American banks be pressured to stop granting short-term credits to Chilean businesses; that agents spread rumors of impending food rationing, bank collapses, and nonexistent plans by Allende to seize private homes and forbid technicians from leaving the country; and that American companies in Chile "foot-drag to the maximum extent possible" in filling orders for spare parts.

"Not a nut or a bolt will be allowed to reach Chile under Allende," Korry warned Minister of Defense Sergio Ossa in a meeting shortly after the election. "We shall do all within our power to condemn Chile and the Chilean people to utmost deprivation and poverty."

It is a tribute to the Chilean political system that despite all the CIA's efforts, FUBELT failed. Neither President Frei nor members of Congress from anti-Allende parties could be persuaded that the threat Allende posed was great enough to require a break with Chile's democratic tradition. As for the idea of promoting a military coup, only a few officers were sympathetic, and they had no realistic hope of success because General René Schneider, the army commander, was fiercely opposed to military interference in politics. For a coup to succeed, Ambassador Korry cabled his superiors in Washington, "General Schneider would have to be neutralized, by displacement if necessary."

In late September the Americans began to focus on Schneider as a key obstacle to their plan. "Anything we or Station can do to effect the removal of Schneider?" CIA planners asked in a cable to Henry Hecksher. "We know this [is a] rhetorical question, but want to inspire thoughts on both ends on this matter."

After receiving that message, American agents in Santiago began meeting with disgruntled Chilean officers. The most enthusiastic was a retired general named Roberto Viaux, an extreme anti-Communist who had been cashiered from the army after leading an abortive uprising against President Frei. During mid-October, CIA agents in Santiago passed Viaux $20,000 in cash to keep him "financially lubricated" with enough money "to buy arms, bribe arsenal commanders to provide arms, or to acquire them in any fashion he can."

On October 13, with less than two weeks remaining before the Chilean Congress was scheduled to install Allende, President Nixon summoned his national security team to the White House and demanded action. According to one participant in the meeting, Nixon "went out of his way to impress all of those there with his conviction that it was absolutely essential that the election of Mr. Allende to the presidency be thwarted." He was frustrated that Korry seemed unable to arrange this, and summoned the ambassador to the White House on October 15.

"That son of a bitch, that son of a bitch!" Nixon was saying to himself, pounding one of his fists into a palm, as Korry entered the Oval Office. When he looked up and saw Korry's startled expression, he composed himself.

"Not you, Mr. Ambassador," he said. "It's that son of a bitch Allende. We're going to smash him."

That afternoon at four-thirty, Kissinger met with Tom Karamessines, the CIA's director of covert operations, to discuss their Chile project. What happened at this meeting has been the subject of considerable debate. Kissinger later claimed that he "turned off" the plot against General Schneider and "called off Track II before it was ever implemented." Minutes of the meeting, however, record no such action. They say that Kissinger approved a decision "to de-fuse the Viaux plot, at least temporarily," but also mention that he authorized a remarkably encouraging message to the general.

"Preserve your assets," the message said. "The time will come when you with all your friends can do something. You will continue to have our support."

After that meeting, Karamessines sent a cable to the CIA station in Santiago reiterating the administration's "firm and continuing policy that Allende be overthrown in a coup." To implement that policy, the cable said, agents in Santiago should use "propaganda, black operations, surfacing of intelligence or disinformation, personal contacts, or anything else your imagination can conjure." The cable also directed agents to wish General Viaux and another group of rebellious officers, headed by General Camilo Valenzuela, "maximum good fortune."

Soon the CIA sent these officers more than good wishes. The bounty came inside a diplomatic pouch that arrived at Arturo Merino Airport, in Santiago, on October 21. It was a package containing three submachine guns, several boxes of ammunition, and six tear gas grenades.

The plot reached its climax two days later. At two o'clock in the morning, on a dead-silent street, Colonel Paul Wimert, the United States military attaché in Santiago, delivered the weapons to Chilean conspirators aligned with Viaux. Six hours later, while General Schneider was on his way to work, a jeep struck his chauffeur-driven car. Five men surrounded it. One smashed the rear window with a sledgehammer. Accounts differ on whether or not Schneider drew his pistol to defend himself, but his assailants opened fire, using weapons of their own rather than those the CIA had supplied. They hit Schneider with three shots. He died at a hospital soon afterward.

"Station has done an excellent job of guiding Chileans to a point where a military solution is at least an option for them," CIA planners in Washington cabled their Santiago agents after hearing of the assassination. "[Station Chief and others involved] are commended for accomplishing this under extremely difficult and delicate circumstances."

The idea behind this murder was that it would set off a wave of instability that would allow anti-Allende officers to stage a coup. It had the opposite effect. This was the first murder of an important Chilean political figure in more than a century, and instead of throwing Chileans into panic and inducing them to call for authoritarian rule, it outraged them. It strengthened the conviction of soldiers and civilians alike that democracy must be allowed to take its course, meaning that Allende should become president. Responding to this consensus, the Chilean Congress met on October 24 and, by a vote of 153 to 24, certified his election. He was inaugurated on November 4.

"We know as much about U.S. policy making toward Chile for the period from September to November 1970 as we do about policy making in any period in recent American history," the political scientist Paul Sigmund has written. "It is a controversial period and one that does not do credit to American ideals, since it includes an effort to prevent a freely elected president from taking office by fomenting a military coup; the assassination of a Chilean general, for which the United States was indirectly responsible; authorization, though not execution, of efforts to bribe the Chilean Congress; subsidization of a quasi-fascist extreme rightist group; and improperly close relationships between the U.S. government and a major corporation."

AT NINE-FORTY ON THE MORNING OF NOVEMBER 6, 1970, JUST TWO DAYS after Allende donned the presidential sash in Santiago, President Nixon convened the National Security Council to discuss ways of deposing him. No one questioned the assumption that this was a wise and necessary thing to do. In fact, there was remarkable unanimity.

"We want to do it right, and bring him down," Secretary of State William Rogers began. "We can put an economic squeeze on him."

"I agree with Bill Rogers," said Secretary of Defense Melvin Laird. "We have to do everything we can to hurt him and bring him down."

After listening to his aides agree with him, Nixon delivered a trenchant monologue explaining why he considered Allende such a threat. It hardly tells the whole story of why he was so intent on carrying out this coup but offers clear insight into his thinking. It is as close as Nixon ever came to explaining why he did it, and an impressive example of the classic realpolitik that was one of his diplomatic hallmarks.

The main concern in Chile is that [Allende] can consolidate himself, and the picture projected to the world will be his success. . . . If we let the potential leaders in South America think they can move like Chile and have it both ways, we will be in trouble. I want to work on this. And on military relations, put in more money. On the economic side we want to give him cold turkey. . . . We'll be very cool and very correct, but doing those things which will be a real message to Allende and others. . . .

Latin America is not gone, and we want to keep it. . . . No impression should be permitted in Latin America that they can get away with this, that it's safe to go this way.

With this declaration, Nixon made clear that there would be no letup in the campaign against Allende. The CIA had already drawn up a plan, headed "Allende After the Inauguration," that proposed the campaign's thesis. It said that if Chile was to suffer "continued economic decline," the country might fall into chaos and "the military would have justification for intervening." Within days of the inauguration, Americans set out to create that justification.

The first blows they struck were economic. Two principal American foreign aid agencies, the Export-Import Bank and the Agency for International Development, acting under classified instructions from the National Security Council, announced that they would no longer approve "any new commitments of U.S. bilateral assistance to Chile." Then the United States representative at the Inter-American Development Bank was instructed to block all proposals for loans to Chile. When the bank's president protested, the administration forced his resignation. The new president reduced Chile's credit rating from B to D. Private banks followed suit, and the Export-Import Bank, citing the reduction, canceled a scheduled $21 million loan intended to pay for new Boeing jets for Chile's national airline. At the World Bank, the American representative arranged for the suspension of a $21 million livestock-improvement loan to Chile, and then announced that the United States would oppose all new World Bank lending to that country.

The cutting of aid, loans, and credits to Chile became known as an "invisible blockade," but it was relatively straightforward. It certainly fell within the right of the United States, or any country, to apportion its aid as it sees fit. Not all of the American campaign against Allende, however, was as straightforward. Between 1970 and 1973, the CIA carried out a wide-ranging series of covert operations in Chile. The historian and archivist Peter Kornbluh has catalogued them.

> More than $3.5 million was funneled into opposition parties and allied organizations. . . . Station operatives conducted a $2 million propaganda campaign, concentrating on Chile's largest newspaper, *El Mercurio*. More than $1.5 million was passed to business, labor, civic and paramilitary organizations organizing protests, demonstrations and violent actions against Allende's administration.

Soon after Allende's inauguration, most of the leading American companies active in Chile, including ITT, Kennecott, Anaconda, Firestone Tire & Rubber, Bethlehem Steel, Charles Pfizer, W. R. Grace, Bank of America, Ralston Purina, and Dow Chemical, joined to form a Chile Ad Hoc Committee. It was dedicated, according to a memorandum prepared after its first meeting, to working with officials in Washington who were "handling the Chile problem." Over the next few months, its members set out on a quiet destabilization campaign of their own that included office closings, delayed payments, slow deliveries, and credit denial. It was so effective that within two years, one-third of Chile's buses and 20 percent of its taxis were out of service due to lack of spare parts.

On July 11, 1971, the Chilean Congress, meeting in joint session, unanimously approved a constitutional amendment authorizing the nationalization of Kennecott, Anaconda, and the smaller Cerro Mining Corporation. Allende proclaimed that the date would henceforth be "National Dignity Day," and to celebrate the first one, he came to El Teniente. In a triumphant speech to a throng of cheering miners, he accused Kennecott and Anaconda of having made immorally high profits in Chile while masses of Chileans lived in poverty. He did not encourage the companies to hope for much in the way of compensation.

"We will pay it if it is just," he promised. "We will not pay what is not just."

Allende later announced that he considered an annual profit of 12 percent per year to be "rightful," and anything higher to be "excessive." By that standard, Cerro, which had been mining in Chile for barely a year and had yet to turn a profit, was guiltless; Chile's comptroller awarded it compensation of $14 million. For Kennecott and Anaconda, though, the situation was quite different. According to Allende's formula, they had made $774 million in excess profit over the past fifteen years. He asked the comptroller to deduct that sum from their due compensation. The comptroller agreed, and since $774 million was more than the book value of their mines, Kennecott and Anaconda were not awarded a cent.

"We used to be the fucker," one of Anaconda's lawyers lamented. "Now we're the fuckee."

Soon after taking this momentous step, the Allende government took another one, assuming management control of the ITT-owned Compania de Teléfonos de Chile. Two days later, ITT's vice president for Washington relations, William Merriam, sent the White House an eighteen-point list of steps it could take to ensure that Allende would not "get through the crucial next six months." Merriam confidently predicted that if these measures were adopted, they would push Chile to "economic chaos."

As Allende was trying to withstand the American campaign, he also faced intense pressure from groups of workers and peasants whose revolutionary passion he had helped to awaken. His rhetoric led many of them to dream of a new social order in which they would enjoy higher wages, better housing, and other amenities of the good life. They pushed him relentlessly toward radicalism, as did militant Chilean leftists who took up their cause. Among them were radicals who embraced Che Guevara's theory that the only way to bring social justice to Latin America was to repress traditional ruling classes, using violence if necessary. Some carried out armed actions, often clashing with police or rightist paramilitary bands. Others led illegal invasions of farms and factories. Allende repeatedly condemned these radicals, ridiculing their "infantile revolutionary ideas" and urging them to devote their energy not to revolution but to "changing Chile's institutions." Yet because they were fellow leftists, he was not willing to crack down on them, and some Chileans blamed him for their excesses.

Although Allende could never move quickly enough to satisfy his most radical supporters, his march toward socialism horrified other Chileans and helped polarize the country. At the same time, the United States was engaged in a multilayered campaign against him. These two forms of pressure—internal and external—reinforced each other and pulled Chile into a downward spiral.

The anti-Allende project had been under way for more than a year when the secrecy surrounding it was spectacularly breached. A muck-raking Washington newspaper columnist, Jack Anderson, obtained twenty-four internal ITT memos that graphically detailed what Anderson called the company's "bizarre plot to stop the 1970 election of left-ist Chilean President Salvador Allende." They told of ITT's offer of $1 million to help the CIA prevent Allende from coming to power; its regular contacts with the CIA, the National Security Council, and the State Department; and its many efforts to "exert pressure on Allende," push Chile to "economic collapse," and bring about "an internal crisis requiring military intervention."

"No one can dream that we are going to pay even half a cent to this multi-national company that was on the verge of plunging Chile into civil war," President Allende declared after the memos were published. Many Americans were equally outraged. "How could it be so—if it is so—that in 1970 an American President could consider the possibility of acting to prevent a democratically elected president of a supposedly friendly country from taking office?" the *Washington Post* asked in an editorial.

Nixon and his aides sought to play down the importance of the "ITT Papers," but the scandal did not fade away. The Senate Foreign Relations Committee established a subcommittee to hold hearings. In its final report, the subcommittee condemned Allende for his nationalization policies but was even harsher on ITT.

> ITT sought to engage the CIA in a plan covertly to manipulate the outcome of the Chilean presidential election. In so doing, the company overstepped the line of acceptable corporate behavior. If ITT's actions in seeking to enlist the CIA for its purposes with respect to Chile were to be sanctioned as normal and acceptable, no country would welcome the presence of multinational corporations.

By the end of 1972, Allende's divisive policies and the American destabilization campaign had combined to throw Chile into grave crisis. Street disturbances became so regular that Allende was forced to replace his police chief and his interior minister. Shopkeepers and truckers staged crippling strikes. Food became scarce. Several cities were put under temporary states of emergency. Against this backdrop, Allende arrived in New York to address the United Nations.

Twenty-one years earlier, Prime Minister Mohammad Mossadegh of Iran had come to the United Nations to present his case against a foreign corporation that controlled his country's basic resource. Allende was in a similar position. His country was a victim of the resource curse, just as Iran had been. The riches that lay beneath their soil came under the control of foreign corporations, and when they tried to reclaim those riches, great powers came down upon them.

At eleven o'clock on the morning of December 4, 1972, after a brief meeting with George H. W. Bush, the American ambassador to the United Nations, Allende strode to the General Assembly podium. His speech eerily echoed Mossadegh's, showing how little the relationships between large corporations and small countries had changed over the course of two decades. Both leaders had come to the UN to fire a volley in what Allende called "the battle in defense of natural resources."

> Our economy could no longer tolerate the subordination implied by having more than eighty percent of its exports in the hands of a small group of large foreign companies that have always put their interests ahead of those of the countries where they make their profits. . . .
>
> These same firms exploited Chilean copper for many years, made more than four billion dollars in profit in the last forty-two years alone, while their initial investments were less than thirty million. . . . My country, Chile, would have been totally transformed by that four billion dollars. . . .
>
> We find ourselves opposed by forces that operate in the shadows, without a flag, with powerful weapons, from positions of great influence. . . . We are potentially rich countries, yet we live in poverty. We go here and there, begging for credits and aid, yet we are great exporters of capital. It is a classic paradox of the capitalist economic system.

In Washington, Nixon was overhauling his Chile team. He had already replaced Ambassador Korry with another career diplomat, Nathaniel Davis, who had been serving in Guatemala. After Allende's United Nations speech, he decided to replace Richard Helms, the CIA director. According to some accounts, he was displeased that Helms had failed to bring Allende down.

To smooth Helms's fall, Nixon named him ambassador to Iran. At his confirmation hearing he blithely replied "No, sir" when asked if the CIA had tried to block the election of Allende in 1970. That two-word statement later led a federal court to convict him of perjury. He called his conviction "a badge of honor."

When Nixon was sworn in for a second term as president, on January 20, 1973, his campaign against Allende was reaching its crescendo. Chilean military commanders prepared to step in and strike the final blow. At every step, their CIA friends urged them on.

"We should attempt [to] induce as much of the military as possible, if not all, to take over and displace the Allende govt," CIA plotters in Langley directed the Santiago station. "The creation of a renewed atmosphere of political unrest and controlled crisis must be achieved in order to stimulate serious consideration for intervention on part of the military."

On April 10, the CIA directed its Santiago station to begin "accelerated efforts against the military target." Three weeks later, the chief of the agency's Western Hemisphere division, Theodore Shackley, told the station to "bring our influence to bear on key military commanders so that they might play a decisive role on the side of the coup forces." These efforts came to premature fruition on June 29, when a handful of officers staged a confused coup that involved tanks stopping for traffic lights as they made their way through Santiago. It was the first time in forty-two years that Chilean soldiers had struck against an elected government. No senior officer supported the uprising, and General Carlos Prats, the army commander, suppressed it easily. Still, it set nerves on edge.

As military conspirators prepared to strike against Allende, they faced the same problem that had confronted them three years before. The army commander, General Prats, successor to the murdered Schneider, was a strict constitutionalist, dedicated to supporting the elected government. That made him a serious obstacle to the plot.

"Only way to remove Prats would appear to be by abduction or assassination," CIA agents in Santiago reported in a cable to Langley.

Allende, in a desperate attempt to head off the inevitable, had begun naming military commanders to his cabinet, and by midsummer of 1973 General Prats was minister of the interior. After Prats crushed the tank revolt in June, *El Mercurio* began a campaign depicting him as treasonably pro-Communist. One day, several hundred wives of Chilean officers, encouraged by CIA operatives, convened in front of his home, supposedly to give his wife a letter protesting his support for Allende.

The gathering erupted into violence, and the national police (called Carabineros) used tear gas to break it up. General Prats was shaken. He asked his fellow generals for a vote of confidence. When they refused, he had no alternative but to resign. He recommended that President Allende name his deputy to replace him, and Allende followed his advice. The new man was General Augusto Pinochet, whom the CIA, according to one of its reports, knew to be a friend.

> Pinochet, previously the strict constitutionalist, reluctantly admitted he now harboring second thoughts: that Allende must be forced to step down or be eliminated ("only alternatives"). . . . Pinochet was in Panama [and] while in Panama, talked with more junior U.S. officers he knew from days at School of the Americas, and was told U.S. will support coup against Allende "with whatever means necessary" when time comes.

Although the CIA had noticed Pinochet's growing willingness to consider the idea of a coup, his colleagues in Chile had not. President Allende and General Prats considered him to be supremely apolitical and not especially ambitious. Both would pay dearly for their miscalculation.

While CIA operatives in Santiago were helping to orchestrate the removal of General Prats, the "40 Committee" was at work in Washington. On August 20 it approved another $1 million for the destabilization campaign in Chile, to be used specifically as subsidies to opposition political parties. That, by the CIA's own reckoning, brought to $6.5 million the total it had spent on covert action against Allende during his presidency. An investigation by the United States Senate later put the figure at $8 million, "with over three million dollars expended in fiscal year 1972 alone."

As the Southern Hemisphere winter drew to an end, the final act in Allende's drama began to unfold. The departure of General Prats, as a Defense Intelligence Agency memo put it, "removed the main mitigating factor against a coup." CIA agents reported to Langley that "the army is united behind a coup, and key Santiago regimental commanders have pledged their support." Truckers staged another nationwide strike, supported in part by CIA funds, and, as a result, basic foodstuffs had to be rationed while produce and grain rotted in warehouses. Bus drivers, taxi drivers, and employees of the Santiago waterworks also struck. Meat became unavailable in Santiago. Basic products like coffee, tea, and sugar were ever harder to find. Allende's naval aide-de-camp was assassinated. Prices raged out of control. Electric power became unreliable. Antigovernment gangs in the countryside dynamited roads, tunnels, and bridges. Finally, on September 9, 1973, a CIA agent named Jack Devine sent his superiors the news they had been awaiting for nearly three years.

"A coup attempt will be initiated on September 11," Devine wrote in a cable. "All three branches of the armed forces, and the *Caribineros,* are involved in this action. A declaration will be read on *Radio Agricultura* at 7 A.M. on 11 September. The *Carabineros* will have the responsibility of seizing President Allende."

AT A BIRTHDAY PARTY FOR GENERAL PINOCHET'S YOUNGER DAUGHTER, ON September 9, Chilean officers made their final decision to strike against President Allende. While the celebrants were playing, Pinochet took one of the guests, General Gustavo Leigh, commander of the Chilean air force, to another part of the house. Waiting for them were two admirals bearing a letter from a senior navy commander, Admiral José Merino. The letter said the navy was ready. So were the army and the air force.

The officers considered several possible dates for the coup. Pinochet said it didn't matter to him, since he had prepared his plan so carefully that all he needed to do was "push a button" and it would be carried out. They chose Tuesday, September 11. Leigh wrote the word "Agreed" on the back of Admiral Merino's letter and signed his name. Then Pinochet signed his name and affixed his seal.

"In this way," Ambassador Davis later wrote, "the decision was made final that the military services would overthrow the government of Chile."

Allende spent these frantic days working on a last-gasp proposal to call a national plebiscite on his rule. Late on the night of September 10, his supporters at the port of Valparaíso noticed unusual naval maneuvers. Then, at one-thirty in the morning, he himself received a message about infantry movements north of Santiago. The night editor of the Communist newspaper *El Siglo* heard enough to rip up his front page. He replaced the planned banner headline, "Plebiscite Will Take Place," with a more urgent one.

"Everyone to Their Combat Posts!" the new headline screamed.

The coup proceeded methodically, just as Pinochet had predicted.

Soldiers across the country had been called to duty at four o'clock that morning, and soon afterward they began securing radio stations, town halls, police stations, and other centers of power. Valparaíso came into rebel hands at seven o'clock, and Concepción, the country's third largest city, followed at eight-fifteen. No shot was fired in either place.

Allende learned of these developments by telephone at his official residence. His bodyguards had made elaborate plans to defend the residence in such an emergency, but he decided not to stay there. He wanted to make his last stand at La Moneda, the presidential palace and traditional seat of Chilean democracy.

A convoy of four blue Fiats and a pickup truck screeched to a halt in front of La Moneda at seven-thirty on the morning of September 11. President Allende was among the first to emerge. Around him were twenty-three bodyguards, each carrying an automatic rifle. The squad also shared two .30 caliber machine guns and three bazookas. Allende carried a Kalashnikov that Fidel Castro had given him. It bore the inscription "To My Friend and Comrade in Arms, Salvador."

The men raced inside. Allende called them briefly together and told them he had resolved to die in La Moneda if necessary. As he was deploying them around the building, Radio Agricultura, a voice of the opposition, interrupted its programming to read a proclamation announcing the coup.

> Bearing in mind first the very grave economic, social and moral crisis that is destroying the country; second, the inability of the government to adopt measures to stop the spread of chaos; and third, the constant increase of armed paramilitary groups . . . the Chilean armed forces and *Carabineros* are united in the historic mission of fighting to liberate the fatherland from the Marxist yoke, and to restore order and constitutional rule.

Soon afterward, Allende took a telephone call from one of the rebel commanders. They had decided to offer him free passage out of the country if he would resign. Allende refused. He probably could not have escaped in any case, since according to tape recordings that surfaced years later, Pinochet was planning to shoot his plane down before it left Chilean airspace. At around nine o'clock he stepped onto the balcony for a final, forlorn look over Constitution Square. Half an hour later, through a makeshift radio hookup, he addressed his last words to his people.

I will not resign. I will not do it. I am ready to resist by all means, even at the cost of my own life. . . . Foreign capital—imperialism united with reaction—created the climate for the army to break with their tradition. . . . Long live Chile! Long live the people! These are my last words. I am sure that my sacrifice will not be in vain. I am sure it will be at least a moral lesson, and a rebuke to crime, cowardice and treason.

Soon after Allende delivered his impassioned farewell, infantry units began advancing on the palace under cover of artillery fire. Defenders fired back, and men on both sides fell. Shortly before noon, two British-made Hawker Hunter fighters roared out of the sky. They swooped down and fired at the palace, striking so accurately—one missile flew right through the palace's main door—that some theorists later suggested that the pilots must have been Americans. Eighteen rockets hit the old building, which burst into flames. Inside, the air filled with smoke and fumes.

Soon after 1:30, as infantrymen finally reached the flaming palace, a group of politicians and doctors who had been inside edged out under a white flag. The infantrymen crashed past them onto the ground floor of La Moneda. By one account, their commander shouted upstairs for Allende to surrender. According to another, Pinochet himself made the final demand, by telephone. What is certain is that Allende refused. By midafternoon, the shooting was over.

"Mission accomplished," General Javier Palacios, who led the assault, reported to his superiors by radio at 2:45. "Moneda taken. President dead."

9

A Graveyard Smell

A CIA officer who called himself Abe was one of the first people David Atlee Phillips met after he reported for duty at Langley, Virginia, in the autumn of 1970. Phillips, a veteran covert operative, had been chosen to help run the CIA's subversive campaign against President-elect Salvador Allende of Chile. Abe briefed him on the plan, which was to sow chaos for a few weeks in the hope of setting off a revolution or military coup. Phillips, who had edited a newspaper in Chile and knew the country well, said he doubted the wisdom of trying to block Allende's rise to power and, besides that, didn't think it could be done. To his surprise, Abe agreed with him.

"I don't understand," Phillips said. "Why should we be doing this, especially when we believe it won't work?"

"Understand?" Abe mused in reply, taking off his bifocals and polishing them. "Some time ago, I returned with Dick Helms from a meeting downtown. On the way back the car was tied up in traffic almost half an hour, and Helms and I talked about the assignment he had just been given. I ended by saying to Helms, 'I don't understand.' Well, you know what Helms said? He looked at me and said, 'Abe, there's something I've had to learn to understand. I've had to learn to understand presidents.' So I guess you don't really need to understand, as long as you understand what the President ordered."

The coups in Iran, Guatemala, South Vietnam, and Chile were all "what the President ordered." They were not rogue operations. Presidents, cabinet secretaries, national security advisers, and CIA directors approved them, authorized by the 1947 law that created the CIA and assigned it "duties related to intelligence affecting the national security." The first thing all four of these coups have in common is that American leaders promoted them consciously, willfully, deliberately, and in strict accordance with the laws of the United States.

"The finger should have been pointed at presidents, and not the intelligence group," Senator Barry Goldwater of Arizona complained after the CIA was vilified for fomenting these coups.

Their second common feature is that in all four cases, the United States played the decisive role in a regime's fall. It did not simply give insurgents tacit encouragement or discreet advice. American agents engaged in complex, well-financed campaigns to bring down the governments of Iran, Guatemala, South Vietnam, and Chile. None would have fallen—certainly not in the same way or at the same time—if Washington had not acted as it did.

Each of these four coups was launched against a government that was reasonably democratic (with the arguable exception of South Vietnam), and each ultimately led to the installation of a repressive dictatorship. They could be seen as at least temporary Cold War victories for the United States, which at the time seemed quite significant. Beyond that, however, it is hard to see them as successful. Part of the reason is that after the Americans won their victories, they proved unable or unwilling to control the regimes they helped install. The United States devoted enormous amounts of time, energy, and money to plots against elected governments but very little to ensuring that the new regimes were democratic or responsive to the needs of their people. Whatever else these operations may have been, they were not victories for democracy. They led to the fall of leaders who embraced American ideals, and the imposition of others who detested everything Americans hold dear.

The reason was straightforward. When people in countries like Iran, Guatemala, South Vietnam, and Chile were free to speak, many criticized the United States and supported political movements that placed their own national interests ahead of those of outside powers. Once these critical voices were forcibly silenced, Americans were able to believe that anti-American feelings had disappeared. The truth was quite different. Those feelings festered and became steadily more intense.

Soon after the coup in Guatemala, Ambassador John Peurifoy appeared before a congressional committee in Washington. In a single pithy sentence, he explained why the United States so resolutely opposed nationalist regimes in developing countries. "Communism is directed by the Kremlin all over the world," he said, "and anyone who thinks differently doesn't know what he is talking about."

That conviction was widely shared in Washington during the Cold War. Presidents and others had no doubt the Soviets were manipulating Mossadegh, Arbenz, and Allende. That turned out to have been wrong. The three leaders had differing views of Marxism—Mossadegh detested it, Arbenz sympathized with it, Allende embraced it—but they were nationalists above all. Each was driven mainly by a desire to recover control over natural resources, not to serve world Communism, as Americans believed. Why did the United States so misjudge them?

The experiences of the first half of the twentieth century deeply shaped generations of American leaders. Bolshevism triumphed in Russia, and then the Nazis tried to conquer the world. Once Nazism was defeated, the Soviet Union began subduing countries in Eastern Europe. In the minds of many Americans, Soviet Communism assumed the role Nazism had played, that of a fanatic ideology bent relentlessly on world domination.

Also still vivid in the Western imagination was the disastrous policy of appeasement that European powers had used during the 1930s in an effort to avoid conflict with the Nazis. Appeasement gave a deceitful enemy time to prepare for an aggressive war. Its failure taught Americans of the World War II generation that some enemies must be ruthlessly opposed. That was certainly true of the Nazis. It may even have been true of international Communism. The great error Americans made was not in overestimating the Soviet threat but in assuming that nationalist challenges were part of it.

"There is a graveyard smell to Chile, the fumes of democracy in decomposition," Ambassador Edward Korry, who as a young journalist had covered Soviet takeovers in Eastern Europe, wrote in a cable as Allende was taking power. "They stank in my nostrils in Czechoslovakia in 1948, and they are no less sickening today."

American leaders were convinced that the Soviets were plotting to take over Asia and Latin America the way they had taken over Eastern Europe. That has proven wrong. Shattered by war, the Soviets had strategic reasons to want buffer states in Eastern Europe. They were less interested in dominating faraway places. No historical evidence has ever emerged to support the Americans' conviction that they were planning to subvert or seize Iran in the 1950s. They were not manipulating or even paying attention to the Arbenz government in Guatemala. The North Vietnamese regime and the National Liberation Front were not their puppets. In Chile, far from goading Allende toward radicalism, they and the Chinese repeatedly urged him to act more moderately.

American leaders might be forgiven for intervening in countries about which they were so ignorant. What is harder to justify is their refusal to listen to their own intelligence agents. The chiefs of the CIA stations in Tehran, Guatemala City, Saigon, and Santiago explicitly warned against staging the coups. Officials in Washington paid no heed. They rejected or ignored all intelligence reports that contradicted what they instinctively believed.

Americans who think about and make foreign policy have traditionally been Eurocentric. Most of what they understand about the world comes from their knowledge of European history and diplomatic tradition. They grasp the nature of alliances, big-power rivalries, and wars of conquest. The passionate desire of people in poor countries to assert control over their natural resources, however, has never been an issue in Europe. This hugely powerful phenomenon, which pushed developing countries into conflict with the United States during the Cold War, lay completely outside the experience of most American leaders. Henry Kissinger spoke for them, eloquently as always, after Chilean foreign minister Gabriel Valdés accused him of knowing nothing about the Southern Hemisphere.

"No, and I don't care," Kissinger replied. "Nothing important can come from the South. History has never been produced in the South. The axis of history starts in Moscow, goes to Bonn, crosses over to Washington and then goes to Tokyo. What happens in the South is of no importance."

This attitude made it easy for powerful Americans to misunderstand why nationalist movements arose in Iran, Guatemala, South Vietnam, and Chile. Behind these movements, they saw only the hand of Moscow. That made intervention seem almost a form of self-defense.

In 1954, President Eisenhower secretly named James Doolittle, a celebrated air force general who had retired and become a Shell Oil executive, to conduct "a comprehensive study of covert activities of the Central Intelligence Agency." In his confidential report, Doolittle concluded that because the Soviet threat was so profound, the United States must fight back with no quarter.

> It is now clear that we are facing an implacable enemy whose avowed objective is world domination by whatever means and at whatever cost. There are no rules in such a game. Hitherto acceptable norms of human

conduct do not apply. If the United States is to survive, longstanding American concepts of "fair play" must be reconsidered. We must develop effective espionage and counter-espionage services and must learn to subvert, sabotage and destroy our enemies by more clever, more sophisticated and more effective methods than those used against us.

Doolittle's view of the Soviet threat was not more extreme than that of many others in Washington. It had an eminently rational basis. In the late 1940s and early 1950s, the Soviets brazenly intervened to impose pro-Moscow regimes on unwilling nations in Eastern Europe. At the same time, nationalist movements in Asia, Africa, and Latin America began challenging the power of Western corporations and governments. American leaders had no doubt that these two developments were part of a single plan devised by the Soviets. They saw upheaval in the developing world through the lens of their European experiences.

John Foster Dulles, Henry Kissinger, and others who shaped United States foreign policy during the Cold War were utterly uninterested in the details of life in individual countries, and cared not the slightest whether the regimes that ruled them were dictatorships, democracies, or something in between. Their world was defined by a single fact, the Cold War confrontation between Moscow and Washington. Nations existed for them not as entities with unique histories, cultures, and challenges but as battlegrounds in a global life-or-death struggle. All that mattered was how vigorously each country supported the United States and opposed the Soviet Union.

Dulles was tragically mistaken in his view that the Kremlin lay behind the emergence of nationalism in the developing world. He could at least, however, claim consistency in his uncompromising opposition to every nationalist, leftist, or Marxist regime on earth. Nixon and Kissinger could not. While they were working obsessively to force Salvador Allende from power—and while they supported anti-Communist dictators from Paraguay to Bangladesh—they were building realistic, cooperative relationships with the Soviet Union and China. The sophisticated pragmatism that guided them in their policy of détente did not extend to countries that were far less threatening to the United States. When they faced challenges from weak, vulnerable nations like Chile, they reacted with blind emotion rather than the cool assessment of long-term interest that guided their approach to Moscow and Beijing.

. . .

AFTER THE 1953 COUP IN IRAN, THE TRIUMPHANT SHAH ORDERED THE execution of several dozen military officers and student leaders who had been closely associated with Mohammad Mossadegh, and also of Hussein Fatemi, Mossadegh's foreign minister. Soon afterward, with help from the CIA and the Israeli intelligence agency, Mossad, the shah created a secret police force called Savak, which became infamous for its brutality. Among its most notorious directors was General Nematollah Nassiri, who as a colonel had played an important role in Operation Ajax.

It would have been too risky for the shah to order Mossadegh executed. Instead he arranged for the old man to be tried for treason and found guilty. Mossadegh was sentenced to three years in prison and the rest of his life under house arrest in his home village of Ahmad Abad. He served his sentence in full and died in 1967, at the age of eighty-five.

Once the shah was back on his throne, he moved to consolidate his power. The first obstacle he faced was Prime Minister Fazlollah Zahedi. Like Mossadegh, Zahedi was a strong figure who believed that prime ministers, not kings, should run Iran. He clashed repeatedly with the shah. Ultimately he lost their confrontation, and took a diplomatic post in Switzerland. From that moment, the shah was free to shape Iran as he wished.

He did so in close cooperation with the United States, which became Iran's most important political, economic, and military partner. This alliance greatly strengthened his government, but it also embittered many Iranians who had long considered the United States a beacon of democracy. The role of the United States in overthrowing Mossadegh and its long, uncritical embrace of the shah led to the rise of anti-Americanism, a new phenomenon in Iran.

"When Mossadegh and Persia started basic reforms, we became alarmed," wrote Supreme Court Justice William O. Douglas, who visited Iran both before and after the coup. "We united with the British to destroy him; we succeeded; and ever since, our name has not been an honored one in the Middle East."

One of the first tangible benefits the United States reaped from Operation Ajax was a share of Iran's oil wealth. The British expected that once Mossadegh was gone, the Anglo-Iranian Oil Company, which they renamed British Petroleum, would resume its old monopoly. To John Foster Dulles, though, that seemed unfair. Americans had, after all, done the dirty work in Iran, and he believed they deserved some compensation.

Dulles commissioned his old law firm, Sullivan & Cromwell, to work out a new arrangement. Under its provisions, British Petroleum ended up with 40 percent of the shares in the new National Iranian Oil Company, American companies received 40 percent, and the remainder was divided among European companies. This consortium agreed to share its profits with Iran on a fifty-fifty basis. In the end, then, the British wound up with considerably less than they would have had if they had accepted Iran's demand for an equal share of oil profits in the late 1940s.

The main results of the 1953 coup were the end of democracy in Iran and the emergence, in its place, of a royal dictatorship that, a quarter of a century later, set off a bitterly anti-American revolution. "Operation Ajax locked the United States into a special relationship with the Shah and signaled the powerful entrance of American intelligence and military activity into Iran," the historian James A. Bill concluded. "The US intervention alienated important generations of Iranians from America, and was the first fundamental step in the eventual rupture of Iranian-American relations in the revolution of 1978–79."

The shah did not tolerate dissent and repressed opposition newspapers, political parties, trade unions, and civic groups. As a result, the only place Iranian dissidents could find a home was in mosques and religious schools, many of which were controlled by obscurantist clerics. Through their uncompromising resistance to the regime, these clerics won the popular support that secular figures never achieved. That made it all but inevitable that when revolution finally broke out in Iran, clerics would lead it.

After the 1953 coup, diplomats and intelligence agents at the American embassy in Tehran fell into the habit of relying for information almost exclusively on the royal court. As a result, they were blind to the growing threat in Iran. In the summer of 1977, as a broad coalition of antishah groups launched its historic challenge to his regime, the CIA predicted, in a confidential assessment, that "the Shah will be an active participant in Iranian life well into the 1980s . . . and there will be no radical changes in Iranian political behavior in the near future."

John F. Kennedy had prodded the shah to change his ways, but the shah outlasted him. Subsequent presidents were happy to take his money and encourage his excesses. Richard Nixon, who with Secretary of State Henry Kissinger developed a strategy of cooperating with dictators who allowed their countries to be used as platforms for the projection of American power, made him an ally. In 1975 Gerald Ford and Kissinger received him in the White House. Two years later, Jimmy Carter did the same.

"If ever there was a country which has blossomed forth under enlightened leadership," Carter said in his banquet toast to the shah, "it would be the ancient empire of Persia."

Soon after that banquet, angry crowds began surging through the streets of Tehran and other Iranian cities crying "Death to the American shah!" That amazed many in the United States. Worse shocks lay ahead! The cleric who emerged as the revolution's guiding figure, Ayatollah Ruhollah Khomeini, turned out to be bitterly anti-Western. His movement became so powerful that at the beginning of 1979, it forced the shah to flee into exile. A few months later, the new Khomeini regime sanctioned the seizure of the United States embassy in Tehran and the taking of American diplomats as hostage.

The hostage crisis deeply humiliated the United States, destroyed Jimmy Carter's presidency, and turned millions of Americans into Iran haters. Because most Americans did not know what the United States had done to Iran in 1953, few had any idea why Iranians were so angry at the country they called "the great Satan."

Years later, one of the Iranian militants involved in the embassy takeover wrote an article explaining why he and his comrades had carried it out. It was, he said, a delayed reaction to Operation Ajax, when CIA agents working inside the American embassy staged a coup that brought the shah back to power after he had fled the country.

"Such was to be our fate again, we were convinced, and it would be irreversible," the former militant recalled. "We now had to reverse the irreversible."

Like many American "regime change" operations, Operation Ajax seemed like a success at first. The United States rid itself of a government it did not like and imposed one that it did. Mohammad Reza Shah, the restored ruler, was loyally pro-American and warmly welcomed Gulf, Standard Oil of New Jersey, Texaco, and Mobil to Iran.

From the vantage point of history, however, this operation had tragic long-term results. It brought Iran under the shah's harsh rule for a quarter of a century. His repression ultimately set off a revolution that brought radical fundamentalists to power. Not satisfied with the humiliation they visited on the United States by holding fifty-four American diplomats hostage for fourteen months, these radicals sponsored deadly acts of terror against Western targets, among them a United States Marines barracks in Saudi Arabia and a Jewish community center in Argentina. Their example inspired Muslim fanatics around the world, including in neighboring Afghanistan, where the Taliban gave sanctuary to militants who carried out devastating attacks against the United States on September 11, 2001. None of this, as one Iranian diplomat wrote half a century after Operation Ajax, might have happened if Mossadegh had not been overthrown.

> It is a reasonable argument that but for the coup, Iran would be a mature democracy. So traumatic was the coup's legacy that when the Shah finally departed in 1979, many Iranians feared a repetition of 1953, which was one of the motivations for the student seizure of the US embassy. The hostage crisis, in turn, precipitated the Iraqi invasion of Iran, while the [Islamic] revolution itself played a part in the Soviet decision to invade Afghanistan. A lot of history, in short, flowed from a single week in Tehran. . . .
>
> The 1953 coup and its consequences [were] the starting point for the political alignments in today's Middle East and inner Asia. With hindsight, can anyone say the Islamic Revolution of 1979 was inevitable? Or did it only become so once the aspirations of the Iranian people were temporarily expunged in 1953?

GUATEMALA IS A FAR SMALLER, WEAKER, AND MORE ISOLATED COUNTRY THAN Iran, but the leader the United States imposed after the 1954 coup, Colonel Carlos Castillo Armas, followed a repressive course much like the shah's. During his first weeks in power, he abolished the banana workers' federation, revoked the Agrarian Reform Law, banned all political parties and peasant groups, and ordered the arrest of thousands of suspected leftists. His secret police chief, who had held the same office under the former dictator Jorge Ubico, outlawed subversive literature, specifically including all works by Dostoyevsky and Victor Hugo. With this burst of repression, the foundation was laid for a police state that plunged Guatemala into bloody tragedy over the following decades.

On October 10, 1954, Castillo Armas summoned Guatemalan voters to the polls. There was one question on the ballot: "Are you in favor of Lieutenant Colonel Carlos Castillo Armas continuing in the Presidency of the Republic for a term to be fixed by the Constituent Assembly?" According to official results, there were 485,531 votes in favor and just 393 opposed.

Castillo Armas was not an especially bright or honest man, and in the years after the coup he became enmeshed in webs of corruption and intrigue. On the evening of July 27, 1957, as he walked down a corridor toward dinner at his official residence, he was shot dead. Seconds later, someone killed the assassin. There was no serious investigation.

An even sadder end awaited Jacobo Arbenz. The man who directed his overthrow, John Foster Dulles, was determined to convince the world that Arbenz had been a Communist all along, and wished him to settle in a Soviet-bloc country. He did everything he could to push Arbenz to that choice. First he arranged for Mexico to send the former president packing. From there Arbenz traveled to Switzerland, where as the son of a Swiss emigrant he was entitled to citizenship. Under American pressure, however, the Swiss found a way to deny him his birthright. Then he moved to Paris, where in a newspaper interview he mused about a possible return to power. His French visa was not renewed. Finally he landed in Prague, just the kind of place Dulles wanted him to choose. He was unhappy there. In the years that followed, ever more depressed, he drifted to Uruguay, Cuba, and back to Mexico. On January 27, 1971, he drowned in a bathtub at his apartment in Mexico City. He was fifty-eight years old.

Despite what Dulles and his comrades believed, American security in no way required Arbenz's overthrow. He was universally expected to step down at the end of his term, in 1957, and several candidates—all more moderate—were already maneuvering to succeed him. Yet he was a passionate reformer, and he fell because his reforms, in the historian Richard Immerman's words, "could not be translated into the Cold War vocabulary of absolutes."

Dulles concluded that he had to destroy the Arbenz government for two reasons: because it was molesting United Fruit and because it seemed to be leading Guatemala out of the American orbit and toward Communism. Historians have argued over which of these motives was more important. The most likely truth is that they merged completely in Dulles's mind. Each reinforced and proved the other.

Four decades after the coup, the CIA hired an independent historian, Nick Cullather, to examine long-secret documents about Operation Success and write a full account of it. After an exhaustive investigation,

Cullather concluded that the United States had overthrown the government of a country about which it knew almost nothing.

> [American] officials had only a dim idea of what had occurred in Guatemala before Jacobo Arbenz Guzmán came to power in 1950. Historians regard the events of the 1940s and 1950s as following a centuries-old cycle of progressive change and conservative reaction, but officers in the [CIA] Directorate of Plans believed they were witnessing something new. For the first time, Communists had targeted a country "in America's backyard" for subversion and transformation into a "denied area." When comparing what they saw to past experience, they were more apt to draw parallels to Korea, Russia or Eastern Europe than to Central America. They saw events not in a Guatemalan context, but as part of a global pattern of Communist activity.

Many Guatemalans were naturally outraged by the coup, and after it became clear that democracy would not return to their country on its own, some turned to revolution. In 1960, groups of soldiers and young officers seized two mid-size barracks in a coordinated uprising. Government forces suppressed it, but some rebel officers took to the hills and joined with peasants to form guerrilla bands. Later a general who had been Arbenz's defense minister formed another rebel group. In the heady months and years after Fidel Castro seized power in Cuba, thousands of Guatemalans took up arms against their government.

To combat this threat, the Guatemalan army used such brutal tactics that all normal political life in the country ceased. Death squads roamed with impunity, chasing down and murdering politicians, union organizers, student activists, and peasant leaders. Thousands of people were kidnapped by what newspapers called "unknown men dressed in civilian clothes" and never seen again. Many were tortured to death on military bases. In the countryside, soldiers rampaged through villages, massacring Mayan Indians by the hundreds. This repression raged for three decades, and during that period, soldiers killed more civilians in Guatemala than in the rest of the hemisphere combined.

Between 1960 and 1990, the United States provided Guatemala with hundreds of millions of dollars in military aid. Americans trained and armed the Guatemalan army and police, sent Green Beret teams to accompany soldiers on antiguerrilla missions, and dispatched planes from the Panama Canal Zone to drop napalm on suspected guerrilla hideouts. In 1968, guerrillas responded by killing two American military advisers and the United States ambassador to Guatemala, John Gordon Mein.

This bloodiest of all modern Latin American wars would not have broken out if not for Operation Success. During the decade when Guatemalans lived under democratic rule, they had legal and political ways to resolve national conflicts. After dictatorship settled over the country, all space for political debate was closed. Tensions that would have been manageable in a democratic society exploded into civil war.

The coup in Guatemala had another effect that, like many consequences of "regime change" operations, did not become clear until years later. During the Arbenz years, scores of curious Latin American leftists gravitated to Guatemala. One of them was a young Argentine doctor named Che Guevara. After the coup, Guevara flew to Mexico. There he met the Cuban revolutionary Fidel Castro. They discussed the events in Guatemala at great length, and from them drew a lesson that has reverberated through all of subsequent Latin America history.

Operation Success taught Cuban revolutionaries—and those from many other countries—that the United States would not accept democratic nationalism in Latin America. It gave them a decisive push toward radicalism. They resolved that once in power, they would not work with existing institutions, as Arbenz had done. Instead they would abolish the army, close Congress, decapitate the landholding class, and expel foreign-owned corporations.

"Cuba is not Guatemala!" Castro liked to shout when he taunted the United States for its inability to overthrow him during the 1960s.

Oddly enough, one of the losers in Operation Success was United Fruit, the company that had drawn Americans into Guatemala in the first place. Sam Zemurray, the visionary who dominated United Fruit for so long, was ailing—he died in 1961—and without him, the company seemed to lose its edge. Its profits fell and it became mired in antitrust litigation, which it finally resolved by surrendering some of its holdings in Guatemala. In 1972, after shifting many of its banana interests to other countries, it sold what remained to Del Monte. By then United Fruit had become part of the United Brands conglomerate, and when United Brands president and board chairman Eli Black killed himself in 1975 as federal prosecutors prepared to indict him for fraud and other crimes, his act mirrored the violence that was part of the company's legacy in Guatemala.

In 1996, under the auspices of the United Nations, Guatemalan military commanders and guerrilla leaders signed a peace treaty. That did little to resolve the huge inequalities of life in Guatemala, where two percent of the people still own half the arable land, but it did end a long, horrific wave of government repression. It also led to the establishment of a Commission on Historical Clarification that was assigned to study the violence and its causes. The commission's report put the number of dead at over 200,000, and said soldiers had killed 93 percent of them.

"Until the mid-1980s, the United States government and U.S. private companies exercised pressure to maintain the country's archaic and unjust socioeconomic structure," the report concluded. They had done that and more. One who seemed to grasp the dimensions of American responsibility for the horror that enveloped Guatemala was President Bill Clinton, who visited the country a few days after the historical commission issued its report.

"For the United States," Clinton told a gathering of civic leaders in Guatemala City, "it is important that I state clearly that support for military forces and intelligence units which engaged in violence and widespread repression was wrong, and the United States must not repeat that mistake."

THE 1963 COUP IN SOUTH VIETNAM HAD A PROFOUND EFFECT IN WASHINGton. It led many policy makers to believe that the United States had assumed a new level of responsibility for South Vietnam. If the idea of pulling American troops out had seemed crazy before the coup, it was even more so afterward. No one, Undersecretary of Defense William Bundy said, could now consider "withdrawing with the task unfinished."

Several of the men involved in planning the coup later came to consider it tragically misbegotten. General Maxwell Taylor wrote in his memoir that from the perspective of history, it could only be seen as "a disaster, a national disaster." Edward Landsdale said it was "a terrible, stupid thing." William Colby, chief of CIA covert actions in East Asia and later director of the agency, called it the "worst mistake of the Vietnam War."

The Americans who approved Diem's overthrow did so because they were determined to win the Vietnam War, and concluded that Diem was an obstacle to victory. After all, some of them told themselves, Diem was an American creation in the first place, and since the United

States had installed him in power, it should have the right to depose him when he proved unmanageable. Distasteful as that course was, it saved Kennedy and his aides from having to face the deeper question of whether the war was winnable at all.

This does not, however, explain how the coup plot took on such momentum in the late summer and fall of 1963. Even some of the men who allowed it to go forward admitted later that they could not understand how it happened. "Nobody was behind it," Robert Kennedy marveled in 1965. "Nobody knew what we were going to do. Nobody knew what our policy was. It hadn't been discussed."

President Kennedy told several of his friends that if he was reelected in 1964, he would pull American troops out of South Vietnam. Whether he would have done so must remain forever unknown. On November 22, just twenty days after Diem was assassinated, Kennedy suffered the same fate. Later that week in Washington, the new president, Lyndon Johnson, showed Senator Hubert Humphrey a portrait of Diem that was hanging on his wall.

"We had a hand in killing him," Johnson said. "Now it's happening here."

General Duong Van Minh, who carried out the coup, succeeded Diem as president of South Vietnam, with General Tran Van Don as minister of defense. Their government was torn by internecine feuds, many of them stemming from anger over the executions of Diem and Ngo Dinh Nhu. It never managed to consolidate itself. After holding power for just three months, it was overthrown in another coup. After that, a succession of military strongmen ruled South Vietnam. Two of them, Generals Nguyen Cao Ky and Nguyen Van Thieu, had played important roles in the 1963 coup.

During the mid-1960s, President Johnson escalated the American commitment to South Vietnam until more than half a million American soldiers were on duty there. The Vietnam War destroyed Johnson's presidency and profoundly shook American society. It ended on April 30, 1975, with ignominious defeat for the United States. A total of 58,168 Americans lost their lives waging it. The Vietnamese toll was far heavier.

Diem's overthrow was a key turning point in the Vietnam War because it drew the United States across a line of commitment. It gave powerful Americans the sense that they had developed a blood bond with South Vietnam, or incurred a debt they needed to repay. "Amer-

ica's responsibility for Diem's death haunted U.S. leaders during the years ahead, prompting them to assume a larger burden in Vietnam," Stanley Karnow wrote. Another historian, Howard Jones, called the coup "President Kennedy's central tragedy."

> His action set the administration on a path that tied the United States more closely to Vietnam, furthered the Communists' revolutionary war strategy by igniting political chaos in Saigon, and obstructed his plan to bring the troops home. . . . Kennedy's legacy was a highly volatile situation in Vietnam that, in the hands of a new leader seeking victory, lay open to full-scale military escalation. President Johnson soon Americanized the war that resulted in the death of a generation.

One intriguing question the coup raises is whether it was simply a step toward the inevitable doom of the American project in Vietnam, or whether it could have been a turning point. With Diem gone, the United States might have encouraged the formation of a broad-based civilian government. Instead, it kept strongmen in power and charged ahead with its war effort. Robert Shaplen, who covered Vietnam for *The New Yorker,* is among those who have wondered what might have been.

> I have always blamed the Americans in part for the failure of the November 1–2 coup d'état to be anything more than just that—it certainly did not lead to a legitimate revolution and it lacked any direction. The Americans had supported the violent change, but neither Washington nor the embassy had any sound ideas about fostering a strong new government that, in the time-worn phrase, would "capture the hearts and minds" of the people. The big war was still ahead, and the United States, having missed an opportunity after the fall of Diem either to get out of Vietnam or to help establish a firmer civilian political structure and a more broadly based economy, became more and more deeply embroiled in an unfolding tragedy.

John Foster Dulles was long dead by the time the United States suffered its final humiliation in Vietnam, but he had had a hand in it. His refusal to negotiate at Geneva in 1954, based on his mistaken view of world Communism, set the tragedy in motion. According to one biography, this was "the most bizarre performance of his Secretaryship. . . .

It created consternation in Paris and London and contributed anew to the growing public image of Dulles as a maladroit, intuitive cold warrior."

It was at Dulles's urging that the United States had blocked the unification of Vietnam in 1956, adopted the Diem regime, and resolved to defend South Vietnam indefinitely. He bequeathed that commitment to the Kennedy administration. It led inevitably to the Diem coup, since Diem was clearly not the right partner for the United States as long as leaders in Washington wanted to fight on until victory.

After propping up Diem for so long and then discarding him so violently, Americans sank into a war that caused incalculable harm to their interests around the world. The coup bound the United States to South Vietnam in an embrace that proved disastrous to them both. In a very real sense, it was Dulles's final legacy.

"Our American friends are remarkable organizers, brilliant technicians and excellent soldiers," Prince Sihanouk of Cambodia observed as the Southeast Asian war reached its peak. "But their incontestable realism stops short of the realm of politics, where the attitude of the ostrich seems to them to conform best to their interests."

AFTER THE COUP IN CHILE ON SEPTEMBER 11, 1973, GENERAL AUGUSTO Pinochet and the other officers who seized power with him moved quickly to consolidate their power. Pinochet soon became the ruling junta's dominant figure. Several of his military rivals died unexpectedly, most notably his minister of defense, General Oscar Bonilla, who was killed in a helicopter crash in 1975. Others chose early retirement. Thus strengthened, Pinochet declared himself president of the junta and then president of the republic.

One of Pinochet's first acts after the coup was to order a nationwide series of raids on leftists and other supporters of the deposed regime. The harshness with which this campaign was conducted, the tens of thousands of people who were arrested, the conditions under which they were held, and the fact that many were never seen again set the tone for what would be years of repression. The regime ordered summary executions for scores of leftist leaders. Many more died at the hands of soldiers and rightist thugs who swept through pro-Allende slums, called *poblaciones,* beating and killing as they rampaged. On October 8, *Newsweek* reported that city morgues in Santiago had received a total of 2,796 corpses since the coup, most with either crushed skulls or execution-style bullet wounds. Four days later, the *New York Times* also placed the death toll in the thousands.

Officials of the Allende government were rounded up and sent to a prison on desolate Dawson Island, in Chile's extreme south. The junta abolished the country's largest labor federation, which had 800,000 members; banned all political parties that had supported Allende; declared Congress in "indefinite recess"; summarily dismissed hundreds of university professors; removed all mayors and city councillors from office; and decreed a new legal code that forbade any appeal of decisions by military courts. Gleeful militiamen made bonfires of leftist books.

A long controversy surrounded the question of whether Allende was killed by rebel soldiers or committed suicide. Some who sympathized with him felt driven to promote the death-in-battle version. As the passage of time allowed a more dispassionate review of the evidence, however, most came to accept the suicide hypothesis. Allende was sixty-five years old when he died. He had been president of Chile for 1,042 days.

Pinochet moved quickly to resolve the conflicts with American companies that had contributed so decisively to hostility between Washington and Santiago. Less than a year after the coup, his government announced an agreement with Anaconda Copper under which the company would receive $253 million in cash and promissory notes for its expropriated assets. Kennecott Copper received $66.9 million. Chile also settled with ITT, paying the company $125.2 million for its interest in the Chilean Telephone Company.

In 1976, Henry Kissinger traveled to Santiago to deliver a speech to the Organization of American States. The day before his public appearance, he met privately with Pinochet to assure him that although his speech would include a few perfunctory references to human rights, it was "not aimed at Chile."

"My evaluation is that you are a victim of all left-wing groups around the world, and that your greatest sin was that you overthrew a government that was going communist," Kissinger told Pinochet. "We welcomed the overthrow of the communist-inclined government here. We are not out to weaken your position."

Several weeks later, on September 21, 1976, a squad organized by the Chilean secret police assassinated Orlando Letelier, who had been Allende's ambassador to the United States and foreign minister, by detonating a bomb in his car as he drove near Dupont Circle in Washington.

His American assistant, Ronni Moffitt, was also killed. No such act of political terror had ever been committed in Washington, and it set off long and bitter condemnation of Pinochet's regime. Later it became clear that Letelier's murder was part of a wider plan, called Operation Condor, to kill opponents of Pinochet who were active outside Chile.

In 1988, after fifteen years as Chile's dictator, Pinochet submitted to a constitutionally mandated plebiscite in which Chileans were asked whether he should remain in power for another decade. The vote was negative. Instead of giving him a legal basis to remain in power, the plebiscite set off a nationwide clamor for change. Pinochet responded by imposing a series of decrees intended to guarantee the permanent power of the military, and then allowed a presidential election. A Christian Democrat, Patricio Aylwin, won. On the day he was inaugurated, January 6, 1990, Chile entered a new era.

One of the new government's first acts was to create the National Commission on Truth and Reconciliation. In 1991 the commission produced a long and thoughtful report. Chile's fall toward dictatorship, it concluded, began when the country found itself caught up in world politics.

> Starting in the 1950s, Chile, like many countries in Latin America, saw the insertion of its domestic politics into the superpower struggle, the so-called "Cold War." . . .
>
> The victory of Popular Unity and President Allende in 1970 was regarded as the triumph of one of the contending superpowers, the USSR, and as a defeat for and threat to the other, the United States. Hence the United States immediately planned and engaged in a twofold policy of intervention in Chile's internal affairs. . . . These developments are directly related to the devastating economic crisis Chile underwent starting in 1972, and were an integral and very important part of the broader crisis that broke out in 1973.

Chile slowly returned to its once-hallowed role as a beacon of democracy in South America. La Moneda, heavily damaged by bombing during the coup, was lovingly restored during the Pinochet years. Later an imposing statue of Allende was placed in front.

While Pinochet was visiting Britain in 1998, he was detained under a warrant issued by the Spanish judge Baltasar Garzón. Courts in France, Switzerland, and Belgium also asked for his extradition. He spent 503 days under house arrest at a villa near London before the British government finally allowed him to return home. Soon after he arrived, he was stripped of the immunity he had enjoyed as a senator-for-life, and faced an array of kidnapping, torture, and murder charges.

In Washington, the Senate Select Committee on Intelligence conducted an exhaustive investigation of the coup against Allende. It praised the CIA for producing accurate reports about Chile, and said the coup became possible because these reports "were either, at best, selectively used or, at worst, disregarded by policy makers when the time came to make decisions regarding U.S. covert involvement in Chile."

> The more extreme fears about the effects of Allende's election were ill-founded; there never was a significant threat of a Soviet military presence; the "export" of Allende's revolution was limited, and its value as a model more restricted still; and Allende was little more hospitable to activist exiles from other Latin American countries than his predecessor has been. . . . Chile was charting an independent, nationalist course.

Thirty-one years after the coup, a government-appointed commission in Chile concluded that during the years of dictatorship, "torture was a state policy, meant to repress and terrorize the population." It identified 27,255 people who were tortured during the years of military rule, and President Ricardo Lagos announced that each of them would receive a lifetime pension. Soon afterward, a judge ordered Pinochet, then eighty-nine years old, placed under house arrest pending trial on charges of kidnapping and murder. The commander of the Chilean army, General Juan Emilio Cheyre, then made a historic admission.

"The Army of Chile has taken the difficult but irreversible decision to assume the responsibility for all punishable and morally unacceptable acts in the past that fall on it as an institution," General Cheyre said. "Never and for no one can there be any ethical justification for human rights violations."

What would have happened in Chile if the United States had not intervened? The Nixon administration's nightmarish prediction—that Allende would have imposed dictatorial rule and led his country into alliance with the Soviet Union—might have materialized, but given the power of the innately conservative military and Allende's own democratic credentials, it was highly unlikely. Civil war, which Pinochet later said he had acted to prevent, was an even more remote possibility.

Chile's long political tradition suggests that the country would have found a less violent, more constitutional way out of its conundrum. Whatever happened, the number of people arrested, tortured, and killed for political reasons during the following years would almost certainly have been far smaller.

"Left to their own devices, the Chileans just might have found the good sense to resolve their own deep-seated problems," the historian Kenneth Maxwell wrote in a review of declassified documents related to the coup. "Allende might have fallen by his own weight, victim of his own incompetence, and not become a tragic martyr to a lost cause."

Despite its remarkable success in reinventing its democracy, Chile remains a shattered nation. The 1973 intervention and the long period of dictatorship that followed have deeply scarred its collective psyche. Many Chileans, like many Americans and others around the world, ultimately came to believe that this was another in a line of American coups that turned out badly for almost everyone involved. Three decades afterward, Secretary of State Colin Powell endorsed this consensus when he answered a question about the overthrow of Allende.

"It is not a part of American history that we are proud of," he said.

THE COUPS IN IRAN, GUATEMALA, AND CHILE HAD MUCH IN COMMON. ALL three countries were blessed with rich natural resources, but those resources fell under foreign control. When nationalist leaders tried to take them back, the United States responded by turning their countries into bloody battlegrounds. Iran, Guatemala, and Chile were brought back into the American orbit, but at a staggering human and social cost.

In important ways, the coup in South Vietnam was unlike the other three. It was staged in a country where the United States was at war, rather than in one where it faced only a theoretical threat. The control of no great natural resource was at stake. Most poignant, the operation in Vietnam was the only time the United States helped overthrow a leader who was a friend rather than a perceived enemy.

The covert coups of the Cold War era were carried out quite differently from the invasions and stage-managed revolutions that the United States used in deposing regimes in the period around 1900. Much of what motivated them, however, was the same. Each country whose government the United States overthrew had something Americans wanted—in most cases, either a valuable natural resource, a large consumer market, or a strategic location that would allow access to resources and markets elsewhere. Powerful businesses played just as great a role in pushing the United States to intervene abroad during the Cold War as they did during the first burst of American imperialism.

Their influence alone, however, was never enough. Americans overthrew governments only when economic interests coincided with ideological ones. In Hawaii, Cuba, Puerto Rico, the Philippines, Nicaragua, and Honduras, the American ideology was that of Christian improvement and "manifest destiny." Decades later, in Iran, Guatemala, South Vietnam, and Chile, it was anti-Communism. During both eras, Americans came to believe it was their right, and even their historical obligation, to lead the forces of good against those of iniquity.

"For us there are two sorts of people in the world," John Foster Dulles once asserted. "There are those who are Christians and support free enterprise, and there are the others."

Dulles spoke for American leaders from Benjamin Harrison to Richard Nixon. All believed that the twin goals of United States foreign policy should be to secure strategic advantage, for both political and commercial reasons, and to impose, promote, or encourage an ideology. The regimes they marked for death were those they considered both economically and ideologically hostile.

These coups might never have been launched, and great damage to four nations as well as to the United States might have been averted, if the White House had not been so vulnerable to the herd mentality, or "groupthink." In each case, the president of the United States and one or two senior advisers made clear that they wished a certain government overthrown. Their determination set the tone for all that followed. Advisers and planners quibbled over operational details, but rarely over the larger question of whether overthrowing a particular government was a good idea. Everyone thought and spoke within understood limits. No one questioned the premise on which these coups were based: that regimes in Iran, Guatemala, South Vietnam, and Chile were either tools of the Kremlin or in imminent danger of falling under Soviet control.

This was the easy way out, an extreme form of intellectual laziness. The rise of nationalism in the developing world was a complex phenomenon. It had a variety of causes, and for Americans to devise a sophisticated, long-term strategy for dealing with it would have been challenging and difficult. Far easier was to categorize nationalism as simply a disguised form of Communist aggression, and seek to crush it wherever it reared its head.

Some of those who directed Cold War interventions, like John Foster Dulles, devoted their lives to the service of American corporate power. Others, like Henry Kissinger, had no real interest in business and even regarded it with disdain. All of them, however, believed that only malicious regimes would try to restrict or nationalize foreign companies.

Directors of large corporations were the first to wish Mohammad Mossadegh, Jacobo Arbenz, and Salvador Allende overthrown. They persuaded leaders in Washington, who had somewhat different interests, to depose them. In each case, government stepped in to lead a parade that had already formed for other reasons. Ideology and economic interest combined to drive the United States to intervention.

The Americans who conceived, authorized, and carried out covert plots against the governments of Iran, Guatemala, South Vietnam, and Chile considered them to have been great victories. From the perspective of history, they do not look that way. In all four countries, they led to increased repression and reduced freedom. Beyond their borders, they also had profound effects. They intensified and prolonged the Cold War by polarizing the world and choking off possibilities for peaceful change. They undermined Americans' faith in the CIA, thereby making the agency less effective. Around the world, they led millions of people to conclude that the United States was a hypocritical nation, as cynical as any other, that acted brutally to replace incipient democracies with cruel dictatorships.

"Until recently, American foreign policy had been seen as morally steadied," Nathaniel Davis, the U.S. ambassador to Chile in 1973, wrote after the coup. "Then came a series of jolts, starting with Iran in 1953, Guatemala in 1954, and Vietnam. . . . The Chilean story produced still another bump in our fall from grace."

PART THREE

Invasions

10

Our Days of Weakness Are Over

A weekend of golf was the logical prescription for what ailed President Ronald Reagan in the autumn of 1983. His decision to send United States Marines to intervene in Lebanon's civil war had set off intense anger in much of the world. So had a series of saber-rattling military maneuvers that the United States was conducting in Central America. In mid-October, a bizarre series of events on the tiny Caribbean island of Grenada, including the summary execution of the prime minister, raised the sudden possibility of American intervention there.

On Friday afternoon, October 21, Reagan left all this behind—or tried to—as he boarded Air Force One for a flight to Augusta, Georgia. With him were a handful of aides and friends, among them Secretary of State George Shultz and national security adviser Robert McFarlane. They hoped to escape from their cares on the rolling fairways and manicured greens of the Augusta National Golf Club. Instead they flew into the worst weekend of Reagan's presidency.

Before leaving Washington that afternoon, Reagan initialed a National Security Decision Directive authorizing military commanders to prepare options for possible action in Grenada. Several hundred American students were attending a medical college there, and some officials feared they might require evacuation. The directive that Reagan signed included an order that a naval task force heading for Lebanon change course and make for Grenada instead. A navy spokesman in Washington assured reporters that the warships would do no more than assist in a possible evacuation.

"There are not going to be any landings or anything like that," he promised.

Reagan and his friends spent Friday evening at the stately, six-bedroom

Eisenhower Cottage, a famous landmark at Augusta National. As they relaxed, officials in Washington were sensing both danger and opportunity in the unfolding Grenada crisis. The island's pro-Cuban government, which the United States mightily disliked, had just been overthrown and its leaders shot. A new clique declared that the old regime was not militant enough, and vowed to impose pure Marxism-Leninism on this small island.

It seemed at least conceivable that the newly empowered radicals might try to capture or harm the American medical students, and this danger lent an air of urgency to the deliberations in Washington. Another factor also fired enthusiasm there. Reagan's advisers immediately realized that this crisis gave the United States an unexpected chance to win a strategic Cold War victory. Americans were hungry for one. Many felt frustrated after a decade of what they considered global humiliation, marked by defeat in Vietnam and the long, agonizing Iran hostage crisis. They voted for Reagan in 1980 because he promised to restore the "standing" of the United States. Grenada gave him his chance.

To proceed with a full-scale invasion of Grenada, instead of simply evacuating American students, the United States needed a fig leaf of legality. Officials in Washington decided that the leaders of other Caribbean countries should be persuaded to call for an American invasion of the island. On Friday, as Reagan was flying to Augusta, Deputy Assistant Secretary of State Charles Gillespie, the administration's chief Caribbean specialist, flew to Barbados, where six Caribbean prime ministers were holding an emergency meeting. Gillespie and Milan Bish, the U.S. ambassador to the Eastern Caribbean, helped guide the meeting to a consensus.

The prime ministers did not sign any document that night. In public they said only that they had decided to punish Grenada with economic sanctions. Privately, though, they gave the Americans good news: they had agreed to request United States intervention. Gillespie immediately notified Washington.

Secretary of State Shultz's telephone at the Eisenhower Cottage rang at 2:45 on Saturday morning. As soon as he heard that his diplomats had succeeded in extracting an appeal for armed help from Caribbean leaders, he woke McFarlane. During the predawn hours, they telephoned several others in the military chain of command. Finally they roused Reagan.

At 5:15, wearing a bathrobe and slippers, the president heard their report. They told him that six Caribbean leaders had agreed to ask the United States to intervene in Grenada and that intervention would also be the best way to safeguard American citizens there. He responded by making two decisions. First, he directed Vice President George H. W. Bush to convene the Special Situation Group that had been hurriedly established to deal with the Grenada crisis. Second, to keep their actions as secret as possible, he, Shultz, and McFarlane would stay in Augusta and keep golfing as if nothing unusual were happening.

The next day something quite unusual did happen, and it unsettled Reagan and everyone in his group. At midafternoon an unemployed pipe fitter crashed his Dodge pickup through a chain-link gate at Augusta National and stormed into the pro shop. There he produced a .38 caliber pistol, fired a shot into the floor, and took five hostages, including two of Reagan's aides. He threatened to kill them unless the president agreed to speak with him. After frantic consultations, Secret Service agents decided to grant his request. They descended on Reagan as he was playing the sixteenth hole, explained the situation, and gave him a radiophone.

"This is the president of the United States," he said into the receiver. "This is Ronald Reagan. I understand you want to talk to me."

There was no reply. Reagan repeated his offer, but the disturbed man on the other end of the line could not bring himself to speak. Secret Service agents then decided to whisk Reagan off the golf course. They rushed him into a limousine and it sped away, closely shadowed by an open convertible packed with agents waving Uzi submachine guns. Soon afterward, the intruder's mother arrived at the golf club and persuaded him to surrender.

Reagan was never in imminent danger, but the standoff lasted for more than two hours and caused great commotion. It gave the president a good excuse to fly back to Washington. Instead he chose to stay at Augusta, and after the excitement died down, he returned to the course, still wearing his sporty yellow sweater.

"I want to play another round of golf," he told his friends. "I want the weekend to end on an 'up' note."

Reagan played his second round, but as soon as he returned to the Eisenhower Cottage, he was pulled back into the fast-developing Grenada crisis. Vice President Bush called to report that the Special Situation Group favored an operation that would not only secure American citizens but restore democratic rule and end Cuban influence. That meant a full-scale invasion and the overthrow of Grenada's government. Without hesitating or asking a question, Reagan agreed.

"If we've got to go there," he told Bush, "we might as well do all that needs to be done."

When Reagan retired that Saturday night in what had once been President Eisenhower's bedroom, he had every right to hope for a good night's sleep. He did not have it. At 2:27 in the morning, McFarlane came to his room to awaken him. With him he carried one of the most devastating reports Reagan would hear during his presidency. The United States Marine Corps headquarters in Beirut had been destroyed in a suicide-bomb attack, leaving hundreds dead. It was among the bloodiest attacks ever on an American military post, and one of the greatest tragedies in Marine Corps history.

The stunned president knew that he had to return at once to Washington. Aides and others who greeted him there were taken aback by his suddenly dissipated appearance. Reagan was seventy-two years old, but until that moment he had always seemed vigorous. A report in the next day's *New York Times* said he looked like "a man under siege."

It is clear that the past 72 hours have taken their toll on the President. He looked exhausted, emotionally drained, even old for the first time in his presidency when he stepped from his helicopter and reached for an umbrella in the pouring rain on the South Lawn of the White House Sunday morning. It was 8:30 a.m., six hours after he had been awakened with the first news of Marine Corps casualties.

As he began to speak to reporters, he took his wife's hand, seeming to need moral support. Her face showed an anguish that aides said was stirred not only by the bombing in Lebanon but also by the incident Saturday at the Augusta National Golf Club in Georgia where a gunman seized several hostages, demanding to speak to the President.

Today Mr. Reagan conceded how heartsick it made him to call families to inform them of the death of marines.

"I don't know of anything that is worse than the job I have, and having to make the calls that I have made," he said, his voice thick with emotion.

It was in this state of mind that President Reagan plunged into a day of emergency meetings with his national security team. The bombing in Lebanon had inflicted another grievous blow on the United States. It intensified the desire of many Americans for some kind of revenge, some flash of vindication or redemption somewhere in the world, some chance to show their national power.

Reagan had already approved the idea of invading Grenada but had not issued any final orders. There was still time to pull back, to limit the operation to a simple evacuation of American citizens. The prime ministers of Guyana, Belize, and the Bahamas were urging this course. Aides asked Reagan whether the Beirut bombing had led him to reconsider his endorsement of the Grenada invasion. On the contrary, he replied, it steeled his will.

"If this was right yesterday," he said, "it's right today."

GRENADA IS THE JUTTING TIP OF AN UNDERSEA VOLCANO THAT SITS ABOUT one hundred miles north of the South American coast. It is just ten miles wide and twenty-one miles long, about the size of Martha's Vineyard, and home to barely 100,000 people. Charming towns with names like Victoria and Grand Roy poke out toward the sea from lush guava, cashew, and tangerine groves that monkeys share with piping frogs and fish-eating bats. In the capital, St. George's, brightly painted colonial homes overlook an azure harbor as lovely as any in the Aegean or Adriatic. Grenadians say they live "just south of paradise, just north of frustration."

A British trader brought nutmeg to Grenada in 1843, and it thrived so well that today this island produces one-third of the world's supply. It also exports cinnamon, ginger, mace, cloves, allspice, pepper, and turmeric. That is appropriate for a country whose people are instinctively poetic, given to the phantasmagorical, and known for zest and passion.

Grenada had been a relatively quiet British colony for more than a century when, at the beginning of 1951, it was paralyzed by a general strike. The strike's chief organizer, Eric Gairy, delighted audiences with his biting attacks on the mulatto aristocracy, and when the British held an election for a home-rule government, he formed a political party and rode it to victory. He dominated Grenada for most of the next quarter century, led it to independence in 1974 (though it remained part of the British Commonwealth), and became one of the weirdest figures in the colorful history of British colonialism.

Gairy manipulated elections, bullied the press, stole public funds, and used a private squad of thugs, the Mongoose Gang, to silence his critics. He was also a cultist, a mystic, a Rosicrucian, and a self-described master of obeah, an African form of sorcery and worship related to voodoo. For years he tried to persuade the United Nations to investigate UFOs, the Bermuda Triangle, and other "strange and inexplicable psychic and related phenomena which continue to baffle man."

As Gairy aged and began losing himself in his spiritual world, a new generation grew up around him. A militant Black Power movement emerged in Trinidad and Tobago and spread throughout the Caribbean. Jamaican voters propelled the fiery socialist Michael Manley to power. At universities in the United States and Britain, Grenadian students joined movements opposing South African apartheid and American involvement in Vietnam. Some were inspired by the "identity politics" and harsh critique of imperialism they heard from radicals like Malcolm X, whose mother was from Grenada. Others embraced Che Guevara's view that leftists must seize power by force rather than submitting to established political rules.

In the 1970s a group of these young visionaries met in St. George's, formed the New Jewel Movement, and began campaigning against Gairy. Several had recently returned from London, including the tall, bearded Maurice Bishop, a recent law school graduate, and Bernard Coard, a radical economist who had written an influential paper called "How the West Indian Child Is Made Educationally Sub-Normal in the British School System." To Gairy they were "these irresponsible malcontents, these disgruntled political frustrates coming from abroad . . . hot and sweaty, and shouting 'Power to the People!'"

Several New Jewel leaders won seats in Parliament, among them Bishop, whose charisma quickly made him the party's most popular figure. He found Parliament unfulfilling, as well he might. It rarely met, and when it did, it was usually for a shouting match followed by votes to ratify Gairy's will. Fed by this frustration, the New Jewel Movement drifted steadily leftward. Coard and his equally militant wife, Phyllis, worked to push it toward orthodox Leninism.

This combination—the evident impossibility of democratic change and New Jewel's increasing radicalism—propelled Grenada into its next era. On March 11, 1979, Gairy flew to New York to discuss "cosmic phenomena" with United Nations Secretary General Kurt Waldheim. Bishop and other New Jewel leaders believed, or claimed to believe, that he had left orders for the Mongoose Gang to kill them all. They decided to strike first. The next morning Radio Grenada awakened islanders with a shocking communiqué.

At 4:15 A.M. this morning, the People's Revolutionary Army seized control of the army barracks at True Blue. The barracks were burned to the ground. After half an hour of struggle, the forces of Gairy's army were completely defeated and surrendered, and not a single member of the revolutionary forces was injured.

That was an exaggeration, since it actually took twelve hours before the last holdouts inside the barracks surrendered. Insurgents had seized the radio station, though, and controlled the day's truth. There were fewer than sixty of them, but they took the defenders by complete surprise, and by day's end they had won. Their first proclamation, which Bishop read on the newly renamed Radio Free Grenada, promised that "all democratic freedoms, including freedom of elections, religion and political opinion, will be fully restored to the people."

Gairy protested loudly from New York, but he had few friends left. The British, despite being unhappy at the first-ever coup in one of their former Caribbean colonies, did not defend him. Most Grenadians were thrilled. Many admired Bishop, who became prime minister and took to calling himself "the people's leader." He could easily have led New Jewel to victory in a free election, and thereby given himself and his government true legitimacy. The new leaders' Marxist principles, however, prohibited them from submitting to anything so quaint as a democratic election.

The small group of men and women who ran New Jewel—there were only forty-five party members at the time of the 1979 coup, and never more than eighty—were idealists. Once in power, they built roads, opened a new high school and several free clinics, developed agriculture and the fishing industry, and cut the unemployment rate. They also abolished Parliament and the constitution, muzzled the opposition press, and drew up a "watch list" of potential enemies to be kept under surveillance. The cornerstone of their ideology, as Bishop outlined it in a 1982 speech to party members, was their belief that they comprised a Leninist "vanguard" entitled to rule by decree.

Just consider, comrades, how laws are made in this country. Laws are made in this country when the Cabinet agrees and when I sign a document on behalf of the Cabinet. And then that is what everybody in the country—like it or don't like it—has to follow. Or consider how people get detained in this country. We don't go and call for no votes. You get detained when I sign an order after discussing it with the National Security Committee of the party, or with a higher party body. Once I sign it— like it or don't like it—it's up the hill for them.

Bishop and his comrades claimed repeatedly that the CIA lay behind every peep of criticism in Grenada. That was not true, but the record of American intervention in the Caribbean and Central America made it easy for some to believe that it was. Only months after New Jewel seized power, arsonists destroyed two offices of the government-owned travel agency. Later there were other mysterious fires, as well as bombings and assassinations. Labor unions became restive. Twenty-six prominent citizens signed a bold petition demanding greater freedom. Tourism declined as travel agents in the United States stopped recommending Grenada as a destination. Some buyers of tropical fruits and spices began looking for supplies elsewhere. Clergymen gave sharp sermons protesting restrictions on public and pastoral freedom. To anyone familiar with American destabilization campaigns in other countries—and every New Jewel leader was—these episodes conjured a familiar pattern. Everything Bishop accused the Americans of doing to subvert his government was, as he loved to point out in his speeches, something they had already done elsewhere.

> We think of the history of U.S. imperialism. We think of the days when gunboats ruled the world, when you landed Marines in somebody's country: Arbenz in Guatemala in 1954, Dominican Republic in 1965 and dozens of other examples. We think of the occupations and the annexations of other people's territories, particularly in our region, in Latin America and the Caribbean. We think of the assassination of Sandino, the patriot of Nicaragua, of Allende, the hero of Chile, of so many other martyrs of this region who had to die at the hands of imperialism. . . .
>
> Sisters and brothers, destabilization is the name given to the most recently developed, or newest, method of controlling and exploiting the lives and resources of a country through bullying, intimidation and violence. . . . This method was used against a number of Caribbean and Third World countries in the 1960s, and also against Jamaica and Guyana in the 1970s. Now, as predicted, it has come to Grenada.

New Jewel leaders proclaimed themselves part of an anti-Yankee alliance that included Castro's Cuba, the Sandinista regime in Nicaragua, and rebels throughout the region who were defying what Bishop called "the vicious beasts of imperialism." They sharply increased the size of Grenada's army and sent officers to Cuba for training. Several hundred Cuban construction workers, some of them trained as members of the militia, arrived to build an airport at Point Salines, a few miles south of St. George's, that would be big enough to accommodate jumbo jets full of tourists—or, as officials in Washington repeatedly pointed out, combat jets. New Jewel leaders signed three military agreements with the Soviet Union that brought them millions of dollars' worth of weaponry at no charge. They struck up friendships with East Germany, Libya, North Korea, and almost every other country in the world that was hostile to the United States.

Grenada overflows with music, rhythm, and rhyme, and during the early 1980s, reggae and calypso bands developed a large repertoire of tunes praising the "revo" and denouncing imperialism. At raucous outdoor poetry readings, crowds shrieked with delight at poems like "The Last Cowboy," written and declaimed by Chris "Kojo" DeRiggs, who was minister of health in the New Jewel government.

> Ronald Reagan, the aging cowboy bandit man
> Cooked up a major bandit plan,
> This man pattern, this comic clown,
> Of movie fame and bushwacking fun
> Announced that he was riding down
> Through his backyard and islands in the sun
> To put more notches in his gun.
> For Ronald Reagan, 'twas not strange
> To go gun-shooting on his range
> To shoot back all dese winds of change.

As the confrontation between Grenada and the United States escalated, another conflict, at least as bitter and tinged with at least as much barely contained aggression, was growing within the ranks of New Jewel itself. Beginning even before the 1979 coup, Maurice Bishop had jousted with his deputy, Bernard Coard. Once they were in power, they and their supporters spent hours, and sometimes whole days and nights, in hand-wringing "self-criticism sessions" debating which among them was following a "right opportunist course" or failing to show the correct "Marxist-Leninist-Stalinist hand."

Coard and his faction insisted that Bishop was too conciliatory, too moderate, too ready to stray from the true Marxist path. They deplored his call for a tactical alliance with business owners, his preference for a mixed economy, and his insistence that Grenada "cannot proceed straight away to the building of socialism." During the summer and autumn of 1983, this rivalry began to consume the New Jewel Movement. Coard's faction slowly wore down Bishop and the other relative moderates. It sought to impose a new system of coleadership under which Coard would hold true power, with Bishop remaining as a figurehead. Bishop was reluctant to agree, but the balance swung against him when General Hudson Austin, the army commander, sided with Coard. On October 13, thus strengthened, the Coard faction voted to place Bishop under house arrest.

This dramatic step electrified Grenada. Over the next few days, people gathered in public squares for spontaneous pro-Bishop rallies. Many shops stayed shut. Five cabinet ministers resigned. Fidel Castro, whom Bishop had visited in Havana just days before, sent an outraged protest. Coard and his group quickly found themselves isolated and friendless.

After six days of house arrest, Bishop was a wreck. He could not sleep, was chain-smoking, and refused to eat for fear of poisoning. Outside, though, some of his most important supporters were agitating on his behalf. On the morning of October 19, Unison Whiteman, a New Jewel leader who had just resigned as foreign minister, was addressing a protest rally at Market Square in St. George's when a chant of "We Want Maurice!" went up. Soon the crowd was on its way to Bishop's home.

At the gate, soldiers loyal to Coard tried to hold their positions. Their commander, a twenty-four-year-old militant who called himself Imam Abdullah, fired several machine-gun bursts into the air. The demonstrators briefly retreated, but then surged forward again.

"Shoot us!" they dared the soldiers. "Kill us!"

The soldiers did not shoot, and within minutes Bishop's supporters were surging into his house. They found him tied to his bed, wearing shorts and a pale green T-shirt. Tied to a bed next to him was his companion, Minister of Education Jacqueline Creft. Their friends quickly freed them, and by ten o'clock both were on their feet.

Coard's house was close by. If Bishop had been thinking more clearly, he might have led his followers there and seized the rebel clique. Instead, lightheaded from the upheaval and deprivation of past days, and perhaps lacking the "iron discipline" of the true Leninist, he turned elsewhere. He brought his compatriots to Fort Rupert, an imposing eighteenth-century fortress, overlooking the harbor, that had been turned into an army barracks. They arrived there at about eleven o'clock, waving placards and in high spirits.

"We got we leader!" they chanted. "Fuck Coard!"

Whiteman called out to the soldiers inside, telling them that the crowd had come in peace and wished to enter. The soldiers were not prepared to open fire on such a multitude, especially not one with Bishop at its head. Fort Rupert fell to a peaceful invasion.

Inside, people crowded around Bishop, shouting questions, suggestions, demands, and warnings. He made a few decisions, including appointing a new army commander to replace General Austin, but had to take breaks to drink water and orient himself. As he struggled to command, Coard and his friends, astonished that Bishop had not immediately arrested them, plotted their countermove.

Shortly before noon, two officers rang the alarm at Fort Frederick, a military base on the outskirts of St. George's. Soldiers quickly assembled on the parade ground. One of the officers told them that counterrevolutionaries had seized Fort Rupert.

"Are you ready to fight for your country?" he demanded.

"Yeah! Yeah!" came the chanted reply.

"Some have to die for some to survive!" the officer shouted. "Every soldier should see blood in your eyes!"

At that moment, Coard himself arrived, accompanied by his wife and other supporters. Officers told them that Bishop's group seemed poised to recover its former power. Some may have feared that this would cost them their lives. They hurriedly withdrew for an impromptu Central Committee meeting. When it was over, one of Coard's closest supporters, Leon Cornwall, emerged and summoned the troops.

"Because of vicious rumors spread by Maurice Bishop, counterrevolutionaries and big businessmen freed him," Cornwall announced. "As a result, these elements must be liquidated." Then, throwing his arms into the air, he shouted, "Central Committee orders!"

"We obey!" the soldiers shouted back. "We obey!"

Moments later, three Soviet-made armored personnel carriers full of soldiers, each mounted with two machine guns, were speeding toward Fort Rupert. The ride took just ten minutes. When the attackers arrived, they found a huge crowd milling around the old fort. Without hesitating, they took up combat positions. Upon command, they loosed a massive barrage of grenades, rockets, and machine-gun fire. Dozens of bodies flew apart as survivors screamed and ran in panic.

"Oh God! Oh God! They turned their guns on the masses!" Bishop cried to his comrades.

After the soldiers finally stopped shooting, they marched methodically through the carnage and into the fort. They called Bishop and his comrades, among them Jacqueline Creft and Unison Whiteman, to come down to the courtyard and surrender. They did, and all eight were lined against a wall.

Imam Abdullah and a couple of his men sped back to Coard's house for final instructions. The eleven members of the Central Committee who were waiting there were not pleased. They had hoped that Bishop and his friends would be killed in at least a simulated battle, but that was no longer possible. Quickly they consulted again. What they decided is still in dispute, but within a few minutes, Abdullah was back at Fort Rupert.

"Comrades, turn round!" he shouted at his eight prisoners after he returned to Fort Rupert. When they did, he took out a piece of paper, waved it at them, and said, "This is an order from the Central Committee, that you shall be executed by fire. This is not my order, it is the Central Committee's." There was only one cry of protest, from Jacqueline Creft.

"Wait! Wait! Hold on! I'm pregnant!" she gasped.

"Prepare to fire!" Abdullah shouted back. "One, two, three, fire!"

Three machine gunners opened fire, and kept shooting until well after all the victims had collapsed. When they finally stopped, the remains of their national leaders lay scattered about the courtyard. One soldier fired a white flare into the air, a message that the deed had been done.

News of these shocking events reached Washington almost immediately. Not everyone there was displeased. Officials who had been waiting for an excuse to intervene in Grenada now had one.

LESS THAN TWENTY-FOUR HOURS LATER, AT EIGHT O'CLOCK ON THURSDAY morning, October 20, the Crisis Pre-Planning Group, whose job was to monitor world trouble spots, met at the Executive Office Building in Washington, across from the White House. Its chairman, Admiral John Poindexter, presented a variety of military options. Driven in part by the strong views of his aide, Lieutenant Colonel Oliver North, and Constantine Menges, a former CIA officer and adviser to the National Security Council, the group decided to endorse a radical course: the invasion of Grenada and the overthrow of its government. It passed that recommendation up to the next highest body, the Special Situation Group.

At midafternoon, the State Department received a note from Prime Minister Tom Adams of Barbados, a conservative anti-Communist who was highly respected in the region, urging that American troops be sent to depose the new Grenadian regime. That lent credibility to the idea. Shortly before five o'clock, the Special Situation Group convened, chaired by Vice President Bush. Its members were sobered to hear that despite all the hostility between Grenada and the United States over the past three years, and despite the cover that hundreds of American students and tourists might provide, there was not a single CIA agent in Grenada. No one had up-to-date information on Grenada's military capacity, or even maps of the island. The latest aerial photos were five months old. CIA operatives in Barbados bombarded their British counterparts with elemental questions like "Who is the leader of the armed forces?" and "Who are Coard's supporters in the cabinet?"

Bush and the others at that meeting endorsed the idea of invading Grenada and sent their National Security Decision Directive to President Reagan, who signed it the next day, before boarding Air Force One for his golfing trip to Augusta. Soon afterward, the commander of a naval task force heading toward Lebanon, Captain Carl Erie, received an urgent message ordering him to turn south, head for a point near Grenada, and prepare for action.

By a quirk of history, the name of Captain Erie's flagship recalled the only other time the United States had assaulted an island nearly this small: USS *Guam*. A few days earlier, the *Guam* and the four other ships in her task force had called at Morehead City, North Carolina, to take aboard the Twenty-second Marine Amphibious Unit. At its heart was an 822-man landing team, fully equipped with .50 caliber machine guns, antitank weapons, grenade launchers, fifty-two jeeps, and a complement of assault and transport helicopters.

The *Guam* was approaching Grenada when Captain Erie received a second message. This one directed him to send a helicopter to Antigua to pick up five men assigned to join their task force. Captain Erie assumed that the five would be diplomats from the State Department. When they stepped onto the deck of the *Guam* at ten o'clock that night, however, they were in uniform. With them they carried news that no one had expected.

President Reagan, these liaison officers reported, had ordered that the marines invade Grenada and overthrow its government. The force aboard the *Guam* would lead the assault. Its overall commander would be Vice Admiral Joseph Metcalf, commander of the Second Fleet. He wished the landing to commence before dawn on Tuesday.

The Special Situation Group met again on Saturday. President Reagan, who participated by telephone from Augusta, gave his curt approval for the invasion. At seven o'clock on Sunday evening, after the devastating bomb attack in Lebanon and a long day of meetings at the White House, he confirmed it by signing a more detailed "smooth copy" of his decision directive. Beside his signature, he wrote a single word: "Go."

Later that evening, General John Vessey, chairman of the Joint Chiefs of Staff, briefed Reagan and other senior officials on the invasion plan. Then he returned to the Pentagon and sent his final orders to commanders aboard the *Guam*. Their mission, code-named Operation Urgent Fury, was to "protect and evacuate U.S. and designated foreign nationals from Grenada, neutralize Grenadian forces, stabilize the internal situation, and . . . assist in the restoration of a democratic government on Grenada."

While the *Guam* and her task force headed for Grenada, American diplomats looked for ways to make their invasion seem legal. They could not work with the main regional body, the Caribbean Community, because several of its member states favored a negotiated solution to the crisis. Instead they turned to a smaller and much weaker group, the seven-member Organization of Eastern Caribbean States. It met in Barbados on Friday night and, guided by two American diplomats, privately gave the United States the request for intervention that it sought. Although the request was legally dubious, since the group's charter requires unanimity for such decisions and no Grenadian representative was present, it gave the Americans valuable cover.

As soon as officials at the State Department learned that Eastern Caribbean prime ministers were prepared to ask for an American invasion, they drafted a letter for the prime ministers to sign. It appealed to the United States "to take action for collective defense and preservation of peace and security against external aggression," and the prime ministers duly signed it on Sunday afternoon. The State Department drew up a similar letter to be signed by the governor-general of Grenada, Sir Paul Scoon, who was Queen Elizabeth II's official representative and the only recognized authority on the island.

These letters were designed to bolster the legal case for an invasion, but legality was never the administration's main concern. Every statement from the White House named the medical students' plight as most urgent. The students, however, refused to play the role of terrorized hostages. When their dean asked them in a poll whether they wished to leave Grenada, 90 percent replied that they did not. Several who telephoned home or were reached by news organizations said they felt quite safe. Senior Grenadian military officers, including General Austin himself, visited the school's campus at True Blue, near St. George's, and guaranteed that it would be protected.

If the students' safety had been America's true concern, a simple evacuation would have sufficed. It would have taken just a few hours for marines to bring out every American on the island. Rescue was never, though, the essential purpose of Operation Urgent Fury. The real motive, in the words of Major Mark Adkin, a British officer who was stationed in Barbados at the time, was "the intense desire of the President and his advisors to improve U.S. prestige, particularly at home and within the armed forces, where morale and self-respect had fallen substantially since Vietnam."

> With Bishop's execution, a fleeting opportunity presented itself to the United States to act dramatically in the Caribbean. . . . The United States needed a success, something to be proud of. . . . Although announced repeatedly as the primary reason for launching Urgent Fury, the safety of U.S. citizens was really one of several pretexts for grabbing an unprecedented opportunity to halt communist expansion in the U.S. backyard. . . . The decision to intervene in Grenada was made on the basis of seizing a fleeting strategic-political advantage, which had the added merit that inevitable military success would raise U.S. flagging morale.

Neither Reagan nor any other American official ever told the British, who considered themselves to be protectors of all Commonwealth countries, that they had made this decision. On Monday, Prime Minister Margaret Thatcher called a cabinet meeting to discuss the Grenada crisis, and then sent a cable to Washington listing Britain's reasons for opposing military action there. She had no idea that Reagan had already ordered it.

As the *Guam* approached its target, Radio Free Grenada was broadcasting furious appeals, calling all citizens to defense posts. Not many responded. Few wished to defend the murderous clique, especially against United States Marines.

Aboard the *Guam,* hundreds of marines spent Monday night preparing to storm Grenada's beaches. As they were checking their weapons and packs, Captain Erie made an unexpected announcement. He had canceled the film that was to be shown in their berthing spaces. In its place he screened another that he thought would put them in the right mood to storm an island. It was *Sands of Iwo Jima,* starring John Wayne.

FOUR TEAMS OF SEAL COMMANDOS FROM THE NAVY, FROGMEN WHO WERE trained in techniques of infiltration, reconnaissance, and concealment, landed on the beaches of Grenada late Monday night. Two were assigned to check conditions at the Point Salines airfield and nearby beaches. A third was assigned to blow up the Radio Free Grenada transmitter. The fourth was to secure Sir Paul Scoon, the governor-general, and bring him to a place where he could sign the letter requesting an invasion.

The first two teams, which had the most urgent task, managed to land their small Sea Fox raiding launches in the pounding surf at Point Salines and slip ashore undetected. They quickly discovered that rocks and coral reefs obstructed the approaches to every nearby beach, making them unsuitable for an amphibious landing. With a three-word code—"Walking Track Shoes"—they radioed this bad news back to the *Guam.*

As soon as commanders heard it, they knew they had to change their plan. Instead of storming the beaches, the first wave of Americans would drop from helicopters. Most heard the news while they were watching *Sands of Iwo Jima.* At three-fifteen on Tuesday morning, soon after the film ended, the first of twenty-one helicopters filled with marines lifted off the deck of the *Guam.* Lightly armed and highly mobile Rangers, flying aboard twelve planes from Hunter Army Airfield in Savannah, Georgia, followed soon afterward.

Dawn was breaking as the planes closed in on the airport at Point Salines. They could not land because defenders had blocked the runway with boulders, bulldozers, and other obstacles, so the Rangers had to jump. When the lead plane descended to five hundred feet, men began dropping through the wet, warm air. After the first few left the plane, a searchlight from below fixed on its fuselage.

"They're firing on us!" the loadmaster cried.

A cascade of cannon and artillery fire exploded around the plane, tearing holes in its skin. Shell fragments ripped across the hold and tracers lit up the sky. Officers aboard the plane quickly made the painful but probably correct decision to abort the jump. The squadron pulled away, back out over the water.

By the time this decision was made, forty Rangers, accompanied by an air force team, had already jumped. They watched from the ground in dismay as their planes flew off, leaving them isolated. A few minutes later, they were relieved to see a Spectre airborne gunship appear and begin firing at cannon emplacements around the airfield. Grenada's rudimentary air defense system was no match for this awesome machine, which carries two six-barrel machine guns and two twenty-millimeter cannons that can fire a total of 17,000 rounds per minute. It laid down a hail of fire that quickly silenced defenders around the airfield.

After that barrage, Ranger commanders decided it was safe for the rest of their troops to jump. Shortly after six o'clock, a single file of C-130 transports made its second approach. Each man inside was laden with weapons and a hundred pounds of ammunition.

"Rangers, be hard!" their commander shouted at them, and with that, the troops began tumbling out into the Caribbean dawn.

Flak exploded around them, tearing holes in parachutes and sending shock waves through the clouds. Despite it all, nearly every Ranger landed safely on the macadam runway. Some set off to find and destroy enemy positions. Others worked to clear the airstrip, dragging away coils of barbed wire and hot-wiring Cuban bulldozers so they could be driven off the tarmac. At seven-forty, the first C-130 landed. It disgorged not just soldiers but jeeps, motorcycles, artillery pieces, and everything else that an army might need to subdue a small island.

One of the key Ranger missions was to secure the medical campus at nearby True Blue. When soldiers arrived there, they found 138 nervous and grateful young men and women. Some troops remained to guard them, though there was no visible threat to their safety.

Americans heard news of the invasion on their morning newscasts. Shortly after nine o'clock, President Reagan strode to a podium at the

White House to face reporters. He told them that Operation Urgent Fury was going well and that the United States "had no choice but to act strongly and decisively" to save Grenada and the region from "a brutal gang of leftist thugs." Later in the day, Secretary of State Shultz explained the decision at greater length.

> There are two basic reasons that determined the President's decision. First was his concern for the welfare of American citizens living on Grenada. . . . Second, the President received an urgent request from the countries closest to the area—the Organization of East Caribbean States—who . . . determined for themselves that there were developments of grave concern to their safety and peace taking place. They brought in Jamaica and Barbados and, along with those two countries, made a request to the United States to help them in their desire to insure peace and stability in their area.

All that Tuesday, bombers and attack jets screeched over St. George's. They hit Cuban barracks, antiaircraft positions on the long volcanic ridge overlooking the town, and every other target they thought might be part of enemy defenses. Given the poor information they had—some troops were reduced to using photocopies of tourist maps—it is no surprise that one of their raids went badly wrong. A pilot scored a direct hit on Grenada's mental hospital, killing more than a dozen patients. Several dozen others, even more dazed than usual, stumbled away from the blazing ruins. They wandered the streets for days as war swirled around them, lending a surreal touch to a military operation that already had a comic-opera aspect.

By midafternoon, after several hours of pounding from jet bombers and helicopter gunships, antiaircraft fire had ceased. Those few Cubans and Grenadians who still wanted to fight had fled into the interior. The roar of arriving transport planes replaced the staccato of gunfire and explosions.

Commandos assigned to blow up the radio transmitter had completed their mission without resistance, but the ones assigned to extract Sir Paul Scoon ran into trouble. They easily found his house—he had posted a sign saying "Welcome US Marines" on his lawn—but before they could bring him out, Grenadian soldiers surrounded the house and began firing at it. The would-be rescuers suddenly found themselves in need of rescue.

Early Wednesday morning, Admiral Metcalf sent 250 marines to break this siege. They accomplished their mission with ease, and by midday Sir Paul was sipping tea aboard the *Guam*. Later that afternoon he was flown back to Point Salines, where American officers escorted him to a nearby house. Waiting for him there was Brigadier Rudyard Lewis, commander of the Barbados Defense Force and the new Caribbean Peacekeeping Force. From his briefcase, Lewis produced the letter that State Department officials had drafted for Sir Paul's signature. It said Grenada was in a "grave and dangerous situation," and appealed for outside help "to facilitate a rapid return to peace and tranquility and a return to democratic rule." Sir Paul happily signed. The letter was backdated by two days, to October 24, the day before the invasion.

As Sir Paul was doing his diplomatic duty at Point Salines, the Eighty-second Airborne was fanning out across southern Grenada. Soldiers met small pockets of resistance, including at several spots in St. George's, but nothing that could challenge their overwhelming superiority of numbers and weaponry. In many places, civilians welcomed them with applause and cold drinks.

"Things were coming so unstuck," one man told an American reporter. "I'm sure we were just snatched in time from the devil's own mouth."

About six thousand American soldiers ultimately landed in Grenada, at least twice the number needed to do the job. Their stay was short. The marines left first, resuming their interrupted trip to Lebanon. The Rangers quickly followed. Just eight days after the invasion, the American force had dwindled to three thousand. By the end of the year, only a few companies of military police remained.

Several members of Congress rushed to visit Grenada to revel in the victory. "A lot of folks around the world feel we are more steady and reliable than heretofore," said one of them, Representative Dick Cheney of Wyoming. Others roundly denounced the invasion, among them Senator Daniel Patrick Moynihan of New York, who doubted "that you restore democracy at the point of a bayonet." Many foreign governments also protested. The United Nations General Assembly overwhelmingly passed a resolution "deeply deploring . . . a flagrant violation of international law."

President Reagan, as was his wont, brushed this criticism aside. When asked how he reacted to news that more than one hundred member states had voted for the United Nations resolution, he replied, "One hundred nations in the United Nations have not agreed with us on just about everything that's come before them where we're involved, and it didn't upset my breakfast at all." He knew he had given Americans a psychological as well as a strategic victory, and had reason to feel proud.

A few weeks later, Reagan gave an emotional speech to the Congressional Medal of Honor Society in New York. Aides took pains to tell reporters that he had written it himself. In a few words, he distilled what he believed the Grenada invasion should teach Americans and the world.

"Our days of weakness are over!" Reagan proclaimed. "Our military forces are back on their feet, and standing tall."

11

You're No Good

A mutilated corpse without a head, stuffed into a canvas bag made for delivering U.S. mail, set off the long chain of events that led the United States to invade Panama and overthrow its leader. The remains were those of an outspoken Panamanian patriot who disappeared on an autumn day in 1985. His head was never found.

The murder of Hugo Spadafora, one of the most flamboyant figures in modern Panamanian history, stunned a country where such crimes are all but unknown. Revulsion rose to a new level when the results of an autopsy on Spadafora's torso were released, showing that he had suffered through hours of unspeakable torture and that his head had been slowly severed while he was still alive. These facts alone, however, were hardly enough to rouse the United States into action. During the mid-1980s, senior American leaders, including President Ronald Reagan, vigorously supported military regimes in Guatemala and El Salvador, whose troops carried out comparable crimes every day. What made the Spadafora murder such a crucial turning point in Panamanian history was that it signaled the regime's slide into irrationality. That is a quality the United States can tolerate in many of its allies but not one whose domain is so close to the Panama Canal.

General Manuel Antonio Noriega, commander of the Panama Defense Forces, had good reason to believe himself above the law. Within Panama he ruled almost by whim. In the wider world, he had accumulated a remarkably diverse set of friends. He collaborated simultaneously with some of Colombia's most powerful drug dealers and the U.S. Drug Enforcement Administration; with the Sandinista army in Nicaragua and guerrillas who were fighting to depose it; with the CIA and the Cuban intelligence service. Wealthy beyond the wildest dreams of an illegitimate child of the Panama City slums, amply supplied with all he needed to feed his considerable private appetites, and with powerful allies around the world, he came to consider himself invulnerable. It took a full-scale military invasion to show him he was wrong.

Noriega rose from the streets, but despite his occasional stage-managed parachute jumps and scuba diving expeditions, he never became anyone's real hero. He was short and stubby, and had a diffident manner, a weak handshake, and a face so badly pockmarked that behind his back, people called him *cara de piña*—pineapple face. Although he was capable of extreme cruelty, he could collapse into tears when he thought danger was approaching. He chose the military as his only realistic chance for advancement in life, and his early career was marked by episodes of rape and other sorts of brutality. Twice he attended courses at the U. S. Army School of the Americas in the Panama Canal Zone. The first course was in jungle warfare, and his performance was abysmal; he finished 147th among 161 students. In his second, though, he was a great success, and rated "outstanding" by his instructor. That course was in counterintelligence. Noriega had found his life's work.

As Noriega was climbing out of Panama City's hardscrabble Terraplen district, Hugo Spadafora, who was six years younger, came of age in the prosperous seaside town of Chitré, a hundred miles to the southwest. From his earliest years, Spadafora lived a life very different from that of the man who would later become his mortal enemy. His father was an immigrant from Italy, a cosmopolitan intellectual who owned a furniture factory and became popular enough to be elected mayor of Chitré. The family sent Hugo to medical school in Bologna, and while he was there, he fell in with a group of leftists who were closely following the progress of anticolonial revolutions in Africa. Fired with enthusiasm for their cause, he decided to offer his medical services to rebels fighting in Portuguese Guinea, now Guinea-Bissau. He spent a year with rebels in the Guinean jungle, impressing them deeply enough so that after they won independence, in 1974, they named a street in the capital after him. Upon returning to Panama, he wrote a book called *Thoughts and Experiences of a Medical Guerrilla*. By the time he was thirty, many Panamanians knew his story and considered him a romantic hero.

In 1968, Panamanian military officers seized power in a bloodless coup. Spadafora joined an underground cell devoted to overthrowing their regime. He was soon arrested. In other Latin American countries he might have rotted in jail or been made to "disappear," but the new

Panamanian strongman, General Omar Torrijos, was not a dictator in the classic mold. Although hardly a paragon of democratic virtue, he was a visionary determined to wrest power from the country's entrenched elite and pull the Panamanian masses out of poverty. Two weeks after Spadafora was arrested, Torrijos summoned him from his cell for a long conversation about revolution, social reform, and the challenges of power. When it was over, he made Spadafora an offer: instead of returning to prison, he could go to a remote spot in the Darién jungle and open a health clinic. Spadafora instantly accepted and plunged into his work with zealous passion. Later Torrijos named him director of medical services in Colón, the country's poorest province, and then promoted him to deputy minister of health. In the late 1970s, bored with the bureaucrat's life, Spadafora asked for and received Torrijos's permission to raise a guerrilla squad to fight alongside Sandinistas, who were rebelling against the dynastic Somoza dictatorship in Nicaragua.

Only a leader as multifaceted as Torrijos could have nurtured the careers of both these men. They represented the two sides of his character and his regime. Like Spadafora, Torrijos was an idealist who scorned the ideologies of left and right, and looked everywhere for ideas that were practical enough to improve the lives of ordinary people. He was also a career soldier who had seized power in a coup, knew he had many enemies, and relied on amoral thugs like Noriega to protect his one-man rule. In 1970 he promoted Noriega to one of the most sensitive of all government posts, chief of G-2, the office of military intelligence.

Spadafora was everything Noriega was not: tall, fair-skinned, highly articulate, improbably handsome, and immensely self-confident. Over the years, as Noriega slipped steadily toward the criminality that would become his hallmark, Spadafora came to detest him. In 1981 he presented a sheaf of evidence to Torrijos.

"Omar, you have to be very careful with Noriega," Spadafora warned Torrijos. "Noriega is controlling you. Noriega is involved with drugs. Noriega is trafficking in arms. Noriega is going to kill you."

Torrijos asked Spadafora to repeat these charges in Noriega's presence, and, with typical fearlessness, Spadafora did so. He accused Noriega to his face not only of smuggling guns and cocaine but of running a lucrative racket in which he had his men spy on wealthy Panamanians so he could learn their private secrets and blackmail them.

"Noriega was shocked," the *Wall Street Journal* reporter Frederick Kempe later wrote. "No one had ever dared confront him so. Everyone knew Spadafora had driven the final nail either into Noriega's coffin or into his own."

Six months later, on July 30, 1981, Torrijos died in a helicopter crash. It was ruled an accident, but more than a few Panamanians suspected foul play. Whatever the truth, the force that had kept Noriega and Spadafora from each other's throats was gone. Their rivalry intensified. It spilled into public view when Spadafora told journalists that he had evidence of Noriega's crimes and would soon present it so Panamanians could learn the truth about this "pseudo-commander who has reached his position and rank through treason and opportunism." Noriega was not amused.

"Hugo could die any day now," he told one of their mutual friends. "Maybe even by swallowing a fishbone."

This looming confrontation was averted, at least temporarily, when Spadafora turned his attention back to Nicaragua. He had become disillusioned with the Sandinista regime he had fought to install, and spent several years trying to organize a force to help overthrow it. But because he refused to cooperate with the CIA, which was directing the anti-Sandinista army known as the contras, he was cut off from vital supplies and military intelligence. Finally he turned his focus back on his homeland, and particularly on Noriega. Against the advice of friends and relatives, he decided to return openly.

At his home in San José, Costa Rica, Spadafora rose early on September 13, 1985. He began his day with yoga exercises, then ate breakfast and set off in a taxi toward the Panamanian border. One of his friends had offered to meet him there and drive him to Panama City, but Spadafora decided to take a bus instead, fearing that if he traveled in a private car, Noriega's men might arrange to kill him in a staged crash. The bus made its first stop in Concepción, a dusty little town about ten miles inside of Panamanian territory. There an officer of the Panama Defense Forces stepped aboard, found Spadafora, and lifted his bag off the rack above his head.

"Come with me," he said simply.

Spadafora rose to follow. As he was leaving the bus, he stopped to show his identity card to the driver.

"So you will know who I am," he said. "I'm Dr. Hugo Spadafora. I'm being detained by this member of the Defense Forces."

The driver asked Spadafora to pay his fare, which was $1.20, and then watched as the two men crossed the town plaza. Another officer joined them. They walked three blocks to the local military post and disappeared behind its gate.

The next day, a Costa Rican farmer who lived near the Panamanian border was rounding up stray chickens when he saw two legs sticking up from a muddy pond. He waded out and found that a human body had been dumped into a sack marked as property of the United States Postal Service. When police arrived, they found that the body had no head. The next day it was identified as that of Hugo Spadafora. It bore clear evidence of torture. The stomach was full of blood that Spadafora had swallowed as his head was being slowly cut off.

"They Executed Spadafora!" screamed the banner headline in the beleaguered opposition newspaper *La Prensa*. It carried a statement from the victim's father, a revered figure in his own right, that set the terms for the conflict that would build for the next four years before exploding into a world crisis.

"The macabre murder of Dr. Hugo Spadafora was planned and coldly executed by the chief of G-2, Colonel Julio Ow Young, carrying out the orders of the commander of the [Defense Forces], General Manuel A. Noriega," the statement said. "We have complete and authentic proof of these facts."

FROM THE DAYS OF SPANISH COLONIAL RULE, PANAMA HAS BEEN PRIZED FOR the short, low-lying route it offers between the Atlantic and Pacific Oceans. In the nineteenth century, officials in Washington began dreaming of a sea route across the Central American isthmus. Their decision to build a canal through Panama instead of Nicaragua led them to foment the bloodless revolution that brought the Republic of Panama into existence. The canal, which opened in 1914, gave the United States sovereignty over the Canal Zone and a unique stake in the new nation. It also led to the steady growth of patriotic nationalism there. This nationalism inevitably took on an anti-Yankee tone. Over the years it led to spasms of violence.

The bloodiest outburst came in 1964, when several hundred Panamanian students marched toward the canal carrying their flag and a banner reading, "Panama Is Sovereign in the Canal Zone." Clashes broke out, and in one of them the Panamanian flag was ripped. That set off three days of rioting in which twenty-two Panamanians and four American soldiers were killed, hundreds were wounded, and $2 million worth of property was destroyed.

The 1964 uprising marked the emergence of a new form of Panamanian nationalism. It was focused on a specific goal: taking back the Canal Zone and giving Panama control of the waterway that is its greatest resource. This movement also became the instrument by which the country's poor, nonwhite majority hoped to take control of their country from the pro-American oligarchs they called *rabiblancos*, or white-tails. The 1968 military coup in which Torrijos seized power was its triumph.

"I do not want to enter history," Torrijos said in one of his first speeches after the coup. "I want to enter the Canal Zone."

In an act of courageous statesmanship, President Jimmy Carter launched an urgent round of talks on the canal's future soon after he took office in January 1977. Later that year, American and Panamanian negotiators reached agreement on two treaties that fundamentally altered the long-standing relationship between their two countries. The United States agreed to withdraw completely from the Canal Zone by 2000 and turn the canal over to Panamanian control. Panama, in exchange, guaranteed the canal's "permanent neutrality." The treaties stirred intense debate, but both countries ultimately ratified them.

These treaties might have led Panama toward stability, but that prospect began evaporating soon after Torrijos perished in 1981. His successors shared his thinly veiled contempt for traditional democracy but not his passion for social justice. By 1983, one of the most notoriously corrupt among them, General Noriega, had emerged as commander of the National Guard—which he renamed the Panama Defense Forces—and the country's strongman. The first figure to dispute his power was Hugo Spadafora, who paid for his brazen challenge with his life.

Noriega was at a dermatology clinic in Geneva when Spadafora was killed, undergoing treatment that he hoped would repair his deeply scarred face. There he received an urgent telephone call from Major Luis Córdoba, head of the unit that had captured Spadafora. Evidently neither man realized that American intelligence agents were eavesdropping.

"We have the rabid dog in our hands," Major Córdoba told his commander.

"And what does one do with a rabid dog?" Noriega asked in reply.

That was the go-ahead soldiers needed in order to begin the long night of torture that ended in Spadafora's decapitation.

A year earlier, Noriega had directed an electoral fraud from which Nicolás Ardito Barletta, a brilliant but colorless Chicago-trained economist, had emerged as president of Panama. Now he demanded that Barletta publicly absolve him of involvement in the Spadafora murder. Barletta refused, and on September 27, 1985, two weeks after the murder, Noriega forced him to resign. He left office with a prophetic warning.

"Listen to me," Barletta told Noriega. "The day will come when you are sorry for what you are doing. Remember my words."

NORIEGA HAD GOOD REASON TO BELIEVE HE COULD RIDE OUT THIS STORM. He had accumulated an extraordinarily diverse and powerful group of friends. Among them were dictators, guerrilla fighters, drug smugglers, and a variety of high-ranking American officials.

The CIA first recruited Noriega as an informer when he was a young cadet at the Peruvian military academy. His salary increased as he rose through the military ranks, and by the time he became chief of military intelligence, it reached $110,000 annually. He was one of the agency's most important "assets" in Latin America, even meeting personally with CIA director George H. W. Bush during a visit to Washington in 1976.

In the early 1980s, Noriega formed a partnership with the drug cartel based in Medellín, Colombia, allowing it free access to clandestine airstrips in Panama from which it shipped vast amounts of cocaine into the United States. For this service, the cartel paid him fees in the range of $100,000 per flight. Typically for Noriega, however, he was also working as a principal informer for the Drug Enforcement Administration. He gave it valuable information that led to the arrest of hundreds of traffickers from rival cartels, and to the seizure of tons of cocaine. Senior American officials sent him flattering letters of commendation.

During this period, Noriega further endeared himself to the Reagan administration by agreeing to help the Nicaraguan contras. While publicly mouthing platitudes about the need for peace and cooperation among Central American countries, he gave the contras invaluable covert support. He welcomed their leaders in Panama, permitted the United States to train their fighters in secret at Panamanian bases, and turned a blind eye when the Americans began using Howard Air Force

Base, in the Canal Zone, for clandestine flights carrying weapons to their bases along the Nicaragua-Honduras border.

After Noriega forced President Barletta out of office, the American ambassador in Panama, Everett Briggs, wanted to begin increasing American pressure on him. His boss, Undersecretary of State Elliott Abrams, a vigorous supporter of the contras, overruled him. Two months later, eager to learn firsthand what the United States thought of him, Noriega traveled to Washington to meet the CIA director, William Casey. Casey had been the chief architect of the contra project, and rather than reprimand Noriega or demand that he change his behavior, he was downright friendly.

"He let Noriega off the hook," a senior State Department official, Francis McNeil, later told a congressional committee. "He scolded Noriega only for letting the Cubans use Panama to evade the trade embargo, but never mentioned narcotics nor, if I remember correctly, democracy."

At the end of 1985, the newly appointed national security adviser, Admiral John Poindexter, came to Panama to meet with Noriega, and although according to some reports he was tougher than Casey had been, he was not forceful enough to impress his host. The Reagan administration was so obsessed with the idea of overthrowing the Sandinistas that it was ready to support even a scoundrel like Noriega as long as he continued to help the contras.

As this became clear to Panamanian opposition figures, they began looking for other ways to influence American policy. One of them, Winston Spadafora, a brother of the murdered dissident, flew to Washington and managed to persuade Senator Jesse Helms of North Carolina, chairman of the Senate subcommittee on Western Hemisphere affairs, to hold hearings on Panama in the spring of 1986. A week before the first scheduled hearing, Abrams called Helms and asked him to cancel it. He said that Noriega was "being really helpful to us" and was "really not that big a problem."

"The Panamanians have promised they are going to help us with the contras," Abrams said. "If you have the hearings, it'll alienate them. It will provoke them, and they won't help us with the contras."

Helms went ahead with his hearings anyway. They led to no spectacular revelations but drew attention to the administration's extraordinary level of tolerance for Noriega. A couple of months later, the *New York Times* published a front-page story by reporter Seymour Hersh headlined "Panama Strongman Said to Trade in Drugs, Arms and Illicit

Money." The *Washington Post* followed the next day with an even more damning story, cowritten by another widely respected reporter, Bob Woodward, that added details about Noriega's crimes and detailed his long relationship with the CIA.

Opinion in Washington slowly began to turn against Noriega. The director of the Drug Enforcement Administration, Jack Lawn, began a quiet investigation of his role in the drug trade, and refused a request from one of Noriega's advocates, Colonel Oliver North of the National Security Council staff, that he call it off. Then two United States senators from opposite ends of the political spectrum, Helms and John Kerry of Massachusetts, introduced an amendment to the 1986 Intelligence Authorization Act that required the CIA to investigate Noriega's involvement in drug trafficking, arms smuggling, money laundering, and the Spadafora murder. Casey was livid.

"You don't understand!" he told Helms in an angry telephone conversation. "You are destroying our policy. There are some things you don't know about, things Noriega is doing for the United States."

The amendment passed anyway, but it had only symbolic effect, since the CIA report on Noriega's activities was bland and inconclusive. As 1987 began, *el man,* as he was called—a play on his initials, *MAN*—had reason to feel secure. He met regularly with American military commanders and with the new American ambassador, Arthur Davis. Confident that he had outwitted his enemies in Washington, he decided to move against his most powerful Panamanian rival, Colonel Roberto Díaz Herrera, who was second in command of the Panama Defense Forces.

The two officers had been on uneasy terms for several years. Both had wanted to succeed Torrijos, and several months after his death, they agreed on a compromise under which Noriega would take the strongman's role until 1987, and then resign to make way for Díaz Herrera. As the date for the transfer of power approached, it became clear that Noriega had no intention of stepping down. That sent Díaz Herrera off on a bizarre adventure that took him beyond politics into the realm of the occult and supernatural.

With its broad racial and cultural mix, including influences from Africa, the Caribbean, and South America, Panama is overlaid with interest in spiritualism. Many people believe in hexes, curses, faith healing, time travel, reincarnation, and astral projection. Few considered it strange that Noriega consulted spiritualists and that he felt safe only when he was near his amulets and charms. No one, however, could have imagined that this aspect of Panamanian life would play a decisive role in bringing him down.

As Díaz Herrera fell under increasing pressure from Noriega, he came into contact with an elderly mystic whose guru was an Indian holy man named Sai Baba. She told him that Sai Baba had the power to "stop rainbows, heal the sick, materialize all kinds of objects, read the past, present and future of everyone, and transform himself into any human or non-human form." He was fascinated, and spent hours poring over a book of Sai Baba's wisdom.

"You must dive deep to get the pearls," the book said.

Díaz Herrera meditated at length on what this and other obscure maxims meant for him. He also began behaving in odd ways. Fellow officers reported that he walked through corridors of La Comandancia, the headquarters of the defense forces, with his arms held out in front of him to absorb psychic energy. He gave up alcohol, stopped seeing his mistresses, took up a diet of natural foods, and lost more than thirty pounds. Using his government expense account, he brought a series of occult practitioners to Panama.

"Noriega is your enemy," one of them told him. "He is evil, and will do everything in his power to destroy you. The big war we talked about is now clear to me. It is between you and him. It will start soon."

That "big war" exploded in June 1987. It began with Noriega dismissing Díaz Herrera from the defense forces; offering him a diplomatic post in Japan, which he refused; and then announcing that he would remain as commander of the defense forces for another five years. Days later, Díaz Herrera struck back with the only weapon he had. He began spilling Noriega's secrets.

In a series of spectacular interviews with reporters from Panamanian newspapers and television stations, Díaz Herrera confirmed many of the most serious charges against his former comrade. He asserted that Noriega had directed the 1984 electoral fraud that put Barletta in office, worked closely with the Medellín drug cartel, and ordered the murder of Hugo Spadafora. Never had anyone so close to Noriega turned against him with such vehemence.

An outraged Noriega denounced this attack as "high treason" and "assassination because it comes from the bosom of the institution." That did nothing to calm the explosion of support for Díaz Herrera that burst forth in the hours after his interviews were broadcast. Scores of supporters, including priests and nuns, crowded into his living room, jostling for space with a swarm of journalists, and spilled out onto the lawn. Winston Spadafora turned up. So did Father Javier Villanueva, a Roman Catholic priest who had emerged as one of Noriega's boldest critics. Through it all, Díaz Herrera remained serene. He sat on a prayer rug in his living room, holding near him a gold-colored plaque that depicted a lotus flower surrounded by symbols of the world's major religions.

"I am a criminal," he confessed. "I am ready to go to jail for my crimes, but I think Noriega should go with me."

These potent charges set off days of anti-Noriega protest. Thousands of people poured onto the streets of Panama City. Noriega responded by sending soldiers to fire tear-gas grenades at them and beat them as they fled.

On June 26, over the objections of the Reagan administration, the United States Senate passed a resolution calling on Noriega to step down while charges against him were investigated. Senator Kerry, who had become chairman of the Senate subcommittee dealing with drugs and terrorism, intensified an investigation of Noriega that he had been pursuing for more than a year. Even after the street protests in Panama City ended and Díaz Herrera faded from the scene—he issued a statement repudiating his charges, then fled the country—the anti-Noriega movement in Washington continued to gain momentum. Two of Noriega's most powerful supporters in the Reagan administration, Elliott Abrams and Oliver North, fell from power as a result of their involvement in the Iran-contra scandal, a covert scheme to sell arms to Iran and use the proceeds to prop up the contras. Then, early in 1988, two grand juries in Florida handed up criminal indictments charging Noriega and more than a dozen others, including Pablo Escobar, the boss of the Medellín cartel, with conspiring to send tons of cocaine into the United States.

These indictments were not the only reason the United States began turning against Noriega. He had embraced a peace plan for Central America—named after Contadora, the Panamanian island where regional leaders launched it—that the Reagan administration strongly opposed. Noriega's friends in Washington began looking for a way to ease him out of power. During 1988 they made a series of overtures to him. At one point, the White House even announced publicly that it would seek to have criminal charges against him dropped if he would agree to retire. Although he came close to accepting this offer, he changed his mind at the last moment. His obstinacy seemed like madness in the face of the forces that were aligning against him, but as the veteran foreign correspondent Tom Buckley later speculated, there may have been method to it.

> Why shouldn't Noriega just retire—and enjoy his millions? That was one idea heard over and over in Panama around this time; everyone assumed the general was finished. But Noriega could not have retired; he would have been murdered by the Medellín cartel. In power, Noriega was useful to them. Out of power, he was dangerous; he knew too much. Staying in power and staying alive were the same for Noriega.

Presidents of Panama never meant much to Noriega. He insisted that they obey his every order, and fired them when they balked. When an opposition figure, Guillermo Endara, won the presidential election held in May 1989, Noriega simply ignored the result and imposed his own candidate instead.

For many years Noriega seemed able to manipulate presidents of the United States almost as easily. Jimmy Carter cut off his CIA stipend but blocked efforts to indict him on drug and arms-smuggling charges. Ronald Reagan ignored his crimes in order to ensure his continued support for the contras. When George H. W. Bush, a former CIA director who was intimately aware of Noriega's activities, took office, in January 1989, Noriega had good reason to believe he had another friend in the White House.

Bush, however, came into office with the handicap of being considered weak and indecisive, and had to deal with what commentators called "the wimp factor." In May, after Noriega imposed his own president against the will of Panamanian voters, Bush announced that he was sending 1,800 troops to American bases in Panama, a step that was intended as a message to Noriega. When a reporter asked the president what he would like the Panamanians to do, Bush replied that they should "just do everything they can to get Mr. Noriega out of there."

During that summer of 1989, American and Panamanian soldiers engaged in an extended test of will. They stopped each other at roadblocks, arrested each other, and sometimes abused each other. Among the newly arrived soldiers was a group of marines who were known as "hard chargers," evidently devoted to provoking confrontations. They found the defense forces in an equally aggressive mood. By autumn, a list the Americans had compiled of injuries their men and women had suffered at the hands of Panamanian soldiers included bruises, broken fingers, and loosened teeth. Their refusal to respond to these abuses with force led some soldiers to suggest that instead of continuing to refer to the United States Southern Command as Southcom, they should start calling it Wimpcom.

In August, at the recommendation of Secretary of Defense Dick Cheney, President Bush named a new commander of Southcom. To those familiar with the American corps of general officers, this was a clear signal that a crackdown was at hand. The new commander, General Max Thurman, spoke not a word of Spanish and readily admitted that he knew nothing about Latin America, but the focused intensity behind his oversize eyeglasses was so renowned that other officers called him "Mad Max" or "Maxatollah." Before he left to assume his command, the chairman of the Joint Chiefs of Staff, Admiral William Crowe, told him he would soon be at war.

"We're going to go," Crowe told him. "Your job is to put that place on alert, get the population down, get things we don't need out of there, and be prepared to go."

Thurman assumed command on Saturday, September 30, 1989. In his inaugural speech, which Noriega attended, he declared that the United States would "not recognize or accommodate with a regime that holds power through force and violence at the expense of the Panamanian people's right to be free." The next evening, however, he turned down a chance to force the strongman from power.

A senior officer in the defense forces, Major Moisés Giroldi, sent word to Thurman that he was planning to stage a coup against Noriega the next day. Giroldi commanded the 200-man unit that controlled La Comandancia, the military headquarters in Panama City, and served as Noriega's inner line of defense. Now he was prepared to strike against his commander. All he asked from the Americans was that they block roads that lead to Panama City from the north, so that Noriega's elite fighting brigade, the Machos del Monte, would not be able to rush in and rescue him.

General Thurman was not interested. He had been sent to Panama to lead an American military action against Noriega, and was in no mood to settle for a "Panamanian solution." Such a solution could remove Noriega, but the Americans wanted something more: the destruction of the Panama Defense Forces. As long as it existed, even without Noriega, it was likely to be a power unto itself, and not necessarily responsive to the United States.

"You had to take down not only Mr. Noriega, but take down elements of his supporting entity—to reduce the PDF to nothing," Thurman said afterward.

At two o'clock on Monday morning, Thurman telephoned General Colin Powell, who had just taken over from Crowe as chairman of the Joint Chiefs of Staff. He easily persuaded Powell that it would be best not to help the plotters. Powell, in turn, shaped the White House response. The Americans would block no roads.

Giroldi never envisioned his coup as an American operation, and did not consider canceling it after learning that the Americans would not support him. He postponed it for just a single day. His men struck as Noriega arrived for work at La Comandancia on Tuesday morning. Within forty minutes, after a series of gun battles, they captured him.

"Some rebels wanted to shoot him on the spot," one reporter wrote afterward. "All watched as Noriega burst into tears and begged for his life. Some of his captors jeered, yelling that a narco-trafficker deserved to die."

Giroldi decided that rather than killing Noriega, he would turn him over to the Americans. He dispatched several of his aides to Fort Clayton, in the Canal Zone, to pass the offer on to General Marc Cisneros, second in command to General Thurman. Cisneros kept them waiting for half an hour, and then, after talking to Thurman by telephone, said he would accept Noriega only under a detailed set of conditions. Meanwhile, the Machos del Monte were racing to Noriega's defense along the very roads that Thurman had refused to block. As they closed in on La Comandancia, Noriega regained his old swagger. He dared Giroldi to kill him, and spat at him in contempt when Giroldi refused.

The Machos del Monte and other troops loyal to Noriega stormed La Comandancia shortly after noon. Within an hour they had recaptured it. They brought the rebel leaders to Noriega. Giroldi wept and pleaded, just as Noriega had done a few hours earlier. The commander was unimpressed.

"I'm tired of these bastards," he told the soldiers who had rescued him.

To emphasize his point, Noriega pulled out his pistol and shot one of the rebels in the face. Then he ordered a slow death for Giroldi. An autopsy later showed that before he was executed, Noriega's men shot off his elbows and kneecaps, broke one of his legs and one of his ribs, and cracked his skull open.

"I blame the Americans for my husband's death," Giroldi's embittered widow said after fleeing to Miami. "They only had to show off their power and equipment, and his coup would have worked."

This episode produced a storm of criticism in Washington. Senator Helms called President Bush, General Thurman, and the rest of the administration's team "a bunch of Keystone Kops." The military analyst Harry G. Summers wrote in his syndicated newspaper column that the American national security apparatus was "in chaos." In the unkindest cut of all, the chairman of the House Select Committee on Intelligence, Representative Dave McCurdy of Oklahoma, said that Bush's failure to act had led to "a resurgence of the wimp factor."

TENSION CRACKLED THROUGH PANAMA CITY IN THE WEEKS AFTER THE FAILED coup, but that did not stop four testosterone-driven marines from driving to the Marriott Hotel on Saturday night, December 16. They were among the "hard chargers," and the prospect of facing off with Panamanian soldiers was hardly enough to keep them from the hotel bar, which often drew sassy *rabiblanca* women. They were disappointed to find it half empty.

On their way back to the Canal Zone, the marines took a shortcut that led them into a barrio of cobblestone streets and dead ends. They became confused and suddenly found themselves at a roadblock. To make matters worse, they saw that they were just a block from La Comandancia.

Their weathered Chevrolet immediately drew a crowd. Soldiers with the scruffy beards and black T-shirts that were trademarks of Noriega's elite Machos del Monte surrounded it. They waved their Kalashnikovs and ordered the marines out of the car.

"Shit, it's the fucking Machos!" one of the marines cursed as he saw them.

"They just locked and loaded!" shouted the driver. "Let's get the hell out of here!"

He pushed the gas pedal to the floor and crashed his car through the roadblock. Soldiers fired at it as it fled into the darkness. One bullet hit Lieutenant Robert Paz, a marine intelligence officer. The driver made for

Gorgas Hospital in the Canal Zone but had trouble finding it. When he finally did, doctors were unable to save Lieutenant Paz.

That was also the night of the annual Christmas party at Fort Amador, in the Canal Zone. Children were singing "Feliz Navidad" when a messenger brought General Cisneros news of the shooting. He waited for the song to end and then announced it, not saying that the victim had died. Then he ordered all officers to report to their duty stations immediately, and advised their spouses to return home and stay behind closed doors.

"That was the beginning," one officer's wife recalled afterward. "From the sixteenth on, you saw your husband occasionally."

By the time Lieutenant Paz was killed, Thurman and his new staff officers had finished drawing up a plan for what was dubbed Operation Blue Spoon, a full-scale American invasion of Panama. Their superiors at the Pentagon had approved it. President Bush was determined that it should go forward. All that had been needed was a spark, an episode that could be cited as the last straw. The Paz killing provided the justification.

The next morning, Bush attended a church service at a military base in Arlington, Virginia. Reporters shouted questions about what he was intending to do in Panama. He made no reply. After the service, he was driven to the White House for brunch. When it was over, he pulled Vice President Dan Quayle aside and told him he had decided to strike against Noriega immediately. Then he summoned his senior advisers to the Oval Office.

General Powell presented the Blue Spoon plan. It was to be a massive invasion by 25,000 troops, about half of them from the Canal Zone and the other half from bases in the United States. They would strike twenty-seven objectives simultaneously, destroy the Panama Defense Forces, capture Noriega, and oversee a quick return to civilian rule. Bush asked if a smaller operation, targeted specifically against Noriega, might be feasible. Powell said it was not, because Noriega moved quickly and American commandos might not be able to find him.

"This guy is not going to lay off," Bush sighed after General Powell finished answering his questions. "It will only get worse. Let's do it."

Powell was back at the Pentagon by four o'clock. His first call was to General Thurman in Panama. "The President said I should be sure to tell you that enough is enough," he told Thurman. "Execute Blue Spoon."

"Roger, sir."

"D-day, twenty December," Powell continued. "H-hour, oh-one-hundred."

"Yes sir," Thurman replied. "I understand my orders."

Monday and Tuesday were days of intense activity at the Pentagon and half a dozen military bases from California to North Carolina. Army Rangers were mobilized, Navy Seal teams prepared for action, and air force commanders marshaled a force of 285 planes to bring the fighters and their equipment to Panama. At one of the last Pentagon planning sessions, General James Lindsay, chief of the Special Operations Command, raised an unexpected concern. He didn't like the name of the operation. How would it feel years from now, he asked his comrades, when veterans would have to tell stories of their exploits in Blue Spoon? It sounded like the title of a jazz tune, or the name of a remote frontier town.

For years, a computer at the Pentagon had been generating the names of American military operations. It spat out Blue Spoon after producing nearly a dozen others for preceding operations in Panama, including Elaborate Maze, Nimrod Dancer, Purple Storm, Sand Flea, Prayer Book, Golden Pheasant, Fissures One, Elder Statesman, and Blade Jewel. This time, commanders overruled the computer. They decreed that the invasion of Panama would henceforth be known as Operation Just Cause.

On Tuesday evening, December 19, as Noriega was sipping Old Parr whiskey with a couple of other officers at a command post in Colón, his telephone rang. He switched on the speakerphone. One of his staff officers was calling from Panama City.

"General, all the indications I'm receiving point to a major military action by the *gringos* sometime tonight," the officer reported.

Noriega pressed for details. Despite all that had happened, he never seriously believed that the Americans would try to dislodge him by force. After hanging up, he poured himself another glass and told his secretary to "make some phone calls, find out what's happening." Then his well-honed survival instinct took hold. He called for his driver and slipped out into the night.

The Panama Defense Forces had 13,000 soldiers, but most of them were police officers, customs agents, or prison guards. Only about 3,500 were trained or armed for combat. They had no hope of resisting the overwhelming power that came down upon them in the predawn hours of December 20.

More than 3,000 Rangers parachuted onto and around airports, military bases, and other objectives in Panama, making this the largest combat airdrop since World War II. In most places, Panamanian defenders surrendered or simply melted away. Those that held out were quickly silenced by the devastating firepower of Spectre gunships.

The invaders' most important target was La Comandancia. Columns of tanks and armored cars closed in on it soon after one o'clock in the morning. Rifle platoons followed close behind. They smashed their way through barricades and poured heavy rifle and rocket fire into the flimsy wooden buildings around them. Many went up in flames. Terrified residents rushed into the streets, some of them only to be cut down by gunfire. Children shrieked as parents pulled them out through clouds of smoke. Guns blazed for much of the night. Not until six o'clock were the Rangers able to move into the smoldering ruins of La Comandancia.

While fighting raged around La Comandancia and other combat units were seizing targets across the country, small squads of American commandos crept through Panama City on special missions. One found and destroyed Noriega's private Learjet, which the Americans feared he would use in trying to flee. Another raided a prison to free an American who had been arrested for collaborating with the CIA.

A third commando squad was to have been sent to find Guillermo Endara, who had won that year's presidential election but had been prevented from taking office, bring him to the Canal Zone with his two running mates, and swear them in to head a new government. Instead of sending this squad, however, American commanders came up with a less risky idea. They simply invited the three men to dinner at Howard Air Force Base on December 19. When the guests arrived, an American diplomat told them that an invasion was imminent and that the United States wanted to hand the government over to them. They were stunned.

"I felt like a big sledgehammer hit my head," Endara said later.

After waiting for several hours, the three men were brought to another American base in the Canal Zone, Fort Clayton. Shortly before two o'clock in the morning, with Panama City in flames, they took their oaths of office. Fort Clayton was the headquarters of the new government for the next thirty hours. Only then, with the victory won, did the Americans allow Panama's new leaders to return to Panamanian territory.

At seven o'clock that Wednesday morning in Washington, President Bush broadcast a message to the nation. He said he had ordered the invasion "only after reaching the conclusion that every other avenue was closed and the lives of American citizens were in grave danger." By the time he spoke, American forces had already secured all of their important objectives. One uncomfortable fact, however, made it impossible for him to declare victory. Noriega was nowhere to be found.

Several commando units were assigned to capture Noriega, but none was ever given a timely enough tip to do so. On Wednesday afternoon, American commanders offered a $1 million reward to anyone who would turn him in. His network of girlfriends, Santería practitioners, and military comrades, though, served him well. The Americans could not find him. World attention quickly focused on this high-stakes cat-and-mouse game.

Although Noriega managed to elude his pursuers for several days, he soon realized that he could not hide indefinitely. Holed up in a small apartment on the edge of Panama City, he became morose. On Sunday afternoon—it was Christmas Eve—he decided to call Monsignor José Sebastián Laboa, the papal nuncio in Panama City. Laboa was an outspoken critic of Noriega and the defense forces, but also a sophisticated diplomat who wished to see this conflict ended without more bloodshed. He agreed to grant Noriega asylum at the *nunciatura,* as the Vatican embassy was known.

Rather than go himself to pick up the deposed dictator, Laboa sent Father Villanueva, the fiery opposition hero who prayed for the soul of Hugo Spadafora at every Mass. Villanueva arrived at the designated spot, a Dairy Queen parking lot, in a four-door Toyota Land Cruiser with darkly tinted windows. He saw no one. Finally, a van that was parked nearby edged toward him and pulled into the space next to his. Noriega emerged, wearing a baseball cap, a T-shirt, and a pair of blue shorts. He slid into the backseat of the Toyota. After the door slammed shut, Villanueva turned around to see the man against whom he had campaigned so long and loudly.

"Do you know who I am?" he asked.

"Yes, unfortunately," Noriega replied curtly.

Both men were silent during the short ride. At the *nunciatura,* Noriega told his hosts that he wished to ask for asylum in Spain. Laboa called the Spanish ambassador, who told him the request was impractical because Spain had an extradition treaty with the United States. Noriega then suggested Mexico, but the Mexican ambassador made himself unavailable.

Monsignor Laboa had promised Noriega never to hand him over to anyone against his will. His task now was to persuade the fugitive that surrendering was his best option. Later he said he never doubted Noriega would ultimately agree.

"He is a man who, without his pistol, is manageable by anyone," the wise nuncio surmised.

The Americans, however, were not in a patient mood. As soon as they learned that Noriega was inside the *nunciatura,* they sent troops to surround it. Then, on the afternoon of Christmas Day, General Thurman himself appeared at the gate. He spent forty minutes trying unsuccessfully to persuade Laboa to surrender his guest. Barely twenty-four hours into the standoff, some frustrated American officials began invoking the specter of Josef Cardinal Mindszenty, who took asylum at the United States embassy in Budapest in 1956 and remained there for fifteen years.

Acting on recommendations from psychological warfare specialists, Thurman ordered a convoy of armored cars to encircle the *nunciatura* as closely as possible, even pulling onto adjacent sidewalks, and gun their engines continually. Then, late on Sunday night, he sent soldiers to burn the brush off a nearby lot and turn it into a helicopter base. Finally, in what became the most surreal aspect of Operation Just Cause, he had enormous speakers placed around the *nunciatura* so that rock music could be continually blared into it at deafening volume. The songs his advisers chose had titles intended as messages to Noriega, among them "I Fought the Law (and the Law Won)," "You're No Good," and "Nowhere to Run."

The Americans may have hoped that this tactic would force Noriega to run out of the *nunciatura* begging for mercy. Instead it led Laboa to announce that he was suspending negotiations until the noise ceased. After several days of stalemate, the Americans shifted to a more diplomatic approach. They moved their armored cars away from the *nunciatura,* disconnected their loudspeakers, and withdrew most of their soldiers. On January 2, Deputy Secretary of State Lawrence Eagleburger arrived in Panama. That same day, Laboa, who until then had left Noriega largely to himself, began encouraging him to think about surrender. He pulled a curtain aside so Noriega could see the angry crowd that had gathered outside, chanting "Murderer!" and "Kill Him!" At one point he even obliquely suggested that Noriega reflect on the fate that befell the Italian dictator Benito Mussolini, who in 1945 was captured by his enemies as he tried to flee, executed, and then hung upside down in a public square.

On the afternoon of January 3, eleven days after entering the *nunciatura*, Noriega finally realized that he had, as the song said, nowhere to run. He asked to attend a Catholic Mass before surrendering. Father Villanueva was indignant at the very idea.

"Does God love this man?" he asked Laboa incredulously.

"Obviously," Laboa replied.

Laboa himself celebrated the Mass that evening. When it was over, Noriega went to his room and put on a neatly pressed tan uniform that one of his mistresses had sent him. Shortly before nine o'clock, he walked toward the door of the *nunciatura*. As he was about to open it, Villanueva spoke to him for the first time since their encounter at the Dairy Queen.

"I will pray for you every day," he said.

"Thank you," Noriega replied.

With that, the defeated strongman walked out. As soon as he was off the embassy's property, American soldiers pounced on him, taped his wrists behind his back, and hustled him into a waiting helicopter. By sunrise the next day, he was in a cell at the Metropolitan Correction Center in Miami.

12

They Will Have Flies Walking Across Their Eyeballs

All of the twenty Afghan fighters who crossed from Pakistan into their homeland on the afternoon of October 21, 2001, should have been ready to trek for endless miles over forbidding mountain ranges. Only nineteen were. Their commander had good reason to require a jeep or a mule. More than a decade earlier, he had been on a guerrilla mission when he stepped on a Soviet land mine. The explosion threw him to the ground and, as he fell, he saw an object shoot past his face. It was his right foot. From that moment, Abdul Haq fought with a broken body.

Haq's small band of rebels did not look as if it could shape the fate of nations. Terrorists directed from Afghanistan had launched spectacular attacks on the United States less than six weeks before, however, and concepts of the possible and the impossible were in disarray. The United States had begun bombing Afghanistan in an effort to destroy its ruling party, the Taliban. Haq thought this was the wrong way to build a new, democratic Afghanistan. He was returning home to offer his compatriots an alternative.

After a long series of meetings with all manner of Afghans at his headquarters in the Pakistani border town of Peshawar, Haq came to believe that he could bring down the Taliban through a combination of military and political strikes. He was even convinced he could lure important Taliban commanders to his side. During a visit to Rome, he sought and received the blessing of the exiled Afghan king, Zahir Shah, who shared his vision of a multiethnic civilian government for their long-suffering country.

Although this mission held great promise, it was also exceedingly dangerous. Haq was entering a country ruled by ruthless fanatics, with the declared intention of overthrowing their regime. He and his men were only lightly armed and needed to reach some secure place before the Taliban found them.

Haq set off before he was ready. He believed that the Taliban movement, deeply despised by most Afghans and suddenly a symbol of world terror, was on the brink of collapse. He wanted to break its hold on the country with as little violence as possible, hoping that this would reduce the power of warlords and foreign governments over the regime that followed. On October 7, however, American cruise missiles began falling on Afghanistan. That gave Haq a sense of urgency. He feared that if a foreign-sponsored bombing campaign pushed the Taliban from power, the nation would sink into chaos. He wanted to make his way into Afghanistan quickly and build a force that would not only fight the Taliban but be ready to take power when it fell.

On the surface, this seemed like the kind of mission the United States would fervently support. Haq was one of the bravest and most celebrated of Afghan rebel commanders. Unlike many of the others, he was worldly, secular, and pro-Western. Margaret Thatcher had received him at Downing Street, and Ronald Reagan had singled him out for a toast at a White House reception, lifting his glass and promising, "Abdul Haq, we are with you." Yet Haq was also an outspoken nationalist. His dream was that once the Taliban was overthrown, it would be replaced by a regime free of all outside influence.

"What we want from you Americans—we want friendship with you," he told one interviewer. "But we cannot salute you. We cannot be your puppet. If you expect us to be your puppet, there will be no difference for us between you and the Soviets."

Comments like that made Haq a pariah in the eyes of powerful Americans. The CIA had given him only modest support during the rebellion against Soviet occupiers in the 1980s, and since he had become no more cooperative in the intervening years, the United States was not inclined to help him fight the Taliban. He went back to war anyway.

Leaders of the Taliban recognized Haq as a potentially potent enemy. In 1999 they sent a squad to assassinate him at his home in Peshawar, but the killers managed only to gun down his wife and eleven-year-old son. So when Haq crossed into Afghanistan on that autumn night, he wanted to punish the Taliban not simply for what it had done to Afghanistan but for what it had done to his own family.

Peshawar has for centuries been a dazzling center of espionage and intrigue. It is so dangerous that a man can be snatched from the streets and made to disappear without a trace, but also so safe that money changers doze in front of great bundles of cash. Vendors in the labyrinthine bazaar sell mountain lion pelts, peacock feathers, juicy melons, and what they say is the world's finest heroin. Spies are everywhere. It is hard to keep a secret in Peshawar.

That was especially true for Abdul Haq. The Taliban had failed to kill him, but it maintained intimate relations with the Pakistani secret service, which also had no use for him. Both groups followed his every move, tapped his telephone, and repeatedly tried to bribe their way into his inner circle.

Because Haq was so talkative, it was probably not necessary for Taliban and Pakistani spies to watch him this closely. Soon after he crossed into Afghanistan, an article about his mission appeared in the *Wall Street Journal*.

> A key anti-Taliban commander has entered the south of Afghanistan with a force of about 100 men to try to open the first ethnic-Pashtun front against the regime. . . . Mr. Haq plans to launch a military assault in the next few days. . . .
>
> While among Afghanistan's most respected commanders from that period [of war against the Soviets], Mr. Haq hasn't received support distributed in recent months by the U.S. Central Intelligence Agency to some anti-Taliban leaders. . . . [He is] among several opposition leaders in Peshawar who have criticized the U.S. bombing. While 16 days of strikes seem to have destroyed much of the Taliban's military hardware and installations, some opposition leaders say the pounding is also gradually alienating Afghans.

On Saturday, October 20, the day before he set out, Haq had met with CIA agents in Peshawar. He told them he hoped to spark a series of defections and military revolts that would bring down the Taliban with a minimum of bloodshed. They were uninterested, as they always were when Haq had an idea. All they offered him in the way of help was a few satellite telephones. He demurred, for two reasons. First, he already had all the phones he needed, courtesy of James and Joseph Ritchie, wealthy American brothers who grew up in Afghanistan and were contributing to his cause. Second, he suspected that the CIA would use global positioning chips embedded in these phones to track his movements, and perhaps pass the information to his enemies.

After slipping into Afghanistan over mountains near the Khyber Pass, Haq began approaching village chiefs and others he thought might help him in his anti-Taliban mission. Several agreed to join his cause, among them a powerful Taliban leader from a district near Jalalabad. Before the final arrangements for this defection could be made, however, Haq received news that a squad of Taliban fighters, sent from Jalalabad to capture him, was approaching. He tried to retreat toward Pakistan but found every escape route blocked. Just six days into his mission, he was suddenly in mortal danger.

Haq had only one remaining hope. Near the valley where he was cornered were two helicopter landing sites the Soviets had built a decade earlier. Using his satellite phone, he called James Ritchie, his American friend and supporter, who was in Peshawar anxiously awaiting news. This news was very bad.

"Can you do something for me?" Haq asked.

Ritchie immediately relayed this SOS to his brother in the United States, who in turn called Robert McFarlane, one of Haq's American sponsors. McFarlane, who still had the web of Washington connections he built up while serving as President Reagan's national security adviser, telephoned agents at the CIA operations center in Langley, Virginia, and also the chief military adviser to the National Security Council, General Wayne Downing. He gave them Haq's precise location and pleaded that they try to save him.

While McFarlane waited by his telephone for a reply that Thursday night, Haq was half a world away in Afghanistan, surrounded by enemies in the morning chill. His fate lay in the hands of the CIA, which should have been his closest ally but which, over the course of nearly twenty years, had turned him down every time he asked for help. The odds were against him.

FOR CENTURIES, THE NAME "AFGHANISTAN" HAS CONJURED UP IMAGES OF isolation and remoteness. It is a forbidding place, locked in the Asian landmass, cut off from the world by towering mountain ranges and governed more by tribal tradition than by law. Its hostility to invaders is legendary, epitomized by the fate of a British-led column that comprised more than 16,000 soldiers and camp followers when it was forced to flee Kabul in 1842, and was reduced to just a single man by the time it reached the British garrison at Jalalabad, ninety miles away.

During the nineteenth century, Russia and Britain jousted for influence over Afghanistan in a high-stakes rivalry that became known as the Great Game. Rivalries like this usually break out when a poor country has a resource that rich countries covet. Afghanistan has no oil, no mineral wealth, and little fertile land, but it does have one asset that has always attracted outsiders: location. It lies astride routes to India, Iran, Central Asia, and China that have been strategic prizes for centuries.

True to its independent tradition, Afghanistan remained neutral in both World War I and World War II. In the postwar years, its leaders sought with considerable success to remain outside the Cold War confrontation. Young officers who overthrew the monarchy in 1973 accepted aid from both the neighboring Soviet Union and the faraway United States. They held power until 1979, when a leftist coalition deposed them.

The new regime found itself unable to consolidate power, partly because it sought to impose far-reaching social reforms and partly because it entered into an alliance with the Soviet Union, a country many Afghans considered imperialistic and anti-Muslim. In the provincial capital of Herat, a protest against the inclusion of women in a literacy campaign turned into a full-scale rebellion. Militants sought out and hacked to death scores of Soviet men, women, and children and jubilantly paraded some of their mangled bodies through the streets on pikes. The government, with Soviet help, took the city back after a ferocious bombing campaign in which twenty thousand people were killed.

This upheaval came while the region was still recovering from the shock of the Islamic revolution in Iran, which radically reshaped the strategic map of the Middle East and Central Asia. Americans considered the revolution a serious geopolitical setback and feared that the Soviets would take advantage of it, perhaps by using Afghanistan as a base for a thrust toward Persian Gulf oil fields. For the Soviets, it revived the old fear that Muslims in their Central Asian provinces might embrace fundamentalism and use it as a banner for separatist rebellion. Worse, it came as the Soviet position in Afghanistan was eroding under pressure from Islamic rebels. At an emergency meeting of the Soviet Politburo on March 17, 1979, Yuri Andropov, the KGB director who would later become the country's leader, urged his comrades to take a hard line.

"Under no circumstances can we lose Afghanistan," he told them.

The United States was also watching the unfolding Afghan crisis.

Rebellions against pro-Soviet regimes did not break out every day, and when one began in Afghanistan, CIA analysts suggested that the agency give it covert support. The longer this rebellion lasted, they reasoned, the weaker the Soviets would become and the more resources they would have to divert to Afghanistan.

At around the same time Andropov was addressing his Politburo in Moscow, the CIA came up with its first plan to aid Afghan guerrillas. This was the beginning of what would become by far the largest and most expensive operation in CIA history. Some consider it to have been a spectacular success. Others believe that in light of subsequent events, what seemed at first like a victory for the United States looks more like a catastrophe.

It is axiomatic that for a guerrilla movement to succeed against a powerful army, it needs a cross-border sanctuary. The map of Central Asia makes clear that Pakistan, whose border with Afghanistan twists for more than one thousand miles, is the logical sanctuary for Afghan rebels. So if the CIA wished to send clandestine aid to the rebels, it would have to strike a deal with Pakistan.

American leaders were falling into a pattern that has shaped the "regime change" era. They saw the chance to score a victory, in this case by bleeding the Soviet Union in Afghanistan. Eager for that victory, they never weighed the potential long-term consequences of their action.

"We had just come off this terrible tragedy, this Vietnam War, and confidence was a bit shaken," Chuck Cogan, a CIA officer who was posted in the Middle East during the 1980s, explained afterward. "There was a great deal of feeling of frustration, that the Soviets were advancing and we were on the defensive. And suddenly this came along as an opportunity to turn that around."

The first moment the Americans could have stopped to reflect on what this intervention might produce came when they confronted the necessity of dealing with Pakistan. Two years earlier, Pakistan's democratic order had been upset when General Zia al-Huq seized power in a military coup. Zia fervently dedicated himself to two goals: building a nuclear bomb and imposing what he called a "genuine Islamic order" in Pakistan. Then, just as the Americans were deciding whether to embrace him as a partner, he proceeded with the hanging of the prime minister he overthrew, Zulfikar Ali Bhutto. So the man the CIA needed most for its Afghan project was a military dictator who had ordered the execution of his predecessor, was promoting a reactionary form of Islam within his own country, and ran a network of agents around the world trying to buy outlawed nuclear material and technology.

Whatever doubts the Americans had about the wisdom of embracing Zia were overwhelmed by their determination to intensify the rebellion in Afghanistan. They approached Zia and asked if he would agree to turn his country into a base for that rebellion. He was willing, but only under an extraordinary set of conditions. The CIA, he said, must deliver no weapons directly to Afghan rebels but send them instead to Pakistan's Inter-Services Intelligence Agency, the ISI, which would in turn pass them to the Afghans. Furthermore, no Americans were to enter Afghanistan or have any contact with guerrilla commanders. The ISI would pass CIA money and guns on to leaders of its own choosing. To all of this the CIA agreed. It subcontracted to Pakistan the job of directing the Afghan rebellion.

"The CIA knew exactly what their role was," General Hamid Gul, director general of the ISI during the peak of the Afghan campaign, told an interviewer after the war ended. "They knew that we were handling the operations. We were in charge of the entire episode, and they were to provide the logistic support. They were not allowed even to travel into our own tribal areas, leave alone going into Afghanistan—so much so that they could not talk to Afghan leaders without my men, ISI men, being present."

Afghanistan was in upheaval when this deal was struck in mid-1979. By autumn, a Communist leader named Hafizullah Amin, who had once attended Columbia University, had taken power. He treated the Soviets coolly, and when he began meeting with American diplomats in Kabul, Soviet leaders in Moscow feared that he was about to abandon them. On November 26, the Politburo secretly decided to send troops to Kabul, kill Amin, and impose a friendlier regime.

On Christmas Eve, thousands of Soviet troops marched over pontoon bridges across the Amu Darya river into Afghanistan, and others landed at the airport in Kabul. Tanks followed in the morning. A squad of KGB commandos stormed Amin's palace, killed him, and placed a new strongman in power. Afghanistan was no longer simply ruled by a pro-Soviet regime; it was under Soviet military occupation.

The implications quickly became clear to strategists in Washington. Until this point, they had been supporting a rebellion that was only indirectly against the Soviet Union. Now they had a chance to engage the Soviets themselves. It took President Jimmy Carter's national security adviser, Zbigniew Brzezinski, just two days to come up with a memo entitled "Reflections on Soviet Intervention in Afghanistan."

> It is essential that Afghanistan's resistance continues. This means more money as well as arms shipments to the rebels, and some technical advice. To make the above possible, we must both reassure Pakistan and encourage it to help the rebels. This will require a review of our policy toward Pakistan, more guarantees to it, more arms aid and, alas, a decision that our security policy toward Pakistan cannot be dictated by our nonproliferation policy. . . .
>
> Our ultimate goal is the withdrawal of Soviet troops from Afghanistan. Even if this is not attainable, we should make Soviet involvement as costly as possible.

Carter embraced this strategy, and so did Ronald Reagan, who succeeded him in 1981. Soon after Reagan took office, he struck a deal with Pakistan under which the United States embraced it as a strategic ally and turned a blind eye to General Zia's sins. American aid poured into Pakistan, a total of more than $6 billion during the 1980s. So did aid to the Afghan rebels, the mujahideen, which rose steadily from $30 million in 1981 to $200 million in 1984. Nearly every cent of it, along with nearly every weapon and bullet, was delivered first to the ISI, which then distributed it to its favored commanders.

The ISI, reasonably enough, channeled American aid to those warlords who were most responsive to Pakistani influence. It particularly favored those who shared Zia's commitment to fundamentalist Islam. While the Americans looked on happily, the ISI sent hundreds of millions of their dollars to obscurantist warlords like Gulbeddin Hekmatyar, a ruthlessly ambitious commander who made a fortune in the drug trade, dreamed of turning Afghanistan into a pure Islamic state, and liked to lead his followers in lusty chants of "Death to America!"

If there was an anti-Hekmatyar among Afghan commanders, a figure who exemplified the values of nationalism and modernity, it was Abdul Haq. Son of a prominent Pashtun family, he was just twenty years old when he was imprisoned in 1978 for organizing guerrilla attacks against the regime in Kabul. His family bribed him out of prison, and after the Soviets invaded at the end of 1979 he went back to war, this time on a larger scale. He scored several great successes, including the destruction of a large Soviet arms depot in Kabul and, soon afterward, a 200-vehicle Soviet convoy. Yet his appeals for a share of the American largesse went largely unanswered. Both the ISI and the CIA considered him too independent. The ISI also found him too secular and too pro-Western.

In 1985, frustrated by the ISI's refusal to support him, Haq took his case directly to Washington. He electrified many powerful Americans, among them Robert McFarlane, Reagan's national security adviser, who pronounced him "extraordinary" and "terrifically impressive." When he returned to Pakistan, however, he found that his reception in Washington had changed nothing. General Zia refused to see him. Milt Bearden, the CIA station chief who arrived in Islamabad in 1986 and became the war's American field marshal, ridiculed him as a showoff and called him "Hollywood Haq."

Others saw him differently. Ahmed Rashid, the preeminent journalistic chronicler of the modern Afghan wars, called Haq "a very charismatic leader" who "built an effective network with people from very different backgrounds." Even the State Department's special envoy to the Afghan rebels, Peter Thomsen, believed the CIA was foolish to support a brutal fundamentalist like Hekmatyar while rejecting a rival who had "enormous support, not only in his own area but around Afghanistan."

> This was the essential proposition: that Hekmatyar was the best fighter and the best organized. He did get favoritism, of course, from the Pakistani ISI, and most of the weapons went to him, but he was rejected and hated by the great majority of Afghans. . . .
> The CIA cut off Abdul and ceased providing him with any weapons. Privately they spread the word that he was a publicist for himself, he was "Hollywood Haq" and didn't have much of a following inside the country.

In the early 1980s, Reagan and several of his closest advisers began to believe that with enough money and weaponry, Afghan guerrillas could actually defeat the Red Army and turn their country into "the Russians' Vietnam." To pay for this campaign, they recruited an unlikely partner: Saudi Arabia. The Saudis were already deeply involved in Pakistan. They had sent Zia large sums of money to open religious schools catering to both impoverished Pakistanis and Afghan refugees. To ensure that these schools taught only the puritanical Wahhabi form of Islam and that students were not exposed to such corrupting subjects as history or science, they also sent hundreds of mullahs, Koran readers, and religious teachers.

Saudi Arabia was intimately tied to the United States because of its role as a vital oil supplier. In 1984, taking advantage of this friendship, President Reagan asked the Saudi royal family for help in Afghanistan. The Saudis saw at once that granting this request would be a way to strengthen their friend Zia in Pakistan, promote groups within Afghanistan that were submissive to Pakistan and its fundamentalist agenda, and at the same time ingratiate themselves to Washington. They agreed to match all American aid to Afghan rebels on a dollar-for-dollar basis.

This commitment, coupled with Reagan's willingness to pour huge amounts of money into the guerrilla cause, led to one of the most far-reaching and costly operations ever mounted by an intelligence agency. In 1986 the CIA sent Afghan guerrillas $470 million, and the next year $630 million—all of it matched by the Saudis. During this period, the lawless border region straddling Pakistan and Afghanistan gave birth to violent forces that would reshape the world in ways no one could then imagine.

Although the massive size of this project is the first thing about it that jumps from the pages of history, another of its aspects was even more extraordinary. Despite the huge amounts of money the United States sent to Afghan guerrillas, it never played or even sought to play a role in deciding who received its gifts. That was left to Pakistan, which had objectives far different from Washington's. The Pakistanis chose to support seven Afghan factions, all of them in varying degrees fundamentalist and anti-Western, and also worked systematically to undermine and destroy others that were leftist, secular, or nationalist.

"For God's sake," one secular Afghan warned the Americans during this period, "you're financing your own assassins!"

As the Afghan war escalated, the world's attention began to focus on the intensifying threat of international terrorism. Hijackers seized an airliner in Beirut and murdered a United States navy diver they found aboard. A few months later, Palestinians hijacked the cruise ship *Achille Lauro* and killed an elderly Jewish American passenger. Gunmen attacked the El Al airport counters in Vienna and Rome, killing nineteen people. In Lebanon, kidnappers abducted the CIA station chief and tortured him to death. Others seized half a dozen Americans and held them as long-term prisoners.

These events, which were highly publicized in the United States, might have led American leaders to reflect on the origins of anti-American terror. Had they done so, they might have wondered whether it was such a good idea to train and equip brigades of fundamentalists fighting in Afghanistan. Few in Washington, however, recognized that while the United States was reeling from an early wave of terror sprung from the Middle East, it was shaping the fighters who would later launch an even more horrific wave.

One of the most far-reaching decisions the ISI made as it built the Afghan rebel army was to recruit militants from other Muslim countries. Many who volunteered were radicals who believed they could do something holy by coming to Afghanistan and joining a jihad against the infidel Soviet occupier. At CIA-sponsored camps inside Pakistan, they were trained in modern techniques of sabotage, ambush, and assault, and in the use of weapons from sniper rifles to time-delayed bomb detonators.

The Saudi millionaire Osama bin Laden was among those who thrived in this milieu. Bin Laden arrived in Afghanistan in the early 1980s, when he was still in his mid-twenties, and served for several months as a guerrilla fighter. After a time he persuaded the ISI to give him a more important assignment. He took up the job of receiving foreign militants who arrived in Afghanistan and channeling them to training camps. It was an ideal post for someone eager to meet jihadis from around the world.

"There were no less than twenty-eight different Muslim countries from where these motivated youth were drawn," General Gul, the ISI chief, said when the war was over. "I would say that if you were to include Pakistanis who also went and participated, it would be no less than fifty thousand young men who went into Afghanistan."

Slowly and inevitably, given its enormous resources, the insurgency grew stronger. Eventually it reached the point where it could seriously challenge the Red Army. In 1986 the new Soviet leader, Mikhail Gorbachev, told the Politburo that this war had become a "bleeding wound" that had to be stanched. At the end of that year, he announced that eight thousand Soviet troops were being called home. Finally, after doing what he could to secure the regime of the Communist Afghan leader Mohammed Najibullah, he withdrew them all. On February 15, 1989, the last Red Army units crossed the Amu Darya back into Soviet territory.

For the Soviets, this adventure had been an unmitigated disaster. It cost them, by their own account, nearly $100 million and the lives of fifteen thousand soldiers. They also lost incalculable amounts of international prestige and strategic power. Within a few years, the Soviet Union collapsed. The defeat it suffered in Afghanistan played a role in speeding its demise.

If anyone lost even more from this war than the Soviets, it was certainly the Afghan people. They were liberated from occupation by a foreign power, but at a cost so staggering as to be almost incomprehensible. One million Afghans were killed during the 1980s. Three million were maimed. Five million fled to refugee camps in neighboring countries. No war ever fought in Afghanistan left such a devastating physical and spiritual legacy.

General Zia was killed in a plane crash in 1988 and so did not live to see the victory, but Pakistan emerged from the war with greatly increased power. It had become a partner of the United States, a king-maker in Central Asia, and the effective master of Afghanistan. Perhaps most important, it gained a decade of invaluable time to work on its nuclear program without having to worry about complaints from the United States.

No one was more thrilled about the Soviet defeat than the Americans. For them, this war had never been about Afghanistan or anything else other than fighting the Soviet Union. By winning it, they achieved their maximum, almost unimaginable goal. Milt Bearden sent a two-word cable to Langley that distilled the surge of pride he and many other Americans felt at their triumph.

"WE WON," it said.

THIS OUTCOME PRODUCED A GIDDY ROUND OF CONGRATULATIONS IN WASH-ington. It took only a short time, however, for American leaders to begin losing interest in Afghanistan. They did so against the urgent advice of some who knew the country best. President Najibullah warned publicly that if the United States did not remain engaged, Afghanistan "will be turned into a center for terrorism." Abdul Haq predicted that it would become "both a training ground and munitions dump for foreign terrorists and at the same time, the world's largest poppy field." Peter Thomsen, the State Department envoy to the newly victorious rebels, wrote in reports to Washington that if secular-oriented commanders like Haq and the Tajik leader Ahmad Shah Massoud were left without support, fundamentalists backed by Pakistan would crush them. No one took these arguments seriously, especially after 1991, when the United States shifted its focus completely to the Gulf War against the Iraqi dictator Saddam Hussein.

"Did we really give a shit about the long-term future of Nangarhar?" Milt Bearden mused years later, referring to one of Afghanistan's provinces. "Maybe not. As it turned out, guess what? We didn't."

Afghan warlords who had defeated the Soviets now turned their aim on Najibullah's government. Yet Najibullah still counted on strong support from Moscow, and his enemies feuded constantly among themselves. He fended them off for more than three years. Once the Soviet Union collapsed, however, he was lost. On April 25, 1992, under an agreement brokered by the United Nations, he agreed to resign. Warlords formed a new government, but it quickly collapsed in recriminations that escalated into violence and ultimately into civil war. This war's most devastating result was the destruction of Kabul in the winter of 1992–93, achieved through months of sustained bombardment by Hekmatyar, who was still Pakistan's favorite warlord.

As the civil war dragged on, the Pakistanis reluctantly concluded that they would never be able to impose Hekmatyar as leader of Afghanistan and decided to forge a new force that would have a better chance of winning. They recruited radical Afghan refugees from the thousands of religious schools in Pakistan, organized them into military units, and trained and armed their leaders. Because each of these recruits had been a *talib*, or religious student, they called their movement the Taliban. By the time it began capturing territory in Afghanistan, at the end of 1994, it had twenty thousand troops under arms and impressive amounts of weaponry. The Saudi government sent it millions of dollars, and whenever it needed more fighters, Pakistan recruited them from its Saudi-sponsored religious schools.

The Taliban also owed a great deal to the United States. Some of its militants had learned the art of war during the 1980s at camps paid for by the CIA. Many others became radicalized in the profundamentalist climate that the CIA encouraged during that period. After the Soviet defeat, they either fought in the civil war or retreated to the austere monasticism of their religious schools in Pakistan. When they reemerged a few years later as a fundamentalist militia, they owed as much to the Americans as to the Pakistanis.

Help from Pakistan and the United States would probably have been enough to lead the Taliban to power, but it had another powerful patron. Early in 1996, Osama bin Laden returned to Afghanistan after several years in Sudan, bringing his Al Qaeda terror group with him. He recognized the Taliban as a movement perfectly in line with his own beliefs and gave it $3 million to fuel its push to final victory. On September 27, 1996, propelled by four powerful friends—Saudi Arabia, Pakistan, the United States, and bin Laden—Taliban forces rolled triumphantly into Kabul. One squad stormed the United Nations compound, where former president Najibullah had been living since his overthrow four years before, seized him, castrated him, hanged him, and then left his body dangling in a public square.

Immediately after seizing Kabul, Taliban militants went on a rampage most unlike those of other conquering armies. They considered all visual imagery blasphemous, so they smashed televisions, destroyed cameras, and ripped photos from walls. To prevent people from listening to music, which they also considered evil, they destroyed all radios and stereo equipment. They banned alcohol and tobacco, forbade dancing, and even outlawed kite flying. Most chilling, they withdrew every conceivable right from women, decreeing that they must not work or study outside their homes and that whenever they appeared in public, they had to be covered with a burka more forbidding than anyone in the modern world had ever seen.

The Taliban regime also embraced bin Laden, and allowed him to establish camps in Afghanistan where militants from around the world could be trained in terror tactics. Theirs was an ideal match. Mullah Mohammed Omar, the Taliban leader, wanted to bring Afghanistan under pure Islamic rule. Bin Laden had the same ambition for the entire Muslim world. Both seethed with hatred of the West. Soon they were running Afghanistan together and turning it into the world's most active breeding ground for terrorism.

Despite all of this, the United States maintained good relations with the Taliban. American officials, according to Martin Ewans, a senior British diplomat who served in the region for years, were "not just muted about, but even dismissive of, the social and judicial excesses that were from an early stage the hallmark of the Taliban's rule." There was a clear reason for this. An American oil company, Unocal, wanted to build a $2 billion pipeline to carry natural gas from the rich fields of Turkmenistan to booming Pakistan, and perhaps on to India. The pipeline would have to run across Afghanistan, and for that reason Unocal was eager to see a government in Kabul—any kind of government—that could pacify the country.

The most prominent American pushing for friendship with the Taliban was Robin Raphel, an assistant secretary of state in the Clinton administration. Her interest was unabashedly commercial. During a visit to Kabul in 1996, she said she hoped to "facilitate U.S. business interests," and warned that if the United States did not deal with the Taliban on the pipeline project, "economic opportunities here will be missed." The American journalist Steve Coll, author of a magisterial work on the modern Afghan wars, wrote that Raphel seemed principally interested in "corporate deal-making."

"In the absence of alternatives, the State Department had taken up Unocal's agenda as its own," Coll wrote. "American tolerance of the Taliban was publicly and inextricably linked to the financial goals of an oil company."

By the time the Taliban took power, Afghanistan had been at horrific war with itself for nearly twenty years. Many Afghans welcomed them despite their excesses, hoping that they would finally bring a measure of peace to the country. This they did. It was a peace of the graveyard, to be sure, enforced by amputations, floggings, and public executions, but for a time, Afghans thought that the Taliban might lead them toward a better future.

Feminists in the United States and elsewhere protested the Taliban's treatment of women, but their anger was not enough to push Afghanistan back onto the world political agenda. It took the country's most famous guest, Osama bin Laden, to do that. On August 7, 1998, terror squads acting at his direction blew up the American embassies in Kenya and Tanzania, killing more than two hundred people. Two weeks later, President Clinton ordered the bombing of a camp in Afghanistan where bin Laden was thought to be living. More than sixty Tomahawk cruise missiles hit the camp, but although about two dozen militants were killed, the terror leader was not among them.

By then, several of the mujahideen armies that had torn Afghanistan apart for so long were re-forming and beginning to attack the Taliban. The country was pulled back into civil conflict by the same warlords who had done so much to wreck it during the 1980s: Hekmatyar; Massoud; the Uzbek leader Abdul Rashid Dostum; and Ismail Khan, based in the western city of Herat. All used weapons the CIA had sent them to fight the Soviets a decade earlier.

Abdul Haq had served as minister of security in the mujahideen government that tried and failed to rule the country after Najibullah resigned but quickly became disgusted with the regime and quit. Deeply frustrated by what was happening to Afghanistan, he decided to leave. For six years he lived quietly in Dubai, running an import-export company. In the summer of 2001, with his waist thicker and his beard grayer, he returned. He saw a chance that the Taliban might fall, and wanted to help shape the new regime.

Haq's plan was to reassemble his Pashtun force and ally it with Massoud's Northern Alliance. Massoud was a figure of dubious repute, but, like Haq, he both rejected fundamentalism and had a genuine popular following. Theirs was a highly promising combination, and the regime knew it. Early in September, two Al Qaeda operatives arrived at Massoud's headquarters posing as journalists. After waiting for several days, they were finally brought to see the rebel leader. Their video camera was actually a bomb, and moments after Massoud sat down for his interview they detonated it. He bled for fifteen minutes and then died.

Two days later, in the bloodiest attack on American soil since the Civil War, Al Qaeda terrorists flew hijacked airplanes into the Pentagon and the World Trade Center in New York. Nearly 3,000 people were killed. In response, President George W. Bush set his sights on Afghanistan.

"WE'RE GOING TO FIND OUT WHO DID THIS, AND WE'RE GOING TO KICK THEIR asses," Bush told Vice President Dick Cheney an hour after the September 11 attacks. Later he told President Vicente Fox of Mexico that all enemies of the United States were now "wanted, dead or alive." Others in the administration echoed his defiance in even more colorful terms.

"We'll rout 'em out," Cofer Black, head of the CIA's counterterrorism center, promised Bush two days after the attacks. "When we're through with them, they will have flies walking across their eyeballs."

Fateful misjudgments by five presidents had laid the groundwork not simply for the September 11 attacks but for the emergence of the worldwide terror network from which they sprung. Jimmy Carter launched the covert CIA project in Afghanistan. During the 1980s, Ronald Reagan spent billions of dollars to arm and train anti-Western zealots who were fighting the Soviets there. George H. W. Bush further inflamed Muslim radicals by establishing permanent American military bases in Saudi Arabia, home to the holiest sites in Islam. Bill Clinton failed to grasp the scope of the threat his predecessors bequeathed to him, and during his presidency, guerrillas who had been trained and armed by the United States a decade earlier completed their transformation into terrorists. George W. Bush ignored repeated warnings that devastating attacks were imminent, including a memorandum from his intelligence advisers, just five weeks before September 11, entitled "Bin Laden Determined to Strike in U.S." He turned out to be the one fated to confront the result of his own blindness and that of his predecessors.

Bush had come into office with less knowledge of the outside world, and less interest in it, than any other modern American president. He had traveled little outside the United States and had not read widely or thought seriously about world history. During his presidential campaign, a reporter asked him his view of the Taliban, and he answered with a blank stare.

"Because of the repression of women," the interviewer hinted. "In Afghanistan."

"Oh, I thought you said some band," Bush replied. "The Taliban in Afghanistan! Absolutely! Repressive!"

On Saturday morning, September 15, 2001, Bush and his principal advisers assembled for a full-day meeting at the Camp David presidential retreat in Maryland. During their morning session, Secretary of Defense Donald Rumsfeld and his deputy Paul Wolfowitz argued that attacking Afghanistan would be too weak a response to the terror attacks and that the United States should turn its focus to Iraq. Others disagreed. During the lunch break, according to *Washington Post* reporter Bob Woodward, Bush "sent a message to the group that he had heard enough debate about Iraq." He wanted to concentrate on Afghanistan first.

Exactly how the Americans would fight in Afghanistan, and to what end, was still unclear. At first, Bush demanded only that the Taliban oust its leader, Mullah Omar, and cut its ties to Al Qaeda. This was the option that the president of Pakistan, General Pervez Musharraf, was eagerly pushing. Pakistan had created and nurtured the Taliban and did not want to lose it. Musharraf urged its leaders to turn bin Laden over to the Americans, or at least expel him from Afghanistan. When they refused, he withdrew Pakistani support for the Taliban and gave the United States permission to launch bombing raids on Afghanistan from Pakistani air bases.

"Policies are made in accordance with environments," he said when asked about his about-face. "The environment changed, our policy changed."

By mid-September, Bush had decided to use American military power to overthrow the Taliban regime. He was not willing, however, to send large numbers of troops. Instead he approved a dual strategy. The United States would conduct an air war, and hire the Northern Alliance to fight on the ground.

Afghan warlords are notorious for their readiness to switch sides, and it is often said that although they cannot be bought, they can be rented. The CIA now wished to rent the Northern Alliance. A ten-man team of CIA officers carrying $3 million in cash for its commanders set off from Washington on September 20. Before the team left, Cofer Black called its leader to his office and told him that besides delivering the cash he had another assignment.

"Get bin Laden," Black said. "Find him. I want his head in a box."

"You're serious?" the agent asked incredulously.

"Absolutely," Black replied. "I want to take it down and show the President."

The CIA officers landed safely at a Northern Alliance landing strip north of Kabul and were brought to a guesthouse in a nearby village. At their first meeting with guerrilla commanders, they stacked half a million dollars on a table. The commanders were impressed, and asked if there was more where that came from. There was much more. Over the next two months, the CIA delivered $10 million to Northern Alliance commanders and another $60 million to an assortment of other warlords.

It took three weeks for the Americans to launch their air war. Military planners struggled to find targets they could hit in a country that had been blasted to ruin by years of war. They were also hesitant to send bombers over Afghanistan until they had teams in place that could rescue downed crew members. Finally, on Sunday afternoon, October 7, Bush sat down behind a desk in the White House Treaty Room, faced a television camera, and told Americans that Operation Enduring Freedom was under way.

On my orders, the United States military has begun strikes against Al Qaeda terrorist training camps and military installations of the Taliban regime in Afghanistan. These carefully targeted actions are designed to disrupt the use of Afghanistan as a terrorist base of operations, and to attack the military capability of the Taliban regime.

More than two weeks ago, I gave Taliban leaders a series of clear and

specific demands: close terrorist training camps, hand over leaders of the
Al Qaeda network, and return all foreign nationals, including American
citizens, unjustly detained in your country. None of these demands were
met. And now the Taliban will pay a price.

This war, and the terror attacks that set it off, would almost certainly
never have occurred if the United States had not armed and trained tens
of thousands of Islamic radicals during the 1980s, and then failed to act
when those radicals began transforming themselves into terrorists. Bush,
however, was not interested in such subtleties—"I don't do nuance," he
once famously declared—and over the next few weeks, he presented the
war to Americans in messianic terms much like those his predecessors
had used in explaining interventions in countries from the Philippines
to Panama. He said the United States was locked in "a momentous
struggle between good and evil," that it was fighting to promote "God-
given values" and "defend freedom and all that is good and just in the
world." America's enemies, he declared on various occasions, "hate us for
our freedoms," "hate us because we love liberty," and "hate us because
we're good."

Air strikes on Afghanistan began as Bush was making his televised
speech. The first round wiped out the Taliban's rudimentary air defenses
and destroyed its primitive military bases but had little effect beyond
that. Many of the compounds that were bombed had been abandoned
days or weeks earlier. Meanwhile, the Northern Alliance and other militias whose services the Americans thought they had purchased were
proving reluctant to fight. At one National Security Council meeting,
Deputy Secretary of State Richard Armitage listened to the same questions he had been hearing for days—What do we bomb? What comes
after the bombing? Is this a CIA or a Pentagon mission?—and finally
reacted in disgust.

"I think what I'm hearing is FUBAR," he told his comrades. Most had
been around the military long enough to recognize that acronym. It
means "Fucked Up Beyond All Recognition."

From his base in Peshawar, Abdul Haq watched the military campaign with dismay. He feared that by using the warlords as their proxies,
the Americans were giving them too much power and ensuring that
they would continue to dominate Afghanistan after this round of fighting ended. Eager to lay the foundation for a civilian regime, he crossed
back into his homeland.

As Taliban fighters closed in on Haq's little band, his American friends tried frantically to save him. The CIA might have sent a helicopter to pluck him out, or dispatched Predator drones, which fly without pilots, to attack the approaching Taliban squad. It did neither. By mid-morning Haq was in the hands of Taliban fighters. They put him in a jeep and begun driving him to Kabul. Before they had gone far, they saw a black Land Cruiser speeding toward them, flashing its lights in a signal for them to stop. Inside was the Taliban interior minister, Mullah Abdul Razak.

"No, he can't go to Kabul," Razak told the fighters when he heard their plan. "We have to terminate this man. He must be executed."

Razak ordered the jeep to follow his Land Cruiser. The small caravan veered off the main road and stopped at a rocky field. Haq was ordered out.

"This is the will of God, and I accept it," Haq said. "I came here to rebuild Afghanistan, not to destroy it."

Those were Haq's last words. As he finished pronouncing them, one of the Taliban fighters walked up behind him and shot him in the back of the head. After he fell, others emptied their rifles into his body. The man who might have been Afghanistan's greatest hope for peace died at the age of forty-three.

Taliban leaders had reason to be hopeful. They had managed to withstand the first wave of American bombing, and two of their most potentially dangerous enemies, Massoud and Haq, were dead. News commentators in the United States were grumbling that Bush had produced a "flawed plan" of "half-measures" that could lead the country into "another stalemate on the other side of the world." Pressure grew on the president to send ground troops. Secretary of State Powell counseled against it.

"I'd rule out the United States going after Afghans, who have been there for five thousand years," he told the other war planners.

By late October, Bush's strategy began paying off. Bribes from the CIA enticed some warlords who supported the Taliban to change sides, and motivated others to attack Taliban positions. Abdul Rashid Dostum's forces, accompanied by American advisers, took the key northern city of Mazar-i-Sharif. Soon afterward, Ismail Khan regained control of Herat after arranging for the defection of six thousand Taliban troops.

These weeks of preparation and war gave bin Laden plenty of time to escape into the network of caves and tunnels—much of it fortified with

CIA money during the 1980s—that lay beneath the rugged border region known as Tora Bora. The Americans, unwilling to risk taking casualties, did not chase him. Instead they asked their Afghan partners to track him down. Few of the Afghans, however, wanted their families to bear the eternal stain of having betrayed such a personage to infidels. They gave the hunt only minimal effort, and never caught their man.

The fight against the Taliban, in which the warlords had a direct stake, went more successfully than the hunt for bin Laden. On November 13, Taliban commanders decided they could no longer defend Kabul and led their men out to refuges elsewhere. Guerrillas from the Northern Alliance streamed in to replace them. They were received ecstatically. People dragged out hidden phonographs and played music for the first time in years. Women ran joyously through the streets without burkas.

In most wars, the capture of the enemy's capital city is considered decisive. Mullah Omar, however, had never moved to Kabul, preferring to stay in Kandahar, the main town in his native region. On December 7, Kandahar fell to a loose coalition of Pashtun militias. That date, eighty-seven days after the terror attacks on the United States, marked the American victory.

Whether it was really a victory, however, is debatable. Americans deposed the regime that had given Al Qaeda its protected base, but by refusing to send more than a few hundred troops to fight in Afghanistan, they allowed terrorist leaders to escape punishment for the crimes of September 11. Then, very quickly, they turned their attention to Iraq.

13

Thunder Run

Some of history's greatest conquerors have paused near Baghdad before assaulting it. None ever assembled as overwhelming a force as the United States Army massed around the ancient city in the spring of 2003. Its commanders had a simple plan. They would encircle Baghdad with tanks to prevent defenders from fleeing, and then send troops in to capture palaces, military bases, and other keystones of Saddam Hussein's dictatorship.

Sitting at his post eleven miles south of the city, Colonel David Perkins, the commander of a mechanized infantry brigade, was eager to avoid what might become a dangerous urban warfare campaign. On April 6 he offered his fellow commanders an alternative. He proposed to smash his way to the center of Baghdad in an audacious "thunder run," using only his own men, a total of fewer than one thousand. They would take this city of five million, he promised, in a single day.

A "thunder run" is normally a quick, daring, and disruptive thrust into and out of enemy territory. Colonel Perkins's men had staged one just the day before, pushing their column of tanks and armored personnel carriers to the Baghdad airport through a gauntlet of fire, killing several hundred defenders, and then withdrawing to safety before nightfall. Hours after that raid, the Iraqi information minister, Mohammed Said al-Sahaf, gave a bombastic press conference denying that any Americans had made it to the airport. Perkins took that as an affront and a challenge. He persuaded his superiors to send him on a "thunder run" far bolder than his last one. This time he would storm into the city center and try to stay there.

"If the condition's right, I can stay the night," he argued. "If I can stay the night, I can stay forever. If I'm in the city and I stay there, the war's over."

Perkins and his officers decided that their objective should be no less a prize than the walled palace complex from which Saddam Hussein ruled Iraq. The complex was a tree-shaded enclave, strictly off-limits to the public, built on two square miles of land at a bend in the Tigris River. Four busts of Saddam Hussein, each of them thirteen feet high, decorated its most imposing edifice, the Republican Palace. Other buildings housed members of Saddam's military and political elite. Just outside the walls lay other tantalizing targets, among them the army's ceremonial parade ground, the information ministry, and the headquarters of the ruling Baath Party.

The only route from Perkins's headquarters to the center of Baghdad was Highway 8, the same road his men had charged through on their first "thunder run." He knew that it was lined with tenacious defenders who would meet his column with hails of rifle and grenade fire. The defenders, however, had shown themselves to be disorganized, unfamiliar with even basic combat tactics, and armed with weapons hardly potent enough to threaten the tanks, armored personnel carriers, and Bradley fighting vehicles that Perkins planned to send against them.

To hold a position in the city center, Perkins would have to take control of this highway. The largest clusters of defenders had dug in around three major interchanges. Perkins understood that capturing these three interchanges was the key to his "thunder run." He and his staff officers circled them on maps and gave each a name. They might have called them One, Two, and Three, or Red, Yellow, and Blue. Instead they chose a trio of names that any American could love: Curly, Larry, and Moe.

The officers who gathered at Perkins's makeshift headquarters on the eve of this daring thrust had been told repeatedly that thousands of infantrymen from the 82nd Airborne and the 101st Airborne divisions would take Baghdad, and that their own role would be simply to support this assault. Perkins told them something very different. Rather than supporting the strike force, they would *be* the strike force.

"We have set the conditions to create the collapse of the Iraqi regime," Perkins told his officers. "They said it would take five divisions to win this war, but there's no question now that we can really do it ourselves tomorrow."

Perkins, a forty-four-year-old West Point graduate from Keene, New Hampshire, devised a plan under which two columns of tanks would race into Baghdad, firing as they charged but not stopping to engage the enemy. A mechanized infantry brigade would follow, dropping combat teams at each of the three intersections. As soon as Curly, Larry, and Moe were in American hands, trucks carrying fuel and ammunition would speed into the city with supplies for the men encamped at Saddam's palace complex.

"Holy shit, we're going straight into fucking Baghdad!" Captain Philip Wolford, the officer assigned to seize the complex, thought as Perkins gave him his orders. "Are you crazy? What are you thinking?"

Late that night, Wolford called his unit commanders to an outdoor meeting. He unfolded a map of Baghdad on the hood of his Humvee and, by the light of several flashlights, explained their mission. If he felt any doubts, he did not betray them. Instead he gave a classic eve-of-battle speech.

"We are going to the heart of Saddam's regime and we are going to take it and keep it," he began. "If they fire one round at us, we fire a thousand back. If they shoot one of us, we kill them all . . . and we make them regret the day they joined the Iraqi army. Talk to your soldiers. Let them know what we expect of them. Tomorrow we fight."

A hazy dawn was breaking as the American column snaked out of its improvised base. It comprised 970 soldiers riding in sixty tanks, twenty-eight Bradleys, and a handful of armored personnel carriers. As it moved, artillery units fired on the obstacles ahead, timing their barrages to hit ten minutes before the convoy arrived. When tank commanders heard explosions at Objective Curly, the first interchange they would have to take, they knew that many defenders had just been killed.

The defending force, a mix of foreign militants and Iraqis with personal loyalty to Saddam Hussein, fought with a courage bordering on fanaticism. They had no helmets, no flak jackets, and almost no weapons more powerful than rifles and grenade launchers. Their combat engineering skills were so rudimentary that they did not seem even to know how to measure trajectories for their few mortars and artillery pieces. They were facing an enemy that counted on awe-inspiring technology and firepower. Nothing within their power could have stopped its advance.

By mid-morning, just as he had hoped, Colonel Perkins was in downtown Baghdad. His men had destroyed dozens of vehicles, some of them packed with explosives and driven by suicide bombers, and killed hundreds of defenders. Inside the palace complex, he gave a live interview to an American television crew that he hoped would prove he was indeed in the city center. Two of his officers, both graduates of the University of Georgia, triumphantly raised a Georgia Bulldogs flag and shouted, "How 'bout them Dawgs?" at each other.

Their jubilation was quickly dampened. First came a report that their headquarters, eleven miles to the south, had come under fire and that an incoming missile had set off a fireball in which several soldiers and two European journalists were killed. Then Perkins heard in turn from his commanders at Curly, Larry, and Moe. Each was pinned down by waves of attackers and all pleaded for reinforcements and artillery support. As Perkins was weighing this news, trying to decide whether it meant he should retreat from the city instead of trying to stay, he heard his least favorite Iraqi, Information Minister al-Sahaf, on the radio.

"The infidels are committing suicide by the hundreds on the gates of Baghdad," al-Sahaf proclaimed. That was all Perkins needed to hear.

"We're staying," he told his officers.

By mid-afternoon, although combat at the three interchanges was still intense, the highway was judged safe enough for transit and the supply convoy set out. It was under fire for much of the way, and lost five trucks to a deadly ambush at Objective Curly. By nightfall, though, Perkins's men were unloading their precious fuel and ammunition. They did not yet control Baghdad, but they held a strong position there and a secure route in and out.

This "thunder run" cost the lives of five American soldiers. It was a brilliantly conceived operation, planned by highly trained tacticians and executed by brave, well-disciplined soldiers using equipment more sophisticated than their enemy could even imagine. Like the entire war plan, however, it was purely military. Neither Perkins nor any other American officer in Iraq—or in Washington—had thought much about what the United States would do with this country after conquering it. The soldiers believed, in the words of David Zucchino, a *Los Angeles Times* reporter traveling with them, that taking Baghdad "would be their ticket home."

> Once Baghdad fell, the war would be over. Their job would be done. There had been virtually no talk of post-war reconstruction and nation building. The division had been given no guidance for the post-combat phase, no orders for what to do with Baghdad once it was in American hands.

The men who staged this "thunder run" were hardly the only ones who thought that taking Baghdad and overthrowing Saddam meant the end of the Iraq war. Barely a week after its success, the top commander of Operation Iraqi Freedom, General Tommy Franks, stepped jubilantly from a C-130 at Baghdad airport and pumped his fist over his head in triumph. In his first meeting with senior officers, he ordered them to start preparing to leave Iraq. He told them that the first units would be pulled out within sixty days and that by September the 140,000 American troops in the country would be reduced to just 30,000.

As the meeting was about to end, General Franks told his officers that he had a surprise for them. An aide flicked on a television monitor, and after a few moments President Bush appeared on the screen. He congratulated the men on their victory, and when he was finished, they lit cigars and posed for a round of victory photos. None realized that this war was just beginning.

THE STORY OF THE IRAQ WAR IS, AND PROBABLY WILL FOREVER BE, ENVELOPED in a single one-word question: Why? President Bush and the handful of advisers with whom he conceived and launched this war explained their motives in a contradictory series of statements that changed as the war proceeded. Each had a particular set of motives, some declared and others left unsaid. The fact that there is so much debate and uncertainty about these motives makes the Iraq war unique in American history. It is the only conflict Americans ever fought without truly knowing why.

Iraq was at the top of the White House agenda from the moment Bush took office in January 2001. At a National Security Council meeting ten days after he was inaugurated, he, Vice President Dick Cheney, and other senior officials were fascinated when CIA director George Tenet showed them a large aerial surveillance photo of a building in Iraq that he said could be "a plant that produces either chemical or biological materials for weapons manufacture." Two days later, at another meeting, Secretary of State Colin Powell was presenting a plan for "targeted sanctions" against Iraq when his principal bureaucratic rival, Secretary of Defense Donald Rumsfeld, interrupted him.

"Sanctions are fine," Rumsfeld said, "but what we really want to think about is going after Saddam. Imagine what the region would look like without Saddam and with a regime that's aligned with U.S. interests."

These were the first skirmishes of the Iraq war. They made clear that key members of the new administration arrived in Washington already determined to wage it. From their first days in office, they cast eagerly about for a justification.

"There was never any rigorous talk about this sweeping idea," Secretary of the Treasury Paul O'Neill recalled afterward. "From the start, we were building the case against [Saddam] and looking at how we could take him out and change Iraq into a new country. And if we did that, it would solve everything. It was all about finding *a way to do it*. That was the tone of it. The President was saying, 'Fine. Go find me a way to do this.'"

The administration's focus on Iraq was so intense that it crowded out even the most pressing foreign policy challenges facing the new administration. Just days after President Bush was inaugurated, his chief counterterrorism specialist, Richard Clarke, wrote an urgent memo to national security adviser Condoleezza Rice, asking for a chance to brief cabinet secretaries and other senior officials on threats posed by the Al Qaeda terror network. It took three months for Rice to schedule the briefing, and she invited second-tier officials rather than members of the cabinet. Clarke told them it was imperative that they make Al Qaeda a top priority, "because it and it alone poses an immediate and serious threat to the United States."

"Well, there are others that do as well, at least as much," Deputy Secretary of Defense Paul Wolfowitz replied. "Iraqi terrorism, for example."

That surprised Clarke. He told Wolfowitz that Iraq was not known to have sponsored even a single act of terrorism directed at Americans, and when he asked the deputy CIA director, John McLaughlin, to back him up, McLaughlin did.

"We have no evidence of any active Iraqi terrorist threat against the U.S.," McLaughlin said.

"You give bin Laden too much credit," Wolfowitz insisted. "He could not do all those things like the 1993 [truck bomb] attack on New York, not without a state sponsor. Just because the FBI and the CIA have failed to find the linkages doesn't mean they don't exist."

The roots of this obsession are to be found in the 1980s, when Iraq was engaged in a horrific eight-year war with Iran. Bitterly anti-American militants had recently seized power in Iran, and President Reagan was eager to ensure that they did not win this war. That meant helping Saddam, which Reagan did in several ways. He sent Donald Rumsfeld, his special Middle East envoy, to meet Saddam and ask him what the United States could do to help his cause. Soon afterward, American intelligence agencies began sending Saddam reports about Iranian troop movements that allowed him to fend off what might have been abject defeat. Over the next seven years, the United States sold Saddam $200 million worth of weaponry, as well as a fleet of helicopters that were supposedly for civilian use but were immediately turned over to the Iraqi army. Washington also gave him $5 billion in agricultural credits and a $684 million loan to build an oil pipeline to Jordan, a project he awarded to the California-based Bechtel Corporation.

Trust between the United States and Iraq faded when Saddam began receiving weaponry from the Soviet Union, but as late as July 25, 1990, after George H. W. Bush had succeeded Reagan in the presidency, relations between the two countries were good. On that date, Saddam summoned the American ambassador in Baghdad, April Glaspie, for what he called "comprehensive political discussions."

"I have a direct instruction from the President to seek better relations with Iraq," Glaspie told him.

Saddam launched into a monologue that gradually turned to his border dispute with neighboring Kuwait, which Iraq had for decades claimed as part of its own territory. He listed a series of supposed outrages that Kuwait had committed against Iraq, ranging from territorial encroachments to the odd charge that Kuwait "is harming even the milk our children drink."

"Our patience is running out," he told Ambassador Glaspie. "If we are unable to find a solution, then it will be natural that Iraq will not accept death."

This was a broad hint, not difficult to decipher, that Saddam was planning to attack Kuwait. The Americans had not objected when he attacked Iran nearly a decade before, and he wanted to be sure they would not object this time either. Glaspie told him what he wanted to hear.

"We have no opinion on the Arab-Arab conflicts, like your border disagreement with Kuwait," she told Saddam.

Eight days later, Saddam sent his army into Kuwait, easily subdued it, and announced that it had become Iraq's nineteenth province. To his great surprise, President Bush reacted with outrage. Kuwait was a key supplier of oil to the United States, and Bush vowed that the Iraqi occupation would "not stand." He spent the next five months painstakingly assembling a coalition of thirty-four nations that shared his determination.

On January 16, 1991, the American-led coalition launched a bombing campaign against Iraq and Iraqi positions in Kuwait. It followed with a land invasion, not only chasing the Iraqi army out of Kuwait but pursuing it most of the way back to Baghdad. Some urged Bush to press on to the capital itself and depose Saddam, but he prudently declined.

By invading Kuwait, evidently under the mistaken impression that the United States would approve, Saddam turned himself into a pariah in the eyes of Washington. Over the next decade, he and the Americans engaged in a running feud. Although crippled by economic sanctions and left with a devastated army, Saddam ordered his soldiers to take potshots at American spy planes whenever they could. None was ever hit, but the Americans replied by bombing every Iraqi missile site they could find. In 1993, after the publication of reports that Saddam had tried to arrange the assassination of former President Bush, American bombers attacked Baghdad itself. They did so again five years later, after Saddam evicted United Nations weapons inspectors.

Saddam survived all of these assaults. Some powerful Americans, especially several who had held important posts in past Republican administrations, found his resilience unbearable. They harbored a deep sense that Saddam had gotten the better of them, and developed a passionate determination to crush him. When Bush's son assumed the presidency at the beginning of 2001, several of these men found themselves back in power. Among them were Cheney, who had been the father's secretary of defense and was the son's vice president; Wolfowitz, who had been a senior defense department official under the father and became the department's second-ranking figure in the son's administration; and Rumsfeld, who had been President Gerald Ford's defense secretary in the 1970s and took that post for a second time in 2001. They returned to office determined to complete what they saw as unfinished business in Iraq.

The new president himself carried this sense of grievance, and this determination, into the White House. He called Saddam "the guy that wanted to kill my dad," and when the idea of invading Iraq was first urged on him after the terror attacks of September 11, 2001, he could not fail to recognize it as a way to have his revenge, complete the job his father had begun, and redeem his family's honor. Richard Clarke, however, found the idea almost criminally irresponsible.

"Having been attacked by Al Qaeda," he told Secretary of State Powell, "for us now to go bombing Iraq in response would be like our invading Mexico after the Japanese attacked at Pearl Harbor."

A few days after the September 11 attacks, Bush was standing by himself in the White House Situation Room when Clarke and a couple of his aides walked by. Clarke later recalled that the president summoned them, closed the door, and gave them an extraordinary order.

"I know you have a lot to do and all," Bush said, "but I want you, as soon as you can, to go back over everything, everything. See if Saddam did this. See if he's linked in any way."

"But, Mr. President," Clarke replied, astonished, "Al Qaeda did this."

"I know, I know, but see if Saddam was involved," Bush insisted. "Just look. I want to know any shred."

"Absolutely, we will look again. But you know, we have looked several times at state sponsorship of Al Qaeda and have not found any linkages to Iraq."

"Look into Iraq," Bush ordered him once more. "Saddam."

Over the months that followed, Bush and his aides pursued a policy that reflected their obsession. Instead of using their great power to crush a terror group responsible for devastating attacks on the United States, they turned it against a dictator who, though odious and brutal, had never attacked Americans or threatened to do so.

"We won't do Iraq now," Bush told Condoleezza Rice four days after the September 11 attacks, "but eventually we'll have to return to that question."

Bush would later justify his focus on Iraq by asserting that Saddam was building chemical, biological, and nuclear weapons that would soon pose a mortal threat to the world. Sometimes his claims came out as a jumble of the scariest words he could find, as when he asserted that Saddam might soon launch an attack using "horrible poisons and diseases and gases and atomic weapons." He was more articulate when composed, as during an interview he gave to a British television network in mid-2002.

"The worst thing that could happen," Bush said, "would be to allow a nation like Iraq, run by Saddam Hussein, to develop weapons of mass destruction, and then team up with terrorist organizations so they can blackmail the world."

No one could disagree with that. For the world to stand idly by while a brutal dictator built weapons of mass destruction and passed them on to terrorists would be not just irresponsible but suicidal. Any nation that launched a preemptive war against such a dictator would be acting in urgent self-defense. Saddam, however, was no such dictator. His military was a pitiful shell, devastated by eight years of war with Iran and more than a decade of economic sanctions, and armed mainly with weapons old enough to be museum pieces. He was also a secular nationalist who had spent his life repressing, and in many cases slaughtering, fundamentalists who sympathized with groups like Al Qaeda. Aging and contained, he posed no imminent threat to anyone other than his own people.

No one close to President Bush ever presented the case for avoiding war in Iraq. Rice had mastered the art of telling him what he wanted to hear. Powell told Pentagon officials that he considered the Iraq project to be "lunacy," but he was much more circumspect when speaking with Bush, saying only that an invasion would not be "as easy as it is being presented." It fell to a private citizen, retired General Brent Scowcroft, who had been national security adviser to Bush's father, to issue an anguished warning. It appeared in the *Wall Street Journal* under the headline "Don't Attack Saddam."

> There is scant evidence to tie Saddam to terrorist organizations, and even less to the Sept. 11 attacks. Indeed Saddam's goals have little in common with the terrorists who threaten us, and there is little incentive for him to make common cause with them. He is unlikely to risk his investment in weapons of mass destruction, much less his country, by handing such weapons to terrorists who would use them for their own purposes and leave Baghdad as the return address. . . .
>
> The central point is that any campaign against Iraq, whatever the strategy, cost and risks, is certain to divert us for some indefinite period from our war on terrorism. Worse, there is a virtual consensus in the world against an attack on Iraq at this time. . . . Ignoring that clear sentiment would result in a serious degradation in international cooperation with us against terrorism. And make no mistake, we simply cannot win that war without enthusiastic international cooperation, especially on intelligence.

Subsequent events proved Scowcroft right. As he predicted, the war against Saddam turned out to be a priceless gift to Islamic radicals like bin Laden. Why did the Bush administration push ahead with this project despite being warned that it would undermine the security of the United States?

Bush and his senior advisers may truly have believed that Iraq possessed or was building weapons of mass destruction, but they were able to reach that conclusion only by shaping a highly politicized process in which, as the chief of the British secret service reported after visiting Washington in the summer of 2002, "the intelligence and facts were being fixed around the policy." Wolfowitz later conceded that the administration decided to push this argument "because it was the one reason everyone could agree on." There were a host of other reasons. Each member of the war party had one or two or three of his or her own. Together they pushed the United States to war.

· Despite Rumsfeld's insistence that the Iraq war had "nothing to do with oil, literally nothing to do with oil," great powers have often intervened in the Middle East when oil supplies are threatened. The United States consumes oil more voraciously than any other country on earth, and President Bush, who came of age among oil barons in Houston and for a time was in the oil business himself, believed fervently that American security depended on free access to Middle East oil. So did Vice President Cheney, who, like Bush, had once been in the oil business. With Iran in hostile hands and the governments of other Persian Gulf states becoming less stable, control of Iraq's vast reserves, which comprise 10 percent of the world's supply, would guarantee the United States a steady flow of oil.

· Giant American corporations stood to make huge profits from this war and its aftermath. Among the greatest beneficiaries was Halliburton, the oil and infrastructure company that Cheney formerly headed, which was awarded billions of dollars in no-bid contracts for projects ranging from rebuilding Iraq's oil refineries to constructing jails for war prisoners. Two other behemoths tied closely to the Republican Party, Bechtel and the Carlyle Group, also profited handsomely. So did American companies that make missiles, combat jets, and other weapons of war, especially the three biggest, Boeing, Lockheed Martin, and McDonnell-Douglas—which among them were awarded $41 billion in Pentagon contracts in 2002 alone. These companies were major contributors to Bush's presidential campaigns, and he named their senior officers to key positions in the Pentagon and elsewhere. In these men's minds, corporate interest and national interest meshed perfectly.

• Officials in the Pentagon saw Iraq as a proving ground for their theories about how the United States could win future wars. The most eager among them was Donald Rumsfeld. He detested the so-called "Powell Doctrine," named for General Powell, which holds that the United States should never go to war without a force large enough to overwhelm any enemy and deal with any problems that might emerge after victory. His contrary theory was that Americans could win wars with fewer soldiers and more technology. That was why he insisted on sending a relatively small force to Iraq, and publicly reprimanded the army chief of staff, General Eric Shinseki, for warning that a much larger one would be needed to stabilize Iraq after Saddam was vanquished.

• During the entire modern era, the United States has been able to use the territory of a large Middle Eastern country to project power through the region. For a quarter of a century that was Iran, but Iran was lost to the West after the Islamic revolution of 1979. The United States then chose Saudi Arabia as its regional proxy, but by the end of the twentieth century, many in Washington were worried about Saudi Arabia's long-term stability. They thought a pro-American Iraq would be an ideal replacement.

• Protecting the Saudi royal family was another benefit some saw in the Iraq invasion. Radicals in Saudi Arabia and elsewhere, most notably Osama bin Laden, were outraged by the presence of American troops in the kingdom. These troops had used Saudi Arabia as a base during the 1991 Gulf War and never left, leaving many Muslims outraged that an infidel army was profaning the land where Islam was born. Wolfowitz realized that their presence was "a source of enormous difficulty for a friendly government" but believed they could not be safely removed until the United States achieved a foothold somewhere else in the Middle East. He described this as "an almost unnoticed but huge" reason for the United States to depose Saddam and replace him with a pro-American regime.

• Many key figures in the Bush administration were vigorous supporters of Israel, and especially of Ariel Sharon and other Israeli hardliners. Stability in the Middle East, they argued, could be achieved only by crushing Israel's enemies. They saw Saddam as among the most dangerous of these enemies and were eager to promote any plan that would result in his overthrow.

• Bush and his aides also saw the Iraq war as a way for the United States to show the world how strong it had become. A swift, overwhelming victory in Iraq, they believed, would serve as a powerful warning to any real or potential foe.

• The final important argument for the war, which became the major one when American inspectors discovered afterward that Saddam had no weapons of mass destruction, was what Bush called his "deep desire to spread liberty around the world." Although he knew little about world history and even less about Islamic and Middle Eastern cultures—or perhaps because of that—he convinced himself of an extraordinary series of propositions. He declared repeatedly that the Western form of democracy, based on individual choice as expressed through political parties and elections, was ideal for every one of the world's societies; that the United States had a duty to spread this system; and that it could be imposed in Iraq after an American invasion. From there, he dared to hope, it would spread throughout the Middle East and transform it into a region of peace and prosperity.

All of these motives combined to lead the Bush administration to war in Iraq. Beneath them lay an intense desire for vindication, for final victory over an adversary who had taunted the United States—and the Bush family—for more than a decade. So the question of why the United States embarked on this war has many answers, but also no answer at all. When it was posed to Richard Haass, who headed the State Department's policy planning staff during the run-up to the war and was in as good a position as anyone to know the truth, he replied with refreshing candor.

"I will go to my grave not knowing that," Haass said. "I can't answer it. I can't explain the strategic obsession with Iraq, why it rose to the top of people's priority list. I just can't explain why so many people thought this was so important to do."

THE PUBLIC DRUMBEAT FOR WAR INTENSIFIED STEADILY DURING 2002. ON January 29, in his State of the Union address, President Bush named

Iraq, along with Iran and North Korea, as part of an "axis of evil" that posed "a grave and growing danger" to the United States and the rest of the world. He called the Iraqi regime one of the most dangerous on earth, and asserted that it was developing, or actively seeking to develop, nuclear, biological, and chemical weapons. "I will not stand by as peril draws closer," he vowed. Six months later he told graduates of the United States Military Academy at West Point that their country was engaged in "a conflict between good and evil" and warned, "If we wait for threats to fully materialize, we will have waited too long."

Bush's determination to depose Saddam deeply alarmed many people in the United States and beyond. A group of world leaders, doubting his dramatic charges about Iraq's arsenal, proposed an alternative approach. They suggested that the United Nations Security Council pass a resolution demanding that Saddam readmit the weapons inspectors who had been in Iraq from 1991 to 1998. If he accepted this demand, they reasoned, the inspectors would be able to determine what weapons Iraq did and did not have. This suggestion threatened to undermine the war plan, and Cheney rejected it.

"A return of inspectors would provide no assurance whatsoever of [Saddam's] compliance with U.N. resolutions," he told the Veterans of Foreign Wars in August. "On the contrary, there is a great danger that it would provide false comfort that Saddam was somehow 'back in the box.' . . . Simply stated, there is no doubt that Saddam Hussein now has weapons of mass destruction."

At a meeting of the National Security Council a week later, General Tommy Franks presented his war plan. After he finished, he turned to Bush and told him something neither he nor almost anyone else in the room wanted to hear. "Mr. President," he said, "we've been looking for Scud missiles and other weapons of mass destruction for ten years and haven't found any yet." Bush passed over this warning as if he had not heard it. A few days later, he told members of Congress at a White House meeting that he considered Saddam a more threatening enemy than Al Qaeda.

"The war on terror is going okay," he said. "We are hunting down Al Qaeda one by one. The biggest threat, however, is Saddam Hussein and his weapons of mass destruction."

Half a century earlier, John Foster Dulles admitted he had no hard evidence that the Guatemalan government was being manipulated by the Kremlin but said he was determined to overthrow it anyway because of "our deep conviction that such a tie must exist." Bush was acting on the same principle. He liked to call himself a "gut player," and prided himself on the acuity of his instinct. Instinct told him that, as he put it at the end of September, "the Iraqi regime possesses biological and chemical weapons." Never did he entertain any contrary evidence.

"I doubt that anyone ever had the chance to make the case to him that attacking Iraq would actually make America less secure and strengthen the broader radical Islamic terrorist movement," Richard Clarke wrote after leaving the administration. "Certainly he did not hear that from the small circle of advisors who alone are the people whose views he respects and trusts."

In the autumn of 2002, the United States Senate and House of Representatives voted by large margins to authorize President Bush to use force in Iraq if he deemed it necessary. Soon afterward, the United Nations Security Council unanimously approved a resolution requiring Saddam to readmit weapons inspectors and allow them free access to any site they wished to visit. To the dismay of some in Washington, he quickly agreed, insisting that Iraq was "a country devoid of weapons of mass destruction." On November 25, inspection teams arrived in Baghdad to resume their work.

Over the months that followed, the chief UN weapons inspector, Hans Blix, and the director general of the International Atomic Energy Agency, Mohammed ElBaradei, released a series of relatively positive reports. They said that although Saddam was not cooperating fully, their teams were working more freely than ever before. Then, on December 7, Iraq submitted a massive report, more than eleven thousand pages long, purporting to prove that it had no outlawed weapons.

"The declaration is nothing, it's empty, it's a joke," Bush told one of his few foreign allies in this war, Prime Minister José María Aznar of Spain, who visited the White House a few days later. "At some point, we will conclude that enough is enough and take him out."

Most of Bush's advisers, recognizing that he had made up his mind to depose Saddam, embraced the idea and urged him on. CIA director George Tenet was among the most enthusiastic. His analysts had found clues suggesting that Saddam might be concealing forbidden weapons, but no hard proof. When Bush asked him on December 19 how confident he was that Iraq had weapons of mass destruction, he abandoned the analytical coolness that distinguishes great spymasters and told the president what he clearly wanted to hear.

"It's a slam-dunk case," Tenet assured him. "Don't worry. It's a slam-dunk."

After hearing this, Bush decided it was time for Secretary of State Powell to address the Security Council, present the evidence against Saddam, and demand a resolution endorsing military action against him. Powell made the speech on February 5, 2003, with Tenet sitting behind him. He told the delegates that he could not reveal "everything that we know" but laid out a chilling case that Saddam had horrific weapons and was likely to use them "at a time and a place and in a manner of his choosing." To strengthen his case, he played tapes of intercepted telephone conversations that sounded vaguely incriminating, showed aerial photographs of suspected weapons factories, and even held up a vial of white powder to illustrate the prospect that Saddam might use anthrax spores in some future attack.

Powell and others in Washington considered this speech to have been a great success, but it did not move the world. President Jacques Chirac of France called Bush soon afterward to tell him that France would vote against his resolution because "war is not inevitable" and there were "alternative ways" to deal with Saddam. The presidents of two other countries with seats on the Security Council, Vicente Fox of Mexico and Ricardo Lagos of Chile, also told him they would vote against it.

For weeks Bush had been insisting that the Security Council vote on his war resolution. When it became clear that the measure could not pass, however, he changed his mind. He would have preferred to depose Saddam with the approval of the United Nations but had long since made up his mind to do it no matter what anyone else said or did. Chirac was mistaken when he told Bush that war was "not inevitable." It had been inevitable since Bush made his private decision more than a year before.

"All the decades of deceit and cruelty have now reached an end," the president declared in a televised address on Monday evening, March 17. "Saddam Hussein and his sons must leave Iraq within forty-eight hours. Their refusal to do so will result in military conflict, commenced at a time of our choosing."

The United States had massed 130,000 soldiers in Kuwait and tens of thousands more nearby. Britain, the only other major power that supported Operation Iraqi Freedom, had 25,000 there, and there were small, symbolic contingents from Poland and Australia. This force was less than half the size of the one the United States had assembled to fight Saddam in the Gulf War a decade before.

According to General Franks's plan, the war would begin with a brief but intense bombing campaign aimed at killing as many Iraqi soldiers as possible, to be followed by an overland invasion. Americans would charge northward along two routes toward Baghdad, nearly three hundred miles away, while the British would veer to the east and take the port city of Basra. Other American units were to have invaded from Turkey in the north, but the Turkish parliament, reflecting overwhelming public sentiment, refused to permit this.

At midday on March 19, the first American advance teams crossed into Iraq. The main force was to cross two days later, but that plan changed suddenly when a CIA agent who had been inside Iraq for weeks sent urgent and startling news to Langley. He said one of his most trusted Iraqi informants had pinpointed a farm near Baghdad where Saddam and his two widely despised sons would be sleeping that night.

As soon as Tenet and Rumsfeld received this report, they sped to the White House and told Bush he had a chance to decapitate the regime with a single stroke. He approved their plan to attack the farm as soon as the convoy carrying Saddam arrived. It pulled in shortly before dawn, just as the informant had predicted, and soon afterward, American bombs and cruise missiles decimated the farmhouse and everything around it. Several hours later came the disappointing news that neither Saddam nor his sons had been killed. They had either not been at the farm or had managed to escape. The only important figure who died in the attack was the Iraqi informant whose tip had triggered it.

That evening, after sharing a dinner of chicken pot pie with his wife, Bush appeared on television to tell the world that the American-led invasion of Iraq had begun, twenty-four hours earlier than originally planned. He said bombs were falling on "selected targets of military importance" and that these strikes were "the opening stages of what will be a broad and concerted campaign." Saddam responded with a broadcast of his own, defying "the criminal junior Bush."

"Go, use a sword!" he urged his people. "Let Iraq live!"

Few Iraqis heeded Saddam's plea. Soldiers by the thousands ripped off their uniforms and melted into the countryside as American columns charged northward. There were skirmishes in a few towns, but for most of the American soldiers, the ride toward Baghdad was free of resistance.

Some units moved at forty miles an hour, so fast that the treads on their amphibious troop carriers began to shred.

Because there was scattered fighting along the route, and because the invading force took casualties, the drive toward Baghdad cannot truly be described as a "cakewalk," the word used in many news dispatches and other accounts. Still, the invading force faced no sustained resistance on the ground, no aerial bombardment, and no chemical or biological attacks. Many soldiers feared they might encounter all of that when they assaulted Baghdad, but because the "thunder run" on April 7 succeeded so spectacularly, no such assault was necessary. That same day Saddam Hussein fled and his regime collapsed. A thirty-nine-year-old Iraqi named Qifa, who had been working for the Ministry of Information, wept with joy and clutched the hand of an American reporter as he tried to grasp the fact that the bloody tyrant was gone.

"Touch me," he pleaded. "Touch me. Tell me that this is real. Tell me that the nightmare is really over."

It was indeed over. General Franks began planning to withdraw American troops, and President Bush reveled in the swiftness and completeness of his triumph. On May 1, forty-three days after the war began, he stepped out of a fighter jet onto the deck of the aircraft carrier *Abraham Lincoln,* anchored a few miles off the coast of California. Dressed in a pilot's flight suit, he strode across the deck like a proud conqueror. Then, in a speech to hundreds of soldiers and sailors and airmen on board, he declared that "major combat operations" in Iraq had ended. He said the war had been "a noble cause" and "a great moral advance," and even compared it to the World War II battles at Normandy and Iwo Jima, where thousands died in a cause most of the world embraced. Behind him hung a giant banner that summarized his speech in two words: "Mission Accomplished."

Bush often asserted that this war was about much more than Iraq. So it was, but not only in the way he meant. It grew from the history of three places far distant from one another that combined to shape the collective psyche of the Bush administration.

The first was Iran. When militant clerics seized power there after the Islamic revolution of 1979, they shook the world in ways even they could not foresee. Their revolution helped provoke the Soviet invasion of Afghanistan, which in turn drew the United States into Afghanistan and created the conditions under which Al Qaeda grew and thrived. It led American leaders to begin searching for a new ally and proxy in the

Muslim Middle East, a search that drew them to Iraq. It also led Saddam to believe he could finally get away with his old dream of seizing territory from Iran and later from Kuwait. He did not succeed, but America's decision to embrace him during his war against Iran was the first phase of a torturous relationship between Washington and Baghdad that culminated in the American invasion of 2003.

Vietnam was the second place where Americans had traumatic experiences that led indirectly to the invasion of Iraq. In Vietnam, as in Iran, the United States suffered a deep humiliation from which it never truly recovered. Bush and many of those around him believed that, a quarter century later, Americans were still suffering from the "Vietnam syndrome," which they defined as a reluctance to use military force abroad and a nagging sense that the United States had lost its power to shape world events. They saw Iraq as a place where they could win a quick, overwhelming victory that would erase those doubts forever.

The third place whose history strangely influenced the course of events in Iraq was Bush's home state of Texas. The first whites in Texas imposed order at the point of a gun and then, with encouragement from Washington, rebelled against Mexico to establish a regime of their own. All schoolchildren in Texas learn about the bravery of these men in the face of overwhelming odds. Even more than most other Americans, Texans absorb a sense that good men with guns can bring order out of chaos. With that conviction, and with the quintessentially American belief that anything can be achieved if one tries hard enough, Bush launched an invasion that seemed successful only for the briefest of moments. Very soon the "Mission Accomplished" banner that hung behind him as he swaggered across the deck of the *Abraham Lincoln* began to look like a cruel joke.

14

Catastrophic Success

On the evening of March 19, 2003, shortly before announcing that the United States was about to launch its long-expected invasion of Iraq, President George W. Bush sat behind an antique desk in the White House and practiced reading his speech. It struck all the appropriate notes, including a declaration that the purpose of this invasion was "to disarm Iraq, to free its people, and to defend the world from grave danger." Some would later point to it as the speech that ripped the United States away from a long tradition of cooperative diplomacy, turning it into an arrogant power that assumed the right to determine which foreign governments could live and which must die. The man who looked down on Bush from a large oil painting on the wall behind him would have understood better than anyone how wrong that was.

Bush rehearsed this speech in the Treaty Room, at the same desk from which he had announced the invasion of Afghanistan seventeen months before. It was one of his favorite rooms in the White House, at least in part because of the imposing painting that is the first thing visitors see when they enter. It depicts President William McKinley, the first great American practitioner of "regime change," watching as diplomats sign the protocol that turned Cuba into a protectorate and Puerto Rico into a colony.

This somber painting, *The Signing of the Protocol of Peace Between the United States and Spain on August 12, 1898,* by the French artist Theobald Chartran, gives the Treaty Room its name. The "protocol of peace" that was signed that day, however, was not an accord between equal states. It was a document of surrender that the United States forced on Spain after defeating its army in Cuba. More important, it was a declaration that the United States was now able and willing to depose foreign governments.

That made it especially appropriate for Bush to use the Treaty Room as he prepared to launch the invasion of Iraq. He and McKinley, sitting symbolically together, represented the continuity of American policy during the long "regime change" century. Bush's decision to invade Iraq was no break with history but a faithful reflection of the same forces and beliefs that had motivated McKinley and most of the presidents who would later sit in his shadow beneath Chartran's historic painting.

Both McKinley and Bush rose to the presidency in eras when Americans were feeling surges of patriotism and religious fervor, and when American corporations were eagerly looking abroad for new markets and sources of raw materials. During their campaigns for the White House, each promised to use American military power with extreme care. Once in office, they justified their overthrow of foreign governments by insisting that the United States sought no advantage for itself and was intervening abroad only "for humanity's sake," as McKinley put it, or, in Bush's words, "to make the world more peaceful and more free."

Neither man was troubled by his ignorance of the countries whose governments he overthrew. McKinley admitted that he had only a vague idea of where to find the Philippines on a map. Bush explained his certainty that the invasion of Iraq would go well by saying, "I rely on my instincts." Both were deeply religious men imbued with the conviction that humanity is locked in a constant struggle between good and evil. Both believed that God was guiding them and that therefore they did not need to ponder abstruse questions of culture and identity before ordering the overthrow of foreign regimes.

The parallels between McKinley's invasion of the Philippines and Bush's invasion of Iraq were startling. Both presidents sought economic as well as political advantage for the United States. Both were also motivated by a deep belief that the United States has a sacred mission to spread its form of government to faraway countries. Neither doubted that the people who lived in those countries would welcome Americans as liberators. Neither anticipated that he would have to fight a long counterinsurgency war to subdue nationalist rebels. Early in the twenty-first century, ten decades after the United States invaded the Philippines and a few years after it invaded Iraq, those two countries were among the most volatile and unstable in all of Asia.

The four invasions the United States launched between 1983 and 2003 were responses to specific challenges, but they were also expressions of deep impulses that have shaped Americans' collective view of the world and their role in it. The results of these invasions, though highly instructive in themselves, are best understood in the context of a century of American "regime change" operations. The idea behind all of them—that Americans have a right and even an obligation to depose regimes they consider evil—is not new but one of the oldest and most resilient of all the beliefs that define the United States.

ALMOST EVERY AMERICAN OVERTHROW OF A FOREIGN GOVERNMENT HAS LEFT in its wake a bitter residue of pain and anger. Some have led to the slaughter of innocents. Others have turned whole nations, and even whole regions of the world, into violent cauldrons of anti-American passion. The invasion of Grenada in 1983 had quite the opposite effect. Of the fourteen countries whose governments the United States has forcibly deposed, Grenada is one of the few in which most citizens were, and have remained, genuinely grateful for intervention.

From the perspective of history, much about Operation Urgent Fury, including its grand-sounding code name, seems almost ludicrous. The imbalance of power between the two combatants had few precedents in the history of warfare. Nonetheless, it was an important episode, mainly because of its relation to what was happening in the rest of the world during the early 1980s.

Ronald Reagan assumed office in 1981 as a wave of leftist militancy was surging through the Caribbean Basin. Marxist revolutionaries had seized power in Nicaragua, others were fighting in El Salvador and Guatemala, and self-described anti-imperialists had been elected to head governments in Jamaica, Guyana, and Surinam. Farther away but even more frightening, radicals in Iran and elsewhere in the Middle East, many of them driven by fundamentalist religious beliefs, were defying the United States in shocking ways. On the very weekend that Reagan ordered the invasion of Grenada, Islamic militants dealt the United States a devastating blow in Beirut. All of this weighed heavily on a nation that was still coming to grips with its defeat in Vietnam a few years before.

If Reagan and his aides had wanted a peaceful solution in Grenada, they might well have been able to arrange one. That would not, however, have given them the victory they sought. The American triumph in Grenada was above all symbolic. It showed the world that the tide of history had not begun to run against the United States, as some had dared to assert. It also gave Reagan the aura of a leader who could crush America's enemies—especially its weak ones.

Fourteen months after the invasion, Grenadians voted in the first free election many had ever known. They overwhelmingly chose sixty-six-year-old Herbert Blaize, a longtime politician who enjoyed clear support from the United States, as prime minister. Blaize was soft-spoken, calm, and bland, but also prudent, honest, and—most important—pro-American. That was precisely the combination of qualities many Grenadians sought after years of upheaval.

The new regime could not avoid the painful duty of bringing to justice those who had organized and carried out the "Bloody Wednesday" massacre that precipitated the invasion. After a series of delays, eighteen suspects were brought to trial. Fourteen were sentenced to hang, among them Bernard and Phyllis Coard, Hudson Austin, Leon Cornwall, and Imam Abdullah, who was tried under his given name, Callistus Bernard. Three others were given long prison terms, and one. was found not guilty. Later the death sentences were commuted to life imprisonment.

During their trial, the defendants outraged many Grenadians by rejecting the court's legitimacy and refusing to take responsibility for the massacre. Only after years in prison did they show even a hint of remorse, in an open letter addressed in 1996 to "all ex-detainees of the People's Revolutionary Government."

We believe and recognize that those of us who were leaders during the Revolution were collectively responsible for your suffering and must fully accept such responsibility. Thus we feel that the least we can do is to express to you our profound regrets and embarrassment, and offer you our sincere and unreserved apologies. . . .

We were morbidly afraid of internal opposition, seeing the hand of the U.S. government behind every manifestation of internal dissent. This state of mind quickly spread to virtually the entire population. In this siege mentality, the civil and human rights of those who opposed us or even disagreed with us, sadly, counted for little. We just did not have the maturity and wisdom at the time to recognize that many who dissented did so not because they were stooges of the U.S. government, CIA agents, or unpatriotic Grenadians, but because of their concerns about the nonexistence of checks and balances and because they felt, correctly, that as citizens they had the right to freedom of expression and the right to participate in the political process. . . .

We have ruled out any future involvement in politics for all time. When leaders have failed as disastrously as we did, the very least they must do is terminate their involvement in politics and lay to rest any political ambitions they may have had.

Three years after this letter was published, one of the convicted killers, Phyllis Coard, was released for health reasons. The rest remained at Richmond Hill prison. In 2004 the Eastern Caribbean Court of Appeals upheld their convictions. Prime Minister Keith Mitchell said most Grenadians breathed "a tremendous sigh of relief" at the ruling, since they were not "ready yet for the release of those persons."

Did the United States have to invade Grenada? If the principal reason was to rescue American students, as President Reagan asserted, then the answer is probably no. The students could, in all likelihood, have been brought home in a straightforward evacuation, and the Grenadian authorities would have been happy to be rid of them. Even Reagan's secondary justification, the desire to expel Cubans and restore democracy, was dubious, because in the chaos following "Bloody Wednesday," it might well have been possible to achieve those goals peacefully.

Two facts, however, snarl back at those who condemn this invasion. First, there was a possibility, albeit remote, that New Jewel leaders who were crazy enough to massacre their own longtime comrades might also have been crazy enough to commit some outrage against Americans. Second, by 1983 the United States had been seared by a decade of defeats and humiliations, from Saigon to Tehran to Managua. Many Americans were eager to reverse that trend and had voted for Ronald Reagan because he pledged to do so. They wanted a victory. When Marxist fanatics in Grenada gave Reagan a chance to score one, he did not hesitate.

Grenada is a tiny country, with a population that could fit inside the Rose Bowl. After the 1983 invasion, for the price of a few Spectre gunships—they cost $132 million apiece—the United States could have turned it into the garden spot of the Caribbean, a showcase of democracy and prosperity. This would have shown that, at least sometimes, the United States stays positively engaged with countries whose governments it overthrows.

The American pattern, almost unbroken over more than a century, is to walk away from these nations. In Grenada, the United States had a chance to do better, at an exceedingly low cost. True to tradition, it let that opportunity pass. American aid to Grenada jumped in the aftermath of the invasion but was barely enough to pay for repairing the damage wrought by the U.S. troops. Before long, the Americans resumed their customary policy of treating Grenada like any other Eastern Caribbean mini-state. That meant it was all but forgotten.

As aid from the United States dropped during the 1990s, Grenada turned to inelegant ways of making money. For a time it sold passports to foreign nationals, giving them the option of using an assumed name if they wished. Financial watchdogs in France placed Grenada on a list of countries that accommodated money launderers.

Many of the countries in which Americans have intervened are large and complex. Americans could have done far more to guide the Philippines or Iran toward stability and freedom, but even the mightiest of efforts by outsiders could not have reshaped nations of such size. In Grenada, they might have. The triumph of Operation Urgent Fury gave the United States a unique chance, one that might have added much to its honor and image in the world. Americans, reflecting the short attention span that shapes their approach to the world, chose not to seize it.

IN THE HOURS AFTER AMERICAN TROOPS INVADED PANAMA AND DEPOSED General Manuel Noriega, Panama City degenerated into violent anarchy. This eminently predictable result of the invasion seemed to take the Americans completely by surprise. It took them several days to realize that by destroying the force that guaranteed public order, they had assumed an obligation to replace it themselves until a new local force could be constituted. By then it was too late.

The main boulevards in Panama City are lined with lavishly stocked department stores, exclusive boutiques, and specialty outlets that sell everything from televisions and stereo equipment to diamond jewelry and Jaguars. Shoppers from around Latin America and the Caribbean fly there to spend money, competing with *rabiblancos* to scoop up the most expensive prizes. The day after the Americans invaded, poor Panamanians finally had their chance.

By mid-morning on December 21, 1989, the shopping district's main streets were clogged with people pushing factory-fresh stoves, refrigerators, and washing machines. Some appeared with carts and filled them to overflowing with frozen meat, cases of alcohol, furniture, and whatever else they could find. It took them less than thirty-six hours to strip

Panama City's famous shopping centers of almost all their goods. The same thing happened in Colón, one of the hemisphere's most active free ports, where swarms of looters smashed freight containers and carried away everything they found. By one estimate, more than $2 billion of merchandise was stolen during these hours. Even a small show of force would have stopped this larcenous frenzy, but American soldiers never appeared.

The other great loss that the American invasion caused was through fires that were set off during the fighting. Many of the buildings in the neighborhood around La Comandancia were made of wood. So were others in the barrios where American soldiers came to flush out snipers and other remnants of the defense forces. Their heavy weapons set off blazes that consumed scores of city blocks and left thousands of people homeless. Just as no one in the American chain of command had thought to deploy troops to prevent looting, no one apparently considered the possibility that Panama City would burn so easily.

Some looters cried *Viva Bush!* as they collected their treasure. They were not, however, the only ones grateful to the United States for its invasion. Many Panamanians had become intensely frustrated with their inability to rid themselves of Noriega and were relieved when American troops landed to depose him. In more than a few places, they welcomed invading troops with applause.

American casualties in Operation Just Cause were light, just 23 killed— 9 by friendly fire—and 347 wounded. The number of Panamanians killed remains uncertain. According to an estimate that Southcom released soon afterward, 314 Panamanian soldiers and 202 civilians lost their lives. Some Americans, and many Panamanians, came to believe that the true numbers were twice that.

When Noriega was brought to trial in Miami, he was as much a war trophy as a criminal defendant. Whether the United States had any right under international law to abduct and try him was questionable. During the first phase of his trial, the evidence against him seemed weak and circumstantial. Prosecutors then produced a surprise witness, Carlos Lehder, a federal prisoner who had been a key figure in the Medellín drug cartel. Lehder had direct knowledge of Noriega's crimes, and his testimony was decisive. On April 9, 1992, the deposed Panamanian leader was convicted of eight drug-related counts and sentenced to forty years in prison.

The new Panamanian president, Guillermo Endara, declared in one of his first public statements that Panamanians would forever celebrate December 20 as the anniversary of their liberation. As months passed, however, many began changing their minds about the invasion. Some were indignant to learn how lavishly the United States had supported Noriega over the years. Others were moved by the sight of homeless families and burned-out neighborhoods. As the first anniversary of the invasion approached, some demanded that it be observed as a "day of mourning." President Endara, acutely aware of his people's changing views but indebted for his position to the United States, struck a compromise by declaring it a "day of reflection."

The fact that Endara had been installed in power by a foreign government, and sworn in on a foreign military base, crippled him from the start. He might have been able to overcome the stigma if he had been a skilled politician or administrator, but he was neither. By the time he left office, in 1994, he was highly unpopular. Neither of the next two presidents, Ernesto Pérez Balladares and Mireya Moscoso, turned out to be much of an improvement.

The election campaign of 2004 proved more exciting than any since the invasion, largely because a candidate with a very familiar name was on the ballot. He was Martín Torrijos, son of the populist general who dominated the country from 1968 to 1981 and whose memory many poor Panamanians still cherished. His victory was in part the closing of a circle, and not only because he was the son of a beloved father.

When Martín Torrijos was fifteen years old, he asked his father for permission to join the brigade Hugo Spadafora was raising to fight alongside Sandinista guerrillas in Nicaragua. His father agreed. The young man did not see combat, but he came to admire Spadafora, and as an adult he cherished Spadafora's memory. When he became president of Panama, he redeemed not only his father's legacy but also that of the romantic hero whose murder nineteen years earlier had shaped the course of Panamanian history.

AFTER THE SEPTEMBER 11, 2001, TERROR ATTACKS IN NEW YORK AND WASH-ington, it was all but inevitable that President George W. Bush would order the overthrow of the Taliban regime in Afghanistan. The Taliban had not only given Osama bin Laden and his comrades the sanctuary from which they planned the attacks but had made them virtual partners in government. By refusing to turn bin Laden over to the United

States or some other power that could punish him, the Taliban regime sealed its fate.

Deciding to act against the Taliban, however, was the easy part. More difficult was choosing what action to take. There were two options, each fraught with long-term danger. Bush chose the less daunting one. His refusal to send American troops into battle allowed terrorist leaders to escape and left much of Afghanistan in the hands of drug barons and fundamentalist warlords. It also kept American soldiers out of harm's way and allowed the United States to stay out of the "nation-building" business.

The alternative would have been to launch a full-scale invasion of Afghanistan and agree to keep large numbers of troops there for at least several years. This option might well have led to the capture of bin Laden and his lieutenants, and perhaps also set Afghanistan on a path toward stability. One leading American expert on Afghanistan, Larry Goodson of the United States Army War College, concluded that while this option would have required "a commitment truly breathtaking in its depth, breadth, intensity and swiftness of application," modern Afghan history shows that "an ounce of nation-building prevention will be worth a pound of military-operation cure."

It was clear as early as the fall of 2001 that the only approach which would not only smash the Taliban and cripple Al Qaeda but also stabilize Afghanistan and foster a healthier regional environment would require perhaps as many as two full divisions worth of U.S. and allied ground forces, swift and massive reconstruction (beginning with road-building), efforts to limit meddling by its neighbors, and possibly even a temporary U.S. military government to administer the country as a trust. Despite the shock of September 11, it remained hard for a U.S. administration that had come into office deeply opposed to such approaches—to say nothing of a senior U.S. military leadership that was skeptical of peacekeeping missions and highly casualty-averse—to adopt such strategies. So other approaches were tried instead, leaving grave problems that midcourse adjustments and half-measures will probably not be enough to solve.

Besides their deep-seated aversion to "nation-building" missions and their desire to minimize American casualties, President Bush and his advisers had two other important reasons to reject the idea of serious, long-term involvement in Afghanistan. The first was that any such involvement could be successful only with broad international support, probably channeled through the United Nations. That would have forced Americans to share power and authority with Europeans and others, an idea that was anathema to the Bush administration.

The central reason that Bush rejected the ambitious option of long-term engagement in Afghanistan, however, was that his attention was focused elsewhere. He understood the importance of stabilizing Afghanistan and would certainly have been happy to capture bin Laden and his henchmen, but his zeal for these projects paled beside his obsession with Iraq and Saddam Hussein. For the United States to embark on a sustained effort to pacify Afghanistan would have required a commitment comparable in scope to the multibillion-dollar, six-year-long campaign it waged to throw the country into chaos during the period of Soviet occupation in the 1980s. Such an undertaking would have made it impossible for the United States to conduct any other major military offensive at the same time. It would have forced Bush to abandon the idea of invading Iraq, something he was not prepared to do.

A century of American "regime change" operations has shown that the United States is singularly unsuited to ruling foreign lands. Americans never developed either the imperial impulse or the attention span that allowed the Spanish, British, French, and others to seize foreign lands and run them for decades or centuries. In Afghanistan, there were two good reasons to make an exception. First, Afghanistan's collapse was partly the result of the devastating war Americans sponsored there during the 1980s, and it might well be argued that this war gave the United States a moral obligation to help rebuild what it had helped destroy. Beyond morality, though, was the urgent practical question of how to keep Afghanistan from again becoming the world's leading heroin producer and a breeding ground for terror. The Bush administration brushed that question aside when it shifted its focus to Iraq.

Just weeks after the Taliban regime fell, at the end of 2001, a group of Afghan leaders assembled in Bonn and agreed to accept America's hand-picked candidate, Hamid Karzai, an English-speaking Pashtun leader who had spent most of the 1990s outside Afghanistan, to head a six-month transitional government. At the end of the transition period, a broader assembly of Afghan leaders—broadened by the United States at the last moment to ensure the desired result—endorsed the choice of

Karzai. Later, in an election that drew a remarkable 70 percent of eligible voters to the polls, he defeated seventeen other candidates to win a full term.

To guide Karzai, the Americans named an ambassador, Zalmay Khalilzad, who had worked for Unocal in its unsuccessful effort to negotiate a pipeline deal with the Taliban. He and Karzai ran the country together, but their good intentions and hard work scarcely made up for the lack of resources Washington gave them. By the time Khalilzad left in 2005 to become ambassador to Iraq, Afghanistan's challenges remained almost as daunting as they were when he arrived.

Outside powers, most notably the United States, proved remarkably stingy when it came to aiding Afghanistan. They sent less aid and fewer peacekeepers per capita than they had sent to Bosnia, Kosovo, East Timor, or Rwanda, the other four places where postwar reconstruction was then under way. This ensured that Afghanistan would remain in ruins; that warlords would continue to control much of the country; that remnants of the Taliban would reemerge as a fighting force; that bin Laden and other terrorist leaders would remain at large; and that the drug trade would become a steadily more important mainstay of the country's economy. Afghanistan produced 3,200 tons of heroin in 2002, 3,600 tons in 2003, and 4,200 tons in 2004—the last figure representing 87 percent of the world total.

The slow emergence of democracy in Afghanistan, reflected by the election of Karzai and later of a national parliament, was a positive step, and Bush was justified in celebrating it. When placed beside the far more ominous developments in areas like security and poppy production, however, it seemed less than overwhelmingly important. The prospect that a democratic regime might be able to establish control over all of Afghanistan's territory remained distant, while the country's transition from failed state to world center of narcoterrorism proceeded with alarming speed.

The American invasion of Afghanistan produced a supremely positive result, the destruction of a regime that had allowed anti-Western terrorists to train and plot freely. It had one other immediate effect. Fighters whom the United States hired to depose the Taliban captured thousands of Afghans and foreigners during their campaign and turned nearly all of them over to American custody. Some were important figures in the Taliban and in Al Qaeda. Others were low-level foot soldiers who happened to be fighting on the wrong side when the United States invaded; and the rest were innocents swept up either by mistake or because someone with a private grudge falsely accused them. Large numbers were jailed at a sprawling prison the Americans built at their base in Bagram, near Kabul, and many were subjected to coercive interrogations that involved rougher treatment than the United States had used since its war in the Philippines. Hundreds were shipped to a prison the United States had constructed at its base in Guantánamo, Cuba, chosen so that they could be subjected to pressures that might not be legal on American soil. President Bush and his senior aides insisted that the harsh interrogation techniques used at Guantánamo were appropriate in light of the continuing threat terrorism posed to the United States. To millions of people around the world, however, they became a symbol of America's rejection of international human rights standards. The ensuing wave of anti-Americanism easily outweighed the value of any intelligence that interrogators may have gleaned in violent interrogations.

Afghanistan's future will be shaped largely by President Bush's fateful decision to invade Iraq rather than concentrate on rebuilding Afghanistan. With pitifully little help from the United States and other countries that set it on its path to disaster, Afghanistan never emerged from its agony. Years after the invasion, it remained one of the world's most dangerously unstable states.

THE AMERICAN OCCUPATION OF IRAQ WENT ALMOST AS BADLY AS THE INVAsion had gone well. Trouble began just hours after Saddam Hussein's regime collapsed, as looters raged through Baghdad and criminals ran amok. Then, six weeks later, the Americans decreed the dissolution not simply of Saddam's secret police and elite Republican Guard but of the entire Iraqi army. That left more than 300,000 young men, all armed and trained in military tactics, without work and seething with anger against the occupier.

No capable security force took the army's place, and civilians at the Pentagon, determined to prove Secretary of Defense Rumsfeld's theory that wars could be won with relatively small numbers of troops, refused to send enough soldiers to patrol the countryside, guard weapons depots, or seal Iraq's borders to keep foreign insurgents out. Within a few months, enemies of the occupation built the most potent insurgent force the United States had faced since its misadventure in Vietnam.

Just 122 Americans lost their lives in the three weeks between March 20,

2003, when the invasion of Iraq began, and April 9, when Saddam's regime collapsed. Bush apparently believed that these would be the only casualties the United States would have to sustain. In the next two years, however, insurgents killed nearly 2,000 more Americans. Many times that number of Iraqis died. No end to the conflict was in sight. Without either a strong figure to hold this deeply fragmented country together, an accord for power sharing among its various groups, or a handover of real power to its citizens, it collapsed into sectarian fratricide and anti-American violence.

The other shock that awaited Americans after they deposed Saddam was that he had, in fact, been telling the truth when he claimed not to have any biological, chemical, or nuclear weapons. An American team called the Iraq Survey Group spent ten months scouring Iraq in search of these weapons, or factories where they might have been produced, but found nothing. When its work was complete, David Kay, who had been its chief inspector, returned to Washington and told the Senate Armed Services Committee that it was "important to acknowledge failure."

"We were almost all wrong," Kay admitted, "and I certainly include myself."

Once it became clear that there was no basis to the claim Bush had used in justifying the war—that Saddam had or was making weapons of mass destruction—he shifted to other rationales. He had not gone to war simply to disarm Saddam, he began saying, but to help Iraqis build a peaceful democracy that would set off a wave of reform across the Middle East. It was an agile change of position but did not address the other, more far-reaching error his administration had made. Although it devoted enormous energy and spent many billions of dollars to depose Saddam, it never devised a plan for what to do after he was gone.

Bush steadfastly refused to acknowledge that he or his administration made serious errors in planning this war and the occupation that followed. He admitted he had not foreseen the insurgency but insisted that when the final story of Operation Iraqi Freedom was written, it would be judged a historic triumph. The closest he ever came to self-criticism was a lament that the operation went too well.

"Had we to do it over again," he said in an interview sixteen months after the invasion, "we would look at the consequences of catastrophic success."

That was the kind of success it was, if any at all. The war turned Iraq into a cauldron of violent anarchy and a magnet for fanatics from around the world. It set off a global wave of anti-American passion that had no precedent in history. Worst of all, it consumed enormous resources that might have been used in the war against Al Qaeda and other terror groups. By taking pressure off these groups, the Iraq war allowed them to continue their worldwide jihad, launching deadly attacks in Indonesia, Spain, Britain, and elsewhere.

Military occupations are by their nature oppressive, and although the abusive tactics that American soldiers used in Iraq may have seemed defensible from the army's perspective, they angered many Iraqis and countless others around the world. This anger rose to a fever pitch when graphic photographs emerged showing that American soldiers at the Abu Ghraib prison, near Baghdad, had treated prisoners in shocking ways. Bush and his defenders deplored these abuses but insisted they were isolated incidents. Just as General Arthur MacArthur had told American troops in the Philippines that they need not bother with "precise observance of the laws of war," Bush decreed that the Geneva Conventions governing the treatment of prisoners did not apply to prisoners taken in Afghanistan or Iraq.

Bush and his advisers pinned much of their hope for Iraq's future on the development of democracy there. Soon after deposing Saddam, they named a "governing council" to help them run the country. The council chose Ayad Allawi, a pro-American politician who had lived outside Iraq for years, to serve as prime minister until a national election could be organized. In the election, which was held on January 30, 2005, Allawi sought a full term. His party lost to one led by Ibrahim al-Jaafari, a member of the country's dominant Shiite community, whose declared ambition was to steer Iraq into a close partnership with Iran.

This result symbolized one of the contradictions inherent in the American plan for Iraq. Bush and his advisers repeatedly insisted that they wanted Iraqis to enjoy the fullest possible democracy, reasoning that any nation whose citizens were free to express themselves would inevitably be pro-American. The truth was less comforting. Many Iraqis not only felt deep anger at the United States for its failures during the occupation but wanted their country to develop close ties to Iran. Iranian fundamentalists had worked for decades to build their influence in Iraq but had had little success until the United States, supposedly their greatest enemy, gave them the chance.

"Throughout Iraq," a senior Iranian intelligence officer gloated after the 2005 election, "the people we supported are in power."

At least some of the enormous problems that enveloped Iraq during the first two years of American occupation could have been avoided. Had the Americans sent enough troops, had they not abolished the Iraqi army, and had they not issued a sweeping ban that prevented almost all former members of Saddam's Baath Party from holding government jobs, they might have been able to prevent the emergence of an insurgency. Another of their failures, however, was even more costly.

A full year before the invasion of Iraq, the State Department had launched an ambitious project called "Future of Iraq," which was aimed at finding ways to establish security and begin the transition to democracy after Saddam was gone. Large teams of experts, including more than two hundred Iraqis representing almost every ethnic and political group in the country, produced thirteen volumes of recommendations about how to rebuild everything from the country's oil industry to its criminal justice system. They brought their recommendations to the Pentagon, along with a list of seventy-five Arabic-speaking specialists who were ready to go to Iraq as soon as Saddam was gone. Secretary of Defense Rumsfeld summarily rejected them and their ideas.

In the most spectacular misjudgment of Operation Iraqi Freedom, Bush and his aides convinced themselves that there would be no serious problems after the invasion. They dismissed those who warned otherwise as whining doubters. Their stubborn blindness turned what might have been a stirring victory into a bloody stalemate that, two years after the declared end of "major combat operations," was costing the United States hundreds of millions of dollars and the lives of one or two soldiers every day.

"There was never a buildup of intelligence that says, [the insurgency] is coming, it's coming, it's coming, this is the end you should prepare for," General Tommy Franks said later. "It did not happen. Never saw it. It was never offered."

American leaders would have done well to reflect on the fate that befell the British when they tried to subdue Iraq after World War I. Iraqis launched a revolt against the colonial regime in 1920. The British sent troops to suppress it but soon found themselves caught in a spiral of horrific violence. Their occupation, which they expected would last for only a few months, dragged on for thirty-five years. When they finally withdrew from Iraq in 1955, they left behind a weak, unrepresentative political system that ultimately produced Saddam Hussein.

"What happened in Iraq," the British historian Niall Ferguson wrote in 2004, "so closely resembles the events of 1920 that only a historical ignoramus can be surprised."

THERE IS NO STRONGER OR MORE PERSISTENT STRAIN IN THE AMERICAN character than the belief that the United States is a nation uniquely endowed with virtue. Americans consider themselves to be, in Herman Melville's words, "a peculiar, chosen people, the Israel of our times." In a nation too new to define itself by real or imagined historical triumphs, and too diverse to be bound together by a shared religion or ethnicity, this belief became the essence of national identity, the conviction that bound Americans to each other and defined their approach to the world. They are hardly the first people to believe themselves favored by Providence, but they are the only ones in modern history who are convinced that by bringing their political and economic system to others, they are doing God's work.

This view is driven by a profound conviction that the American form of government, based on capitalism and individual political choice, is, as President Bush asserted, "right and true for every person in every society." It rests on the belief that Western-style democracy is the natural state of all nations and that all will embrace it once the United States removes artificial barriers imposed by regimes based on other principles. By implication, it denies that culture and tradition shape the human psyche, that national consciousness changes only slowly, and that even great powers cannot impose their beliefs on others by force.

Early leaders of the United States did not hold this view. George Washington wrote that for nations, as for people, self-interest is always "the governing principle" and that no country, specifically including the United States, should be "trusted further than it is bound by interest." That is a timeless truth. When the United States acts in the world, it acts, as other nations do, to defend its interests. Americans, however, do not like to hear or believe that their government has such self-centered motives. Generations of American leaders have realized that they can easily win popular support for their overseas adventures if they present them as motivated by benevolence, self-sacrificing charity, and a noble desire to liberate the oppressed. The blessings of freedom that McKinley said he wanted to bestow on Cubans, Puerto Ricans, and Filipinos, that

William Howard Taft said the United States would bring to Central America, and that later presidents claimed they were spreading from Iran to Grenada are the same ones that George W. Bush insisted his invasion of Iraq would bring to people there.

"If the self-evident truths of our founding are true for us," Bush declared soon after the Iraq invasion, "they are true for all."

Generations of Americans have eagerly embraced this belief, largely because it reinforces their self-image as uniquely decent people who want only to share their good fortune with others. More sophisticated defenders of the regime change idea make a better argument. They recognize that the United States considers principally its own interests when deciding whether to overthrow foreign governments, but insist that this is fine because what is good for the United States is also good for everyone else. In their view, American power is intrinsically benign because the political and economic system it seeks to impose on other countries will make them richer, freer, and happier—and, as a consequence, create a more peaceful world.

A clear truth lies behind this belief in the transformative value of American influence. For more than a century, Americans have believed they deserve access to markets and resources in other countries. When they are denied that access, they take what they want by force, deposing governments that stand in their way. Great powers have done this since time immemorial. What distinguishes Americans from citizens of past empires is their eagerness to persuade themselves that they are acting out of humanitarian motives.

For most of the "regime change" era, the United States did little or nothing to promote democracy in the countries whose governments it deposed. Presidents McKinley, Theodore Roosevelt, and Taft claimed to be interested in doing so, but in truth they were willing to support any governing clique, no matter how odious, as long as it did America's bidding. Later, in Iran, Guatemala, and Chile, the United States covered itself in even greater shame by overthrowing democratically elected leaders and leaving tyrants in their place. During the George W. Bush era, however, the United States began taking its democratic rhetoric more seriously. It tried, though not always wholeheartedly, to guide Afghanistan along the road toward a new political system. In Iraq, it threw itself into the task even more vigorously, devoting huge resources to the most ambitious "nation-building" project America had ever undertaken.

Part of the reason for this change was that the stakes were far higher. When Honduras or Nicaragua, for example, fell under the rule of pro-American dictators after the United States overthrew their governments, only the citizens of those countries suffered. By some measures, especially those related to business and commerce, the United States actually benefited. If disaster was to overtake the Bush administration's Iraq project, however, the whole world, and especially the United States, would suffer grievously.

Bush and his advisers leapt into Iraq because they saw that success there—which they defined as replacing Saddam's tyranny with a peaceful, democratic, capitalistic, and pro-American regime—would bring enormous benefits. They dared to hope that besides giving the United States a new strategic platform in the Middle East and a reliable source of oil, such a regime would become a beacon of democracy for the entire region. These goals were so tantalizing that the Bush administration refused to assess coldly and realistically the chances that they could be achieved.

Americans believe, perhaps more fervently than anyone else on earth, that everything is possible if one works hard enough to achieve it. That may be true when people confront challenges posed by nature, science, or even other people. Transforming long-established cultures, however, is a much more daunting task. Attempting to do so and failing can bring terrible consequences.

Most American-sponsored "regime change" operations have, in the end, weakened rather than strengthened American security. They have produced generations of militants who are deeply and sometimes violently anti-American; expanded the borders that the United States feels obligated to defend, thereby increasing the number of enemies it must face and drawing it ever more deeply into webs of foreign entanglement; and emboldened enemies of the United States by showing that despite its awesome power, it has a soft and vulnerable underbelly.

It is understandable, though perhaps not forgivable, that the Bush administration's enthusiasm for invading Iraq led it to ignore the potential consequences of failure. More puzzling was its unwillingness to reflect on the danger of success. Ever since the dawn of the "regime change" era, the United States has had to face the reality that when foreign countries become democratic, they do not necessarily become pro-American. On the contrary, they often assert their independence by refusing to allow foreign troops on their soil, restricting the rights of foreign-owned corporations, and placing their own national interest above all others. In Iraq, true democracy might also lead to the establishment of a religious state permeated with more hatred of the United States and Israel than Saddam ever harbored. The dangers of success there are almost as great as the dangers of failure.

Each country in the world has legitimate interests of its own, and sometimes they conflict with American interests. That is why the crucial moment in almost every "regime change" operation comes when Americans have to decide whether they should return true sovereignty to the nation whose government they have deposed. In many places, that would mean accepting a new regime that will not serve, and may well wish to undermine, American political, military, and economic interests. The temptation to prevent such regimes from taking power is naturally great. In many countries it has led the United States to impose leaders who are pro-American but unpopular, a course that inevitably leads to trouble.

Presidents from McKinley to Bush have deluded themselves into believing that people living in subject nations would embrace American influence. Many have done just the opposite. Their resentment festered and often turned to violence that pulled the United States into repeated interventions. Each of these interventions radicalized more people. They ultimately led millions around the world to support anti-American movements like those that have erupted in countries from Nicaragua to Iraq.

George W. Bush and his supporters never wavered in their belief that the United States has the right to wage war whenever it deems necessary, regardless of how loudly domestic critics or foreign leaders might protest. "At this moment in history, if there is a problem, we're expected to deal with it," Bush explained. "We are trying to lead the world." American leaders made clear, however, that they did not accept the right of other countries to act this way. Those other nations, they warned, would abuse this right by waging wars of conquest or self-aggrandizement, something they insisted the United States would never do.

Countries that have the power to interfere in foreign lands almost always do so. Military historians since Thucydides, who wrote that nations feel "an innate compulsion to rule when empowered," have observed that no state ever acquires great military strength without

Greed

using it. As a country grows more powerful, it inevitably becomes greedy and succumbs to the temptation to take what it wants. Time and again over the course of history, greed has led great nations to overreach and sow the seeds of their decline.

"I dread our *own* power and our *own* ambition," the British statesman Edmund Burke presciently warned when his country was master of a vast empire. "I dread our being too much dreaded. It is ridiculous to say that we are not men, and that, as men, we shall never wish to aggrandize ourselves."

The United States has been a world power since the end of the nineteenth century. By using its might to overthrow foreign governments, it acted not in a new or radical way but in accordance with a long-established law of history. When no power restrained it, it did not restrain itself.

Several other factors led the United States to embrace the idea of "regime change." One was the desire to find a means of shaping world events that did not involve old-style colonialism. Another was the rise of giant corporations able to finance election campaigns and buy political power, a phenomenon that is nowhere more pronounced than in the United States. Perhaps the most deeply rooted was the unique combination of beliefs that give Americans a messianic desire to combat evil forces in the world, a conviction that applying military power will allow them to reshape other countries in their image, a certainty that doing so is good for all humanity, and a fervent belief that this is what God wants the United States to do.

One of the most immutable patterns of history is the rise and fall of empires and great nations. Some Americans, however, believe their country to be so far beyond comparison with any other country or empire that has ever existed that it has passed beyond the reach of history. This belief has allowed them to embark on ambitious "regime change" projects with supreme confidence that they would succeed, and equal confidence that no matter how badly the projects might turn out, the United States would not suffer because its power is so overwhelming.

For most of the twentieth century, and even more as the twenty-first century dawned, the United States commanded enough military might to defeat any nation or group of nations on the battlefield. The history of this period, however, shows that military power, even combined with political and economic power, is not enough to bend the will of nations. In almost every case, overthrowing the government of a foreign country has, in the end, led both that country and the United States to grief.

There are, and probably will always be, governments that threaten global order, sometimes in terrifying ways. The world community, unavoidably led by the United States, has an urgent responsibility to contain and reduce those threats. The blunt instrument of "regime change," however, almost never does so. When the United States assumes the right to decide which regimes pose urgent threats, and then acts violently to crush them, it destabilizes the world rather than stabilizing it.

Too often, "regime change" operations have been simply a substitute for thoughtful foreign policy. In most cases, diplomatic and political approaches would have worked far more effectively. They are subtler, more difficult to design, and take longer to bear fruit, but they do not plunge nations into violence and do not drive millions of people to resent the United States.

Modern history makes eminently clear that when the United States engages with oppressive and threatening regimes, using combinations of incentives, threats, punishments, and rewards, those regimes slowly become less dangerous. The most obvious examples are China and the former Soviet Union, but the same approach has been highly effective in countries from South Korea to South Africa. Nations the United States confronts only with threats and pressures, and isolates from the international system, like Iran, Cuba, and North Korea, never emerge from their cocoons of repression and anti-Americanism.

Deft combinations of measures to build civil society, strengthen free enterprise, promote trade, and encourage diplomatic solutions to international problems have worked wonders in many countries. These measures require patience, willingness to compromise, and recognition that all nations have legitimate interests, including security interests. They are most effective when they are the product of global consensus. Because the United States is not always patient and not always willing to compromise, recognize other countries' interests, or work on an equal basis with other nations, it impulsively turns to the option of forcible "regime change." Driven by shifting combinations of frustration, anger, and fear, it lashes out in ways that bring quick satisfaction but often create problems greater than the ones it seems to resolve.

Americans have a spectacularly successful story to tell the world, and the world, despite its growing resentment of the United States, is still eager to hear it. As American presidents have invested hundreds of billions of dollars in weaponry and other blunt tools, however, they have systematically closed American diplomatic posts, libraries, and cultural centers around the world. During the Cold War, millions of people were exposed to American ideals through this dense information network, and many came to admire the United States deeply. Once the Cold War ended, Americans seemed to believe that they no longer needed to teach anyone about their way of life. They came to accept two great fallacies. First, they assumed that the collapse of Communism would lead people around the world to agree that the American political and economic model was best for everyone. Second, they imagined that their overwhelming military power would allow them to crush any power that dissented from this consensus.

If it were possible to control the course of world events by deposing foreign governments, the United States would be unchallenged. It has deposed far more of them than any other modern nation. The stories of what has happened in the aftermath of these operations, however, make clear that Americans do not know what to do with countries after removing their leaders. They easily succumb to the temptation to stage coups or invasions but turn quickly away when the countries where they intervene fall into misery and repression.

The fundamental reason why countries invade other countries, or seek forcibly to depose their governments, has not changed over the course of history. It is the same reason children fight in schoolyards. The stronger one wants what the weaker one has. Most "regime change" operations fit within the larger category of resource wars. When the United States intervenes abroad to gain strategic advantage, depose governments it considers oppressive, or spread its political and religious system, it is also acting in its commercial self-interest. The search for markets, and for access to natural resources, is as central to American history as it has been to the history of every great power in every age.

The United States rose to world power more quickly than almost any nation or empire ever has. Filled with the exuberance and self-confidence of youth, it developed a sense of unlimited possibility. Many

Americans came to believe that since they had been so successful in building their country, they not only could duplicate that success abroad but were called by Providence to do so. Responding to this call, and to their belief that they are entitled to a large share of the world's resources, they set out to overthrow foreign governments. Most of these adventures have brought them, and the nations whose histories they sought to change, far more pain than liberation.

NOTES

page   **1:** A HELL OF A TIME UP AT THE PALACE

10   Colburn reports to Thurston: Thurston, Lorrin A., *Memoirs of the Hawaiian Revolution* (Honolulu: Advertiser Publishing, 1936), p. 245.
Hawaiian society very successful: Bushnell, O. A., *The Gifts of Civilization: Germs and Genocide in Hawaii* (Honolulu: University of Hawaii Press, 1993), p. 14.

11   Natives react to ships: Bushnell, p. 133.
Illnesses of Hawaiians: Bushnell, pp. 23, 131; Schmitt, Robert C., *Historical Statistics of Hawaii* (Honolulu: University Press of Hawaii, 1977), p. 232.

12   Natives are ignorant and stupid: Bushnell, p. 16.
Streets now deserted: McKee, Linda, "Mad Jack and the Missionaries," *American Heritage,* Apr. 1971, p. 33.

14   Treaty with President Grant: Russ, William Adam, *The Hawaiian Revolution (1893–94)* (Selinsgrove, Pa.: Susquehanna University Press, 1959), p. 11.
Treaty brings Hawaii under American influence: Russ, pp. 11–12.
Hawaiians infuriated: Dougherty, Michael, *To Steal a Kingdom: Probing Hawaiian History* (Waimanalo, Hawaii: Island Style, 1992), pp. 130–31.
Number of plantations tripled: Dougherty, p. 131.
Sugar exports soared: Schmitt, pp. 418–20.

15   Russ on influence of whites: Russ, pp. 15–17.
Planters in depths of despair: Dougherty, p. 163.

16 · Queen on bayonet constitution: Allen, Helena G., *The Betrayal of Liliuokalani: Last Queen of Hawaii, 1838–1917* (Honolulu: Mutual, 1982), p. 207.
Judd advice to queen: Allen, p. 233.

17   Thurston describes meeting in Washington: Thurston, pp. 231–32.
Navy will cooperate: Russ, p. 42.
Thurston doubts queen will quit: Thurston, p. 234–36.

18   Census of 1890: Russ, William A., "The Role of Sugar in Hawaiian Annexation," *The Pacific Historical Review,* Dec. 1943, p. 341.
Queen addresses legislature: Allen, Helena G., *Sanford Ballard Dole: Hawaii's Only President, 1844–1926* (Glendale, Calif.: Arthur H. Clark, 1988), p. 184.

18   Ministers in a blue funk: Thurston, p. 247.

Intelligent part of the community: Allen, *Betrayal*, p. 287.

19   Committee of Safety formed: Twigg-Smith, Thurston, *Hawaiian Sovereignty: Do the Facts Matter?* (Honolulu: Goodale, 1998), p. 147.

Cooper urges annexation: Thurston, p. 250.

20   Queen sends supporters home: Daws, Gavan, *Shoal of Time: A History of the Hawaiian Islands* (Honolulu: University of Hawaii, 1968), pp. 271–72.

Sub-meeting: Thurston, p. 251.

Presidential inquiry: Blount, James H., *Report of U.S. Special Commissioner James H. Blount to U.S. Secretary of State Walter Q. Gresham Concerning the Hawaiian Kingdom Investigation*, http://libweb.hawaii.edu/digicoll/annexation/blount.

21   Rebels won't sit on a volcano: Russ, p. 75.

Thurston declines leadership: Allen, *Betrayal*, p. 289; Daws, p. 274.

22   Wilson fails to discourage rebels: Thurston, pp. 253–54.

Rebels write appeal to Stevens: Russ, *Hawaiian Revolution*, p. 77.

23   Queen promises no changes in constitution: Russ, *Hawaiian Revolution*, p. 80.

Male white foreign element: Allen, *Betrayal*, p. 290.

Thurston speech: Thurston, pp. 262–63.

Unanimous understanding: Thurston, p. 267.

Fit companion for a hog: *Honolulu Daily Bulletin*, Jan. 17, 1893.

24   Peterson and Parker visit Stevens: Russ, *Hawaiian Revolution*, p. 76.

Stevens will land troops: Russ, *Hawaiian Revolution*, p. 81.

Stevens's note to Wiltse: House Executive Document 48, 53rd Congress, Second Session, p. 487.

25   Rickard argues with Thurston: Thurston, p. 270.

Parker appeal: Russ, *Hawaiian Revolution*, p. 83.

26   Immediate approval of Dole: Damon, Ethel M., *Sanford Ballard Dole and His Hawaii* (Palo Alto, Calif.: Pacific Books, 1957), p. 248.

27   Dole recalls offer: Allen, *Sanford Ballard Dole*, p. 188.

Dole expects short presidency: Allen, *Sanford Ballard Dole*, p. 189.

Stevens tells Dole he has great opportunity: Damon, p. 250.

28   Stevens warns against attack by queen's forces: Blount.

Rebel proclamation: Damon, pp. 191–95.

Ministers write about treasonable persons: Russ, *Hawaiian Revolution*, p. 92.

29   Stevens recognizes new regime: Russ, *Hawaiian Revolution*, p. 105.

Queen's resignation statement: Allen, *Betrayal*, p. 294.

2: BOUND FOR GOO-GOO LAND

31   Cubans forbidden to celebrate independence: *New York Times*, Dec. 28–29, 1898.

32   1898 was watershed year: Pérez, Louis A., Jr., *The War of 1898: The United States and Cuba in History and Historiography* (Chapel Hill: University of North Carolina Press, 1998), p. ix.

Cleveland on seizing territory: Nevins, Allan (ed.), *Letters of Grover Cleveland, 1850–1908* (Boston: Houghton Mifflin, 1933), pp. 491–92.

32   Turner on expansion: Turner, Frederick Jackson, "The Problem of the West," *Atlantic Monthly*, Sept. 1896.

33   Mahan says America must look outward: Mahan, Alfred Thayer, "The United States Looking Outward," *Atlantic Monthly*, Dec. 1890.

34   Gresham sees symptoms of revolution: LaFeber, Walter, *The New Empire: An Interpretation of American Expansionism, 1860–1898* (Ithaca, N.Y.: Cornell University, 1963), p. 200.
       Carlisle on selling surplus: LaFeber, p. 181.

35   Martí warns of United States: Foner, Philip S., *The Spanish-Cuban-American War and the Birth of American Imperialism, 1895–1902* (New York: Monthly Review Press, 1972), p. 13.

36   *New York Journal* on Weyler: Walker, Dale L., *The Boys of '98: Theodore Roosevelt and the Rough Riders* (New York: Tom Dougherty, 1998), p. 37.

37   Any president with a backbone: Pérez, p. 80.
       Maceo and Rubens oppose intervention: Pérez, p. 20.

38   Teller Amendment: Pérez, p. 21.
       García on Teller Amendment: Healy, David F., *The United States in Cuba, 1898–1902* (Madison: University of Wisconsin Press, 1963), p. 31.
       Newspapers embrace cause: Dierks, Jack Cameron, *A Leap to Arms: The Cuban Campaign of 1898* (Philadelphia: J. B. Lippincott, 1970), pp. 25–26; Walker, p. 85.

39   War without misgivings: Millis, Walter, *The Martial Spirit: A Study of Our War with Spain* (Boston: Houghton Mifflin, 1931), p. 160.
       Splendid little war: Boot, Max, *The Savage Wars of Peace: Small Wars and the Rise of American Power* (New York: Basic Books, 2002), p. 102.
       Newspapers favor violating Teller Amendment: Pérez, p. 28.

40   Misconceptions of Cuban rebels: Pérez, pp. 81–97.

41   Shafter on self-government: Healy, p. 36.

42   Gómez laments intervention: Pérez, p. 23.
       Wood on delegates: Healy, p. 148.

43   Editorial on violating promise: *New York Evening Post*, Feb. 1, 1901.
       Havana was in turmoil: Healy, p. 169.

44   Wood sees no independence left: Healy, p. 178.
       Roosevelt and Lodge on taking Puerto Rico: Carrión, Arturo Morales, *Puerto Rico: A Political and Cultural History* (New York: W. W. Norton, 1983), p. 134.
       Hanna reports Puerto Ricans are jubilant: Carrión, p. 133.

45   Puerto Rico has eight days of independence: Carrión, p. 125.
       Miles reassures Puerto Ricans: Barnes, Mark R., "The American Army Moves on Puerto Rico," www.spanamwar.com/puerto.

46   Casualties in Puerto Rico: Barnes.
       Davis says war was a picnic: Barnes.
       Davis calls it a fête de fleurs: Carrión, p. 136.
       Evening Post report: Carrión, p. 140.

47   McKinley's views obscured in fog: Smith, Ephraim K., "William McKinley's Historical Legacy: The Historiographical Debate on the Taking of the Philippine Islands," in Bradford, James C. (ed.), *Crucible of Empire: The*

Spanish-American War and Its Aftermath (Annapolis: Naval Institute Press, 1993), p. 205.

47 God guides McKinley to take Philippines: Boot, p. 105; Millis, pp. 525–26.
McKinley knew Filipinos not at all: Welch, Richard E., Jr., *Response to Imperialism: The United States and the Philippine-American War, 1899–1902* (Chapel Hill: University of North Carolina Press, 1979), p. 10.
McKinley on darned islands: Kohlsaat, H. H., *From McKinley to Harding: Personal Recollections of Our Presidents* (New York: Charles Scribner's Sons, 1923), p. 68.
Karnow on pivotal point: Karnow, Stanley, *In Our Image: America's Empire in the Philippines* (New York: Ballantine, 1990), p. 79.
Dewey meets Aguinaldo: Karnow, pp. 13–14.

48 Anderson wishes amicable relations: Nearing, Scott, and Joseph Freeman, *Dollar Diplomacy: A Study in American Imperialism* (New York: Modern Reader, 1969), p. 197.
Welch on McKinley and Aguinaldo: Welch, pp. 15–16.

49 Hoar sees vulgar empire: Karnow, p. 113.
Amazing coincidence: Welch, p. 19.
We come as ministering angels: *Congressional Record,* 55th Congress, Third Session, p. 838.

50 McKinley cannot turn Philippines over: LaFeber, Walter, "That 'Splendid Little War' in Perspective," *Texas Quarterly,* no. 11 (1968), pp. 97–98; Welch, pp. 5–10.
Letters home: Poole, Fred, and Max Vanzi, *Revolution in the Philippines: The United States in a Hall of Cracked Mirrors* (New York: McGraw-Hill, 1984), p. 171.

51 *Philadelphia Ledger* report: Poole and Vanzi, p. 180.
Capture of Aguinaldo: Boot, pp. 117–19.

52 Bound for goo-goo land: Boot, p. 99.
Balangiga massacre: Boot, p. 120; Linn, Brian McAllister, *The Philippine War, 1899–1902* (Lawrence: University Press of Kansas, 2000), pp. 305–21.

53 Smith wants no prisoners: Poole and Vanzi, p. 184.
Water cure: Linn, p. 223.

54 *Plain Dealer* on water cure: Welch, p. 146.
Criticism of U.S. actions in the Philippines: Karnow, pp. 191–93; Welch, pp. 121–25, 138, 141.
Mark Twain on redesigning flag: *North American Review,* Feb. 1901.
Actions defended: Welch, pp. 140–44.

55 Torture inquiry was sleight of hand: Welch, p. 145.
Death toll in Philippines: Nearing and Freeman, p. 199.

3: FROM A WHOREHOUSE TO A WHITE HOUSE

57 Report favoring Nicaragua route: U.S. Senate, *Report of the Inter-Oceanic Canal Commission,* Senate Executive Document 15, 46th Congress, First Session, pp. 1–2.

58 Cromwell can smile sweetly: *New York World,* Oct. 4, 1908.

58   Cromwell donates to Republican Party: McCullough, David, *The Path Between the Seas: The Creation of the Panama Canal, 1870–1914* (New York: Simon and Schuster, 1977), p. 291; DuVal, Miles P., Jr., *Cádiz to Cathay: The Story of the Long Diplomatic Struggle for the Panama Canal* (New York: Glenwood Press, 1968), p. 147.
      Momotombo stamp: Image at www.iomoon.com/momotombo.

59   Leaflets sent to senators: Image in DuVal, p. 163; McCullough, pp. 147–48.
      Cromwell's fee: DuVal, p. 121; McCullough, p. 291.
      Canal price reduced to $40 million: Dobson, John M., *America's Ascent: The United States Becomes a Great Power, 1880–1914* (DeKalb: Northern Illinois University Press, 1978), p. 155.

60   Stamp played decisive role: McCullough, p. 152.
      Morgan cites corrupt lobby: *New York Times*, June 26, 1902.
      American officials praise Zelaya: Berman, Karl, *Under the Big Stick: Nicaragua and the United States Since 1848* (Boston: South End Press, 1986), p. 142.
      Findling on Zelaya: Findling, John Ellis, "The United States and Zelaya: A Study in the Diplomacy of Expediency" (Doctoral dissertation, University of Texas at Austin, 1972), p. 133.
      Roosevelt sees two alternatives: Brands, H. W., *T. R.: The Last Romantic* (New York: Basic Books, 1997), p. 483.

61   Intervention in Panama was brazen and successful: Boot, p. 134.
      Roosevelt's explanations: Boot, pp. 133–34; Brands, p. 488.

62   Zelaya's complacency: Findling, p. 132.

63   Emery concession: Findling, p. 184; Berman, p. 143.

64   Roosevelt praises Zelaya: Berman, p. 142.
      Roosevelt Corollary: Zimmerman, Warren, *First Great Triumph: How Five Americans Made Their Country a World Power* (New York: Farrar, Straus and Giroux, 2002), pp. 440–41.

65   Emery claim resolved: Findling, pp. 83–84; Berman, pp. 143–44.
      Zelaya seeks loan from Europe: Findling, p. 189.
      Zelaya on beggarly Peru: Musicant, Ivan, *The Banana Wars: A History of United States Military Intervention in Latin America from the Spanish-American War to the Invasion of Panama* (New York: Macmillan, 1960), p. 138.
      American campaign against Zelaya: Musicant, p. 137; Findling, pp. 209, 215.

66   Cost of revolution: Denny, Harold Norman, *Dollars for Bullets: The Story of American Rule in Nicaragua* (New York: Dial Press, 1929), p. 79.
      Cannon and Groce: Denny, pp. 79–80; Berman, pp. 145–46; Findling, pp. 212–14.

67   Knox asks Central American countries to invade Nicaragua: Findling, pp. 214–15.

68   Nicaraguan response to Knox Note: Findling, pp. 218–19.
      Taft sends warships and marines: Berman, p. 147.
      Zelaya resignation speech: Selser, Gregorio, *La restauración conservadora y la gesta de Benjamín Zeledón: Nicaragua–USA, 1909–1916* (Managua: Aldilá, 2001), p. 105.

69   Moffett bans fighting: Denny, pp. 85–87.
      Butler at Bluefields and Rama: Musicant, p. 141; Schmidt, Hans, *Maverick Marine: General Smedley Butler and the Contradictions of American Military History* (Lexington: University Press of Kentucky, 1987), pp. 41–42.
70   Denny on beginning of American rule: Denny, p. 90.
71   Lee Christmas is a Dumas hero: *New York Times,* Jan. 15, 1911.
72   Christmas and Bonilla speed away: Langley, Lester D., and Thomas Schoonover, *The Banana Men: American Mercenaries and Entrepreneurs in Central America, 1880–1930* (Lexington: University Press of Kentucky, 1995), p. 128.
      Zemurray background: Whitfield, Stephen J., *Strange Fruit: The Career of Samuel Zemurray,* in *American Jewish History,* March 1984, pp. 307–23.
73   Bonilla needs help from *El Amigo*: Langley and Schoonover, p. 119.
      Zemurray would unlikely stop intrigues: Langley and Schoonover, pp. 123–24.
74   Military campaign in Honduras: Langley and Schoonover, pp. 114–40; LaFeber, Walter, *Inevitable Revolutions: The United States in Central America* (New York: W. W. Norton, 1983), pp. 43–45.
75   Cooper cable to Washington: Langley and Schoonover, p. 134.
76   Historian on bankers and banana men: Marvin Barahona, quoted in Langley and Schoonover, p. 144.
      Bonilla, Christmas, and Zemurray after charges are dropped: Langley and Schoonover, pp. 148–49.
77   United Fruit throttled competitors: Kepner, Charles David, Jr., and Jay Henry Soothill, *The Banana Empire: A Case Study of Economic Imperialism* (New York: Russell & Russell, 1935), p. 336.

4: A BREAK IN THE HISTORY OF THE WORLD

78   Roosevelt feels proud: *New York Times,* Dec. 17, 1907.
      Great White Fleet: Hart, Robert A., *The Great White Fleet: Our Nation's Attempt at Global Diplomacy in the Twilight of Its Innocence, 1907–1909* (Boston: Little, Brown, 1965); McKinley, Mike, *The Cruise of the Great White Fleet* (Washington: Naval Historical Center, at www.history.navy.mil); *New York Times,* Dec. 15, 1907; Zimmerman, Warren, *First Great Triumph: How Five Americans Made Their Country a World Power* (New York: Farrar, Straus and Giroux, 2002), pp. 2–6.
80   Lodge wants large policy: Foner, Philip S., *The Spanish-Cuban-American War and the Birth of American Imperialism, 1895–1902* (New York: Monthly Review Press, 1972), p. 304.
      Bryce sees stupendous change: Cabán, Pedro A., *Constructing a Colonial People: Puerto Rico and the United States, 1898–1932* (Boulder: Westview, 1999), p. 34.
      Lodge urges annexation of Canada: Pratt, Julius W., *Expansionists of 1898: The Acquisition of Hawaii and the Spanish Islands* (Chicago: Quadrangle, 1964), p. 207.
      Roosevelt muses about attacking Spain: Phillips, Kevin, *William McKinley* (New York: Times Books, 2002), p. 92.

81   Portuguese leaders worry about Azores: Dell'Orto, Giovanna, "We Are All Americans" (Doctoral dissertation, University of Minnesota, 2004), p. 108.

Beard on realpolitik: Beard, Charles A., *The Idea of National Interest* (Chicago: Quadrangle, 1934), p. 107.

Reports from European correspondents: Dell'Orto, pp. 82–84.

Americans never worried about diplomatic questions: *Frankfurter Zeitung*, Jan. 2, 1899, quoted in Dell'Orto, p. 94.

82   Godkin on imperialism: Beisner, Robert L., *Twelve Against Empire: The Anti-Imperialists, 1898–1900* (New York: McGraw-Hill, 1968), pp. 74–75.

Roosevelt calls Godkin a liar: Beisner, p. 56.

Roosevelt letter to Lodge: Tuchman, Barbara, *The Proud Tower: A Portrait of the World Before the War, 1890–1914* (New York: Ballantine, 1962), p. 147.

Roosevelt on unhung traitors: Beisner, p. 237.

83   Aggressive national egoism: Smith, Joseph, *The Spanish-American War: Conflict in the Caribbean and Pacific, 1895–1902* (London: Longman, 1994), p. 217.

Kipling poem: *McClure's Magazine*, Feb. 1, 1899.

McKinley on oppression at our very doors: Pérez, Louis A., Jr., *The War of 1898: The United States and Cuba in History and Historiography* (Chapel Hill: University of North Carolina Press, 1998), p. 111.

84   Beveridge on disappearance of debased civilizations: Stephanson, Anders, *Manifest Destiny: American Expansion and the Empire of Right* (New York: Hill and Wang, 1995), p. 98.

Cochrane on Aryan races: Stephanson, p. 89.

Clark on enduring our shame: Russ, William Adam, *The Hawaiian Republic (1894–98) and Its Struggle to Win Annexation* (Selinsgrove, Pa.: Susquehanna University Press, 1992), p. 318.

85   Newspapers react to Hawaiian revolution: Russ, *Hawaiian Republic*, pp. 113–17.

New government takes power: Russ, *Hawaiian Revolution*, pp. 100–11; Allen, Helena G., *Sanford Ballard Dole: Hawaii's Only President, 1844–1926* (Glendale, Calif.: Arthur H. Clark, 1988), pp. 198–200.

Proclamation by Stevens: Russ, *Hawaiian Revolution*, p. 128.

Queen's report to Foster: Russ, *Hawaiian Revolution*, p. 145.

86   Alexander on war necessity: Russ, *Hawaiian Republic*, p. 305.

87   Russ on why Hawaii was annexed: Russ, *Hawaiian Republic*, pp. 300, 372.

88   Akaka on Senate resolution: *Honolulu Star-Bulletin*, Nov. 23, 1993.

Gorton on Senate resolution: *Seattle Post-Intelligencer*, Nov. 1, 1993.

89   American policy makers delude themselves: Benjamin, Jules R., *The United States and the Origins of the Cuban Revolution: An Empire of Liberty in an Age of National Liberation* (Princeton: Princeton University Press, 1990), p. 99.

90   Castro speech: Benjamin, p. 215.

Eisenhower is baffled: Benjamin, p. 216.

91   Muñoz Rivera on invasion of Puerto Rico: Trías Monge, José, *Puerto Rico: The Trials of the Oldest Colony in the World* (New Haven: Yale University Press, 1997), p. 52.

92   Henna on Mr. Nobody: Trías Monge, p. 40.

92   Sugar and coffee exports: Brau, M. M., *Island in the Crossroads: The History of Puerto Rico* (Garden City, N.J.: Zenith, 1968), p. 88.
      Puerto Ricans become steadily poorer: Trías Monge, p. 83.
      Historian on foreign corporations: Caban, p. 217.

94   Islands or canned goods: Karnow, *In Our Image: America's Empire in the Philippines* (New York: Ballantine, 1990), p. 129.

95   Eisenhower recommends withdrawal from Philippines: Bonner, Raymond, *Waltzing with a Dictator: The Marcoses and the Making of American Policy* (New York: Times Books, 1987), p. 32.

96   Manglapus blames United States: Poole, Fred, and Max Vanzi, *Revolution in the Philippines: The United States in a Hall of Cracked Mirrors* (New York: McGraw-Hill, 1984), p. 341.

97   Reagan doesn't know anything more important: Karnow, p. 414.

98   Zelaya dies in New York: *New York Times,* May 19, 1919.

99   Sandino on Zeledón's death: Kinzer, Stephen, *Blood of Brothers: Life and War in Nicaragua* (New York: G. P. Putnam's Sons, 1991), p. 27.
      State Department dismisses Sandino: Denny, Harold Norman, *Dollars for Bullets: The Story of American Rule in Nicaragua* (New York: Dial Press, 1929), pp. 324–25.
      Sandino says he won't live much longer: Kinzer, p. 31.

100   Mule costs more than a congressman: Langley, Lester D., and Thomas Schoonover, *The Banana Men: American Mercenaries and Entrepreneurs in Central America, 1880–1930* (Lexington: University Press of Kentucky, 1995), p. 171.
      Fruit companies own most land: Merrill, Tim L. (ed.), *Honduras: A Country Study* (Washington: Federal Research Division, Library of Congress, 1993), p. 6.

101   1,000 miles of railroad: Acker, Alison, *Honduras: The Making of a Banana Republic* (Boston: South End Press, 1988), p. 24.
      Country of the seventies: LaFeber, Walter, *Inevitable Revolutions: The United States in Central America* (New York: W. W. Norton, 1983), p. 177.

102   Eli Black scandal and suicide: McCann, Thomas, *An American Company: The Tragedy of United Fruit* (New York: Crown, 1976), pp. 1–3.

103   Root on effect of building canal: LaFeber, p. 37.

104   Roosevelt says countries must behave: LaFeber, p. 37.
      Lodge on consolidation: Pratt, p. 207.

5: DESPOTISM AND GODLESS TERRORISM

111   Dulles and Eisenhower examine world drama: Kluckhohn, Frank L., *The Man Who Kept the Peace: A Study of John Foster Dulles* (New York: Columbia Heights, 1968), p. 26.

112   Dulles habits at home: Kluckhohn, pp. 123–26.
      Foster asks Cromwell to hire Dulles: Beal, John Robinson, *John Foster Dulles: A Biography* (New York: Harper & Brothers, 1957), p. 55.

113   Early foreign assignments for Dulles: Kluckhohn, p. 12.
      Dulles may have been a world watcher: Pruessen, Ronald W., *John Foster Dulles: The Road to Power* (New York: Free Press, 1982), pp. xiii–xiv, 104.

113   Clients at Sullivan & Cromwell: Preussen, pp. 60–69; Lisagor, Nancy, and Frank Lipsius, *A Law unto Itself: The Untold Story of the Law Firm Sullivan & Cromwell* (New York: William Morrow, 1988), pp. 67, 100.

114   Sullivan & Cromwell ties to Nazis: Lisagor and Lipsius, pp. 32–33, 132–37; Mosley, Leonard, *Dulles: A Biography of Eleanor, Allen, and John Foster Dulles and Their Family Network* (New York: Dell, 1979), pp. 104–8.
         Enemy of the Reds: Beal, photo of Dulles car.

115   Only religious leader to become secretary of state: Gearson, Louis L., *John Foster Dulles* (New York: Cooper Square, 1967), p. xi.
         Dulles sees religious heritage and duty to help others: Van Dusen, Henry P., *The Spiritual Legacy of John Foster Dulles: Selections from His Articles and Addresses* (Philadelphia: Westminster, 1960), pp. 80–87.
         Dulles flies to Paris: Drummond, Roscoe, and Gaston Coblentz, *Duel at the Brink: John Foster Dulles' Command of American Power* (Garden City, N.Y.: Doubleday, 1960), p. 30.
         Dulles was out of touch: Goold-Adams, Richard, *The Time of Power: A Reappraisal of John Foster Dulles* (London: Weidenfeld and Nicolson, 1962), p. 14.

116   Hoopes on Dulles: Hoopes, Townsend, *The Devil and John Foster Dulles* (New York: Atlantic Monthly Press, 1973), p. 38.
         Dulles scarcely knew meaning of compromise: Gaddis, John Lewis, *Strategies of Containment: A Critical Appraisal of Postwar American National Security Policy* (New York: Oxford University Press, 1982), pp. 14, 160.
         Dulles trained in adversarial terms: Gaddis, p. 136.

117   Dulles positions in 1952 campaign: *New York Times,* July 10, 1952.

118   Iran's misery caused by oil company: Goode, James F., *The United States and Iran: In the Shadow of Mussadiq* (New York: St. Martin's Press, 1997), p. 31.
         We English have experience: Elm, Mostafa, *Oil, Power, and Principle: Iran's Oil Nationalization and Its Aftermath* (Syracuse, N.Y.: Syracuse University Press, 1992), p. 103.

119   Persian oil vital to our economy: Elm, p. 112.
         Adjectives applied to Mossadegh: Abrahamian, Ervand, "The 1953 Coup in Iran," *Science and Society,* Summer 2001.

120   Mossadegh is man of the year: *Time,* Jan. 7, 1952.
         Roosevelt meets with British counterparts: Roosevelt, Kermit, *Countercoup: The Struggle for the Control of Iran* (New York: McGraw-Hill, 1979), pp. 107–8.

121   Tudeh threat was not real: Behrooz, Maziar, "The 1953 Coup in Iran and the Legacy of the Tudeh," in Gasiorowski, Mark J., and Malcolm Byrne, *Mohammed Mossadeq and the 1953 Coup in Iran* (Syracuse, N.Y.: Syracuse University Press, 2004), pp. 102–23; Abrahamian.
         Coordination between Mossadegh and Tudeh could not have existed: Ghods, M. Reza, *Iran in the Twentieth Century: A Political History* (Boulder: Lynne Rienner, 1989), pp. 110, 125.

122   National Security Council meeting: Department of State, *Foreign Relations of the United States, 1952–1954.* Vol. 10: *Iran 1952–1954* (Washington: Government Printing Office, 1989), p. 693.

122   Petroleum considerations were involved: Bill, James A., *The Eagle and the Lion: The Tragedy of American-Iranian Relations* (New Haven: Yale University Press, 1988), p. 81.

123   Coup plan: Accounts in Abrahamian; Bill; Diba, Farhad, *Mohammad Mossadegh: A Political Biography* (London: Croon Helm, 1986); Doril, Stephen, *MI6: Inside the World of Her Majesty's Secret Intelligence Service* (New York: Free Press, 2000); Elm; Gasiorowski and Byrne; Goode; Katouzian, Homa, *Mussadiq and the Struggle for Power in Iran* (London: I. B. Tauris, 1999); Kinzer, Stephen, *All the Shah's Men: An American Coup and the Roots of Middle East Terror* (New York: Wiley, 2003); Prados, John, *Presidents' Secret Wars: CIA and Pentagon Covert Operations Since World War II* (New York: William Morrow, 1986); Roosevelt; Woodhouse, C. M., *Something Ventured* (London: Granada, 1982); and Zabih, Sepehr, *The Mossadegh Era: Roots of the Iranian Revolution* (Chicago: Lake View, 1982). The CIA's long-secret internal report on the coup, "Overthrow of Premier Mossadeq of Iran, November 1952–August 1953," is at www.nytimes.com.
       Dulles on getting rid of that madman: Roosevelt, p. 8.
       Goiran quits: Gasiorowski and Byrne, p. 231.
       Dispatches from Grady and McGhee: Bill, James A., and William Roger Louis (eds.), *Mussadiq, Iranian Nationalism, and Oil* (London: I. B. Tauris, 1988), p. 302.

124   Press plays supporting role: Ghods, pp. 220, 245.
       Mossadegh's commitment to rights benefited his enemies: Ghods, p. 95.

126   First coup attempt fails: Gasiorowski and Byrne, pp. 248–49; Kinzer, pp. 5–16; Roosevelt, pp. 149–73.

127   Mossadegh refuses Communist help: Author's interview with former Tehran mayor Nosratollah Azimi, June 23, 2002; Lapping, Brian, *End of Empire* (London: Granada, 1985), p. 215.

128   Roosevelt has farewell meeting with shah: Roosevelt, pp. 199–202.

6: GET RID OF THIS STINKER

129   People began dying: Reuters dispatch from Guatemala City, Oct. 20, 1995.
       United Fruit tied to United States government: Ambrose, Stephen E., *Ike's Spies: Eisenhower and the Espionage Establishment* (Garden City, N.Y.: Doubleday, 1981), p. 223; Immerman, Richard H., *The CIA in Guatemala: The Foreign Policy of Intervention* (Austin: University of Texas Press, 1982), p. 125; Marchetti, Victor, and John Marks, *The CIA and the Cult of Intelligence* (New York: Knopf, 1964), p. 376.

130   Ubico called anyone a Communist: Immerman, p. 33.
       Ubico showers United Fruit with concessions: Ambrose, p. 218; Immerman, p. 124; Schlesinger, Stephen, and Stephen Kinzer, *Bitter Fruit: The Untold Story of the American Coup in Guatemala* (Garden City, N.Y.: Doubleday, 1982), p. 70; Rabe, Stephen G., *Eisenhower and Latin America: The Foreign Policy of Anticommunism* (Chapel Hill: University of North Carolina Press, 1988), p. 45.

131   Arévalo's inaugural speech: Schlesinger and Kinzer, p. 34.
       Arévalo's farewell: Schlesinger and Kinzer, p. 47.

132   Arbenz inaugural address: Schlesinger and Kinzer, p. 52.

133   Dispute over compensation for United Fruit: Gleijeses, Piero, *Shattered Hope: The Guatemala Revolution and the United States, 1944–1954* (Princeton: Princeton University Press, 1991), p. 164.

134   Bernays on public relations: Bernays, Edward, *Biography of an Idea: Memoirs of a Public Relations Counsel* (New York: Simon and Schuster, 1965), pp. 745, 761.
    Bernays on Guatemala: Bernays, pp. 9, 31.
    Press campaign: Immerman, p. 113.

135   Lodge and McCormack: Immerman, p. 117.
    Products of the Cold War ethos: Immerman, p. 81.
    Communists in Guatemala: Rabe, pp. 48, 57.

136   Such a tie must exist: Department of State, *Foreign Relations of the United States 1952–54*, vol. 4: *The American Republics* (Washington: Government Printing Office, 1984), doc. 30.
    Ruthless agents: Rabe, p. 46.

137   Change in passivity: *New York Times,* Nov. 8, 1953.
    Normal approaches will not work: Schlesinger and Kinzer, p. 139.
    Start a civil war: Schlesinger and Kinzer, p. 117.

138   Hunt recruits Spellman: Interview with Hunt, at www.gwu.edu/~nsarchiv/coldwar/interviews/episode-18/hunt1.html.

139   Toriello speech in Caracas: Schlesinger and Kinzer, pp. 143–44.

140   Arms from Czechoslovakia: Schlesinger and Kinzer, pp. 147–58; Immerman, pp. 155–60.
    Gruson pulled out of Guatemala: Salisbury, Harrison, *Without Fear or Favor* (New York: Times Books, 1980), pp. 478–80.
    O'Neill transferred: Wise, David, and Thomas B. Ross, *The Invisible Government* (New York: Random House, 1964), p. 194.

141   Murphy opposes coup: Immerman, p. 159.
    We are on the road: Immerman, pp. 157–58.

142   Looks like this is it: Schlesinger and Kinzer, p. 15.
    State Department statement: *New York Times,* June 20, 1954.
    Arbenz radio speech: Schlesinger and Kinzer, pp. 19–20.

143   Eisenhower approves more planes: Ambrose, p. 230; Eisenhower, Dwight D., *Mandate for Change: The White House Years, 1953–1956* (Garden City, N.Y.: Doubleday, 1963), pp. 425–26; Wise and Ross, pp. 178–79.

144   Toriello cable to Dulles: Phillips, David A., *The Night Watch: Twenty-five Years of Peculiar Service* (New York: Atheneum, 1977) p. 46; Schlesinger and Kinzer, p. 184; Wise and Ross, pp. 190–91.
    Peurifoy visits Díaz: Immerman, pp. 174–75; Schlesinger and Kinzer, pp. 195–96.

145   Arbenz radio speech: Schlesinger and Kinzer, pp. 199–200.
    Peurifoy will crack down, arranges new regime: Schlesinger and Kinzer, pp. 205–16.
    Dulles radio address: Department of State, Intervention of International Communism in the Americas, Publication 5556 (Washington: Department of State, 1954), p. 32.

7: NOT THE PREFERRED WAY TO COMMIT SUICIDE

149   Monk's suicide: Browne, Malcolm, *Muddy Boots and Red Socks: A Reporter's Life* (New York: Times Books, 1993), pp. 8–12.

150   Ho declares independence: Langguth, A. J., *Our Vietnam: The War, 1954–1975* (New York: Touchstone, 2000), p. 59.

Ho looks to United States: Langguth, p. 59.

151   Not unless autos collide: Langguth, p. 72.

152   Landsdale rescues Diem: Maitland, Terrence, and Stephen Weiss, *The Vietnam Experience: Raising the Stakes* (Boston: Boston Publishing, 1982), p. 126.

153   Campaign to entice Vietnamese southward: Karnow, Stanley, *Vietnam: A History* (New York: Viking, 1983), p. 221.

Kattenburg recalls Dulles meeting: Public Broadcasting System, *Vietnam: A Television History*, episode 2, "America's Mandarin, 1954–1963."

Diem family: Maitland and Weiss, pp. 2, 63–65.

154   Eisenhower never mentioned it: Maitland and Weiss, p. 169.

155   Aid was overwhelmingly military: Karnow, p. 259.

Johnson on Vietnam and Diem: Karnow, pp. 214, 250.

Diem complains: Hammer, Ellen J., *A Death in November: America in Vietnam, 1963* (New York: E. P. Dutton, 1987), p. 37.

156   Reluctant protégé: Karnow, p. 284.

Nhu wants to live in peace: PBS, *Vietnam: A Television History.*

Twentieth-century Asians protesting: *New York Times*, Sept. 11, 1963.

157   Let them burn: Karnow, p. 281.

Vietcong control in 1963: Langguth, p. 139.

158   Cable to Lodge: Karnow, p. 286–87.

159   Taylor would never have approved cable: Langguth, p. 225.

160   Government is coming apart: Karnow, p. 288.

Lodge sees no turning back: Halberstam, *The Best and the Brightest* (New York: Penguin, 1969), p. 324.

Kennedy interview on CBS: PBS, *Vietnam: A Television History.*

161   Kattenburg and Robert Kennedy doubt war can be won: Karnow, p. 292.

Conein: Halberstam, *Best and Brightest*, p. 350; Jones, Howard, *Death of a Generation: How the Assassinations of Diem and JFK Prolonged the Vietnam War* (Oxford: Oxford University Press, 2003), pp. 387, 392.

162   Conein had a lot of dental work: Karnow, p. 295.

163   Richardson has doubts and is transferred: Karnow, p. 297; Halberstam, *Best and Brightest*, p. 241.

Doubts expressed at October 29 meeting: Prados, John (ed.), *The White House Tapes: Eavesdropping on the Presidents* (New York: New Press, 2003), pp. 110–33.

165   Prados on meeting: Prados, pp. 95–96.

166   Conein arrives with cash and sends coded message: Karnow, p. 305.

Lodge telephone conversation with Diem: Hammer, pp. 288–89; Halberstam, *Best and Brightest*, p. 355.

167   Pull them up at the roots: Hammer, p. 297.

168   Nhu asks why soldiers use such a vehicle: Jones, p. 429.

168   Bodies arrive, Don asks why victims are dead: Halberstam, *Best and Brightest,* p. 298; Hammer, p. 298.

Conein does not want to see bodies: Karnow, p. 311.

169   Taylor on Kennedy's reaction: Taylor, Maxwell D., *Swords and Plowshares* (Cambridge, Mass.: Da Capo, 1990), p. 301.

169   Bundy on the preferred way: Jones, p. 434.

Forrestal on killings: Hammer, p. 301.

Hammer on killings: Hammer, p. 301.

They were in a difficult position: Collier, Peter, and David Horowitz, *The Kennedys* (New York: Summit, 1984), p. 309.

8: WE'RE GOING TO SMASH HIM

170   Edwards asks if U.S. will do anything: Kornbluh, Peter, "The *El Mercurio* File," *Columbia Journalism Review,* Sept.–Oct. 2003.

171   Geneen proposes million-dollar contribution: U.S. Senate, *Covert Action in Chile, 1963–1973,* 94th Congress, 1st Session (Washington: Government Printing Office, 1975), p. 12.

McCone is conduit while on two payrolls: Hersh, Seymour, *The Price of Power: Kissinger in the Nixon White House* (New York: Summit, 1983), p. 267; Uribe, Armando, *The Black Book of American Intervention in Chile* (Boston: Beacon, 1974), p. 40.

Edwards and Pepsi interests: Louis, J. C., *Cola Wars* (New York: Dodd, Mead, 1980), p. 222–25.

172   Nixon had been triggered into action: Kissinger, *White House Years* (Boston: Little, Brown, 1979), p. 673.

Nixon is anxious and frantic: Petras, James F., *How Allende Fell: A Study in U.S.–Chilean Relations* (Nottingham: Spokesman, 1974), p. 221.

173   Helms scribbles list: Kornbluh, Peter, *The Pinochet File: A Declassified Dossier on Atrocity and Accountability* (New York: New Press, 2003), p. 36.

174   Background of ITT in Chile: *New York Times,* March 3, 1972.

Alliance for Progress settles on Chile: U.S. Senate, *Covert Action,* p. 4.

175   CIA spends $3 million for Frei: U.S. Senate, *Covert Action,* p. 1.

CIA activities after Frei's election: U.S. Senate, *Covert Action,* pp. 17–19.

176   Chile receives military aid: Boorstein, Edward, *Allende's Chile: An Insider's View* (New York: International Publishers, 1977), p. 76.

Korry sees fiduciary responsibility: Korry testimony to U.S. Senate investigators, at www.aardibrary.org/publib/church/reports/vol7.

Nixon will not downgrade military: Kornbluh, p. 119.

Spoiling campaign: U.S. Senate, *Covert Actions,* pp. 19–23, 43; Kissinger, p. 666.

Rockefeller interest in Chile: Hersh, p. 266; Isaacson, Walter, *Kissinger: A Biography* (New York: Simon & Schuster, 1992), p. 289.

177   Rockefeller hears that Allende is Communist dupe: Rockefeller, David, *Memoirs* (New York: Random House, 2002), p. 432.

Eagleburger on American principles: Isaacson, p. 764.

Kissinger is not interested: Uribe, p. 33.

178   40 Committee meets on March 25: U.S. Senate, *Covert Action,* p. 20.
      ITT donates to Alessandri campaign: U.S. Senate, *Covert Action,* p. 13.
      President came down very hard: Hersh, p. 274.

179   Kissinger speech in Chicago: U.S. Senate, *Covert Action,* p. 27.
      Allende would present massive problems: U.S. Senate, *Covert Action,* p. 27.
      Frei is a too gentle soul: Kornbluh, p. 13.
      Track II: Kornbluh, pp. 38–39; U.S. Senate, *Covert Action,* pp. 25–26.
      Contact the military: Kornbluh, pp. 58–59.

180   Don't stand by and watch country go Communist: *New York Times,* Sept. 11, 1974.
      Several express doubts: Kornbluh, pp. 8–11.
      Constant pressure from White House: Kornbluh, p. 14.

181   CIA cable suggests three tools: Kornbluh, pp. 49–56.
      We provide formula for chaos: Kornbluh, p. 1.

182   Not a nut or a bolt: Kornbluh, pp. 17–18; U.S. Senate, *Covert Action,* p. 33.
      CIA inquires about removing Schneider: United States Senate, *Alleged Assassination Plots Involving Foreign Leaders,* Report 94–465, 94th Congress, 1st Session (Washington: Government Printing Office, 1975), p. 241.
      Viaux paid to buy arms: Isaacson, p. 282; Kornbluh, p. 23.
      Nixon went out of his way: Kornbluh, p. 24.
      That son of a bitch: Kornbluh, p. 25; Hersh, p. 284.

183   Kissinger claims he called off Track II: Kissinger, pp. 674–77.
      Kissinger approves message to Viaux: Kornbluh, p. 25.

184   Station has done an excellent job: Kornbluh, p. 73.
      Sigmund on policy making: Sigmund, Paul E., *The Overthrow of Allende and the Politics of Chile, 1964–1976* (Pittsburgh: University of Pittsburgh Press, 1977), p. 48.
      Nixon meets National Security Council: Kornbluh, pp. 119–20.
      First blows were economic: U.S. Senate, *Covert Actions,* pp. 33–35.

185   Americans seek removal of IDB chairman: Kornbluh, p. 83.

186   Catalogue of covert operations: Kornbluh, p. 88.
      Ad hoc committee: United States Senate, *The International Telephone and Telegraph Company and Chile, 1970–1971* (Washington: Government Printing Office, 1973), p. 12.
      Buses and taxis out of service: U.S. Senate, *Covert Action,* p. 33.
      We will pay if it is just: *New York Times,* July 12, 1971.

187   Anaconda lawyer's lament: Moran, Theodore H., *Multinational Corporations and the Politics of Dependence: Copper in Chile* (Princeton: Princeton University Press, 1974), p. 153.
      Merriam sends list to White House: Sobel, Lester A. (ed.), *Chile and Allende.* New York: Facts on File, 1974, p. 118.
      Allende condemns leftists: Sobel, p. 47.

188   No one can dream that we will pay: Davis, Nathaniel, *The Last Two Years of Salvador Allende* (Ithaca, N.Y.: Cornell University Press, 1985), p. 288.
      How could it be so?: Kornbluh, p. 97.
      Senate subcommittee report: U.S. Senate, *ITT and Chile,* p. 18.

190   Helms considers conviction a badge of honor: *New York Times,* Sept. 7, 1991.

190   Induce as much of the military as possible: Kornbluh, p. 106.

CIA seeks accelerated efforts: Kornbluh, pp. 108–9.

Prats suppresses uprising: Boorstein, p. 231; Sobel, p. 131; Rojas Sandford, Robinson, *The Murder of Allende and the End of the Chilean Way to Socialism* (New York: Harper & Row, 1975), pp. 162–63.

191   CIA knew Pinochet as friend: Kornbluh, pp. 136–37.

40 Committee approves another $1 million: Kornbluh, pp. 144, 152.

CIA and Senate estimates of anti-Allende spending: Central Intelligence Agency, CIA Activities in Chile (Washington: Central Intelligence Agency, 2000), at www.derechos.org/nizkor/chile/doc/hinchey.html; U.S. Senate, *Covert Action*, p. 42.

Final act begins to unfold: Birns, Laurence (ed.), *The End of Chilean Democracy: An IDOC Dossier on the Coup and Its Aftermath* (New York: Seabury, 1973), p. 194; Kornbluh, p. 111.

CIA supports trucker strike: *New York Times,* Sept. 20, 1974; U.S. Senate, *Covert Action*, pp. 2, 31.

192   Devine reports coup will happen: Kornbluh, p. 112.

Davis on how decision was made: Davis, p. 222.

Events of September 11, 1973: Birns, pp. 35–41; Davis, pp. 231–306; Dorfman, Ariel, *Exorcising Terror: The Incredible Unending Trial of General Augusto Pinochet* (New York: Seven Stories, 2002), pp. 35–41; Sigmund, pp. 3–8, 242–47; Verdugo, Patricia, *Interferencia secreta: 11 Septiembre de 1973* (Santiago: Editorial Sudamericana, 1998), pp. 47–196; Vergara, José Manuel, and Florencio Varas, *Coup: Allende's Last Day* (New York: Stein & Day, 1975), pp. 38–90; Rojas Sandford, pp. 1–5, 37–47, 190–219.

194   Allende's last words to his people: Birns, pp. 31–32.

Mission accomplished: Vergara and Varas, p. 95.

9: A GRAVEYARD SMELL

195   Phillips told to understand what the president ordered: Phillips, David A., *The Night Watch: Twenty-five Years of Peculiar Service* (New York: Atheneum, 1977), pp. 222–23.

196   Goldwater on pointing the finger: Jeffreys-Jones, Rhodri, *The CIA and American Democracy* (New Haven: Yale University, 1989), p. 248.

Peurifoy on Kremlin: Eisenhower, Dwight D., *Mandate for Change: The White House Years, 1953–1956* (Garden City, N.Y.: Doubleday, 1963), p. 424.

197   Korry cable as Allende takes power: *New York Times,* Sept. 13, 1998.

198   Nothing important can come from the south: Hersh, Seymour, *The Price of Power: Kissinger in the Nixon White House* (New York: Summit, 1983), p. 263. Doolittle report: www.foia.cia.gov/browse_docs_full.asp?doc_no=0000627859.

200   Douglas on basic reforms: Bill, James A., *The Eagle and the Lion: The Tragedy of American-Iranian Relations* (New Haven: Yale University Press, 1988), p. 94.

201   Dulles commissions his old law firm: Lisagor, Nancy, and Frank Lipsius, *A Law unto Itself: The Untold Story of the Law Firm Sullivan & Cromwell* (New York: William Morrow, 1988), p. 210.

201   Operation Ajax locked the United States in: Bill, p. 94.
     CIA predicts no radical changes: Sick, Gary, *All Fall Down: America's Tragic Encounter with Iran* (New York: Penguin, 1986), p. 92.

202   Carter toasts shah: *Washington Post*, Nov. 18, 1977.
     Militant explains hostage taking: Zahrani, Mostafa T., "The Coup That Changed the Middle East: Mossadegh v. the CIA in Retrospect," *World Policy Journal*, Summer 2002.

203   Iran would be a mature democracy: Zahrani.

204   Reforms could not be translated into Cold War vocabulary: Immerman, Richard, *The CIA in Guatemala: The Foreign Policy of Intervention* (Austin: University of Texas Press, 1982), p. 186.

205   Assessment of CIA's independent historian: Cullather, Nick, *Secret History: The CIA's Classified Account of Its Operations in Guatemala, 1952–1954* (Stanford, Calif.: Stanford University Press, 1999), pp. 8–9.

206   Guevara influenced by events in Guatemala: Immerman, pp. 186–96; *La Hora Cultural* (Guatemala City), June 26, 2004.

207   Clinton says support for repression was wrong: *Washington Post*, March 11, 1999.
     Taylor, Landsdale, and Colby regret coup: Jones, Howard, *Death of a Generation: How the Assassins of Diem and JFK Prolonged the Vietnam War* (Oxford: Oxford University Press, 2003), p. 428.

208   Nobody was behind it: Hammer, Ellen J., *A Death in November: America in Vietnam, 1963* (New York: E. P. Dutton, 1987), p. 185.
     We had a hand in killing him: Hammer, p. 309.
     America's responsibility haunted U.S. leaders: Karnow, Stanley, *Vietnam: A History* (New York: Viking, 1983), p. 278.

209   Kennedy's central tragedy: Jones, p. 456.
     Shaplen blamed the Americans: Maitland, Terrence, and Stephen Weiss, *The Vietnam Experience: Raising the Stakes* (Boston: Boston Publishing, 1982), p. 89.
     Most bizarre performance by Dulles: Drummond, Roscoe, and Gaston Coblentz, *Duel at the Brink: John Foster Dulles' Command of American Power* (Garden City, N.Y.: Doubleday, 1960), p. 120.

210   Sihanouk on Americans: *New York Times*, Sept. 9, 1964.

211   Kissinger tells Pinochet he is victim of left-wing groups: Rogers, William D., and Maxwell, Kenneth, "Fleeing the Chilean Coup: The Debate over U.S. Complicity," *Foreign Affairs*, Jan.–Feb. 2004.

213   Extreme fears were ill-founded: U.S. Senate, *Covert Actions*, p. 28.

214   Chileans might have found good sense: Maxwell, Kenneth, "The Other 9/11: The United States and Chile, 1973," *Foreign Affairs*, Nov.–Dec. 2003.
     Not a part we are proud of: *Washington Post*, Feb. 21, 2003.

215   *Two kinds of people:* Dulles Oral History Project, Princeton University, interview with former French foreign minister Christian Pineau; cited in Morgan, Roger, *The United States and West Germany, 1945–1973: A Study in Alliance Politics* (London: Oxford University Press, 1974), p. 54.

216   Our fall from grace: Davis, Nathaniel, *The Last Two Years of Salvador Allende* (Ithaca, N.Y.: Cornell University Press, 1985), p. xi.

10: OUR DAYS OF WEAKNESS ARE OVER

219   There are not going to be any landings: O'Shaughnessy, Hugh, *Grenada: Revolution, Invasion and Aftermath* (London: Sphere, 1984), p. 158.

221   I want to play another round: O'Shaughnessy, p. 162.

222   Do all that needs to be done: Adkin, Mark, *Urgent Fury: The Battle for Grenada* (Lexington, Mass.: Lexington, 1989), p. 120.
Reagan looks like a man under siege: *New York Times*, Oct. 24, 1983.

223   If this was right yesterday: Adkin, p. 121.
Gairy regime: Payne, Anthony, et al., *Grenada: Revolution and Invasion* (New York: St. Martin's Press, 1984), pp. 5–9; Schoenhals, Kai P., and Richard A. Melanson, *Revolution and Intervention in Grenada: The New Jewel Movement, the United States, and the Caribbean* (Boulder: Westview, 1985), pp. 13–32.

224   Gairy's interest in strange phenomena: Searle, Chris, *Grenada: The Struggle Against Destabilization* (London: Writers and Readers, 1983), p. 11.
Irresponsible malcontents: Searle, p. 15.

225   Radio Grenada announces coup: O'Shaughnessy, p. 77.
Only sixty rebels: Deskin, Martin (ed.), *Trouble in Our Backyard* (New York: Pantheon, 1983), p. 13.
Bishop promises democracy: O'Shaughnessy, p. 79; Scoon, Paul, *Survival for Service: My Experiences as Governor of Grenada* (London: Macmillan Caribbean, 2003), p. 36.
Gairy had few friends left: Scoon, pp. 39–40.
Just consider how laws are made: Seabury, Paul, and Walter A. McDougall (eds.), *The Grenada Papers: The Inside Story of the Grenadian Revolution and the Making of a Totalitarian State—as Told in Captured Documents* (San Francisco: Institute for Contemporary Studies, 1984), p. 71.

226   Think of history of U.S. imperialism: Searle, p. 33.

227   Vicious beasts of imperialism: Kinzer, Stephen, "Report from Grenada: Little Country, Big Revolution," *The Nation*, Feb. 7, 1981.
Last cowboy: Searle, pp. 97–98.
Split in New Jewel: Adkin, pp. 13–29; Payne, pp. 105–31; Seabury, pp. 281–321; Schoenhals and Melanson, pp. 60–77.

230   Shooting of Bishop and others: Adkin, pp. 59–81; O'Shaughnessy, pp. 114–41; Payne, pp. 135–44; Schoenhals and Melanson, pp. 77–81.

231   No maps or aerial photos: Spector, Ronald H., *U.S. Marines in Grenada, 1983* (Washington: History and Museums Division, Marine Corps, 1987), p. 2.
CIA unprepared: Adkin, pp. 118–19, 129–30.
Marines board in North Carolina: Spector, p. 1.
Erie receives message: Spector, p. 2.

232   Reagan signs smooth copy: Adkin, p. 106.
Vessey briefs Reagan: Adkin, p. 126.

233   Austin and others guarantee students' safety: *New York Times*, Oct. 28, 1983.
A fleeting opportunity presented itself: Adkin, pp. 106–9, 115.

234   Walking Track Shoes: Spector, p. 6.
Invasion: Adkin, pp. 167–312; Harding, Stephen, *Air War Grenada* (Missoula, Mont.: Pictorial Histories, 1984), pp. 21–48; *Newsweek*, Nov. 7, 1983; Payne, pp. 148–61; Russell, Lee E., *Grenada 1983* (London: Osprey, 1985),

pp. 9-35; Spector, pp. 6–25; Schwarzkopf, Norman, *It Doesn't Take a Hero: The Autobiography of General Norman Schwarzkopf* (New York: Bantam, 1992), pp. 244–58; *Time*, Nov. 7, 1983.

236   Reagan and Shultz explain invasion: *New York Times*, Oct. 25, 1983.

237   Scoon signs backdated letter: Adkin, pp. 99, 256, 365; Scoon, p. 145.
Things were coming unstuck: *Time*, Nov. 7, 1983.
We are more steady and reliable: *New York Times*, Oct. 29, 1983.

238   Reagan gives emotional speech: *New York Times*, Dec. 13, 1983.

11: YOU'RE NO GOOD

240   Noriega performance in American courses: Dinges, John, *Our Man in Panama: How General Noriega Used the U.S.—and Made Millions in Drugs and Arms* (New York: Random House, 1990), pp. 38–89.

241   Spadafora accuses Noriega, Kempe comments: Kempe, Fred, *Divorcing the Dictator: America's Tangled Affair with Noriega* (New York: G. P. Putnam's Sons, 1990), p. 128.

242   Rivalry intensifies: Buckley, Tom, *Panama: The Whole Story* (New York: Simon and Schuster, 1991), p. 26; Dinges, pp. 182–83; Kempe, pp. 129–30.

243   Killing of Spadafora: Buckley, pp. 26–29; Dinges, pp. 217–39; Kempe, pp. 132–50; Weeks, John, and Phil Gunson, *Panama: Made in the USA* (London: Latin America Bureau, 1991), pp. 59–60.
1964 riots: Martínez Ortega, Aristides, "Panama Explodes: The 1964 Flag Riots," in Wheaton, Philip E., *Panama Invaded: Imperial Occupation Versus Struggle for Sovereignty* (Trenton, N.J.: Red Sea, 1992), pp. 68–76.

244   We have the rabid dog: Dinges, p. 239.

245   The day will come when you are sorry: Kempe, p. 143.
Noriega stipend reaches $110,000: *Newsweek*, Jan. 15, 1990.
Noriega allows use of bases to aid contras: *Newsweek*, Jan. 15, 1990.

246   He let Noriega off the hook: Dinges, p. 233.
Noriega involved in drug traffic: Dinges, pp. 14–16, 133–34, 149–50, 184–85; Kempe; pp. 75–80; Weeks and Gunson, pp. 50–55.

247   Panamanians have promised to help with the contras: Dinges, p. 237.
You are destroying our policy: Dinges, p. 253.
Panamanians interested in occult: *New York Times*, June 18, 1987.

248   Díaz Herrera: Buckley, pp. 68–75; Dinges, pp. 261–63; Kempe, pp. 207–11.

249   I am a criminal: Buckley, p. 84.
White House offers to drop indictments: Gilboa, Eytan, "The Panama Invasion Revisited: Lessons for the Use of Force in the Post–Cold War Era," *Political Science Quarterly*, vol. 110, no. 4, p. 539.

250   Why Noriega can't retire: Buckley, p. 97.
Carter blocked Noriega indictment: Gilboa.
Injuries inflicted by Panamanian soldiers: Buckley, p. 161.

251   We're going to go: Buckley, p. 193.

252   Reduce the PDF to nothing: *Panama Deception*, Rhino Video, 1993.
Giroldi coup: Buckley, pp. 197–220; Dinges, 369–94; Weeks and Gunson, pp. 86–88.
Some wanted to shoot him on the spot: Buckley, p. 202.

253   Giroldi's widow blames U.S.: Dinges, p. 393.
      Summers and McCurdy reactions: *Washington Post,* Oct. 7, 1989.
254   This guy is not going to lay off: Buckley, p. 231; Dinges, p. 99.
255   Blue Spoon becomes Just Cause: Dinges, p. 101.
      Indications point to major military action: Murillo. L. E., *The Noriega Mess: The Drugs, the Canal, and Why America Invaded* (Berkeley: Video Books, 1995), p. 27.
256   Invasion: Briggs, Clarence E., *Operation Just Cause: Panama, December 1989: A Soldier's Eyewitness Account* (Harrisburg, Pa.: Stackpole, 1990), pp. 48–137; Donnelly, Thomas, et al., *Operation Just Cause: The Storming of Panama* (New York: Lexington, 1991), pp. 135–379; McConnell, Malcolm, *Just Cause: The Real Story of America's High-Tech Invasion of Panama* (New York: St. Martin's Press, 1991), pp. 23–300; Taw, Jennifer Morrison, *Operation Just Cause: Lessons for Operations Other Than War* (Santa Monica: Rand, 1996), pp. 3–29.
      Endara takes oath of office: Buckley, p. 234; McConnell, p. 100; *Time,* Jan. 1, 1990; Weeks and Gunson, p. 13.
257   Noriega enters Vatican embassy and surrenders: Buckley, pp. 243–54; Dinges, pp. 364–65; Kempe, pp. 398–417; *Newsweek,* Jan. 8 and 15, 1990; *Time,* Jan. 8 and 15, 1990.

12: THEY WILL HAVE FLIES WALKING ACROSS THEIR EYEBALLS

261   We want friendship with you: British Broadcasting Corporation, *Afghan Warrior: The Life and Death of Abdul Haq.*
262   Commander has entered Afghanistan: *Wall Street Journal,* Oct. 24, 2001.
263   Haq is trapped: Author's interviews with Joseph Ritchie (June 13, 2005) and Robert McFarlane (July 1, 2005).
264   Under no circumstances can we lose: Coll, Steve, *Ghost Wars: The Secret History of the CIA, Afghanistan, and bin Laden, from the Soviet Invasion to September 10, 2001* (New York: Penguin, 2004), p. 40.
265   We had just come off this tragedy: BBC.
266   CIA knew what its role was: BBC.
267   Essential that resistance continues: Coll, p. 51.
      Hekmatyar ruthless and anti-American: BBC; Ewans, Martin, *Afghanistan: A Short History of Its People and Politics* (New York: HarperCollins, 2002), p. 213.
268   This was the essential proposition: BBC.
269   Hundreds of millions to guerrillas: Coll, p. 151.
      Financing your own assassins: Coll, p. 182.
270   No less than twenty-eight countries: BBC.
      War had become a bleeding wound: Ewans, p. 233.
271   Bearden cable: Coll, p. 185.
      Najibullah warns of terrorism: Coll, p. 234.
      Haq foresees terrorists and poppy field: BBC.
272   Long-term future of Nangarhar: Coll, p. 173.
273   U.S. maintains good relations with Taliban: Ewans, p. 256.
274   State Department takes up Unocal agenda: Coll, p. 330.

275   We're going to find out who did this: Woodward, Bob, *Bush at War* (New York: Simon and Schuster, 2002), p. 18.

       Wanted dead or alive: Woodward, p. 97.

       We'll rout 'em out: Woodward, p. 52.

276   I thought you said some band: *New York Times,* June 16, 2000.

       Bush sent a message to the group: Woodward, p. 85.

277   I want his head in a box: Woodward, p. 141.

278   U.S. locked in momentous struggle: Woodward, pp. 35, 45, 131.

       Why enemies hate us: Tanner, Stephen, *The Wars of the Bushes: A Father and Son as Military Leaders* (Philadelphia: Casemate, 2004), p. 164.

       Armitage on what I'm hearing: Woodward, p. 244.

279   Haq's last moments: BBC; *New York Times,* Oct. 26–28, 2001; *Wall Street Journal,* Oct. 24, 2001; *Washington Post,* Oct. 29, 2001.

       News commentators were grumbling: Woodward, p. 279.

       Rule out going after Afghans: Woodward, p. 275.

13: THUNDER RUN

281   If the condition's right: Perkins interview on *Frontline,* http://www.pbs.org/wgbh/pages/frontline/shows/invasion/interviews/perkins.html.

282   We have set the conditions: Zucchino, David, *Thunder Run: The Armored Strike to Capture Baghdad* (New York: Atlantic Monthly Press, 2004), p. 80.

283   Going straight into Baghdad: Zucchino, p. 87.

       Heart of Saddam's regime: Zucchino, p. 90.

284   Once Baghdad fell: Zucchino, p. 82.

285   Franks visit: *New York Times,* Oct. 19, 2004.

       Sanctions are fine: Suskind, Ron, *The Price of Loyalty: George W. Bush, the White House, and the Education of Paul O'Neill* (New York: Simon and Schuster, 2004), p. 85.

286   Never any rigorous talk: Suskind, p. 86.

       Wolfowitz disagrees with Clarke: Clarke, Richard A., *Against All Enemies: Inside America's War on Terror* (New York: Free Press, 2004), pp. 231–32.

287   Ambassador meets with Saddam: *New York Times,* Nov. 23, 1990.

289   Horrible poisons and diseases: *Washington Post,* Oct. 8, 2002.

       Worst thing that could happen: Woodward, Bob, *Plan of Attack* (New York: Simon and Schuster, 2004), p. 120.

290   Scowcroft warns against attack: *Wall Street Journal,* Aug. 25, 2002.

291   Nothing to do with oil: Purdum, Todd, *A Time of Our Choosing: America's War in Iraq* (New York: Times Books, 2003), p. 245.

       $41 billion in contacts: Hartung, William D., *How Much Money Are You Making on the War, Daddy?: A Quick and Dirty Guide to War Profiteering in the Bush Administration* (New York: Nation Books, 2003), p. 120.

292   Wolfowitz on protecting Saudi royal family: *Newsday,* Aug. 28, 2003; *Vanity Fair,* July 2003.

293   I will go to my grave: Lemann, Nicholas, "Remember the Alamo: How George Bush Reinvented Himself," *The New Yorker,* Oct. 18, 2004.

294   Cheney opposes return of inspectors: Woodward, *Plan,* pp. 165, 195.

294   Franks hasn't found any yet: Woodward, *Plan*, p. 173.
        Bush passes over this warning: Suskind, p. 73.
        War on terror is going okay: Woodward, *Plan*, p. 186.
295   Bush calls himself a gut player: Prados, John, *Hoodwinked: The Documents That Reveal How Bush Sold Us a War* (New York: New Press, 2004), p. 12.
        Instinct told him Iraq has weapons: Woodward, *Plan*, p. 195.
        I doubt anyone had the chance: Clarke, p. 244.
        A country devoid of weapons: Keegan, John, *The Iraq War* (New York: Knopf, 2004), p. 112.
        The declaration is empty: Woodward, *Plan*, p. 240.
296   It's a slam-dunk case: Woodward, *Plan*, p. 249.
        Chirac sees alternative ways: Woodward, *Plan*, p. 313.
297   Bush approves plan to attack Saddam's farm: Woodward, *Plan*, p. 384.
        Use a sword: Purdum, p. 111.
298   Touch me: Purdum, p. 210.

14: CATASTROPHIC SUCCESS

301   To make the world more peaceful: Prados, John, *Hoodwinked: The Documents That Reveal How Bush Sold Us a War* (New York: New Press, 2004), p. 32.
303   Open letter to ex-detainees: www.pipeline.com/~rgibson/grenada.
304   Cost of Spectre: http://www.af.mil/factsheets/factsheet.asp?fsID=71.
        Looting and fires in Panama City: Panama Deception, Wheaton, Philip E. (ed.), *Panama Invaded: Imperial Occupation Versus Struggle for Sovereignty* (Trenton, N.J.: Red Sea, 1992), pp. 13–34.
306   Looters shout *Viva Bush!: Time*, Jan. 1, 1990.
        American tally of death toll in Panama: Dinges, John, *Our Man in Panama: How General Noriega Used the U.S.—and Made Millions in Drugs and Arms* (New York: Random House, 1990), pp. 287, 298.
307   Some want day of mourning; Endara calls day of reflection: Buckley, Tom, *Panama: The Whole Story* (New York: Simon and Schuster, 1991), pp. 258, 263.
308   Ounce of prevention: Goodson, Larry, "Afghanistan's Long Road to Reconstruction," *Journal of Democracy*, vol. 14, no. 1 (2003).
        It was clear as early as 2001: Goodson.
310   Eighty-seven percent of world poppy production: Goodson.
311   122 Americans killed: Keegan, John, *The Iraq War* (New York: Knopf, 2004), p. 204.
312   Had we to do it over again: *Time*, Sept. 6, 2004.
313   People we supported are in power: Galbraith, Peter, "Bush's Islamic Republic," *New York Review of Books*, Aug. 11, 2005.
314   Future of Iraq project: Phillips, David L., *Losing Iraq: Inside the Postwar Reconstruction Fiasco* (Boulder: Westview, 2005), pp. 35–40.
        There was never a buildup of intelligence: *New York Times*, Oct. 20, 2004.
315   Ferguson on parallels to 1920: London *Sunday Telegraph*, Oct. 4, 2004.
        A peculiar, chosen people: Melville, Herman, *White-Jacket* (Oxford: Oxford University, 2000), p. 151.

315   Right and true for every person: *New York Times,* Sept. 20, 2002.
        Washington on self-interest: Monten, Jonathan, "The Roots of the Bush
        Doctrine: Power, Nationalism, and Democracy Promotion in U.S. Strategy,"
        International Security, Spring 2005.
316   Self-evident truths are true for all: Federal News Service, May 21, 2003.
318   At this moment in history: Jervis, Robert, "Understanding the Bush Doc-
        trine," *Political Science Quarterly,* Autumn 2003.
319   I dread being too much dreaded: Morgenthau, Hans, *Politics Among Nations*
        (New York: Knopf, 1979), pp. 169–70.

BIBLIOGRAPHY

Acker, Alison. *Honduras: The Making of a Banana Republic*. Boston: South End Press, 1988.

Adams, Brooks. *The Law of Civilization and Decay: An Essay on History*. New York: Macmillan, 1896.

Adams, Richard. *Crucifixion by Power: Essays on Guatemalan National Social Structure, 1944–1966*. Austin: University of Texas Press, 1970.

Adkin, Mark. *Urgent Fury: The Battle for Grenada*. Lexington, Mass.: Lexington, 1989.

Aguilera, Pilar, and Ricardo Fredes (eds.). *Chile: The Other September 11*. Melbourne: Ocean, 2003.

Aitken, Thomas, Jr. *Poet in the Fortress: The Story of Luis Muñoz Marín*. New York: New American Library, 1964.

Aker, Frank, and Morgan Norval. *Breaking the Stranglehold: The Liberation of Grenada*. Falls Church, Va.: Gun Owners Foundation, 1984.

Alger, Russell. A. *The Spanish-American War*. New York: Harper & Brothers, 1901.

Allen, Helena G. *The Betrayal of Liliuokalani: Last Queen of Hawaii, 1838–1917*. Honolulu: Mutual, 1982.

———. *Sanford Ballard Dole: Hawaii's Only President, 1844–1926*. Glendale, Calif.: Arthur H. Clark, 1988.

Ambrose, Stephen E. *Ike's Spies: Eisenhower and the Espionage Establishment*. Garden City, N.Y.: Doubleday, 1981.

Ambursley, Fitzroy, and James Dunkerly. *Grenada: Whose Freedom?* London: Latin America Bureau, 1984.

Anderson, Thomas P. *Politics in Central America: Guatemala, El Salvador, Honduras and Nicaragua*. New York: Praeger, 1982.

Auchincloss, Louis. *Theodore Roosevelt*. New York: Times Books, 2001.

Aybar de Soto, José. *Dependency and Intervention: The Case of Guatemala in 1954*. Boulder: Westview, 1978.

Bacevich, Andrew J. *American Empire: The Realities and Consequences of U.S. Diplomacy*. Cambridge, Mass.: Harvard University Press, 2002.

Bachrach, Deborah. *The Spanish-American War*. San Diego, Calif.: Lucent, 1991.

Barahona, Amaru. *Estudio Sobre la Historia de Nicaragua: Del Auge Cafetalero al Triunfo de la Revolución*. Managua: Inies, 1989.

Barreto, Amilcar Antonio. *Vieques, the Navy, and Puerto Rican Politics.* Gainesville: University Press of Florida, 2002.

Beaglehole, J. C. (ed.). *The Journals of Captain James Cook on His Voyages of Discovery.* Vol. 3, part 1: *The Voyage of the Resolution and Discovery, 1776–1780.* Cambridge: Cambridge University Press, 1967.

Beal, John Robinson. *John Foster Dulles: A Biography.* New York: Harper & Brothers, 1957.

Beale, Howard K. *Theodore Roosevelt and the Rise of America to World Power.* New York: Collier, 1956.

Beals, Carleton. *Banana Gold.* New York: Arno, 1970.

Beard, Charles A. *The Idea of National Interest.* Chicago: Quadrangle, 1934.

Beisner, Robert L. *Twelve Against Empire: The Anti-Imperialists, 1898–1900.* New York: McGraw-Hill, 1968.

Bemis, Samuel Flagg. *The Latin American Policy of the United States.* New York: Harcourt, Brace, 1943.

Benjamin, Jules R. *The United States and the Origins of the Cuban Revolution: An Empire of Liberty in an Age of National Liberation.* Princeton: Princeton University Press, 1990.

Berding, Andrew H. *Dulles on Diplomacy.* Princeton: D. Van Nostrand, 1965.

Berman, Karl. *Under the Big Stick: Nicaragua and the United States Since 1848.* Boston: South End Press, 1986.

Bernays, Edward. *Biography of an Idea: Memoirs of a Public Relations Counsel.* New York: Simon & Schuster, 1965.

Bill, James A. *The Eagle and the Lion: The Tragedy of American-Iranian Relations.* New Haven: Yale University Press, 1988.

————, and William Roger Louis (eds.). *Mussadiq, Iranian Nationalism, and Oil.* London: I. B. Tauris, 1988.

Birns, Laurence (ed.). *The End of Chilean Democracy: An IDOC Dossier on the Coup and Its Aftermath.* New York: Seabury, 1973.

Bisignani, J. D. *Hawaii Handbook.* Emeryville, Calif.: Moon Publications, 1999.

Blachman, Morris J., et al. *Confronting Revolution: Security Through Diplomacy in Central America.* New York: Pantheon, 1986.

Black, George. *The Good Neighbor: How the United States Wrote the History of Central America and the Caribbean.* New York: Pantheon, 1988.

Blair, John M. *The Control of Oil.* New York: Pantheon, 1976.

Blount, James H. *The American Occupation of the Philippines, 1898–1912.* New York: G. P. Putnam's Sons, 1912.

————. *Report of U.S. Special Commissioner James H. Blount to U.S. Secretary of State Walter Q. Gresham Concerning the Hawaiian Kingdom Investigation.* http://libweb.hawaii.edu/digicoll/annexation/blount.

Bohlen, Charles. *Witness to History, 1929–1969.* New York: Norton, 1973.

Bolger, Daniel P. *Americans at War 1975–1986: An Era of Violent Peace.* Novato, Calif.: Presidio, 1988.

Bonner, Raymond. *Waltzing with a Dictator: The Marcoses and the Making of American Policy.* New York: Times Books, 1987.

Boorstein, Edward. *Allende's Chile: An Insider's View.* New York: International Publishers, 1977.

Boot, Max. *The Savage Wars of Peace: Small Wars and the Rise of American Power.* New York: Basic Books, 2002.

Bouscaren, Anthony Trawick. *The Last of the Mandarins: Diem of Vietnam.* Pittsburgh: Duquesne University Press, 1965.

Bowers, Claude G. *Beveridge and the Progressive Era.* Boston: Houghton Mifflin, 1932.

Bradford, James C. (ed.). *Crucible of Empire: The Spanish-American War and Its Aftermath.* Annapolis: Naval Institute Press, 1993.

Brands, H. W. *Bound to Empire: The United States and the Philippines.* New York: Oxford University Press, 1992.

——. *The Reckless Decade: America in the 1890s.* New York: St. Martin's Press, 1995.

——. *T. R.: The Last Romantic.* New York: Basic Books, 1997.

——. *What America Owes the World: The Struggle for the Soul of Foreign Policy.* Cambridge: Cambridge University Press, 1998.

Brau, M. M. *Island in the Crossroads: The History of Puerto Rico.* Garden City, N.J.: Zenith, 1968.

Briggs, Clarence E. III. *Operation Just Cause: Panama, December 1989. A Soldier's Eyewitness Account.* Harrisburg, Pa.: Stackpole, 1990.

Briody, Dan. *The Halliburton Agenda: The Politics of Oil and Money.* Hoboken, N.J.: Wiley, 2004.

——. *The Iron Triangle: Inside the Secret World of the Carlyle Group.* Hoboken, N.J.: Wiley, 2003.

Brizan, George. *Grenada: Island of Conflict.* London: Zed Books, 1984.

Brown, Charles Henry. *The Correspondents' War: Journalists in the Spanish-American War.* New York: Scribner, 1967.

Browne, Malcolm. *Muddy Boots and Red Socks: A Reporter's Life.* New York: Times Books, 1993.

Buckley, Tom. *Panama: The Whole Story.* New York: Simon and Schuster, 1991.

——. *Violent Neighbors.* New York: Times Books, 1984.

Bushnell, O. A. *The Gifts of Civilization: Germs and Genocide in Hawaii.* Honolulu: University of Hawaii Press, 1993.

Butler, Smedley D. *War Is a Racket.* Los Angeles: Feral House, 2003.

Cabán, Pedro A. *Constructing a Colonial People: Puerto Rico and the United States, 1898–1932.* Boulder: Westview, 1999.

Campbell, Ian C. *A History of the Pacific Islands.* Berkeley: University of California Press, 1989.

Carr, Raymond. *Puerto Rico: A Colonial Experiment.* New York: New York University Press, 1984.

Carrión, Arturo Morales. *Puerto Rico: A Political and Cultural History.* New York: W. W. Norton, 1983.

Central Intelligence Agency. *CIA Activities in Chile.* Washington: Central Intelligence Agency, 2000. www.derechos.org/nizkor/chile/doc/hinchey.html.

Chace, James. *Endless War: How We Got Involved in Central America—and What Can Be Done.* New York: Vintage, 1984.

Chidley, Donald Barr. *La Guerra Hispano Americana, 1896–1898.* Barcelona: Ediciones Grijalbo, 1973.

Childs, Marquis. *Eisenhower, Captive Hero: A Critical Study of the General and the President.* New York: Harcourt Brace Jovanovich, 1958.

Clark, Sebastian. *Grenada: A Workers' and Farmers' Government with Revolutionary Proletarian Leadership.* New York: Pathfinder, 1980.

Clarke, Richard A. *Against All Enemies: Inside America's War on Terror.* New York: Free Press, 2004.

Clarridge, Duane, with Digby Diehl. *A Spy for All Seasons: My Life in the CIA.* New York: Scribner, 1997.

Cline, Ray S. *Secrets, Spies and Scholars: Blueprint of the Essential CIA.* Washington: Acropolis, 1976.

Coletta, Paulo E. (ed.). *Threshold to American Internationalism: Essays on the Foreign Policy of William McKinley.* New York: Exposition, 1970.

Coll, Steve. *Ghost Wars: The Secret History of the CIA, Afghanistan, and bin Laden, From the Soviet Invasion to September 10, 2001.* New York: Penguin, 2004.

Collier, Peter, and David Horowitz. *The Kennedys.* New York: Summit, 1984.

Comfort, Mildred H. *John Foster Dulles, Peacemaker.* Minneapolis: T. S. Dennison, 1960.

Conniff, M. L. *Panama and the United States: The Forced Alliance.* Athens: University of Georgia Press, 1991.

Cook, Blanche Wiesen. *The Declassified Eisenhower: A Divided Legacy of Peace and Political Warfare.* New York: Penguin, 1981.

Cosmas, Graham. *An Army for Empire: The United States Army in the Spanish-American War.* Columbia: University of Missouri Press, 1971.

Cottam, Richard W. *Nationalism in Iran.* Pittsburgh: University of Pittsburgh Press, 1979.

Cox, Isaac Joslin. *Nicaragua and the United States, 1909–1927.* Boston: World Peace Foundation, 1927.

Cramer, Floyd. *Our Neighbor Nicaragua.* New York: Frederick A. Stokes, 1929.

Crapol, Edward P. *James G. Blaine: Architect of Empire.* Wilmington, Del.: Scholarly Resources, 2000.

Crile, George. *Charlie Wilson's War: The Extraordinary Story of the Largest Covert Operation in History.* New York: Atlantic Monthly Press, 2003.

Crowther, Samuel. *The Romance and Rise of the American Tropics.* New York: Doubleday, Doran, 1927.

Cullather, Nick. *Secret History: The CIA's Classified Account of Its Operations in Guatemala, 1952–1954.* Stanford, Calif.: Stanford University Press, 1999.

Cushman, Mike (ed.). *Subversion in Chile: A Case Study in U.S. Corporate Intrigue in the Third World.* Nottingham: Spokesman, 1972.

Damon, Ethel M. *Sanford Ballard Dole and His Hawaii.* Palo Alto, Calif.: Pacific Books, 1957.

Danner, Mark. *Torture and Truth: America, Abu Ghraib, and the War on Terror.* New York: New York Review Press, 2004.

Davis, Nathaniel. *The Last Two Years of Salvador Allende.* Ithaca, N.Y.: Cornell University Press, 1985.

Davis, Richard Harding. *Notes of a War Correspondent.* New York: Charles Scribner's Sons, 1910.

Daws, Gavan. *Shoal of Time: A History of the Hawaiian Islands.* Honolulu: University Press of Hawaii, 1968.

Dell'Orto, Giovanna. "We Are All Americans." Doctoral dissertation, University of Minnesota, 2004.

Dementyev, Igor Petrovich. *USA, Imperialists and Anti-Imperialists: The Great Foreign Policy Debate at the Turn of the Century.* Moscow: Progress Publishers, 1979.

Denny, Harold Norman. *Dollars for Bullets: The Story of American Rule in Nicaragua.* New York: Dial Press, 1929.

Department of State. *A Brief History of the Relations Between the United States and Nicaragua, 1909–1928.* Washington: Government Printing Office, 1928.

———. *Foreign Relations of the United States, 1952–54.* Vol. 4: *The American Republics.* Washington: Government Printing Office, 1984.

———. *Foreign Relations of the United States, 1952–1954.* Vol. 10: *Iran, 1952–1954.* Washington: Government Printing Office, 1989.

———. *Foreign Relations of the United States, 1961–1963.* Vol. 4: *Vietnam, August–December 1963.* Washington: Government Printing Office, 1991.

———. *Intervention of International Communism in the Americas.* Publication 5556. Washington: Government Printing Office, 1954.

Deskin, Martin (ed.). *Trouble in Our Backyard.* New York: Pantheon, 1983.

De Vylder, Stefan. *Allende's Chile: The Political Economy of the Rise and Fall of Unidad Popular.* Cambridge: Cambridge University Press, 1976.

Diba, Farhad. *Mohammad Mossadegh: A Political Biography.* London: Croon Helm, 1986.

Dierks, Jack Cameron. *A Leap to Arms: The Cuban Campaign of 1898.* Philadelphia: J. B. Lippincott, 1970.

Diffie, Bailey W., and Justine Whitefield Diffie. *Porto Rico: A Broken Pledge.* New York: Vanguard, 1927.

Dinges, John. *Our Man in Panama: How General Noriega Used the U.S.—and Made Millions in Drugs and Arms.* New York: Random House, 1990.

Divine, Robert. *Eisenhower and the Cold War.* New York: Oxford University Press, 1981.

Dobson, John M. *America's Ascent: The United States Becomes a Great Power, 1880–1914.* DeKalb: Northern Illinois University Press, 1978.

Dodds, Archibald John. "The Public Services of Philander Chase Knox." Doctoral dissertation, University of Pittsburgh, 1950.

Dolan, Edward F. *Panama and the United States: Their Canal, Their Stormy Years.* Danbury, Conn.: Franklin Watts, 1990.

Dole, Richard, and Elizabeth Dole Porteus. *The Story of James Dole.* Aiea, Hawaii: Island Heritage, 1990.

Dole, Sanford B. *Memoirs of the Hawaiian Revolution.* Honolulu: Advertiser Publishing, 1936.

Donnelly, Thomas, et al. *Operation Just Cause: The Storming of Panama.* New York: Lexington, 1991.

Donovan, John C. *The Cold Warriors: A Policy-Making Elite.* Lexington, Mass.: Heath, 1974.

Dorfman, Ariel. *Exorcising Terror: The Incredible Unending Trial of General Augusto Pinochet.* New York: Seven Stories, 2002.

Doril, Stephen. *MI6: Inside the World of Her Majesty's Secret Intelligence Service.* New York: Free Press, 2000.

Dougherty, Michael. *To Steal a Kingdom: Probing Hawaiian History.* Waimanalo, Hawaii: Island Style, 1992.

Doyle, Edward, et al. *The Vietnam Experience: Passing the Torch.* Boston: Boston Publishing, 1981.

Drake, Paul. *Socialism and Populism in Chile, 1932–1952.* Champaign: University of Illinois Press, 1977.

Drummond, Roscoe, and Gaston Coblentz. *Duel at the Brink: John Foster Dulles' Command of American Power.* Garden City, N.Y.: Doubleday, 1960.

Du Berrier, Hilaire. *Background to Betrayal: The Tragedy of Vietnam.* Boston: Western Islands, 1965.

Dudley, Michael Kioni, and Keoni Kealoha Agard. *A Call for Hawaiian Sovereignty.* Honolulu: Na Kane O Ka Malo Press, 1993.

Dulebohn, George Roscoe. *Principles of Foreign Policy Under the Cleveland Administration.* Philadelphia: University of Pennsylvania Press, 1941.

Dulles, Allen. *The Craft of Intelligence.* New York: Harper & Row, 1963.

Dulles, Foster Rhea. *America's Rise to World Power, 1898–1954.* New York: Harper & Row, 1954.

DuVal, Miles P., Jr. *Cádiz to Cathay: The Story of the Long Diplomatic Struggle for the Panama Canal.* New York: Glenwood Press, 1968.

Dyal, Donald H. *Historical Dictionary of the Spanish American War.* Westport, Conn.: Greenwood Press, 1996.

Eisenhower, Dwight D. *Mandate for Change: The White House Years, 1953–1956.* Garden City, N.Y.: Doubleday, 1963.

Elwell-Sutton, L. P. *Persian Oil: A Study in Power Politics.* London: Lawrence and Wishart, 1955.

Elm, Mostafa. *Oil, Power, and Principle: Iran's Oil Nationalization and Its Aftermath.* Syracuse, N.Y.: Syracuse University Press, 1992.

Engelhardt, Tom. *The End of Victory Culture: Cold War America and the Disillusioning of a Generation.* New York: Basic Books, 1995.

EPICA Task Force. *Panama: Sovereignty for a Land Divided.* Washington: EPICA, 1976.

Etchison, Don L. *The United States and Militarism in Central America.* New York: Praeger, 1975.

Eulate Sanjurjo, Carmela. *La España Heroíca y la América Magnánima.* Madrid: Editorial Naval, 1951.

Ewans, Martin. *Afghanistan: A Short History of Its People and Politics.* New York: HarperCollins, 2002.

Falcoff, Mark. *Modern Chile, 1970–1989: A Critical History.* New Brunswick. N.J.: Transaction, 1989.

Fall, Bernard (ed.). *The Two Vietnams.* New York: Praeger, 1963.

Farhang, Mansour. *U.S. Imperialism from the Spanish-American War to the Iranian Revolution.* Boston: South End Press, 1981.

Feinberg, Richard E. *The Triumph of Allende: Chile's Legal Revolution.* New York: New American Library, 1972.

Ferguson, James. *Grenada: Revolution in Reverse.* London: Latin American Bureau, 1990.

Ferrell, Robert H. *The Eisenhower Diaries.* New York: W. W. Norton, 1981.

Findling, John Ellis. "The United States and Zelaya: A Study in the Diplomacy of Expediency." Doctoral dissertation, University of Texas at Austin, 1972.

Finn, Janet L. *Tracing the Veins: Of Copper, Culture, and Community, from Butte to Chuquicamata.* Berkeley: University of California Press, 1998.

Fitzgerald, Frances. *Fire in the Lake: The Vietnamese and Americans in Vietnam.* New York: Vintage, 1972.

Foner, Philip S. *The Spanish-Cuban-American War and the Birth of American Imperialism, 1895–1902.* New York: Monthly Review Press, 1972.

Foster, Lynn V. *A Brief History of Central America.* New York: Facts on File, 2000.

Gaddis, John Lewis. *Strategies of Containment: A Critical Appraisal of Postwar American National Security Policy.* New York: Oxford University Press, 1982.

Gardner, Lloyd C. *A Different Frontier: Selected Readings in the Foundations of American Economic Expansion.* Chicago: Quadrangle, 1966.

—— (ed.). *Imperial America: American Foreign Policy Since 1898.* New York: Harcourt Brace Jovanovich, 1976.

Garraty, John A. *Henry Cabot Lodge: A Biography.* New York: Knopf, 1953.

Gasiorowski, Mark J., and Malcolm Byrne (eds.). *Mohammed Mossadeq and the 1953 Coup in Iran.* Syracuse, N.Y.: Syracuse University Press, 2004.

Gearson, Louis L. *John Foster Dulles.* New York: Cooper Square, 1967.

Gerassi, John. *The Great Fear in Latin America.* New York: Macmillan, 1963.

Gettleman, Marvin E. (ed.). *Vietnam: History, Documents, and Opinions on a Major World Crisis.* Greenwich, Conn.: Fawcett, 1965.

—— et al. (eds.). *Vietnam and America: A Documentary History.* New York: Grove Press, 1985.

Ghods, M. Reza. *Iran in the Twentieth Century: A Political History.* Boulder: Lynne Rienner, 1989.

Gibney, Frank. *The Pacific Century: America and Asia in a Changing World.* New York: Macmillan, 1992.

Girvan, Norman. *Copper in Chile: A Study in Conflict Between Corporate and National Economy.* Kingston, Jamaica: University of the West Indies, 1972.

Gleijeses, Piero. *Shattered Hope: The Guatemala Revolution and the United States, 1944–1954.* Princeton: Princeton University Press, 1991.

González Vélez, Isaura. *Mini-bibliografía Selectiva: El Tratado de París.* Mayagüez: Universidad de Puerto Rico, 1989.

Goode, James F. *The United States and Iran: In the Shadow of Mussadiq.* New York: St. Martin's Press, 1997.

Goold-Adams, Richard. *The Time of Power: A Reappraisal of John Foster Dulles.* London: Weidenfeld and Nicolson, 1962.

Gould, Louis L. *The Spanish-American War and President McKinley.* Lawrence: University Press of Kansas, 1982.

Graff, Henry F. *American Imperialism and the Philippine Insurrection: Testimony Taken from Hearings in the Philippine Islands Before the Senate Committee on the Philippines—1902.* Boston: Little, Brown, 1969.

————— (ed.). *Grover Cleveland*. New York: Times Books, 2002.

Greenberg, Karen J., and Joshua L. Dratel. *The Torture Papers: The Road to Abu Ghraib*. Cambridge: Cambridge University Press, 2005.

Grose, Peter. *Gentleman Spy: The Life of Allen Dulles*. Boston: Houghton Mifflin, 1994.

Gruber, Ruth. *Puerto Rico: Island of Promise*. New York: Hill and Wang, 1960.

Guhin, John Michael. *John Foster Dulles: A Statesman and His Times*. New York: Columbia University Press, 1972.

Halberstam, David. *The Best and the Brightest*. New York: Penguin, 1969.

Hammer, Ellen J. *A Death in November: America in Vietnam, 1963*. New York: E. P. Dutton, 1987.

Hammond, Thomas T. *Red Flag over Afghanistan: The Communist Coup, the Soviet Invasion, and the Consequences*. Boulder: Westview, 1984.

Hanson, Earl Parker. *Puerto Rico: Ally for Progress*. Toronto: Van Nostrand, 1962.

Harding, Stephen. *Air War Grenada*. Missoula, Mont.: Pictorial Histories, 1984.

Harrison, James Pinkney. *The Endless War: Vietnam's Struggle for Independence*. New York: McGraw-Hill, 1982.

Hart, Robert A. *The Great White Fleet: Our Nation's Attempt at Global Diplomacy in the Twilight of Its Innocence, 1907–1909*. Boston: Little, Brown, 1965.

Hartung, William D. *How Much Money Are You Making on the War, Daddy?: A Quick and Dirty Guide to War Profiteering in the Bush Administration*. New York: Nation Books, 2003.

Hauberg, Clifford A. *Puerto Rico and the Puerto Ricans*. New York: Twayne, 1974.

Healy, David F. *Drive to Hegemony: The United States and the Caribbean, 1898–1907*. Madison: University of Wisconsin Press, 1988.

—————. *The United States in Cuba, 1898–1902*. Madison: University of Wisconsin Press, 1963.

—————. *U.S. Expansionism: The Imperialist Urge in the 1890s*. Madison: University of Wisconsin Press, 1970.

Heilbroner, Robert, and Aaron Singer. *The Economic Transformation of America, 1600 to the Present*. Fort Worth: Harcourt Brace, 1999.

Hersh, Seymour. *Chain of Command: The Road from 9/11 to Abu Ghraib*. New York: HarperCollins, 2004.

—————. *The Dark Side of Camelot*. Boston: Little, Brown, 1997.

—————. *The Price of Power: Kissinger in the Nixon White House*. New York: Summit, 1983.

Hogan, Michael J. *The Panama Canal in American Politics: Domestic Advocacy and the Evolution of Policy*. Carbondale: University of Illinois Press, 1986.

Hoganson, Kristin L. *Fighting for American Manhood: How Gender Politics Provoked the Spanish-American and Philippine-American Wars*. New Haven: Yale University Press, 1998.

Hoopes, Townsend. *The Devil and John Foster Dulles*. New York: Atlantic Monthly Press, 1973.

Horsman, Reginald. *Race and Manifest Destiny: The Origins of American Racial Anglo-Saxonism*. Cambridge, Mass.: Harvard University Press, 1981.

Hunt, E. Howard. *Undercover: Memoirs of an American Secret Agent*. New York: Berkley, 1974.

Immerman, Richard H. *The CIA in Guatemala: The Foreign Policy of Intervention.* Austin: University of Texas Press, 1982.

Independent Commission of Inquiry on the U.S. Invasion of Panama. *The U.S. Invasion of Panama: The Truth Behind Operation "Just Cause."* Boston: South End Press, 1991.

Isaacson, Walter. *Kissinger: A Biography.* New York: Simon & Schuster, 1992.

Jacobs, W. Richard, and Ian Jacobs. *Grenada: The Route to Revolution.* Havana: Casa de las Americas, 1980.

Jeffreys-Jones, Rhodri. *The CIA and American Democracy.* New Haven: Yale University Press, 1989.

Jervis, Robert. "Understanding the Bush Doctrine." *Political Science Quarterly,* Autumn 2003.

Johnson, Chalmers. *Blowback: The Causes and Consequences of American Empire.* New York: Henry Holt, 2000.

Jonas, Susanne. *The Battle for Guatemala: Rebels, Death Squads, and U.S. Power.* Boulder: Westview, 1991.

—— and David Tobis (eds.). *Guatemala.* New York: North American Congress on Latin America, 1974.

—— et. al. (eds.). *Guatemala: Tyranny on Trial.* San Francisco: Synthesis, 1984.

Jones, Howard. *Death of a Generation: How the Assassinations of Diem and JFK Prolonged the Vietnam War.* Oxford: Oxford University Press, 2003.

Judis, John B. *The Folly of Empire: What George W. Bush Could Learn from Theodore Roosevelt and Woodrow Wilson.* New York: Lisa Drew, 2004.

Julien, Claude. *America's Empire.* New York: Pantheon, 1971.

Kane, John. "American Values or Human Rights?: U.S. Foreign Policy and the Myth of Virtuous Power." *Presidential Studies Quarterly,* Dec. 2003.

Kaplan, Amy, and Donald E. Pease (eds.). *Cultures of United States Imperialism.* Durham, N.C.: Duke University Press, 1993.

Karnes, Thomas L. *The Tropical Enterprise: The Standard Fruit and Steamship Company in Latin America.* Baton Rouge: Louisiana State University Press, 1978.

Karnow, Stanley. *In Our Image: America's Empire in the Philippines.* New York: Ballantine, 1990.

——. *Vietnam: A History.* New York: Viking, 1983.

Karp, Walter. *The Politics of War: The Story of Two Wars Which Altered Forever the Political Life of the American Republic (1890–1920).* New York: Harper & Row, 1979.

Katouzian, Homa. *Mussadiq and the Struggle for Power in Iran.* London: I. B. Tauris, 1999.

Keegan, John. *The Iraq War.* New York: Knopf, 2004.

Kempe, Fred. *Divorcing the Dictator: America's Tangled Affair with Noriega.* New York: G. P. Putnam's Sons, 1990.

Kennedy, Paul M. *The Rise and Fall of the Great Powers: Economic Change and Military Conflict from 1500 to 2000.* New York: Random House, 1987.

Kepel, Gilles. *Jihad: The Trail of Political Islam.* Cambridge, Mass.: Belknap, 2002.

Kepner, Charles David, Jr., and Jay Henry Soothill. *The Banana Empire: A Case Study of Economic Imperialism.* New York: Russell & Russell, 1935.

Kinzer, Stephen. *All the Shah's Men: An American Coup and the Roots of Middle East Terror.* New York: Wiley, 2003.

———. *Blood of Brothers: Life and War in Nicaragua.* New York: G. P. Putnam's Sons, 1991.

Kissinger, Henry. *White House Years.* Boston: Little, Brown, 1979.

———. *Years of Upheaval.* Boston: Little, Brown, 1982.

Kluckhohn, Frank L. *The Man Who Kept the Peace: A Study of John Foster Dulles.* New York: Columbia Heights, 1968.

Knight, Franklin. *The Caribbean: The Genesis of a Fragmented Nationalism.* New York: Oxford University Press, 1990.

Kohlsaat, H. H. *From McKinley to Harding: Personal Recollections of Our Presidents.* New York: Charles Scribner's Sons, 1923.

Kolko, Gabriel. *The Roots of American Foreign Policy: An Analysis of Power and Purpose.* Boston: Beacon, 1969.

Kolko, Joyce. *The Limits of Power: The World and United States Foreign Policy, 1945–1954.* New York: Harper & Row, 1972.

Konstam, Angus. *San Juan Hill 1898: America's Emergence as a World Power.* Oxford: Osprey, 1998.

Kornbluh, Peter. *The Pinochet File: A Declassified Dossier on Atrocity and Accountability.* New York: New Press, 2003.

Koster, R. M., and Guillermo Sanchez. *In the Time of the Tyrants: Panama, 1968–1990.* New York: Norton, 1990.

La Croix, Sumner. *Economic History of Hawai'i.* http://www.eh.net/encyclopedia/?article=lacroix.hawaii.history

LaFeber, Walter. *Inevitable Revolutions: The United States in Central America.* New York: W. W. Norton, 1983.

———. *The New Empire: An Interpretation of American Expansionism, 1860–1898.* Ithaca, N.Y.: Cornell University Press, 1963.

———. *The Panama Canal: The Crisis in Historical Perspective.* New York: Oxford University Press, 1989.

———. "That 'Splendid Little War' in Historical Perspective." *Texas Quarterly,* no. 11 (1968).

Landis, Fred Simon. "Psychological Warfare and Media Operations in Chile, 1970–1973." Doctoral dissertation, University of Illinois at Urbana-Champaign, 1975.

Langguth, A. J. *Our Vietnam: The War 1954–1975.* New York: Touchstone, 2000.

Langley, Lester. *Banana Wars: An Inner History of American Empire, 1900–1934.* Lexington: University Press of Kentucky, 1983.

———. *The United States and the Caribbean, 1989–1934.* Athens: University of Georgia Press, 1980.

———, and Thomas Schoonover. *The Banana Men: American Mercenaries and Entrepreneurs in Central America, 1880–1930.* Lexington: University Press of Kentucky, 1995.

Lapper, Richard. *Honduras: State for Sale.* London: Latin American Bureau, 1985.

Lapping, Brian. *End of Empire.* London: Granada, 1985.

Leech, Margaret. *In the Days of McKinley.* New York: Harper & Brothers, 1939.

Lewis, Gordon K. *Grenada: The Jewel Despoiled*. Baltimore: Johns Hopkins University Press, 1987.

Lewy, Guenter. *America in Vietnam*. New York: Oxford University Press, 1978.

Liliuokalani. *Hawaii's Story by Hawaii's Queen*. Rutland, Vt.: Charles E. Tuttle, 1964.

Linn, Brian McAllister. *Guardians of Empire: The U.S. Army and the Pacific, 1902–1940*. Chapel Hill: University of North Carolina Press, 1997.

———. *The Philippine War, 1899–1902*. Lawrence: University Press of Kansas, 2002.

Lisagor, Nancy, and Frank Lipsius. *A Law unto Itself: The Untold Story of the Law Firm Sullivan & Cromwell*. New York: William Morrow, 1988.

Livezey, W. E. *Mahan on Sea Power*. Norman: University of Oklahoma Press, 1947.

Lodge, Henry Cabot. *The War with Spain*. New York: Harper and Brothers, 1899.

Lohrbach, Kurt. *Holy War, Unholy Victory: Eyewitness to the CIA's Secret War in Afghanistan*. Washington: Regnery Gateway, 1993.

Loomis, Albertine. *Grapes of Canaan. Hawaii 1820: The True Story of Hawaii's Missionaries*. Honolulu: Hawaiian Mission Children's Society, 1966.

Louis, J. C. *Cola Wars*. New York: Dodd, Mead, 1980.

Loveman, Brian. *Chile: The Legacy of Hispanic Capitalism*. New York: Oxford University Press, 1988.

MacEoin, Gary. *No Peaceful Way: Chile's Struggle for Dignity*. New York: Sheed and Ward, 1974.

Mahan, Alfred Thayer. *The Influence of Sea Power on History 1660–1783*. Boston: Little, Brown, 1898.

Mahoney, James. *The Legacies of Liberalism: Path Dependence and Political Regimes in Central America*. Baltimore: Johns Hopkins University Press, 2001.

Maitland, Terrence, and Stephen Weiss. *The Vietnam Experience: Raising the Stakes*. Boston: Boston Publishing, 1982.

Mann, James. *Rise of the Vulcans: The History of Bush's War Cabinet*. New York: Viking, 2004.

Marchetti, Victor, and John Marks. *The CIA and the Cult of Intelligence*. New York: Knopf, 1964.

Martin, John Bartlow. *U.S. Policy in the Caribbean*. Boulder: Westview, 1978.

Matthews, Herbert, and Hiram Hilty. *Understanding Cuba*. Philadelphia: American Friends Service Committee, 1960.

Matthews, Thomas. *Puerto Rican Politics and the New Deal*. Gainesville: University of Florida Press, 1960.

May, Ernest R. *American Imperialism: A Speculative Essay*. New York: Atheneum, 1968.

———. *Imperial Democracy: The Emergence of American as a Great Power*. Chicago: Imprint, 1991.

May, Glenn A. *Battle for Batanga: A Philippine Province at War*. New Haven: Yale University Press, 1991.

McCann, Thomas. *An American Company: The Tragedy of United Fruit*. New York: Crown, 1976.

McConnell, Malcolm. *Just Cause: The Real Story of America's High-Tech Invasion of Panama*. New York: St. Martin's Press, 1991.

McCormick, Thomas J. *China Market: America's Quest for Informal Empire, 1893–1901*. Chicago: Quadrangle, 1967.

McCullough, David. *The Path Between the Seas: The Creation of the Panama Canal, 1870–1914*. New York: Simon and Schuster, 1977.

McMahon, Robert J. *The Limits of Empire: The United States and Southeast Asia Since World War II*. New York: Columbia University Press, 1999.

Meeks, Brian. *Caribbean Revolutions and Revolutionary Theory: An Assessment of Cuba, Nicaragua and Grenada*. London: Macmillan Caribbean, 1993.

Méndez Saavedra, Manuel. *1898: La Guerra Hispano Americana en Caricaturas*. San Juan, P.R.: M. Méndez Saavedra, 1992.

Merk, Frederick. *Manifest Destiny and the Mission in American History: A Reinterpretation*. New York: Vintage, 1966.

Merrill, Tim L. (ed.). *Honduras: A Country Study*. Washington: Federal Research Division, Library of Congress, 1993.

Merry, Sally Engle. *Colonizing Hawaii: The Cultural Power of Law*. Princeton: Princeton University Press, 2000.

Metcalfe, June M. *Copper: The Red Metal*. New York: Viking, 1944.

Miller, Richard Hayes, ed. *American Imperialism in 1898: The Quest for National Fulfillment*. New York: Wiley, 1970.

Miller, Stuart Creighton. *"Benevolent Assimilation": The American Conquest of the Philippines, 1899–1903*. New Haven: Yale University Press, 1982.

Millis, Walter. *The Martial Spirit: A Study of Our War with Spain*. Boston: Houghton Mifflin, 1931.

Miner, Dwight Carroll. *The Fight for the Panama Route: The Story of the Spooner Act and the Hay-Herrán Treaty*. New York: Octagon, 1971.

Monten, Jonathan. "The Roots of the Bush Doctrine: Power, Nationalism, and Democracy Promotion in U.S. Strategy." *International Security*, Spring 2005.

Moran, Theodore H. *Multinational Corporations and the Politics of Dependence: Copper in Chile*. Princeton: Princeton University Press, 1974.

Morgan, Howard Wayne. *America's Road to Empire: The War with Spain and Overseas Expansion*. New York: Wiley, 1968.

———— (ed.). *Making Peace with Spain: The Diary of Whitelaw Reid, September–December, 1898–1965*. Austin: University of Texas Press, 1965.

Morgan, Roger. *The United States and West Germany 1945–1973: A Study in Alliance Politics*. London: Oxford University Press, 1974.

Morgenthau, Hans. *Politics Among Nations*. New York: Knopf, 1979.

Morris, Charles. *The War with Spain: A Complete History of the War of 1898 Between the United States and Spain*. Philadelphia: J. B. Lippincott, 1899.

Morris, James [Jan]. *Pax Britannica: The Climax of an Empire*. London: Penguin, 1979.

Morris, James A. *Honduras: Caudillo Politics and Military Rulers*. Boulder: Westview, 1984.

Mosley, Leonard. *Dulles: A Biography of Eleanor, Allen, and John Foster Dulles and Their Family Network*. New York: Dell, 1979.

Munro, Dana. *The Five Republics of Central America: Their Political and Economic Development and Their Relations with the United States*. New York: Oxford University Press, 1918.

————. *Intervention and Dollar Diplomacy, 1900–1921*. Westport, Conn.: Greenwood Press, 1964.

Munthe, Turi (ed.). *The Saddam Hussein Reader: Selections from Leading Writers on Iraq.* New York: Thunder Mouth, 2002.

Murillo. L. E. *The Noriega Mess: The Drugs, the Canal, and Why America Invaded.* Berkeley: Video Books, 1995.

Musicant, Ivan. *The Banana Wars: A History of United States Military Intervention in Latin America from the Spanish-American War to the Invasion of Panama.* New York: Macmillan, 1960.

Nearing, Scott. *The American Empire.* New York: Rand School of Social Sciences, 1921.

——, and Joseph Freeman. *Dollar Diplomacy: A Study in American Imperialism.* New York: Modern Reader, 1969.

Nevins, Allan. *Grover Cleveland: A Study in Courage.* New York: Dodd, Mead, 1932.

—— (ed.). *Letters of Grover Cleveland, 1850–1908.* Boston: Houghton Mifflin, 1933.

Newhouse, John. *Imperial America: The Bush Assault on the World Order.* New York: Knopf, 2003.

Nixon, Richard M. *RN: The Memoirs of Richard Nixon.* New York: Grosset & Dunlap, 1978.

Nofi, Albert A. *The Spanish-American War, 1898.* Conshohocken, Pa.: Combined Books, 1996.

Nogales, Rafael de. *The Looting of Nicaragua.* New York: Robert McBride, 1928.

Noriega, Manuel, and Peter Eisner. *America's Prisoner: The Memoirs of Manuel Noriega.* New York: Random House, 1997.

North, Oliver, and William Novak. *Under Fire: An American Story.* New York: HarperCollins, 1991.

Nyrop, Richard F. (ed.). *Panama: A Country Study.* Washington: Government Printing Office, 1981.

O'Brien, Thomas F. *The Revolutionary Mission: American Business in Latin America, 1900–1945.* New York: Cambridge University Press, 1996.

O'Connor, Richard. *Pacific Destiny: An Informal History of the United States in the Far East, 1776–1968.* Boston: Little, Brown, 1969.

Offner, John L. *An Unwanted War: The Diplomacy of the United States and Spain over Cuba, 1895–1898.* Chapel Hill: University of North Carolina Press, 1992.

O'Shaughnessy, Hugh. *Grenada: Revolution, Invasion and Aftermath.* London: Sphere, 1984.

Pan, Stephen, and Daniel Lyons. *Vietnam Crisis.* New York: Twin Circle, 1966.

Parmet, Herbert. *Eisenhower and the American Crusades.* New York: Macmillan, 1972.

Passalacqua, Juan Manuel García, and Carlos Rivera Lugo. *Puerto Rico y los Estados Unidos: El Proceso de Consulta y Negociación de 1989 y 1990.* San Juan, P.R.: Editorial Universidad, 1989.

Pastor, Robert. *Not Condemned to Repetition: The United States and Nicaragua.* Boulder: Westview, 1987.

Paterson, Thomas G. "United States Intervention in Cuba, 1898: Interpretations of the Spanish-American-Cuban-Filipino War." *OAH Magazine of History,* Spring 1998.

Paye, Walter. "The Guatemalan Revolution 1944–54." *Pacific Historian,* Spring 1973.

Payne, Anthony, et al. *Grenada: Revolution and Invasion*. New York: St. Martin's Press, 1984.

Pearce, Jenny. *Under the Eagle: U.S. Intervention in Central America and the Caribbean*. London: Latin American Bureau, 1982.

Peckenham, Nancy, and Street, Annie (eds.). *Honduras: Portrait of a Captive Nation*. New York: Praeger, 1985.

Pérez, Louis A., Jr. *The War of 1898: The United States and Cuba in History and Historiography*. Chapel Hill: University of North Carolina Press, 1998.

Perkins, Dexter. *Hands Off: A History of the Monroe Doctrine*. Boston: Little, Brown, 1941.

———. *A History of the Monroe Doctrine*. Boston: Little, Brown, 1955.

Perkins, Whitney T. *Constraint of Empire: The United States and Caribbean Interventions*. Westport, Conn.: Greenwood Press, 1981.

Perlo, Victor, and Kumar Goshal. *Bitter End in Southeast Asia*. New York: Marzani & Munsell, 1964.

Petras, James F. *How Allende Fell: A Study in U.S.–Chilean Relations*. Nottingham: Spokesman, 1974.

Phillips, David A. *The Night Watch: Twenty-five Years of Peculiar Service*. New York: Atheneum, 1977.

Phillips, David L. *Losing Iraq: Inside the Postwar Reconstruction Fiasco*. Boulder: Westview, 2005.

Phillips, Kevin. *William McKinley*. New York: Times Books, 2002.

Poole, Fred, and Max Vanzi. *Revolution in the Philippines: The United States in a Hall of Cracked Mirrors*. New York: McGraw-Hill, 1984.

Post, Charles Johnson. *The Little War of Private Post*. Boston: Little Brown, 1960.

Prados, John. *Hoodwinked: The Documents That Reveal How Bush Sold Us a War*. New York: New Press, 2004.

———. *Presidents' Secret Wars: CIA and Pentagon Covert Operations Since World War II*. New York: William Morrow, 1986.

——— (ed.). *The White House Tapes: Eavesdropping on the Presidents*. New York: New Press, 2003.

Pratt, Julius W. *Expansionists of 1898: The Acquisition of Hawaii and the Spanish Islands*. Chicago: Quadrangle, 1964.

Pringle, Henry F. *Theodore Roosevelt*. New York: Harcourt, 1931.

Pruessen, Ronald W. *John Foster Dulles: The Road to Power*. New York: Free Press, 1982.

Purdum, Todd. *A Time of Our Choosing: America's War in Iraq*. New York: Times Books, 2003.

Qintana, Carlos. *Nicaragua: Ensayo sobre el imperialismo de los Estados Unidos, 1909–1927*. Managua: Vanguardia, 1987.

Rabe, Stephen G. *Eisenhower and Latin America: The Foreign Policy of Anticommunism*. Chapel Hill: University of North Carolina Press, 1988.

Rashid, Ahmed. *Taliban: Militant Islam, Oil and Fundamentalism in Central Asia*. New Haven: Yale University Press, 2001.

Rickover, Hyman G. *How the Battleship Maine Was Destroyed*. Washington: Department of the Navy, Naval History Division, 1976.

Robinson, Linda. *Intervention or Neglect: The United States and Central America Beyond the 1980s*. New York: Council on Foreign Relations, 1991.

Rockefeller, David. *Memoirs*. New York: Random House, 2002.

Rodríguez González, Agustín. *La guerra del 98: Las campañas de Cuba, Puerto Rico y Filipinas*. Madrid: Agualarga, 1998.

Rojas Sandford, Robinson. *The Murder of Allende and the End of the Chilean Way to Socialism*. New York: Harper & Row, 1975.

Roosevelt, Kermit. *Countercoup: The Struggle for the Control of Iran*. New York: McGraw-Hill, 1979.

Ropp, Steve C. *Panamanian Politics: From the Guarded Nation to the National Guard*. New York: Praeger, 1982.

Rositzke, Harry. *The CIA's Secret Operations: Espionage, Counterespionage, and Covert Action*. New York: Reader's Digest Press, 1977.

Rossett, Peter, and John Vandermeer (eds.). *Nicaragua: Unfinished Revolution*. New York: Grove Press, 1986.

Russ, William Adam. *The Hawaiian Republic (1894–98) and Its Struggle to Win Annexation*. Selinsgrove, Pa.: Susquehanna University Press, 1992.

———. *The Hawaiian Revolution (1893–94)*. Selinsgrove, Pa.: Susquehanna University Press, 1959.

Russell, Lee E. *Grenada 1983*. London: Osprey, 1985.

Saar, Eric, and Viveca Novak. *Inside the Wire: A Military Intelligence Soldier's Eyewitness Account of Life at Guantánamo*. New York: Penguin, 2005.

Salisbury, Harrison. *Without Fear or Favor*. New York: Times Books, 1980.

Salisbury, Richard. *Anti-Imperialism and International Competition in Central America 1920–1929*. Wilmington, Del.: Scholarly Resources, 1989.

Sampson, Anthony. *The Sovereign State of ITT*. New York: Stein and Day, 1973.

Schirmer, Daniel B. *Republic or Empire: American Resistance to the Philippine War*. Cambridge, Mass.: Schenkman, 1972.

Schlesinger, Stephen, and Stephen Kinzer. *Bitter Fruit: The Untold Story of the American Coup in Guatemala*. Garden City, N.Y.: Doubleday, 1982.

Schmidt, Hans. *Maverick Marine: General Smedley Butler and the Contradictions of American Military History*. Lexington: University Press of Kentucky, 1987.

Schmitt, Robert C. *Historical Statistics of Hawaii*. Honolulu: University Press of Hawaii, 1977.

Schneider, Ronald. *Communism in Guatemala, 1944–1954*. New York: Praeger, 1959.

Schoenberg, Robert J. *Geneen: The Biography of Harold Geneen, Who Made ITT into the Most Successful Conglomerate in History*. New York: W. W. Norton, 1985.

Schoenhals, Kai P., and Richard A. Melanson. *Revolution and Intervention in Grenada: The New Jewel Movement, the United States, and the Caribbean*. Boulder: Westview, 1985.

Scholes, Walter V., and Marie V. Scholes. *The Foreign Policies of the Taft Administration*. Columbia: University of Missouri Press, 1970.

Schoonover, Thomas. *Uncle Sam's War of 1898 and the Origins of Globalization*. Louisville: University Press of Kentucky, 2003.

Schwarzkopf, Norman. *It Doesn't Take a Hero: The Autobiography of General Norman Schwarzkopf*. New York: Bantam, 1992.

Scoon, Paul. *Survival for Service: My Experiences as Governor of Grenada*. London: Macmillan Caribbean, 2003.

Scranton, Margaret. *The Noriega Years*. Boulder: Westview, 1991.

Seabury, Paul, and Walter A. McDougall (eds.). *The Grenada Papers: The Inside Story of the Grenadian Revolution and the Making of a Totalitarian State—as Told in Captured Documents*. San Francisco: Institute for Contemporary Studies, 1984.

Searle, Chris. *Grenada: The Struggle Against Destabilization*. London: Writers and Readers, 1983.

————. *Words Unchained: Language and Revolution in Grenada*. London: Zed, 1984.

Secretariat-General of the Government, Republic of Chile. *White Book of the Change of Government in Chile, 11th September 1973*. Santiago: Empresa Editorial Nacional Gabriela Mistral, 1973.

Selser, Gregorio. *Nicaragua de Walker a Somoza*. Mexico City: Mex Sur Editorial, 1984.

————. *La Restauración Conservadora y la Gesta de Benjamin Zeledón: Nicaragua–USA, 1909–1916*. Managua: Aldilá, 2001.

Sick, Gary. *All Fall Down: America's Tragic Encounter with Iran*. New York: Penguin, 1986.

Sigmund, Paul E. *The Overthrow of Allende and the Politics of Chile, 1964–1976*. Pittsburgh: University of Pittsburgh Press, 1977.

————. *The United States and Democracy in Chile*. Baltimore: Johns Hopkins University Press, 1993.

Smith, Bradford. *Yankees in Paradise: The New England Impact on Hawaii*. Philadelphia: J. B. Lippincott, 1956.

Smith, Joseph. *The Spanish-American War: Conflict in the Caribbean and Pacific, 1895–1902*. London: Longman, 1994.

Smith, Peter H. *Talons of the Eagle: Dynamics of U.S.–Latin American Relations*. Oxford: Oxford University Press, 2000.

Sobel, Lester A. (ed.). *Chile and Allende*. New York: Facts on File, 1974.

Spector, Ronald H. *U.S. Marines in Grenada, 1983*. Washington: History and Museums Division, Marine Corps, 1987.

Spurr, David. *The Rhetoric of Empire: Colonial Discourse in Journalism, Travel Writing, and Imperial Administration*. Durham, N.C.: Duke University Press, 1993.

Stannard, David E. *Before the Horror: The Population of Hawaii on the Eve of Western Contact*. Honolulu: University of Hawaii Press, 1989.

Stang, Alan. *The Actor: The True Story of John Foster Dulles, Secretary of State from 1953 to 1959*. Boston: Western Islands, 1968.

Stephanson, Anders. *Manifest Destiny: American Expansion and the Empire of Right*. New York: Hill and Wang, 1995.

Storey, Moorfield. *The Conquest of the Philippines by the United States*. New York: Putnam, 1926.

Suskind, Ron. *The Price of Loyalty: George W. Bush, the White House, and the Education of Paul O'Neill*. New York: Simon and Schuster, 2004.

Sweeney, Jerry K. (ed.). *A Handbook of American Military History from the Revolutionary War to the Present*. Boulder: Westview, 1996.

Tanner, Stephen. *The Wars of the Bushes: A Father and Son as Military Leaders*. Philadelphia: Casemate, 2004.

Tate, Merze. *The United States and the Hawaiian Kingdom: A Political History*. New Haven: Yale University Press, 1965.

Taw, Jennifer Morrison. *Operation Just Cause: Lessons for Operations Other than War.* Santa Monica: Rand, 1996.

Taylor, Charles Carlisle. *The Life of Admiral Mahan.* New York: Doran, 1920.

Taylor, Maxwell D. *Swords and Plowshares.* Cambridge, Mass.: Da Capo, 1990.

Tebbel, John. *America's Great Patriotic War with Spain: Mixed Motives, Lies and Racism in Cuba and the Philippines, 1893–1915.* Manchester Center, Vt.: Marshall Jones, 1996.

———. *The United States and the Caribbean Republics, 1921–1933.* Princeton: Princeton University Press, 1974.

Thurston, Lorrin A. *Memoirs of the Hawaiian Revolution.* Honolulu: Advertiser Publishing, 1936.

Timmerman, Kenneth R. *The Death Lobby: How the West Armed Iraq.* New York: Houghton Mifflin, 1991.

Tompkins, E. Berkeley. *Anti-Imperialism in the United States: The Great Debate, 1890–1920.* Philadelphia: University of Pennsylvania Press, 1970.

Travis, Helen, and A. B. Magil. *What Happened in Guatemala.* New York: New Century, 1954.

Trías Monge, José. *Puerto Rico: The Trials of the Oldest Colony in the World.* New Haven: Yale University Press, 1997.

Tuchman, Barbara. *The Proud Tower: A Portrait of the World Before the War, 1890–1914.* New York: Ballantine, 1962.

Turner, Frederick Jackson. "The Problem of the West." *Atlantic Monthly,* Sept. 1896.

Twigg-Smith, Thurston. *Hawaiian Sovereignty: Do the Facts Matter?* Honolulu: Goodale, 1998.

United States Senate. *Alleged Assassination Plots Involving Foreign Leaders.* Report 94-465. 94th Congress, 1st Session. Washington: Government Printing Office, 1975.

———. *Covert Action in Chile 1963–1973.* 94th Congress, 1st, Session. Washington: Government Printing Office, 1975.

———. *Final Report of the Select Committee to Study Governmental Operations with Respect to Intelligence Activities.* Report 94-755. 94th Congress, 2nd Session. Washington: Government Printing Office, 1974.

———. *The International Telephone and Telegraph Company and Chile, 1970–1971.* Washington: Government Printing Office, 1973.

———. *Report of the Inter-Oceanic Canal Commission.* Senate Executive Document 15, 46th Congress, 1st Session, 1876.

Uribe, Armando. *The Black Book of American Intervention in Chile.* Boston: Beacon, 1974.

Valenzuela, Arturo. *The Breakdown of Democratic Regimes: Chile.* Baltimore: Johns Hopkins University Press, 1978.

Vandercook, John W. *King Cane: The Story of Sugar and Hawaii.* New York: Harper & Brothers, 1939.

Van Dusen, Henry P. *The Spiritual Legacy of John Foster Dulles: Selections from His Articles and Addresses.* Philadelphia: Westminster, 1960.

Verdugo, Patricia. *Allende: Cómo la Casa Blanca Provocó su Muerte.* Santiago: Catalonia, 2003.

————. Interferencia secreta: 11 Septiembre de 1973. Santiago: Editorial Sudamericana, 1998.

Vergara, José Manuel, and Florencio Varas. *Coup: Allende's Last Day*. New York: Stein & Day, 1975.

Walker, Dale L. *The Boys of '98: Theodore Roosevelt and the Rough Riders*. New York: Tom Dougherty, 1998.

Walker, Martin (ed.). *The Iraq War: As Witnessed by the Correspondents and Photographers of United Press International*. Washington: Brassey's, 2004.

Walters, Vernon. *Silent Missions*. Garden City, N.Y.: Doubleday, 1978.

Watson, Bruce, and Tsouras, Peter (eds.). *Operation Just Cause: The U.S. Intervention in Panama*. Boulder: Westview, 1991.

Watterson, Henry. *History of the Spanish American War*. Hartford, Conn.: American Publishing, 1898.

Weeks, John, and Phil Gunson. *Panama: Made in the USA*. London: Latin America Bureau, 1991.

Weil, Thomas, et al. *Area Handbook for Panama*. Washington: Government Printing Office, 1972.

Welch, Richard E., Jr. *Response to Imperialism: The United States and the Philippine-American War, 1899–1902*. Chapel Hill: University of North Carolina Press, 1979.

Welch, Richard J. *The Presidencies of Grover Cleveland*. Lawrence: University Press of Kansas, 1988.

Wheaton, Philip E. (ed.). *Panama Invaded: Imperial Occupation Versus Struggle for Sovereignty*. Trenton, N.J.: Red Sea, 1992.

Wheeler, Burton K. *Dollar Diplomacy at Work in Mexico and Nicaragua*. Washington: Government Printing Office, 1927.

White, Trumbull. *United States in War with Spain and the History of Cuba*. Philadelphia: International Publishing, 1898.

Wilcox, Marrison. *A Short History of the War with Spain*. New York: Frederick A. Stokes, 1898.

Wilkerson, M. M. *Public Opinion and the Spanish-American War: A Study in War Propaganda*. Baton Rouge: Louisiana State University Press, 1932.

Wilkins, Mira. *The Emergence of Multinational Enterprise: American Business Abroad, from the Colonial Era to 1914*. Cambridge, Mass.: Harvard University Press, 1970.

Williams, William Appleman. *The Roots of the Modern American Empire: A Study of the Growth and Shaping of Social Consciousness in a Marketplace Society*. New York: Vintage, 1969.

Wilson, Charles Morrow. *Empire in Green and Gold: The Story of the American Banana Trade*. New York: Henry Holt, 1947.

Wilson, Hazel. *Last Queen of Hawaii: Liliuokalani*. New York: Knopf, 1963.

Wimmel, Kenneth. *Theodore Roosevelt and the Great White Fleet: American Sea Power Comes of Age*. Washington: Brassey's, 2000.

Wise, David, and Thomas B. Ross. *The Invisible Government*. New York: Random House, 1964.

Wolff, Leon. *Little Brown Brother: How the United States Purchased and Pacified the Philippine Islands at the Century's Turn*. Garden City, N.Y.: Doubleday, 1961.

Woodhouse, C. M. *Something Ventured*. London: Granada, 1982.

Woodward, Bob. *Veil: The Secret Wars of the CIA, 1981–1987*. New York: Simon and Schuster, 1987.

———. *Bush at War*. New York: Simon and Schuster, 2002.

———. *Plan of Attack*. New York: Simon and Schuster, 2004.

Woodward, Ralph Lee. *Central America: A Nation Divided*. New York: Oxford University Press, 1976.

Yergin, Daniel. *The Prize: The Epic Quest for Oil, Money and Power*. New York: Simon and Schuster, 1991.

———. *Shattered Peace: The Origins of the Cold War and the National Security State*. Boston: Houghton Mifflin, 1977.

Zabih, Sepehr. *The Mossadegh Era: Roots of the Iranian Revolution*. Chicago: Lake View, 1982.

Zaide, Gregorio F. *The Philippine Revolution*. Manila: Modern, 1954.

Zelaya, José Santos. *La Revolución de Nicaragua y los Estados Unidos*. Madrid: B. Rodríguez, 1910.

Zimmerman, Warren. *First Great Triumph: How Five Americans Made Their Country a World Power*. New York: Farrar, Straus and Giroux, 2002.

Zinn, Howard. *A People's History of the United States, 1492–Present*. New York: HarperCollins, 1999.

Zucchino, David. *Thunder Run: The Armored Strike to Capture Baghdad*. New York: Atlantic Monthly Press, 2004.

ACKNOWLEDGMENTS

This book surveys a period of more than a century, and deals with events in fourteen countries scattered around the globe. Few if any writers are easily conversant with all of the events and personalities it describes. I drew the accounts in this book from the work of hundreds of historians, journalists, and others. My bibliography is not only a jumping-off point for readers who want more information about the episodes I describe but also a tribute to authors whose work shaped and guided my own.

To ensure that my accounts of "regime change" operations were as accurate as possible, I asked specialists to review each chapter. All of them made corrections, suggestions, and comments that greatly improved my text. Their only compensation was the satisfaction of serving truth. I am deeply in their debt.

Professor Pauline King of the University of Hawaii reviewed the chapter on Hawaii. Professor Louis A. Pérez of Duke University, Professor Silvia Álvarez Curbelo of the University of Puerto Rico, and Professor Maria Luisa Camagay of the University of the Philippines reviewed sections of my chapter on the Spanish-American War.

The historian, novelist, and former Nicaraguan vice president Sergio Ramírez and the Nicaraguan economist Edmundo Jarquín reviewed material about their country. Professor Mario Argueta of the National University of Honduras did the same for my account of events there.

I counted on comparably expert guidance for my accounts of the four Cold War coups. The author and historian Farhad Diba reviewed my chapter on Iran. Professor Susanne Jonas of the University of California at Berkeley and Edelberto Torres Rivas of the Facultad Latinoamericano de Ciencias Sociales in Guatemala City reviewed the Guatemala chapter. Professor Mark Bradley of Northwestern University reviewed the chapter on South Vietnam. The historian and archivist Peter Kornbluh, the Chilean author Ariel Dorfman, Professor Peter Winn of Tufts University, and Professor Paul Sigmund of Princeton University reviewed the chapter on Chile.

The independent scholar Wendy Grenade reviewed my chapter on the invasion of Grenada. Professor Steven Ropp of the University of Wyoming reviewed the chapter on Panama. The author and journalist Ahmed Rashid reviewed my Afghanistan chapter. Thom Shanker of the *New York Times,* who closely covered the invasion of Iraq, reviewed my account of it. David Zucchino of the *Los Angeles Times* and the scholar-diplomat David L. Phillips also read portions of what I wrote about Iraq.

I did not make every change that these experts suggested, so any remaining errors are my own responsibility. Their contribution to this book, however, was invaluable.

So were those of others who read all or part of my manuscript and offered insightful comments. Elmira Bayrasli, Sacha Brown, James Linkin, David Shuman, James M. Stone, and Chris Robling all gave trenchant advice and helped in various ways to shape the text.

Kate Barrett, a talented graduate of the Medill School of Journalism at Northwestern University, contributed important research on Afghanistan. Grace Lewis and other librarians at the public library in Oak Park, Illinois, worked tirelessly to locate obscure books and articles. My agent, Nancy Love, provided faithful encouragement. Alex Ward deftly managed my transition from *New York Times* reporter to private citizen, counting on the generous cooperation of Bill Keller and other *Times* editors. Jeff Roth spent hours locating photos. Paul Golob edited the manuscript with a light but authoritative hand, and Brianna Smith worked on it at every stage.

Writing this book was an all-consuming exercise that required me to withdraw from most human society for an extended period. Those closest to me understood my obsession, and cheered me on rather than resenting my intense focus on figures from Queen Liliuokalani to Saddam Hussein. I am most grateful to them.

INDEX

ABOUT THE AUTHOR

STEPHEN KINZER is a longtime foreign correspondent who has reported from more than fifty countries on four continents. He has served as the *New York Times* bureau chief in Turkey, Germany, and Nicaragua. Before joining the *Times*, he was Latin America correspondent for *The Boston Globe*. His previous books include *All the Shah's Men: An American Coup and the Roots of Middle East Terror*, *Crescent and Star: Turkey Between Two Worlds*, and *Blood of Brothers: Life and War in Nicaragua*. He is also the coauthor of *Bitter Fruit: The Untold Story of the American Coup in Guatemala*. He lives in Oak Park, Illinois.